Whose Antigone?

Whose Antigone?

The Tragic Marginalization of Slavery

TINA CHANTER

SUNY PRESS

Cover art: (L to R) Kamal Angelo Bolden and La Shawn Banks in Remy Bumppo Theatre Company's production of *The Island*. Photo by Johnny Knight.

Published by State University of New York Press, Albany

Printed in the United States of America

For information, contact State University of New York Press, Albany, NY
www.sunypress.edu

Production by Ryan Morris
Marketing by Anne M. Valentine

Library of Congress Cataloging-in-Publication Data

Chanter, Tina, 1960–
Whose Antigone? : the tragic marginalization of slavery / Tina Chanter.
p. cm.
Includes bibliographical references and index.
ISBN 978-1-4384-3755-2 (hardcover : alk. paper)
ISBN 978-1-4384-3754-5 (pbk. : alk. paper)
1. Sophocles. Antigone. 2. Slavery in literature. 3. Antigone (Greek mythology) in literature. 4. Feminism in literature. I. Title.

PA4413.A7C47 2011
882'.01—dc22 2010041946

10 9 8 7 6 5 4 3 2 1

Contents

Preface

The figure of Oedipus has been read by Sigmund Freud, Jacques Lacan, and their followers as an inaugural myth, originating a psychic complex that has come to be foundational for Western thought. Oedipus is the one who knows, but whose knowledge fails him, the solver of riddles, one for whom his own identity presents an irresolvable enigma, the stranger and the one who is too close—the one who is blinded to the very proximity of his own blood kin. Oedipus commits incest and murders his father. One of the major tasks of this book is to reread Sophocles' Oedipal cycle, challenging some of the fundamental tenets that have come to specify its founding role in literature, philosophy, and psychoanalytic thinking.

If feminist theorists have reoriented readings of the Oedipal cycle in significant ways, not least by focusing their interpretations on Antigone rather than Oedipus, in other ways some of the most influential readings retain an important continuity with G. W. F. Hegel. Hegel's admiration for the heroes of Greek tragedy—and Antigone enjoys pride of place amongst them—is mediated both by his attempt to contain the threat that emergent feminism presents in his age and by his insistent aversion to interrogating both the limitations of the emerging democracy of Athens and the colonial commitments of his own age. To the extent that Hegel's critics reiterate this aversion in their rehabilitation of Antigone, they too fail to acknowledge the paradox that the literary heroes of the Western tradition emerged from an Athenian culture that required the exclusion of certain members from its polity, even while depending on their labor as a necessary prerequisite for the freedoms afforded those granted full political rights. The dependence of male members of the aristocracy—including tragic poets such as Sophocles—upon certain individuals (foremost among them slaves and women) who were deprived of basic political freedoms, even as they catered to the necessities of life for those who enjoyed such freedoms, is a founding paradox that was constitutive of life in fifth century BCE Athens. One of the ways in which this paradox expressed itself was in the performative constraints it imposed upon the theatrical productions of Greek tragedy, in which female characters such as Antigone would have been played by male actors.

If the significance of these performative constraints has not always been taken seriously, there is a sense in which other gendered dimensions of *Antigone* have taken on such a dominant role in interpretations of the play that they have been allowed to eclipse equally pressing dynamics that demand attention. The focal point of my argument concerns the need to expand the debate over the significance of Antigone's challenge to Creon beyond the concerns of family, kinship, and gender, themes that have come to dominate the post-Hegelian critical literature. Or rather, the point is to construe family and kinship in a way that is not restricted to, or does not privilege, gender as an isolated category. This entails challenging Hegel's crucial intervention, which has served as the inspiration for a number of decisive critical interpretations of Sophocles' *Antigone*, including those of Jacques Derrida, Lacan, Luce Irigaray, and Judith Butler. In the wake of Hegel's own understanding of the play in terms of a conflict between the ethical demands of the family on the one hand and the state on the other, Butler frames her important discussion of *Antigone* as a response both to Hegel and Lacan. She succeeds in establishing the heteronormative biases not only of Hegel and Lacan, but also of more recent feminist critiques of German idealist and psychoanalytic readings of *Antigone*. Yet even as Butler and Lacan question and recast in different ways the basic dichotomy within which Hegel approaches *Antigone*, that of family and state, precisely to the extent that they resituate this opposition, there is a sense in which they reinscribe its centrality.

This book contends that there is another discourse in which the Oedipal cycle is implicated, one that has been overlooked, in part due to the colonial commitments of the tradition of German idealism that has been so dominant in setting the terms for the interpretation of Greek tragedy. This discourse is one in which definitions of citizenship, political rights, foreigners, slavery, and enemies figure writ large. It is a discourse reflective of an Athenian culture, supported by a fledgling but limited democracy, which is trying to assert its dominance in the face of its enemies.

By broadening the purview of questions beyond that of family and kinship, or rather by challenging the restrictive terms according to which these concepts have been understood, I ask how these themes have been developed in a particular direction that might have obscured or downplayed other concerns at stake both in Sophocles' *Antigone*, and in the theoretical, interpretive tradition to which the Oedipal cycle has given rise. These concerns will prove to be entangled with the questions of kinship and gender that have taken precedence in recent debates, but taking them seriously will also require a reconfiguration not only of these contemporary questions but also of standard interpretations of *Antigone* as a tragedy. At issue then is to refrain from imposing modern, Western, identity categories such as "race," "gender," or "class" onto a context that preceded the reification of such categories, where issues of kinship, marriage, exchange, slavery, citizenship, foreignness, and so on, were not carved up into the discrete categories that contemporary discourse tends to impose on them. Building on, but also challenging, the readings of Hegel, Martin Heidegger, Derrida, Lacan, Irigaray and Butler, Jean-Pierre Vernant, and others, while at the same time problematizing some of the philosophical and psychoanalytic assumptions and blind spots of the tradition in which these readings are ensconced, my effort will be both to situate the Oedipal cycle in relation to the historical and social context out of which it arises, and to show where and how that context informs the text in ways that have been neglected and underplayed. This will be a question of sifting through the available evidence concerning the legal, ethical, and political context, at the same time as interrogating why certain aspects of this context have been played down by the dominant, European, theoretical reception of Sophocles' plays, while others have come to dictate the terms of its reception. A European, colonialist framework continues to drive Western, philosophically and psychoanalytically inspired readings of the Oedipal cycle, invested in retaining the invisibility of the founding paradox upon which I suggest a good number of post-Hegelian interpretations are premised.

During the period in which Sophocles wrote the Oedipal cycle, attempts to draw up legal definitions about who was entitled to marry whom were intimately bound up not only with demarcating the concept of strangers from that of Athenian citizens, but also with the determination of who should be a citizen and who should not, and with who should be a slave and who should be free. The exchange of women within a group of men, the boundaries of which were newly circumscribed, had everything to do with the circulation and containment of wealth, and with attempts to ensure the political and military prominence of Athens. Questions of mastery over self, others, the body, and the body politic were intricately bound up with one another, and the desire for freemen to maintain mastery over the self was formulated in tension with the desire not to be construed at any cost or in any way as slavish.[1] A constellation of factors were related to one another in complex ways, including controlling the movements of women across geographical boundaries, monitoring the circumstances under which Athenian women gave birth, establishing the legitimacy of male citizens and the identity of slaves, and overseeing the inheritance of wealth.

A complex nexus of historical forces, including a recent shift in marriage practices—away from exogamy and toward endogamy—its legal corroboration, and its implications for foreigners and slavery, constitutes the background against which Sophocles conceives of the Oedipal cycle. This background can be read as informing Sophocles' exploration of the implications of Oedipus's incestuous marriage to Jocasta, his self-imposed exile, Antigone's rejection of Haemon as a potential husband, and her insistence upon distinguishing the status of Polynices from that of a slave in her burial of him. Once one starts to look, textual evidence abounds for Sophocles' deep concern with questions such as what makes a slave a slave, how does a woman who is not a slave differ from a slave, and how is it that kings can be distinguished from slaves. Given this, some of the received parameters within which critics have interpreted *Antigone* bear revisiting.

Although a good deal of commentary has concerned itself with why Antigone determines that the brother she insists upon burying, thereby flouting King Creon's edict, is irreplaceable in a way that distinguishes him from any husband or son she might have—had her literary life not been destined to end prematurely—there is a dearth of critical literature on another demarcation Antigone draws. A central task of the book is to demonstrate that Antigone's discrimination of her brother Polynices from a slave is part of a larger complex of themes concerning the status of outsiders, foreigners, and slaves that informs the Oedipal cycle, the significance of which has been largely neglected by the philosophical and psychoanalytic traditions. Situating the Oedipal cycle in its legal and social context, including the ramifications of the Periclean law of 450–51 BCE that refined the requirements for Athenian citizenship by stipulating that in order to qualify as an Athenian citizen both parents must be Athenian born, I show how the imperative of distinguishing insiders from outsiders, citizens from non-citizens, and freemen from slaves, permeates Sophocles' exploration of the Oedipal family.[2] At the same time, the significance of Antigone's insistence upon burying her brother needs to be assessed in the light of contrasting Persian practices of exposing corpses precisely in order that they can be consumed as carrion by vultures. Antigone's distinction of her brother from a slave is also a delineation of a free, cultured individual from a barbarian, non-Athenian slave.[3]

While theorists have begun to excavate the importance of the richly diverse, international, dramatic tradition of appropriating *Antigone*, perhaps most notably Barbara Goff and Michael Simpson, they have tended to do so in a way that leaves intact the dominant psychoanalytic Oedipal myth, rather than arguing that this myth itself, as developed by Freud and Lacan, has helped to formulate some of the blind spots that need to be demystified.[4] Even while critics have brought to bear incisive analyses of the rich dramatic tradition of plays appropriating and recasting the Oedipal cycle, they have not questioned as much as they might the Oedipal myth as it has been inherited through Western psychoanalysis. Consequently, at the level of drawing upon received interpretations of the Oedipal complex, such critics continue to privilege theories of sexual difference and incest at the expense of the other issues raised by Sophocles' *Antigone.* Theoretical investments have thereby, sometimes inadvertently, contributed to the obfuscation of the questions surrounding slavery and citizenship that I argue are not only central to playwrights such as Fémi Òsófisan, but also—albeit it different ways—integral to Sophocles' concerns. The Oedipal model, as inflected through Freud and Lacan, cannot be taken up and applied to colonial issues, as if it constituted an adequate hermeneutical tool that operates independently of those very issues its dominance has helped to eclipse.[5]

The concerns highlighted by the literary and theatrical appropriations of *Antigone* within African contexts turn out to be in profound communication with those embedded in Sophocles' own preoccupations, concerns that have been made unavailable for questioning, submerged by the prevailing tenor of Hegel's idealist reading of tragedy. This reading saw fit to privilege the dichotomy of state versus family, to read Antigone as a purified ethical heroine, to situate her as representative of the private, domestic, religious sphere, as opposed to the public, political, and civic sphere, and thus to contain, quell, and tame any threat posed by women's demands to be considered political subjects. The political realm thereby fortified itself, resisting the claims of feminism that were beginning to make themselves heard, and resignifying itself as resolutely masculine.

Yet if Antigone's interpretive legacy can be read, in part, as symptomatic of a philosophical attempt to justify and rationalize women's political subordination in the context of nineteenth century Europe, Hegel's reading of tragedy also exhibits another source of anxiety that betrays a less articulate unease. If Hegel confronts the challenge that feminism was beginning to pose to the equilibrium of the state by reigning in the restless, disruptive spirit of femininity that Antigone epitomizes for him, he also attempts to outlaw another topic that threatens to disrupt the narrative of civilized, masculinized, and progressive rationality to which he is committed, a narrative that cites Athens as an origin, and construes Europe—and more particularly Germany—as the inheritor and arbiter of its ancient Greek legacy. As I show in detail in Chapter 2, Hegel outlaws slavery as a subject for tragedy altogether, in a gesture of refusal and indirection that betrays a pervasive discomfort about the imperial ambitions of Europe and its deep implication in new world slavery, together with an unwillingness to confront the ethical questions thereby posed.

Heeding neither Hegel's dictum to outlaw slavery as a legitimate topic for tragedy, nor his requirement to eschew topics that he regards as unaesthetic, postcolonial dramatists have turned repeatedly to Greek tragedy in order to articulate predicaments that are fraught with the burden of drawing on a tradition that has been imposed by cultural and military dictate, and yet which is turned against itself under the pens of playwrights such as Athol Fugard and Fémi Òsófisan.[6] Tragic commitments, including those of empire and colonialism, are thereby made to subvert themselves. In Òsófisan's *Tègònni*, Antigone appears on stage with bodyguards, since the roads she has traveled throughout history are unsafe.[7] Each time she plays her part, she must die. Òsófisan's exploration of the mythical status of Antigone in the context of colonial Nigeria is also an interrogation of the multiple re-births of Antigone across the ages and in diverse continents. If Antigone becomes a symbolic sister to *Tègònni*, not only does their relationship complicate traditional familial lines of kinship, it also labors under the burden of colonial, racial, oppression. "What colour is mythology?"

asks Antigone, responding to the meta-theatrical dilemma into which Òsófisan casts his characters. The question is one that haunts this book.

Tègònni takes up and recasts questions posed in Sophocles' *Antigone* about who is expected to marry whom, and who deserves a proper burial, and transposes them into the context of a modern-day Nigeria, beset with problems of economic exploitation and political corruption, problems which themselves arose in a context that was structured by European imperialist ambitions, a colonial regime and a legacy of slavery. The play negotiates questions of race and gender, and explores the tensions created by the conflict of competing cultural traditions, confronting the issue of cultural authorization. *Tègònni* opens up a perspective on *Antigone*, its transmission, its legacy, and its reception—one could almost say its mythology—that reflects on how the stories of Oedipus and Antigone have been handed down to us, and how their transmission is redolent of imperial ambitions. In doing so, it grants access to a dimension of this transmission that has been played down by theorists who, even in their attempts to distance themselves from his legacy, are still beholden to a framework essentially inherited from Hegel, a framework that privileges the family/state antithesis, and assumes the priority and authority of a political state that defines its membership exclusively.

It does not seem accidental that playwrights have turned again and again to *Antigone* when political states exhibit the symptoms of political crisis. I suggest that Antigone's ongoing relevance derives in part from the fictions of sovereignty that continue to unfold, fictions that make it difficult to unearth the complex array of issues that I argue structure Sophocles' *Antigone*, and which Antigone's continual renaissance, especially in the African dramas I consider here, helps to uncover. The effort of this book is to allow the theatrical accomplishments of playwrights such as Fémi Òsófisan, and the theoretical innovations of those contesting abuses of justice—whether in the guise of postcolonial theory or in the shape of addressing the significance of slavery in ancient Greece—to facilitate a new trajectory for reading *Antigone*. Discussion is devoted to Òsófisan's *Tègònni* in Chapter 4, and in Chapter 3 to *The Island*, a collaborative play by Athol Fugard, John Kani, and Winston Ntshona, set in apartheid South Africa.[8]

The Island was inspired by an actual performative appropriation of *Antigone*, a play that was performed at Robben Island, where Nelson Mandela was imprisoned.[9] *The Island* explores the gendered dynamics of cross-dressing in a way that transposes, resituates, and reinvents the performative constraints of classical Greek theatre, and in doing so it makes those constraints available for questioning in new ways. It also renews the way in which the character of Antigone confronts the meaning of justice. As her character refuses to cede ethical authority to a state structured by apartheid, Antigone is transfigured, and her call for justice is renewed. This call becomes a claim that challenges the right of a state to proceed upon the basis of the corrupt principle that race should disqualify individuals from full and equal political and economic participation in the state. As such, it recalls Sophocles' own underlying concerns, even as it transposes them into modern discourses of racial identity.

The Island reframes questions of exclusion and the parameters according to which a state rests upon those it excludes even as it excludes—and thereby in a certain way includes—them. The principle of justice, the importance of friendship, the question of how kinship bonds should be construed, all central to Sophocles' *Antigone*, also infuse *The Island*. So too the question of torture—one that is interrogated by Sophocles' *Oedipus Rex*—and the inhuman treatment of humans who are consigned to physical labor, are integral to *The Island*, which thereby brings to the fore, even as it reconstitutes them, issues that help to structure the context in which Sophocles' *Antigone* was conceived.

As Edith Hall points out, "Every era of classical scholarship looks into the ancient world and finds in it reflected its own contingent socio-political preoccupations."[10] Consistent with this, my approach to *Antigone* is no doubt inflected by recent efforts to render feminist theory accountable for its relative silence—at least until recently—on questions surrounding race. This is not to assume that race as a concept operates in the same way in an ancient Greek context as in contemporary contexts, nor even that it makes sense to think of race as a concept for the Greeks, given the particular way in which scientific concepts of race have, of late, been discredited, after the consolidation of race as a concept in a post-Darwinian era. However, the twentieth century plays I consider here, and the political contexts with which they engage, which include postcolonial exploitation and apartheid, help bring to the surface certain tensions, questions, and preoccupations configured around slavery and barbarians in distinction to citizens, to which Sophocles might well have been responding in his own time.[11]

Issues concerning slavery and colonialism have been rendered if not invisible, at least thematically insignificant, by a tradition of scholarship that has continued to influence feminist reclamations of the figure of Antigone, in so far as they have focused on this character to the exclusion of considerations of how she situates herself in relation to slavery. I am neither suggesting that contemporary concerns are fundamentally the same as those of Sophocles' *Antigone*, nor that those abiding concerns have reemerged in their essential form, having suffered a long period of immersion.[12] The argument is neither that the issues of slavery or colonialism, or what it means to be considered an outsider, are eternal or unchanging, nor that Sophocles' Oedipal cycle is really about the question of slavery, to the exclusion of other issues.[13]

New world slavery is differently configured from slavery in ancient Athens due in part to its inflection through the prism of racc and racism, concepts which emerge in their own peculiar historical set of circumstances, and which, for a while, became inextricably linked with biological determinism.[14] Yet the practice of playing down the significance of new world slavery in modern world colonialism and imperialism has served to deflect attention away from the structuring presence of slavery in the Athenian Empire. The precise contours by which this structuring presence designated and enforced the marginality of slaves in ancient Athens, at the same time as substantially informing the life of the polis, will be sketched below. This sketch is intended to set the scene in which slavery operated as one aspect of a complex set of forces shaping Athenian culture and politics. My focus on rescuing the slave/free dichotomy from the oblivion to which it has been consigned is occasioned not because I think it operates in abstraction from other crucial polarities structuring the Athenian social imaginary, but because it is a theme that has been largely neglected in the critical literature on *Antigone.*

When we try to tackle the problem of whether or not the ancients thought in racial terms, and if they did, how far their ideas might be considered precursors of modern ideas of race, we immediately confront a quagmire. Not only are definitions of race and racism highly contested, but the very categories that help to do the work of attempting to define race and racism bear the trace of contemporary, scientist assumptions, which do not accord with ancient philosophy, religion, or culture. The varied attempts to reach adequate definitions of terms such as race, racism, racialism, and ethnicity often assume unproblematically an array of concepts that are themselves the product of a modern mindset.[15] Even attempts to interrogate the political, social, and cultural significations informing how concepts such as barbarian functioned for the ancient Greeks must carefully negotiate their position in doing so. We are reminded by some that it is useless, unproductive, or misguided to imagine we can say anything meaningful, anything worth saying, about what the Greeks actually thought, or about objective reality; rather, we must restrict ourselves to the invented, subjective ideology of the Greeks. "There is a world of difference" observes Hall "between saying that the Greeks *were* the descendants of Egyptians and Phoenicians, and saying that the Greeks *thought* that they were descended from Egyptians and Phoenicians."[16] Similarly, Paul Cartledge implicitly assumes a distinction between subjective and objective when he, quite appropriately, bemoans the lack of source material written by anyone other than the ruling elites—the fact that the slaves of ancient Greece are "unutterably silent" is a "horrible and tragic fact, given the many hundreds of thousands of slaves that existed at all periods of classical antiquity"—but then goes on with comparative equanimity to suggest that this actually suits his purposes very well, since he is concerned with how the Greeks represented slaves for their own purposes, and not, the implication is, with what the lives of slaves were actually, objectively speaking, like. As he says, what is at stake is "the ideology of slavery, the way in which slaves and slavery were represented by, for, and to the literate, slave-holding element of the Greek citizen estate."[17]

My point is not to question the suggestion, made by Hall, Cartledge, and others, that, in part due to the lack of source material from slaves themselves, any reconstruction of the role and significance of slaves in ancient Greek culture will say more about how slaves were perceived by those who owned them and ruled over them—and perhaps even more about us and about our contemporary preoccupations—than it will about the slaves in ancient Athens themselves. One can easily see why Hall and Cartledge emphasize the ideological construction of slaves and barbarians, and the ways in which such a construction tells us more about the self-representation and self-understanding of Greeks (or maybe even more about ourselves) than it does about anything else. The idea that a certain representation of those who come to inhabit the place of the other serves the interests of those who construct this other has become familiar enough, especially in the light of Edward Said's work on Orientalism.[18] My point is that the very distinctions to which both Hall and Cartledge appeal in order to establish how the Greeks represented themselves, and how slavery played into their self-representations, distinctions such as subjective versus objective, are themselves the product of a philosophical worldview that would not have pertained in ancient Greece. Therefore, while it might be helpful to employ notions such as ideology—notions that assume a distinction between what is subjectively perceived and objectively certifiable, even as they complicate the very distinction between how a subject represents the world and what is objectively true about that world—a certain amount of caution must be utilized in applying such notions to a culture that would not have assumed a subject-object split, would not have carved up the world into subjective and objective spheres, and would not have automatically privileged scientific thinking, nor the objective ideal that accompanies it in its contemporary manifestations, over other culturally embedded ways of thinking. In other words, in negotiating the complex ways in which the Greeks might have related to their own mythology, it is not altogether clear how helpful it is to employ terms such as ideology, which assume (even if these terms are employed in ways that seek to reconfigure or overcome) a series of distinctions which might come second nature to us, but would not have done to the Greeks.

The same problem emerges elsewhere. It has become commonplace to trace the modern concept of race back to Georges-Louis Buffon (1707–1788), but in his book *The Invention of Racism in Classical Antiquity* Benjamin Isaac locates the fifth century BCE as the point of origin of the "environmental theory" central to Buffon's work.[19] Isaac attributes to the ancients a "proto-racism" on the basis of the fact that even if they "lacked the biological elements of modern racism," they nonetheless harbored racism understood as "a construct of ungrounded theories and discriminatory commonplaces elaborated with the specific aim of establishing the superiority of one group over another, based on presumed physiological characteristics" (IR, 37). The story Isaac tells distinguishes modern racism from proto-racism by appealing to modern racism as an off-shoot of Darwinism (see IR 5 and 29).

The dimensions of the problem become clear when we consider that the very concepts used to distinguish modern racism from proto-racism are themselves the products of a modern mindset, in so far as the modern concept of race is identified with ideas about biological determination. Yet at the same time, these days there is widespread agreement that race, as a scientific concept, does not exist. The importance of establishing its existence as a social construct is maintained by some, but biologically and scientifically its existence has been discredited. We have a situation, then, in which efforts to trace the development of the concepts of race and/or racism (in contrast, for example, to ethnic prejudice) find themselves embroiled in a two-step argument. First there is the effort to distinguish ancient views of barbarians, for example, from modern ideas about race that attribute biological differences to groups and which imagine such differences to be determinative of distinct racial groups. The point is made that while the Greeks might not have seen race as biologically determinative, there were certain elements of their thinking that anticipated later views on race, for example their beliefs about environment, including climate, and beliefs about heredity. The salience of skin color, it is pointed out, does not become decisive until Enlightenment thinking (see IR, 13). The first leg of this argument is invested in showing that while there are certain continuities between the way the Greeks thought of barbarians, and modern concepts of race, there are also discontinuities, notably the role (or lack thereof) played by skin color as an indicator of race, and the relevance of ideas about certain racial traits being thought of as biologically determinative.

When ideas on race were pressed into service in order to justify African-American slavery, or in order to rationalize the Nazi treatment of Jews, Charles Darwin's work on the heritability of traits in relation to human species and subspecies was appropriated. The prevalent view of race was that it was biologically grounded. Now, and this is the second step of the argument—and where it gets complicated—those who want to insist on the importance of interrogating the development of the concept of race, and yet at the same time claim that race is not a scientific concept, find themselves doing a delicate balancing act. On the one hand they are in agreement with social theorists who not only concede that race is not a valid scientific concept, but argue rather that it is an ideological concept that still has salience precisely because of its vice-like grip on the public imagination. As such the concept needs to be thought of, and developed as, a social concept, since it has such importance in organizing our lives. In endorsing the importance of race as a social—not a scientific—concept, such positions, implicitly or explicitly, tend to argue for the imperative of taking not only scientific, but also (and especially, in the case of race) social concepts seriously, particularly when those concepts, like race, happen to play such decisive roles in determining the fabric of our lives. Race organizes, for example, where people live (residential segregation), where they go to school (educational discrimination), how much money they make (the racial glass ceiling), how much money banks are willing to lend them (institutional racism), and how seriously their concerns are taken by social and governmental agencies (organized racial inertia masquerading as often as not as color-blindness).

In arguing for the continuing salience of race as an organizing category of social, economic, and political life, theorists of race refuse to concede that the only important realities are material, scientifically measurable, empirically verifiable ones. That is, they refuse to concede that science is the last court of appeal, as important as it might be for scientists to come to some kind of consensus about the non-existence of race as a scientific concept. The fact that race continues to infiltrate so many important areas of our lives, whether or not it is a scientifically verifiable as a concept, makes it imperative to think about its continued impact, and therefore also makes it imperative to develop a nuanced and sophisticated concept of race as a social construct that retains enormous purchase over the ways we think and operate, even if it has no scientific grounding. It is part of the social imaginary, and as such its power cannot be underestimated.

In so far as they can be shown to rest on prejudice rather than appealing to any biologically determinative ground, the pre-scientific views that Aristotle and other ancient Greeks articulate about barbarians appear to be—let's concede the usual terms of debate for a moment—ideologically driven. Yet this ideological drive is precisely what interests social theorists who want to maintain the concept of race in order to designate its social, rather than its scientific, reality, in order to interrogate racial ideologies. Ironically, then, in some senses, we appear to have traveled in a full circle. If race did not exist as a (scientific) concept as such for the ancient Greeks—at least not in the sense that gained popularity in a post-Darwinian era, when it became associated with biologically heritable traits—neither is it said to exist now, according, to the influential and persuasive arguments of social theorists, except as a social construct.[20] To attribute to the ancient Greeks a proto-racism on the basis of the fact that whatever racially discriminatory views they inclined toward did not yet exhibit the scientism that would come to characterize post-Darwinian views of race, and then to throw in one's lot with contemporary theorists who deny the existence of race as a scientific concept, is to inhabit somewhat uneven conceptual ground. It is to claim that since the Greeks did not adhere to a biologically based conception of race they cannot be said to embrace race in the sense that post-Darwinians did, although they can be said to have anticipated it in important ways. Moreover, the post-Darwinians, who developed scientific conceptions of race, it now turns out, were wrong to construe race as a scientific concept. The consensus that race is not a scientific concept results in a view of race that largely conforms to the beliefs about barbarians that would have been circulating amongst the Greeks—at least insofar as their non-scientific status goes—in which case we seem to have retrospectively deprived ourselves of the grounds on which any distinction between a proto-racism attributed to the Greeks, and scientific racism might be made.

When Isaac distinguishes between modern racism and the proto-racism he attributes to the ancients, he embraces concepts without addressing the specifically modern assumptions that they imply. Consider the appeal to the concepts of "determinism," "human will," "control," "outside," and inside" in the following passage:

> The essence of early racism, as distinct from most other forms of hostility towards others, is that it seeks the cause for the differences between groups of peoples in either physiological or genetic determinism. This means that the presumed collective characteristics are unalterable by human will. They are claimed to be constant and to derive from factors over which people have no control, be it from the outside (climate and geography) or from the inside (genetic or physiological). (IR 36)

In appealing to the notions "determinism" and "human will," and understanding determinism in terms of "factors over which people have no control" whether these factors are external ("from the outside") or internal ("from the inside"), Isaac—despite agreeing that race does not exist as a scientific concept—seems to implicitly assume a post-Cartesian metaphysics, one that takes for granted the differentiation of an inner mind as opposed to an outer body, and aspires to notions of certainty grounded in science, the ideal of which is posited as mathematical. One need only consult E. R. Dodds, *The Greeks and the Irrational*, in order to get an inkling of the difficulty of superimposing assumptions emanating from essentially modern conceptions of consciousness, free will, individuality, and so forth, onto a culture whose literature is replete with Greek heroes who can be infused with divine *atē*, overcome with divine frenzy, or infected with mania at any given moment.[21] However we explain the relationship of mortals to gods, it is clear that it simply will not work to assume a mechanistic world in which cause and effect can be reduced to scientifically observable phenomena. Where characters in Greek mythology are routinely visited by divine inspiration, when the entire course of tragic action is shaped by an oracle, when a city traces back what it construes as its autochthonous ancestry to gods, or where community is such an important part of defining ethical and political action according to Aristotle, we can assume neither an individualism that carves up the world into ideally rational, atomistic subjects as distinct from objects, nor a behaviorist worldview in which we react to environment as if we were automata.

We cannot assume the authority of an inner mental rationalism that triumphs over external or material forces any more than we can reduce the world to a network of causes and effects, where we become the playthings of nature. I am not suggesting that any of the critics I discuss, and from whom I draw, are naively adopting either of these reductive worldviews, only that the options that modern thinking tends to confront us with assumes these views as the dichotomous endpoints within which the spectrum of explanations tends to fall, and in terms of which positions tend to be cashed out. While efforts such as that of Isaac remain helpful in trying to establish the relationship between how the processes according to which ancient Greeks rendered certain groups as other than themselves might relate to more recent ways of thinking of race, such efforts are weighed down by the conceptual difficulties to which I am pointing.

The issue is complicated still further by the fact that while there is not yet, in ancient Greek thinking, a hard and fast disciplinary compartmentalization into science versus humanities, there is an attempt to systematize knowledge under distinct headings. Aristotle theorizes about poetics, politics, physics, animals, and so on, moving from one to another with apparent alacrity, and thereby defying modern expectations of specialization, yet at the same time he reserves his attention for one topic as distinct from another, adhering to his own version of classifying topics, which does not accord with contemporary Western disciplinary boundaries. We see in Aristotle the beginnings of an attempt to systematize knowledge, and a move away from attributing to the gods an all pervasive influence on human action—although he still embraces a religious outlook to some extent—and toward what we would recognize as a more scientifically ordered world. We see Aristotle distinguish voluntary from involuntary action, in his attempt to explain ethical responsibility, but we do not see him making use of a vocabulary of inner versus outer. In other words, Aristotle's approach to the systemization of knowledge, building on Plato, begins to move away from a universe in which the relationship of mortals to gods is all-consuming, and we can retroactively identify elements of ancient Greek thinking as anticipating modern metaphysical thinking, but we should not make the mistake of importing modern, analytical assumptions into the world of the ancient Greeks lock, stock, and barrel.

One more caveat is required here, to mark the fact that my own understanding, as a continental philosopher, of the received philosophical genealogy that gives rise to what might broadly be identified as a phenomenological and poststructuralist heritage (traceable through figures such as Heidegger, Derrida, Michel Foucault, Luce Irigaray, Julia Kristeva, Emmanuel Levinas, Maurice Merleau-Ponty, and Jean-Paul Sartre) is part of a tradition that has constructed itself around the label "continental philosophy." This tradition is not immune from promulgating Eurocentric versions of philosophical legacies, which have played a part in the erasure of the questions I want to establish as crucial to an intellectually responsible, philosophically rigorous, and contextually informed interpretation of *Antigone*. In this sense my attempt is to rethink some of the assumptions that have helped to structure the tradition of continental philosophy, a tradition that traces itself back in some ways to the Greeks, but which acknowledges a certain reading of the Greeks that some continental philosophers have begun to challenge.[22] To point to the relevance of the slippage in the social imaginary of classical Athens between barbarian and slave to a play such as *Antigone* is itself to disrupt to a certain extent the orthodox interpretative legacy that has established itself as continuous with Hegel, Heidegger, Derrida, and Lacan. To extend this line of enquiry in order to legitimate questions that have tended to fall out of the orbit of the questions that the ritual citation of this distinguished intellectual heritage has authorized, is to take seriously, for example, the ramifications of Creon's exposure of Polynices' corpse in the context of Persian burial practices and to think through its significance for how barbarian practices figure into Athenian mythology.

As Herodotus reports, "the dead bodies of Persians are not buried before they have been mangled by bird or dog," or as Strabo reports the Magi "leave their bodies to be eaten by birds."[23] Again, Strabo reports "a similar custom at Taxila, now in Pakistan: 'Aristobolus mentions some novel and unusual customs at Taxila: . . . the dead are thrown out to be devoured by vultures.' " The point here is not whether or not the exposure of dead bodies "on high towers called Towers of Silence" where the bones were "stripped by birds"—an exposure that the inaugural (but belatedly presented) scene of Oedipus's first days as an infant might be said to mimic, since as an infant he is exposed on a mount—in fact corresponded to common burial practices amongst the Persians.[24] As Cartledge says, "Non-Greeks are 'Other,' therefore they must expose of the dead in 'other' ways" (GP 174). There is evidence that burial was indeed common in Persia. Yet the fact that the exposure of dead bodies constituted part of the mythical imaginary that Greeks entertained in relation to Persians suggests a relevant context in terms of which Polynices' exposed corpse in *Antigone* might be read. Creon expressly says that he wants to shame Polynices by having his corpse eaten by "birds" and "dogs."[25] The fact that it has not, for the most part, been read in this light is itself relevant to the question of how a tradition of reading *Antigone* has constructed itself according to certain parameters, leaving certain questions off the conceptual map that defines authorized interpretations in continental philosophy circles.

Sophocles' description in *Antigone* of the screeching birds that circle Polynices suggests that this conceptual map stands in need of disruption. The sounds of the birds constitute unintelligible signs for the transgendered Teiresias—and in light of the issues played out in *Antigone* around femininity, masculinity and barbarian identity his or her sexuality itself becomes food for thought.[26] The blind Teiresias, trained in the art, cannot interpret the sounds the birds make as intelligible signs. As Hall points out, in order to describe the screeching of the birds Sophocles uses a cognate of the word *barbaros,* "which originally referred solely to language, and simply meant 'unintelligible.' "[27] The word is onomatopoeic, evoking the allegedly cacophonous sounds of barbarian language. It may well be, then, that Sophocles had Persian practices of exposing the dead in mind in evoking barbarian sounds—which for the Greeks, especially in Athens which prided itself on the importance of civil discourse, rhetorical skill, and an emergent rationality—betokened a lack of civilization. To be unable to speak the Greek tongue was, essentially, to be considered deficient or uncivilized. In his description of the birds that are polluting the city of Thebes, a city that traces its ancestry back to Phoenicians, a city in which everything is turned upside down in *Antigone*, where the dead are left unburied and the living are buried alive, Sophocles references the barbarian threat, inhuman sounds that pervert intelligible meaning. The very order of things is under threat.

Against this background, Antigone's efforts to distinguish her brother from a slave resonate with the mythical Greek imaginary in which Persians exposed their dead. The equation of barbarians with slaves in the ancient Greek imaginary calls for the distinction Antigone is concerned to affirm: Antigone, a member of the royal line of descent, daughter of Oedipus, whose origins are surrounded with uncertainty, Antigone, whose father seeks to establish whether or not he was born a slave, Antigone, whose birth is plagued by an oracle that concerns a hereditary curse, which itself might well be read as a reference to the heritability of slavery, feels obligated to defend her brother from Creon's reduction of him to a traitor, to a barbarian—symbolically, therefore, to a slave.[28]

According to Wm. Blake Tyrrell and Larry J. Bennett proper burial was the expected norm in Athens. They refer to an Attic law that Aelian cites, which prescribes burial: "whoever comes upon an unburied corpse of a human, by all means throw earth upon it, and then bury it looking to the sunset" (RS 131). This sheds light on Antigone's dusting of Polynices' corpse with earth, and perhaps even her return to perform what, as commentators have pointed out, amounts to a second burial attempt.[29] As Tyrrell and Bennett note, citing Parker in a formulation that becomes decisive in the light of the questions I pursue below, a token act of burial "was required by virtue of the body's being that of a human" (RS 131).[30] We will see that the Greeks worked in a number of ways to raise questions about the humanity of slaves, whose status, at least if we are to take Aristotle's discussion of slavery in the *Politics* seriously, seemed to hover somewhere between that of animals and tools.[31] Given Creon's efforts to reduce Polynices to nothing but a traitor, and therefore as in some senses "worse" than a barbarian/slave, the status of Polynices' humanity is very much at stake in Antigone's burial of his corpse.

Tyrrell and Bennett go on to point out that while burial was the norm, "burial within the territory of Attica was never automatic" and that one of the crimes that would have been responsible for its denial was treason. They cite Xenophon in support of the claim that the "bodies of . . . traitors . . . were cast beyond the borders of the territory" (RS 131), and Lycurgos who says that the "remains of such offenders could be dug up and cast from Attica 'so that there not lie in the country the bones of someone who betrayed the country and city' " (RS 131). Even in such cases, however, Tyrrell and Bennett go on to note, "it was generally understood that the bodies of such men would be retrieved by their *philoi* [loved ones], and, if possible, buried secretly in Attica. Although 'it was not permitted to bury the bones of one exiled for treason' in Attica, the body of Themistocles was retrieved and buried secretly in his mother earth (Thucydides 1.138.6). From historical practice, it seems, Athenians would have allowed Polyneices' family to bury him in Attica, although not publicly" (RS 131). Antigone, of course, insists on declaiming her burial of her brother, and it is perhaps her loud declaration of her act, her insistence on airing her grievance, her refusal to adhere to the cannons of silence prescribed for women, in contrast to the secrecy surrounding the concession that family could bury even traitors, which gives cause for most offense.

Antigone's insistence not merely in burying her brother, but also in proclaiming the validity of her action is as much an assertion of Polynices' humanity as it is anything else. Her differentiation of Polynices from a slave is an affirmation of his humanity at the expense of the imputed sub-humanity of slaves. This, at least, constitutes an important strand of my argument, one that I believe can be sustained with a plethora of textual, historical and theoretical arguments, the persuasiveness of which I will attempt to establish.

Although, as I noted earlier, each of us necessarily brings to a text our own contemporary preoccupations—and in this sense we are necessarily entrenched to some extent in contemporary assumptions—it is also important to recognize significant, sometimes dramatic, differences between contemporary conceptual biases, and those characteristic of the period under consideration. Clearly we cannot hope to get inside the minds of ancient Greeks; equally, while their ways of thinking and living will remain somewhat impervious to us, it remains important to do what we can to try to entertain plausible scenarios about their interpretive schema. It seems important not to be content with simply constructing the Greeks as irredeemably other, and to give up on understanding them. The fact that, in the case of ancient Athens, a certain, idealized construction of Athenian culture has been so pervasively influential in setting up Western European ideals, including philosophical and political ideals, renders it all the more imperative that the subtext of this idealized construction be interrogated. If certain blindly dogmatic positions have settled into orthodoxies, such that the culture of fifth century BCE Athens, which has attained such prominence in Western imaginaries, has come to be articulated in the shadow of what sometimes appears to be willful ignorance of the structuring impact of slavery, the shadowy others of ancient Greece—and of *Antigone* specifically—demand attention.

Notwithstanding the difficulty of working through the conceptual thicket of the construction of continental philosophy, its specific configuration as it has been bequeathed to the interpretative legacy of *Antigone*, the blind spots that have resulted, and the current state of race theory and historiography, what can be said with a relative degree of confidence is that the idea of common descent or origin has been central to the concept of race, and that the ancient Greek appeal to *genos* reflects this idea. Even if ideas of common ancestors or pure descent have proved to be mythical, their importance in informing the popular imaginary cannot be ignored (see Isaac IR 25). Nicole Loraux has shown the ancient Greek fascination with myths of autochthony, myths which not only conceive of humans as born of the earth but are also concerned, as Herodotus puts it, with those who "stay in the same place" as opposed to emanating from elsewhere; Oedipus's displacement to Corinth comes to mind.[32] The chain of events set in motion by the oracle that warns of Lauis's death at the hands of a son by Jocasta removes Oedipus from Thebes, transports him to Corinth, and imports him to Thebes once more, a city he now enters as if a stranger.

Whereas the Athenians posited Ericthonios as their "autochthonous hero," as "born from the soil of Attica," as Loraux puts it, the Thebans identified the Phoenician Kadmos as their founder.[33] While the myth of human origins that Thebes tells itself therefore celebrates, in Loraux's words, a "foundational alterity, other cities and regions [Athens among them] opted for the reassuring celebration of the same by the same."[34] As Loraux notes, such foundation myths are "less concerned with providing a version of the beginnings of humankind than with postulating the original nobility of a founder: as Erechtheids the autochthonous Athenians liked to remember that the palace of Erechtheus was also the temple of Athena."[35] At stake, then, was the "passage to the human . . . what makes the son of a god into the first human?"[36] In turn, myths that elaborated noble origins were caught up with rivalry between Greek cities. As Hall says, citing Froma Zeitlin, "Athenians liked to emphasize the tradition of the Thebans' barbarian origins and, moreover, in tragedy displaced their own stasis and internal strife to other, historically hostile, Greek cities: the tragic Thebes is counterculture, a mirror opposite of the tragic Athens (Zeitlin 1986). Thebes houses tyrants, incest, stasis, and sexual deviationists, whereas the Athens of tragedy is nearly always an idealized polis, free from internal conflict and led by democratically minded kings."[37] The idea of Thebes as a counterculture proves pertinent to the reading suggested throughout this book.

The interest in protecting and preserving the clarity and legitimacy of kinship structures in the Athenian polis was closely connected to the desire to distinguish between slaves and free citizens, a structuring theme in the fabric and organization of Athens. As N. R. E. Fisher says, "the distinction between slave and free was one of the most fundamental and determining antitheses in the structures of thought and moral values of the Athenians (and probably of other Greeks)."[38] Reflecting Aristotle's arguments in the *Politics*, Peter Garnsey maintains, "Slavery both provided the economic necessities of life for a number of Athenians, and gave them the freedom to pursue 'the good life' in the sphere of politics."[39] While these two observations can serve as introductory statements about the structuring presence of slavery in fifth century BCE Athens, there is more to be said, both about slavery as a structuring antithesis for the Athenian way of life, and about the sense in which the slavery of some facilitated for others the form of life that consisted of living well and flourishing, the free pursuit of *eudaimonia* that Aristotle spells out in the *Nicomachean Ethics*.[40]

In order to pursue a life of politics or of philosophy—or indeed to be able to create tragedies—the free, male citizens of Athens depended on slaves to attend to the menial, material necessities of life. As Cartledge puts it, slavery provided "the privileged Greek citizens with the necessary leisure (*skholē*) for their *praxis* of politics and philosophical contemplation" (GP 142). Cartledge elaborates five polarities that structure Greek thought, each of which mutually implicates and intercuts with the others. These polarities are citizen-alien, Greek-barbarian, men-women, free-slave, and gods-mortals. In exploring how these polarities function, Cartledge pursues an approach that builds on the legacy of structuralism, in the tradition of Claude Lévi-Strauss, Jean-Pierre Vernant, and Charles Segal. "The narrating of myths" Cartledge reminds us ". . . is famously seen by Lévi-Strauss as a method of mediating contradictions between deeply structured binary polarities such as men v. women and mortals v. gods" (GP 16).

I suggest that the way in which Cartledge envisages the sets of binaries he maps out, illuminating though it is, needs some refinement, or at least some tweaking. He cites approvingly Charles Segal's specification that "it is not a 'static system of polarities' that we have to deal with, but 'overlapping sets of dynamic interrelations, complex transformations and shifting tensions, viewed in the context of history, social institutions, ritual and political life' " (GP 16).[41] To affirm that the mutually implicating binaries he explores to such good effect can be adequately described as "overlapping" does not in fact do justice to the account that Cartledge goes on to provide, in so far as the image preserves the integrity and independence of the different pairs of binaries.

As Cartledge's own account demonstrates, it is not just that these binaries intercut, intertwine, or intersect with one another; rather they are constructed in terms of one another, fabricated with the help of one another. They blend into one another, feed off one another, do metaphorical work for one another, borrowing from one another, helping to constitute one another, and bolstering one another up, so that one pole of a pejorative polarity functions in support of another and vice versa. So, for example, as Cartledge observes, " 'Female' was considered categorically inferior to 'male,' and it was an essential part of

Greek heterology that male barbarians should have been construed as naturally effeminate" (GP 12).[42] Here it is evident that the men-women polarity does not just intercut with the Greek-barbarian polarity, but helps to construct it and inform it. That, as Cartledge goes on to say, referring to Aristotle's *Politics*, "women are not (deemed to be) by nature equal to men" and therefore "cannot be citizens" (GP 124) is held by Aristotle to be a mark of the superiority of the Athenian political way of life over that of barbarians, a superiority that includes a condemnation of the fact that women's inequality with men appeared to be less entrenched in non-Greek cultures. Borrowing from a prejudice against women, which itself is formulated in a way that posits a dichotomy between Greeks and barbarians, Aristotle thereby construes both women and barbarians as inferior to Greek males. Feeding into the construction of the Greek male, as we will see, are assumptions specific to Athens about entitlements to freedom and about criteria that are imagined to qualify only free men as citizens.

The opposition between men and women conceived here in terms of the opposition citizen-non-citizen (the latter constituting a polarity made up of nuances Cartledge does not allow for, since his opposition citizen-alien does not take account of the need to distinguish between *astoi, politai,* and *xenoi*—or between those who are resident Athenians, such as women, but excluded from functioning in any civic capacity—and in this sense not active, political citizens—fully participating citizens, and those who derive from elsewhere, from somewhere outside Athens).[43] Yet, paradoxically, the men-women polarity also relies on an implicit analogy between resident aliens or metics (non-Athenian residents of Athens) and women, both of whom are considered unsuited for the responsibilities and privileges of citizenship.[44] Though in some sense part of, included within, the polis, in another sense, women, resident aliens (or metics), and slaves are excluded from it. As we will see further, the chain of associations that dictated who was "in the club" of Athenian citizenry, as Cartledge phrases it, and who was out, appealed to stereotypes about the slavish nature of barbarians, or foreigners who did not speak Greek.[45]

That Aristotle finds it necessary to clarify that "the female and the slave are by nature distinct" suggests that there might be some reason to doubt this, and the fact that he goes on to assert that "among barbarians the female and the slave have the same rank" suggests the degree to which Aristotle's view of distinctions he casts as natural—including (and perhaps especially) the distinction between slaves and females—is bound up with establishing the Greek, or more specifically Athenian, way of life as superior to that of barbarians.[46] At the same time it indicates that questions of appropriate virile conduct and sexual roles are, in Aristotle's mind, a mark of the level of civilization he thinks has been attained by respective peoples.[47] Proper control over women is associated with proper control over slaves, in classical Athens, and both are implicated in having the best form of government.

If the way in which the difference between women and men was conceived as intricately bound up with the differentiation between citizens and non-citizens (and therefore reliant upon assumptions about the common traits of those disqualified from citizenry), so too the citizen-alien binary was very much informed by the free-slave binary. As Cartledge observes, in a remark that takes account of how the citizen-alien binary was constituted in part by the free-slave binary for the Classical Greeks: " 'slave' was by extension the antithesis of 'citizen,' since a Greek citizen was by definition free" (GP 133). In turn, there was a virtual equation of slavery and barbarians. Cartledge goes on to say "In so far as Greekness was identified with freedom—spiritual and social as well as political—and slavery was equated with being barbarian, Greek civilization, culture and mentality could be said to have been based, ideologically, on slavery" (GP 142).[48] As Cartledge also stipulates, "For the Greeks, Persians were slaves because, being barbarians, they were naturally slavish" (GP 113). Whether the ostensible slavishness of barbarians was imputed to Persians because they were barbarians (and therefore allegedly naturally slavish), or whether their reputed slavish nature was due to the fact that the Athenians routinely made barbarians into slaves, confining them to the work they judged appropriate for slaves, and then justifying enslaving them because of the work to which they had been confined, is not a question Aristotle allows himself to confront.[49] Aristotle does, however, cover all his bases, often providing multiple and mutually incompatible explanations and justifications for slavery, betraying inadvertently perhaps a not so deeply buried anxiety about the inadequacy that pervades the many conflicting grounds he adduces.[50]

For Aristotle, as Cartledge says, the "nature of [the work of craftsmen and farmers] allegedly rendered their souls servile and slavish, whereas 'political' ruling was by definition something practised by, over, and for entirely free men" (GP 125). It does not take much to see how, having rendered the Athenian way of life—as symbolized by the free, male, adult citizen—practically synonymous with freedom, Aristotle can construe the Athenians as suited to rule over barbarians. The latter are symbolized by those supposedly effeminate males who are constructed as naturally slavish—as proven by their apparent incapacity to rule appropriately over barbarian women—and as such are thought to be appropriately ruled by those whose talents prove themselves worthy political rulers, those whose political structures assure appropriate governance over "their" women: the Athenians. What is presented as appropriate governance over Athenian women turns out to be a rather thinly veiled effort to control the inheritance of citizenship; in other words, it turns out to be a question of surveillance over women's sexual activity for the purposes of ensuring the reproduction of legitimate citizens, the legitimacy of which, by definition, was exclusive of those constructed as slavish barbarians.

The spectacular circularity of the thought process justifying slavery in relation to other beliefs at the heart of the social fabric of Athenian life is breathtaking. Male barbarians are said to be effeminate, which helps to bolster up the argument that they are naturally slavish. Their ostensible effeminacy assumes the inequality of women to men, at the same time as it presupposes that women's inferiority allies women with slaves. The fact that male barbarians are thought to be incapable of controlling what are construed as "their" women is taken to be a sign of their political incompetence, their weakness as rulers, while their ostensible effeminacy (and therefore alleged similarity to women) already functions as grounds for suspicion of their allegedly inherently slavish natures. Neither women nor slaves are deemed eligible for citizenship, an ineligibility which itself is ascribed on the basis of the imputed slavish nature of male barbarians, and the alignment of slaves with women, that suggests both need to be ruled over, as Cartledge puts it ironically, "for their own good" (GP 124).[51] Male barbarians, the implication is, are insufficiently despotic in their rule over women, an inadequacy that is used to indicate their failure as political rulers, and a mark of their own purportedly slavish natures.[52] The series of embedded implications that make up these dovetailing assumptions encloses the binaries Cartledge defines in a self-sustaining economy that, if not impervious to challenge, certainly resembles a veritable conceptual labyrinth that resists navigation.

Adding to this complexity is the reputedly natural role that Aristotle assigns to the polis—and, Cartledge suggests, most Greeks would have agreed upon the "indispensability of the polis framework" (GP 123). The political organization that takes the form of the polis appears to seal the all but hermetically closed system of cultural inferences that links women, barbarians, non-citizens, and slaves. The freedom that is assumed to be so central to, and definitive of, the life of an adult, Athenian, male citizen cannot be separated from the Greek belief in the polis as the sole political organization in which human life can flourish (for some) to its full potential. The polis functions only by reserving the right to specify who may pursue, and who must be excluded in advance from pursuing, the true human potential that the polis makes possible; among those who are excluded from political participation—denied citizenship—are slaves, who are (for the most part) drawn precisely from those whose lives are said to be conducted in a politically inferior way, namely barbarians. Moreover, the exclusion of slaves from the political life of the polis facilitates the inclusion of those who participate in its political life.

It is not just, as Cartledge says, that "although other forms of community could provide the means of bare subsistence or existence, only the polis could enable mankind to live the true morally good life, the life of 'well-faring' (*eudaimonia*)" (GP 123). It is also that the dependence of this full and flourishing life made possible by the polis was subtended by the ideological exclusion of those not recognized as worthy or capable of pursuing such a life, those consigned to tasks the execution of which, and the material products of which, precisely made possible the pursuit of allegedly worthy goals by others. In other words, those consigned to bare life within the polis—male and female slaves and free women—freed up others to formulate their goals as worthy, to formulate the end of life in terms of realizing their full potential as human, by relegating others to lives not considered worthy or capable of living up to that full human potential. If, as Cartledge says, "zōön politikon designates a living creature designed by its nature to realize its full, human potential, its 'end' (*telos*) . . . within and only within the political framework constituted by polis" (GP 123), and if the polis was designed so that those who realized their full human potential did so at the expense of those denied the opportunity to do so, then, as Giorgio Agamben formulates it, "bare life has the peculiar privilege of being that whose exclusion founds the city of men."[53] Within the polis, the labor performed by those excluded from politics rendered possible the formulation of political and social ends that underwrite their constitutive exclusion. In Chapter 5 I attend to Agamben's understanding of those excluded others of the polis that are also in some way included, a formulation that helps shed light on *Antigone*, even if, I will suggest, *Antigone* helps complicate and problematize the terms of Agamben's formulation. As Moira Fradinger suggests, for Creon, "the rotting corpse" of Polynices "signifies the ever present internal 'enemy' of Thebes who justifies Creon's measures to prevent the spawning of further enemies. Essential to the operation of inclusion/exclusion is that the corpse is *one of their own*. Creon insists on Polynices' ties to the family: 'He was prepared to destroy *his* land and the gods of his *race*, to feed on *kindred* blood and reduce other *kindred* to slavery' " (Fradinger's italics).[54]

The city of men, as Agamben puts it, is defined by a group of people capable of realizing their full human potential by requiring others to inhabit a subordinate realm constructed in such a way as to prevent them from realizing theirs. Perhaps unsurprisingly, in order to justify such a construction, the Greeks construed the people they required to inhabit this marginal zone as subhuman. One of the terms that, according to Cartledge "unambiguously" designated slaves was *andrapodon*, a term that was "formed by analogy with a standard Greek word for cattle, *tetrapoda* or 'four-footed things,' and so provides as perfect an illustration as could be hoped for of the normative Greek construction of slaves as subhuman creatures" (GP151).[55] This construction served therefore to enable adult, male, Athenian citizens to construe themselves as free, and as natural rulers over slaves—most of whom were barbarians—and over women, whose insubordinate state among barbarians was in turn used to rhetorically justify the equation of barbarians with slaves.

In the light of the analogy with cattle upon which the term *andrapodon* relies, the significance of the riddle of the Sphinx that Oedipus solves comes into relief in a way that has been largely overlooked. What creature, asks the sphinx, goes on four, two, and three feet?[56] Rarely have commentators drawn what appears to be an implication that surfaces once one takes into account the salience of the slave-culture upon which Athenian supremacy was built, and the uncertainty surrounding the circumstances of Oedipus's familial origins.[57] Inscribed at the heart of the riddle that Oedipus solves is whether or not he is a slave or a king; the arbitrariness of—and lack of clarity surrounding—the solution at which he arrives serves to highlight the arbitrariness of the marking of some individuals, rather than others, as suitable for the institution of slavery. Cultural markers are assigned to do the work of making certain peoples eligible for slavery, and the distinction between cultures and peoples has everything to do with Oedipus's anxiety about his origins. His "fear," as Frederick Ahl puts it, "of being ignobly born," is played out in an exchange with a Corinthian and a slave who herds sheep, an exchange in which, as Ahl points out, "interrogation under torture becomes an imminent threat."[58] As we will see further, torture was an accepted practice for slaves, and its institution was one of the defining differentiating factors between slaves and non-slaves. As Ahl points out, if a disagreement between a free man and a slave arose, evidence from slaves was only accepted in classical Athens under torture so that Sophocles' exploration of a slave's interrogation under threat of torture serves as a platform on which Sophocles can put on display and interrogate the process by which so-called evidence was extracted, and thereby explore the conventions according to which trials were conducted, at the same time as contemplating the mores according to which slaves were treated as subhuman. Oedipus is concerned to establish the legitimacy of his heritage when he asks whether the child born to Laius, and given to a slave belonging to Laius, was, "a slave or born of Laios' own blood."[59] The slave entrusted with instructions to expose the infant defied his master, a defiance which sets in motion the confusion that ensues in the Oedipal cycle between the identity of a slave and that of a king, a defiance, therefore, that questions the order of authority in Thebes, the symbolic other of Athens, both that of slave to master, and that of subject to king.[60]

Oedipus wants to establish whether he was born a slave, and in doing so, he also brings into question the leadership of Thebes he has assumed. Since according to Pausanius, Laius, as Ahl points out, had "several . . . illegitimate sons by concubines," the question Oedipus raises, and the anxiety it betrays both about his origins, and about the legitimacy of his leadership as king, assumes a context that, on its own terms, makes his question perfectly explicable.[61] Oedipus wants to know if he was one of the illegitimate sons that Laius is reputed to have had. Ironically, it is precisely his legitimacy—the fact that Jocasta, rather than a concubine, was his mother—that resulted in his being given to a slave in order to be exposed, since the oracle according to which Laius and Jocasta act when they order Oedipus's abandonment specifies that Laius would be killed by a son by Jocasta, rather than by anyone else.[62] Oedipus's legitimacy (as king and as son of Laius) is intricately bound up, it would seem, with questions surrounding the legitimacy of slaves. The legitimacy of slaves, in turn, is intricately bound up with the legitimacy of marriage, and Oedipus's marriage to Jocasta has compromised his own legitimacy as a father and thus thrown into crisis any possibility of the children he generates establishing clearly and definitively the logic of their inheritance. Included among the consequences of the impasse to which this leads the children of Oedipus is the mortal combat in which Eteocles and Polynices engage over who should rule Thebes, the enmity between Ismene and Antigone over the question of burying Polynices against Creon's edict, and the death of Antigone as a result of her burial of Polynices. Antigone's suicide marks the end of the Oedipal line: no children issue from the children of Oedipus, and none shall be forthcoming from the wife or sons of Creon either, all of whom are dead by the end of the play named for *Antigone*, while Creon himself is a broken man, whose lack of foresight for the polis, and lack of appreciation for the mutual dependence of politics and *philoi* has led to the destruction of his own family. Antigone's distinction of her brother Polynices from a slave, as we will see further, can be read as an effort to differentiate him from the uncertainties surrounding the birth of Oedipus.

The familial and sovereign lines of Oedipus the father and Oedipus the king are profoundly confused, and this confusion cannot be rectified without implicating fundamental questions about the legitimacy of the political and cultural ordering of Thebes, the symbolic Other of Athens. The role of the symbolic father, in the Lacanian sense, has indeed been catastrophically interrogated by its founding, literary father, Oedipus, such that no amount of consolidating can conceal its fragility, despite the stalwart work of Lacanians to shore it up. In staging the intricacies of inheritance, the freighted question of origins, and the importance of establishing one's birthright, Sophocles is confronting the tangled web of dependencies that constitutes marriage protocols, specifies lineage, and determines who is granted citizenship and who is not, who is free, and who is enslaved in the Athens of his time. In transposing these questions to Thebes, he holds out the possibility that in Athens this tangled web might be sifted through and straightened out. So tangled were the threads of the web, readers of *Antigone* are still sorting through them, delineating them. So important were the questions Sophocles raised, they still generate conceptual impasses that haunt our interpretive efforts.

Excluded from the pursuit of the good life that the polis made possible, slaves and women were in another way included—but included as subordinate—as their labor was necessary in order to free up citizens to conduct their lives in ways that allowed them to enquire into and reflect upon the goals that were considered worth pursuing. Precisely what could be the worth of goals defined on the basis of the exclusion of those whose labor facilitated this pursuit, and thus were inscribed as inferior? Questions such as this appear to have been off limits for most Athenians. How were such limits imposed on the reflective purview of the contemplative life such that reflection did not extend to questioning the conditions that enabled such contemplation to flourish—a condition that enslaved some men and women so that others had the leisure to pursue a free life? Cartledge answers the question in this way with regard to Aristotle: so much was slavery "part of the air that the Greeks breathed" (GP 142) that it did not occur to him to challenge it.[63] Cartledge goes on, "Aristotle's gloss on the ordinary free Greek's view of slavery could be woven seamlessly into his anti-conventionalist, teleological view of the good life for mankind within the polis" so that he "could imagine no alternative" (GP 142)—aside, that is, as Bernard Williams puts it, from the invention of "self-propelling tools."[64]

Williams corroborates Cartledge's view when he observes that Aristotle's defense of a theory of natural slavery is premised on the desire to defend the form of life as conducted in the polis: "It is necessary for life in the polis, and the polis is a natural form of association."[65] Williams adds that Aristotle "argues not merely that it is natural that someone or other should be a slave, but that there are people for whom it is natural that they, rather than someone else, should be slaves."[66] The people who turn out to be natural slaves, according to Aristotle, as we have seen, are the barbarians, and Asiatics are singled out in this respect as those who, claims Aristotle, "endure despotic rule without any resentment."[67] In order to argue why certain people are suited to slavery, while others are suited to rule over them, Aristotle has recourse to a number of analogies, comparing slaves at various points not only to women and children but also to tools and animals, and appealing to the way in which the soul should rule over the body.[68] In an argument taken to be essential to his position, Aristotle maintains that a slave is deficient in reason.[69] A slave can "apprehend" reason but not "possess it."[70]

As Fisher points out, Aristotle's reasoning here "does not cohere" with his later argument that Asiatics are not lacking in logos, or what H. Rackham translates "reason," but rather are lacking in spirit (*thumos*), and that they are naturally more slave-like than the Greeks.[71] The "Greek race" (*genos*) is said to be midway between those of Europe, and the people of Asia, as the Greek race is both "spirited and intelligent; hence it continues to be free and to have very good political institutions, and to be capable of ruling all mankind."[72] It is hard to avoid Fisher's conclusion that this amounts to the view that "it is in general wrong for Greeks to be enslaved, but proper for non-Greeks."[73]

Having invoked a Greek "genos" in the context of defending the freedom of the Greeks, Aristotle—perhaps in order to mark his esteem for the Athenian political way of life above that of others, as well as to attempt to justify that there are some people that need "to be guided in virtue"—then goes on to acknowledge that there exists a "diversity among the Greek races (ἔθνη) compared to one another."[74] Side by side with the emergence of a PanHellenic consciousness, as Hall reminds us, there is also considerable rivalry among Greek city-states, and this helps to explain why Aristotle pursues his arguments about slavery in a way that both seeks to establish the superiority of Greeks in general over barbarians—and in particular over Asiatics—while at the same time reserves for the Athenian way of life a respect that differentiates the Athenian polis from other poleis.[75]

Hall has argued for the prevalence of the Hellene/barbarian polarity in tragedy. At the same time she has indicated that this polarity functions ideologically both as a way of establishing the supremacy of the political form of life characteristic of the Athenian polis over political forms of organization elsewhere, and in concert with the idea that barbarians are naturally slavish.[76] "The polarization of Hellenism and barbarism even presupposes that a generic bond exists not only between all Greeks, but between all non-Greeks as well" says Hall, citing a number of tragedies in which "the entire barbarian *genos*" is invoked.[77] Cartledge agrees with Hall when he cites the Greek victory in the Persian wars (480–79 BCE) as the decisive event that entrenched the polarity of Greeks and barbarians (see GP 13). Henceforward, as Wilfred Nippel says, "instead of statements about the Persians, Thracians, Scythians and Egyptians, there appeared others on Barbarians understood as a uniform *genos* [race or family] to whom were attributed cumulatively determined models of behaviour."[78] If a generalized *genos* was attributed to barbarians in Greek tragedy, we also find a generalized *genos* attributed to Greeks in Aristotle's notorious attempt to defend a theory of natural slavery. Aristotle appeals to a Greek "race" (*genos*), for example, in an effort to establish why it is that Asiatics are allegedly more suited to slavery than are the Greeks, whose predisposition, as we have seen, on Aristotle's view, is supposedly to rule—and Athenians, it would seem, for him, are still more predisposed to rule than other Greeks.

One consideration Aristotle includes in his attempt to justify slavery, one that is not usually the focus of critical attention, is the "natural instinct to desire to leave behind one another being of the same sort of oneself."[79] As we saw, Loraux notes that the Athenian myth of its autochthonous origins is a myth that celebrates sameness, rather than alterity.[80] Not only are arguments concerning the natural proclivity of some to rule over others, and the lack of reason (or spirit) in barbarian peoples invoked by Aristotle, but also, implicitly, the desire to populate the world in the image of oneself—linked, we can add—to the desire for free men to ensure that their children remain free and do not suffer the fate of enslavement. It is precisely on this point, however, that nature is found to be lacking. For nature, Aristotle reasons, should produce slaves with appropriately stooped bodies, since the tasks they perform (manual crafts and agriculture) involve stooping, but nature does not always comply (see Cartledge GP 140). As Garnsey puts it, "The problem of pinning down the natural slave would be less acute if there were firm, visible criteria by which he could be identified. It would be a straightforward matter, says Aristotle, if the natural slave had a distinctive physique. But nature slipped up."[81] It intended to differentiate between the bodies of freemen and slaves, such that free bodies are upright, but since this does not always work out, nature needs to be supplemented. So, Cartledge suggests, Aristotle has recourse to a theory that differentiates between slaves and free persons with reference not merely to their bodies, but to their souls: "whereas it is not so simple to identify securely the nature of a person's *psukhē,* his or her posture is immediately and irrefutably apparent" (GP 140). One can discern, here, Plato's influence regarding the nature of souls. If the souls of those belonging to the three classes of persons Plato distinguishes from one another in the *Republic* can do the work that nature tried but failed to do with regard to distinguishing slavish from non-slavish bodies (on Aristotle's interpretation), then all will be well. It is up to nature to ensure that some souls are naturally suited to slavery, while others are not. Problem solved.

The underlying tensions that structure Aristotle's vacillation with regard to whether and how the bodies and souls reflect slavish natures show him grappling with debates that will come to characterize later efforts to classify peoples into races, to provide exhaustive taxonomies, and to point to physical and/or mental capacities that supposedly prove the inferiority of some groups of people in relation to others, in order to justify the subordination of allegedly inferior peoples. Responding to some unidentified interlocutor, Aristotle's strained reasoning appears to betray the conclusion that Fisher draws, cited above, that Aristotle's efforts are directed toward establishing why barbarians, but not Greeks (and especially not Athenians), should be slaves, when, acknowledging the relevance of just-war theory, he refuses to entertain the possibility that nobility deserve to become "slaves and the descendants of slaves" in the following argument:

> [S]ome persons, doing their best to cling to some principle of justice (for the law is a principle of justice), assert that the enslavement of prisoners of war is just; yet at the same time they deny the assertion, for there is the possibility that wars may be unjust in their origin and one would by no means admit that a man that does not deserve slavery can be really a slave—otherwise we shall have the result that persons reputed of the highest nobility are slaves and the descendants of slaves if they happen to be taken prisoners of war and sold.[82]

Aristotle's differentiation of nobility from slaves here seems to confirm that his arguments about slavery—the contorted form of which are evident in this passage—are driven by the need to defend the Athenian system of chattel slavery as much as they are motivated by anything else. Aristotle advances the view that the Greek polis, and more especially that of the Athenians, is the supreme political organization, and is symptomatic of why Greeks (and more particularly Athenians) are suited to rule over others; by construing Greeks as generally more fit to rule over barbarians. Aristotle's views on slavery are complicit with the ambitions of sustaining the Athenian empire. His emphasis on distinguishing nobility from slaves cannot help but convey a self-interest in preserving the status quo, in which social stratification demands the careful separation of slaves from non-slaves. As Cartledge says, "Aristotle was faithfully representing the ideology of the Greek ruling classes and the ideas of the ruling classes were Greece's ruling ideas" (GP 164-5).[83]

The need to delineate clearly between nobility on the one hand, and slaves and their descendants on the other hand, rests upon the clear demarcation of kinship lines. This need to preserve the sanctity and purity of kinship lines was at the heart of protecting the Athenian way of life, including its system of chattel slavery, where slaves were understood as animate tools, living property, or property with souls.[84] The labyrinthine argumentation Aristotle constructs in defense of chattel slavery—which Cartledge takes to be "largely representative" of Athenians in general—such that slaves are "ensouled" (*empsukhon*) property (GP 136)—analogous to multi-tasking tools, depends, as Cartledge expresses it, on *genos* in two ways. First, it rested on an allegedly natural condition of the soul, and secondly on heredity. It "depended on a 'natural' condition of *psukhē*, which should be male, free, and Greek; and, secondly, it should be transmissible by—and usually solely by—heredity" (GP 125). In a formulation that takes account of the Periclean law, but which glosses over a difference between men and women vis-à-vis citizenship that will need to be elaborated, Cartledge goes on to observe (in a formulation that refers back to the standard view of *genos* as articulated by Aristotle): "A state like democratic Athens that required double descent (citizenship parentage on both sides) took this standard view to its logical limits, adding for good measure the ideological glue of autochthony" (GP 125).

If Williams and Cynthia Patterson clarify what is at issue in the distinction between male citizens and the women who functioned as legal conduits to convey citizenship, Loraux, as indicated, has done a great deal to elucidate the importance of the Athenian myth of autochthony. As William says, "Athenian women were not citizens, but the 'women of Athens.' At the same time, there was a relevant difference between being such a woman and not being so, since the Periclean rule required a male citizen to be *ex amphoin aston*—as it cannot be translated, 'a citizen on both sides.' "[85] Williams' point is that while Athenian women themselves could not be citizens in the sense of functional civic persons able to make political decisions, serve in political office, or as jurors, for example, the all-important fact that they lived within the city boundaries, that they were, in this sense, Athenian rather than barbarian, enabled them to confer citizenship upon their male children. Excluded from citizenship themselves, legitimate mothers/wives were nonetheless indispensable for conferring male citizenship.[86] In an exhaustive and important study of the significance and impact of Pericles' law Patterson clarifies that although the law is usually taken to concern marriage, in fact the evidence of the law itself suggests simply that "Athenians are only those with two Athenian parents."[87] Patterson goes on to suggest that "the law would have severely discouraged marriages between Athenians and foreigners" and to note the related "Athenian fear (realistic or not)," to which she understands Pericles' law to be a response, "that Athenians were no longer Athenians—a fear which developed alongside the 'obsessive' idea that Athenians were a special and distinct group of people, autochthonous and 'unmixed' with barbarians."[88] The practice of adoption—the fate of Oedipus at Corinth—is cited as a cause of this Athenian fear.

Myths concerning origins and descent were inextricably linked to the ancient Greek belief in gods. As indicated by Cartledge's insistence upon exploring not only the Greek-barbarian, men-women, citizen-alien, and free-slave binary polarities, but also the antithesis gods-mortals, the social roles attributed to slaves or women functioned in tandem with religion. We have already begun to see this to some extent in considering Greek perceptions of barbarian burial practices, which did not necessarily accord seamlessly with actual burial practices, but which certainly served the purpose of othering barbarians, thereby cementing the Greek belief in the lack of civilization characteristic of barbarian ways of life, including religious conventions concerning the burial (or non-burial) of the dead. We have also begun to see that the extent to which Greek ideas about barbarians are equated with their ideas about slaves, and that the existence of slaves was a fact, the necessity of which in Athenian culture was taken for granted. Williams suggests that "considerations of justice and injustice were immobilised by the demands of what was seen as social and economic necessity."[89]

Disputing the adequacy of the conventional explanation provided for slavery in sixth century BCE Athens, that of war and conquest, as neither necessary nor sufficient, M. I. Finley adduces the following three necessary conditions. First, there was a "sufficient concentration" of "private ownership of land" in an "overwhelmingly agrarian" world "to need extra-familial labour for the permanent work-force." Second, there was "a sufficient development of commodity production and markets," and third, a "negative condition" obtained—there was "the unavailability of an internal labour supply, compelling the employers of labour to turn to outsiders."[90] Finley explains Athens' turn to "slave outsiders" as a source of labor with reference to the fact that the "élite" had "lost their older forms of involuntary labour. . . . The peasantry had won their personal freedom and their tenure on the land through struggle, in which they also won citizenship, membership in the community, the *polis*."[91] Consistent with this, Garnsey cites Solon's reforms as a catalyst in the adoption of slavery in Athens: "Athenians . . . in the late archaic period had need of slaves because the reforming law-giver Solon in the early sixth century outlawed debt-bondage and other forms of dependent labour affecting the free residents of Attica, thus depriving rich Athenians of their workforce."[92] After Solon's laws, traditionally dated, in 594 BCE, according to Fisher, "No Athenian was henceforth to be enslaved in Athens."[93]

The outsider status of slaves consisted both in the fact that the slave originated from outside Athens, and in the deprivation of kinship affiliation—a deprivation that has particular pertinence to the Oedipal cycle, in which kinship ties are overdetermined in a hyperbolic fashion. The kinship roles that become so compounded in the royal Oedipal family, to the point that the family line is finally extinguished, in one way presents us with a mirror opposite of the total kinlessness imposed on slaves, their rootlessness, their deracinated, outsider status. Yet in another way, as we have begun to see, it is the unusual circumstances of the birth of Oedipus—circumstances which, when Oedipus tries to reconstruct them yield a high degree of uncertainty—that give rise to the intensely compounded familial symbolic functions to which each member of the Oedipal family becomes answerable. That Sophocles has Oedipus, in his attempted reconstruction of the events surrounding his birth, exposure, and transition to Corinth, rely on the testimony of a slave whom he threatens with torture suggests Sophocles' interest in reflecting on the Athenian practice of extracting evidence from slaves through torture, and in raising the question of the reliability of such evidence. That Sophocles has Oedipus displaced to Corinth—a known slave center—suggests that he is playing on the idea of the contingency of circumstances that lead to slaves becoming slaves, perhaps with respect to the restrictive conditions imposed upon the criteria for citizenry in Athens, a polis in which no Athenian could become a slave.

"The slave," says Finley, was always a deracinated outsider—an outsider first in the sense that he originated from outside the society into which he was introduced as a slave, second in the sense that he was denied the most elementary of social bonds, kinship."[94] As Fisher puts it, slaves "remain permanently foreign, 'outsiders,' having no social identity. Those who are enslaved during adult life often have their previous identity formally removed in the process of sale; they are stripped of their clothes, their former names, their kin, their nationality, and even their personality. Patterson calls this process 'social death,' after which a new life begins with a different name and identity and very few, if any, rights. Such an experience was bound to be traumatic, and to a degree that is hard to imagine."[95] In the words of Garnsey, "The slave was kinless, stripped of his or her old social identity in the process of capture, sale and deracination, and denied the capacity to forge new bonds of kinship."[96] As Garnsey goes on to say, "most slaves in Athens were 'barbarians,' or foreigners, from Thrace, the Black Sea Region, Asia Minor and Syria."[97] In the context of the status of slaves as deracinated outsiders, the fact that, along with Chios, the city-state of Corinth—where Oedipus is adopted by King Polybus and Queen Merope without knowing his true familial origins—was known as a slave center, takes on a peculiar significance.[98]

The decisive difference, as Finley formulates it, between slavery and other forms of labor (such as debt-bondage) lies in the fact that in slavery, it is not merely "*labour power*" that is the commodity, but the "*labourer himself* is the commodity."[99] Finley goes on, "The slave, by being a slave, suffered not only 'total loss of control over his labour' but total loss of control over his person and his personality."[100] In this "reduction of human beings to the category of property" Finley identifies the inherent "ambiguity" in slavery.[101] It is on account of this ambiguity that Finley explains the need to resort to corporal punishment and torture.

> If a slave is a property with a soul, a non-person and yet indubitably a biological human being, institutional procedures are to be expected that will degrade and undermine his humanity and so distinguish him from human beings who are not property. Corporal punishment and torture constitute one such procedure.[102]

The slave's "answerability with his body" extended not only to beating and torture, but also to "their unrestricted availability in sexual relations."[103] Such availability gave all the more reason for the men who were Athenian citizens to establish firm control over the sexual availability of their Athenian wives.

This book concerns itself with a founding paradox embedded in and informing the return of German idealism to the Greeks, a return that celebrates the heroic status of Oedipus and Antigone, citing them as its literary precursors, at the same time as it cites Athens as originary. A longstanding resistance continues to assert itself in even some of the most important and influential critical interpreters of *Antigone* to thinking through the fact that dominant approaches to *Antigone* are implicated in the ritual conceptual, literary, and historical citation of a tragic hero penned by a tragic poet, who authored his plays in the context of a fledgling democracy that was in fact supported by a system of chattel slavery. My aim is to read the symptoms of this resistance in the reception of *Antigone* as much as it is to reread Sophocles by engaging the paradox to which this resistance bears witness.

In attending to the significance of *Antigone*'s multiple rebirths, with particular reference to the historical and political legacy of recent appropriations of the play, I am careful not to simply overturn the construction of Antigone as representing the family in opposition to Creon's representation of the state. Butler is correct to insist on the sense in which Antigone throws into productive crises not only the categories of both the familial and the political, but also the sense in which Antigone can represent any institution in an uncomplicated way. Antigone brings into question the narrowly authoritarian terms in which Creon construes the interests of the polis, interrogating the vision of the political that such a view presupposes, and the naturalized hierarchies that support it. If Antigone can be re-read as figuring the political, she must be read as calling for a renewal of the political itself. The fate under which Antigone labors might exempt her from making any political contribution to the state as it is dramatically framed by the play, yet precisely the way in which she takes up this exemption alters her position of subjugation, at the same time as it reveals the pretension of Creon's absolute claims. In question is the emergence of the political, legal and ethical authority of the state as a state, its parameters and its casualties.

Even as Antigone calls attention to this logic of exclusion in one way, she participates in it, usurps it, or reinvents it for her own ends in another way, assuming her aristocratic privilege as she refuses to allow her brother, Polynices, to suffer the indignity of being treated as a slave. In this assumption, she lends legitimacy to the institution of slavery. Daughter of Oedipus, she is, after all, a member of the royal aristocracy.[104] Her insistence upon her right to bury Polynices is also an effort to usher her brother into a community that celebrates his humanity, which takes shape as a demand that the privileges of her high birth be granted to her despite her status as a woman. This demand is articulated, however, in such a way as to exploit and reinforce a distinction between those who can lay claim to an undisputed humanity, and slaves, who cannot.

Acknowledgments

A shorter version of Chapter 2 appeared in Hegel's *Philosophy and Feminist Thought—Beyond Antigone?* ed. Kimberly Hutchings and Tuija Pulkkinen (Basingstoke: Palgrave Press, 2010) 61–85. I am grateful to Palgrave/Macmillan Press for granting permission to reprint this chapter.

List of Abbreviated Titles Cited in Text for Quick Reference

GP	Cartledge, *The Greeks: A Portrait of Self and Others*
HS	Agamben, *Homo Sacer*
I, II [Volume nos.]	Hegel, *Aesthetics* (see ch. 2 note 8 for further details)
IR	Isaac, *The Invention of Racism in Classical Antiquity*
I	Fugard, Kani and Ntshona, *The Island*
RS	Tyrrell and Bennett, *Recapturing Sophocles' Antigone*
T	Òsófisan, *Tègònni, an African Antigone*

1

Introduction

The Shadowy Others of *Antigone*'s Legacy

The Sophoclean tragic cycle stands as exemplary for Western culture in so many diverse ways, the exemplarity of which has been expounded by various philosophical, psychoanalytic, and literary figures, some of whom have themselves founded schools of thought (Aristotle, Hegel, Freud). Yet all too rarely have the exponents of Sophocles' Oedipus or Antigone been willing or able to take on and think through the paradox that these literary, philosophical, psychoanalytic heroes were penned by an aristocratic author whose "leisure" time to conceive, write, and perform his exemplary tragedies was bought at the expense of a system of chattel slavery that in some circles is considered in bad taste even to mention. In other circles the historical fact of Athenian slavery tends to be minimized, peremptorily dismissed, or excused on the pretext that if the suffering of some enabled the genius of others, if Athens was built on a system of slavery, and if that is what it took to produce the literary heroes who have become heroes of more than one empire, then so be it.[1] The achievements of ancient Athenian society are glorified in a manner that encourages a certain evasion of our own implication in empires built on slavery and colonialism. In the following I suggest that slavery is very much at issue, even in tragedies, such as *Antigone*, whose interpretive legacy might imply otherwise.

Sophocles' *Oedipal Cycle* can be read as negotiating, reflecting, and differentiating between two different models of marriage: an archaic model based upon exogamy, and the newly emergent one that was more characteristic of the limited democracy of the city of Athens in the fifth century BCE, which tended toward endogamy. Central to the question of whether to marry outside or inside a group is how that group is constituted: who qualifies as someone outside the group, and how are such identities distinguishable from those inside the group? How are the boundaries of the group delineated? What constitutes heterogeneity, and what homogeneity? What is the role of birth, lineage, culture, politics, language, or rationality? What does it mean to be an outsider or a foreigner? What does it mean to be an insider? What is the province of law, what is that of convention, and how does one inform the other?

Since the issue of how to constitute a group is at stake, so too is the issue of how one's membership of a particular group is determined, and how group identity is passed on. Questions of purity or impurity, recognition and misrecognition, and the possibility of contamination figure writ large. The need to forge or enforce certain distinctions, to stipulate legality, conventions of rule and governance, and the determination of political rights—all these issues are fairly obviously at play in Greek tragedy. Thrown into the mix, but often subordinated to the concerns that most interpretive legacies have treated as self-evident, is the paradox that the Oedipal cycle, and the tragic dramas more or less cotemporaneous with it, is written during a period when aristocratic, archaic rule is giving way to democratic rule in Athens, and yet the democracy that was emerging based itself upon a slave society.

My observation about the paradox between democracy and slavery is not, of course, unprecedented. According to Yvon Garlan, "Considered theoretically indispensable to the fulfillment of free men, servile labor . . . does appear to have played a determining role . . . in places where we can form the clearest picture, that is, in classical Athens . . . it is . . . undeniable that chattel slavery in classical Athens and communal servitude of one type or another elsewhere did constitute the 'basis' of Greek society or—to put it another way—the necessary element for it to affirm its identity."[2] In an article originally published in 1941, Gregory Vlastos comments on "the real contradiction in Athenian society: a free political community that rested on a slave economy" and goes on to say "that a consistent democratic philosophy would repudiate slavery altogether."[3] As Page du Bois observes however, Vlastos distanced himself from his earlier arguments in a 1959 postscript, "undoubtedly affected by the postwar climate of the United States in the Eisenhower fifties."[4] My focus here is on how slavery and related themes play out in Sophocles' *Antigone.*

Written over a period of time that has come to be differentiated from the earlier, archaic, mythical time that it narrates, Sophocles' Oedipal cycle both enacts and interrogates the transition from archaic to classical culture. Self-consciously looking over his shoulder, Sophocles begins at the end of his narrative drama, as it were, with *Antigone*, returns to its beginning, with *Oedipus Rex*, and ends in the middle of the action, with *Oedipus at Colonus*. Moving back in time, in order to move forward, going back to the beginning, with a retroactive gesture that approaches the present with a newly informed perspective, Sophocles spirals back to an originating moment that has always already been put in question as originary. The literary construction of the Oedipal cycle thereby refuses any straightforward causal approach to history, introducing a model of temporality that might be interpreted in a traumatic vein, one that requires a working through of certain impasses, ruptures, and repetitions.

Sophocles presents his audience with an Antigone whose array of symptoms requires interpretation. Yet hermeneutic authority has, perhaps inevitably, been granted to those who have proven themselves invested in taking on some of the textual impasses that arise in a reading of *Antigone* at the expense of others, thereby participating in and inventing a history and politics of interpretation that perpetuates and reinvigorates certain blind spots, even as others come to be creatively and provocatively alleviated and recast. Institutional, theoretical, and disciplinary legacies intersect with one another in ways that predispose critics to position themselves within this politics of interpretation in more or less defensive ways. When entrenched positions are questioned, their proponents are liable to respond in ways that rearticulate old hegemonic patterns, while those who have issued challenges, having absorbed to a certain extent the theoretical assumptions of the interlocutors they set out to engage, are susceptible to a measure of complacency about the critical purchase of their own inherited discourses.

Antigone has thus been endowed with a death wish, with an unnatural attachment to her dead brother—an attachment that has been read in Oedipal terms, one that she elevates above all other familial connections, including Haemon and Ismene. She has been read as if she exhibited an abnormal aversion to marriage, to femininity, and to her reproductive destiny. Yet what such readings leave aside is the profound confusion into which Oedipus's parricide and incest throws his family and his city, a confusion that is reflected by the order in which the plays are written, and which is both generational and conceptual. In *Antigone*, everything appears to be in disarray, not least conventional roles.

Given the expectation that women married young and perpetuated the family line, Antigone's refusal of marriage, her substitution of Polynices for Haemon, and her subsequent symbolic marriage to death, are seen as calling into question the economy of exchange, or what Gayle Rubin has called the "traffic in women."[5] According to this system, the exchange of women from their birth family to the family into which they marry was orchestrated by the male guardian or *kurios*. In Antigone's case, Creon has become, by default, both the *kurios*, the one who expects to give away the bride, and the father of the one who expects to receive her—a doubling of identity that echoes all the other doubled identities that structure the Oedipal myth.

In a world where women are silenced and marginalized, confined indoors for the most part, seen as unfit for politics, excluded from decision making, in need of constant male guardianship, incapable of acting as legal subjects, ostensibly given to the pleasures of Eros, and therefore subject to close scrutiny to ensure the legitimacy of male heirs, Antigone's character breaks all the rules.[6] She flouts the authority of Creon, her *kurios,* or familial guardian, and her king, she refuses marriage and childbearing altogether, she insists on the superiority of her beliefs, and she threatens the established balance of power between male and female, king and subject.[7] She will not be governed by Creon's rule at any level.[8] She will be mastered by no one but herself, preferring death to compromise, preferring death to life.

No sooner is this said than the full complexity of the symbolic challenge, definitive of the kinship relations that situate Antigone, begins to impose itself. For, as Derrida has observed so appositely, and with such devastating irony, hers is no ordinary family.[9] Creon is both king and uncle to Antigone, whose relationship to Oedipus and Polynices suffers from a profound generational confusion. If Oedipus is both son and husband to Jocasta, both father and brother to Antigone, Antigone is both sister and aunt to Polynices. As the daughter of Oedipus, Antigone is sister to Polynices and Eteocles, and as the half sister of Oedipus, she is aunt to her brothers. She is the daughter of a previous king (Oedipus), but she is also (via Jocasta) his half sister. She is the sister/aunt of previous kings, who mutually contest one another's right to be king (Polynices and Eteocles), and the wife-to-be of King Creon's son (Haemon). Creon has inherited the throne as a function of the unwavering refusal of Athenian inheritance law to recognize women as legal subjects, and of Athenian culture to view women as subjects capable of competent decision making or of political leadership. Antigone's violation of Creon's edict is as much a marking out of the structure that ensures the exchange of women as it is a refusal to obey Creon's edict, or to marry Haemon. For how can Antigone be exchanged from one *oikos* to another, when she is already included in the *oikos* to which she is destined? Acting as her legal guardian, her *kurios*, in the wake of the death of Oedipus, Creon would have to give his niece Antigone away to his own son. The generational distinction between father and son is precisely that which Oedipus has conflated; in Antigone's case, the distinction between the function of the father, in this case Creon, as the one who, according to convention, should give Antigone away, and his son, in this case Haemon, the one who should receive her, is obscured.[10] Oedipus's act of incest has rendered the distinction between the father as donor and recipient as son inoperative. Unless this distinction is clarified, the *oikos* into which Antigone would be received is the very same as that which cedes her—an impressive blockage indeed!

Antigone's refusal to be the object of exchange between Creon and Haemon, her refusal to make the transition from virgin to wife, marks a breakdown of her passage from one household to another, a breakdown that is inscribed not merely in her obstinacy, but in the logic of her excessively compounded identity—for which, true to Hegel's reading of tragedy—Antigone takes responsibility. In refusing to follow through on her proposed marriage to Haemon, Antigone draws attention to and renders problematic the endogamous trend of marriage practices that are ascendant in Athens, the difficulty within the Oedipal family of separating the father from the son, and the status of women in the exchange that is expected of them in marriage. In this particular family, the logic of gift-giving is exposed as aporetic; some might say that aporetic relations are at the heart of such a logic at the best of times. In this sense Antigone's refusal to be the object of exchange points out a more general problematic within the logic of the exchange system, in which women must pass from one guardian to another. Antigone raises the question of the nature of the gift as such to which Marcel Mauss and Derrida, among others, have drawn attention. Antigone's blocked passage metonymically evinces not merely her refusal to be exchanged by Creon, but rather the impossibility of this exchange in her particular case, an impossibility predicated on the failure of the Oedipal family to maintain a distinction between the symbolic role of the father and that of the son. More importantly it points out the impossibility of a system that looks exclusively inward, threatening to become ever more incestuous, ever more exclusionary, ever more allergic to outsiders, ever more protective of its borders—a system that is in danger, we might say, of autoimmunity.[11]

So concerned is Athens to patrol its borders, so concerned is it to protect its wealth from foreign interlopers, and so concerned is Creon to consolidate wealth, that—Sophocles' hyperbolic representation of this incestuous family suggests—both polis and oikos are in danger of undermining their own systems of exchange, of administering their own poison to precisely the body politic on which there is such a premium to protect from outside corruption. Measures adopted to ensure the stability of the polis are liable to stagnate it. Athens is in danger of an infection that spreads not from without, but from within, and it is Creon, as much as Oedipus, who constitutes the threat. Ignorant of who he is and what he has done, Oedipus dramatically figures a contamination of Thebes. He poses a danger to the security of the polis, threatening its stability, and passing on the confusion of his identity to his children, who do not fail to follow out the ramifications of Oedipal ignorance about the meaning of his identity and the significance of his deeds. Killing each other in mutual combat, Polynices and Eteocles bequeath their familial confusion to Antigone, who confronts it, abruptly arresting the logic of the apparently inevitable familial curse, opting out, refusing to play any of the roles that might have been expected of her. Faced first with the consequences of the multiple familial identities of Oedipus, and then with the threat of impurity that Polynices' exposed corpse represents, Antigone puts a stop to the logic of misplaced identity and morality gone awry, blocking the impulse to turn ever more inward, challenging the need to consolidate boundaries by keeping it all within the family. To say that Antigone is acting out, that she is too stubborn, is to miss the point: she is what she is, but in becoming so resolutely that which she is, by adhering obstinately to the extremely limited role allotted to her as a woman, she also disrupts what it means to be a woman. By insisting upon inhabiting so vigorously the role of outsider that her accompaniment of her blind father through wild terrain had already (and not yet) made of her, by insisting upon the performance of religious burial ritual that constituted the one remaining public sphere of women's influence, Antigone does not so much enact as become woman in her own way.[12] She becomes other than the obedient, passive woman that Creon and his ilk wants her to be.

The democracy that is struggling to emerge in fifth century BCE Athens is burdened with the attempt to reassess its geopolitical boundaries, an effort it takes on in part through the avid formulation and definition of legal discourses, intended to circumscribe and secure the city. What does it mean to belong, politically, linguistically, or culturally? How far does lineage, or birth determine one's status? Interspersed with the formalization of custom as public law, of which Hegel made so much, is the formulation of symbolic, familial law, of which Freudian and Lacanian psychoanalysis has made so much (and of which Hegel made so little).[13] What does it mean to recognize a member of one's family as such, and how far is one's identity determined by failures of recognition? Such questions are embedded in Sophocles' preoccupations. So too, I would maintain, however implicitly, is the paradox that not only remained unthinkable for the Greeks—whether because it was invisible, because it was too difficult to confront, or because it was unquestioningly accepted (perhaps all of these for different constituencies)—but also irresolvable for Hegel and his philosophical associates, as well as psychoanalytic devotees, a paradox that has constituted a site of aversion for even the most ingenious of Sophocles' contemporary interpreters.

If Oedipus is the exemplary hero, and if his exemplariness has been traditionally said to inhere in the manner in which he faces up to the dilemma in which he finds himself, are there not perhaps also exemplary evasions that he performs, enigmas that remain to be unraveled? If Oedipus turns out to play the role of both prosecuting judge and criminal, subject and object, investigator and object of investigation, perhaps there is a sense in which his ambiguous duality resonates beyond the particular crimes of which he commits himself. He can also be read as calling attention to the logic according to which free men set themselves up as kings, rulers, and lawgivers, while their freedom—including their freedom to rule free men—is premised upon the subjugation, in the form of slavery, of others. Emphasizing the way in which excessive attempts at control over the city turn into failure not only of the ruler's attempt to govern the city, but also for the sovereign attempt to govern the self, Froma Zeitlin has suggested that central to tragedy are the issues of power over the self, over others, over the city, and over one's own body.[14] The question of self control, and the desire to avoid being associated with slavery at all costs, was crucial for Athenian citizens (all of whom were men, if the term citizen is taken to include full political rights), both in terms of being master of oneself, rather than working for another, and in terms of not being slavishly dependent on bodily appetites or desires.[15] As Fisher says, in Athens "An important part of what being a citizen meant was not being manhandled by other citizens." In this context he quotes Demosthenes as follows:

> If you (the jury) wished to look into what makes the difference between a slave and a free man, you would find that the greatest distinction was that in the case of slaves it is the body which takes responsibility for all their offences, whereas it is possible for free men, however great their misfortunes, to protect their bodies.[16]

Yet in his misfortune, far from protecting his body, Oedipus impales himself, marking himself as infirm forever, becoming other to himself in the process, and thereby differentiating himself from the too close proximity or sameness that has indelibly marked his familial relationships. When Jocasta implores Oedipus to desist from further enquiry after the messenger from Corinth tells him that he was a foundling, Oedipus assumes that Jocasta is worried about the possibility that she will discover that he is of low birth. He is afraid that he might turn out to be the son of a slave.[17] Could it be that, once he discovers the true reason for Jocasta's attempt to dissuade him, Oedipus blinds himself not just because he cannot bear to look upon what he has done, but also because in scarring his body, he inflicts upon himself his fear that he is nothing but a slave? He inscribes upon his own body the scars that double those of his birth, marking him out as doubly defiled, in a world where bodily scarring would usually have been reserved for those who were subject to the control of their masters. The beating of slaves, whose bodies in an important sense were not their own, was commonplace in fifth century BCE Athens. The body of Oedipus had already been marked shortly after his birth, as a result of his feet being bound together.[18] Lacking the fleet-footed movement of Achilles, Oedipus' bodily movement is marred by a deficiency. He is not as itinerant as others, does not move as quickly as others away from his family, at least not by his own locomotion. Or rather he returns home too quickly, unlike Odysseus's slow and circuitous progress. At the foot of his body, his feet are marked, and he himself marks his face, putting out his own eyes and obliterating his vision, mimicking physically the blindness that afflicted him about his own history, origins, and people. From top to bottom he is a marked man. Marked, or tattooed like a slave, at the foot of his body with an emblem of a divine, Dionysiac curse, since Laius had drunk too much and impregnated Jocasta, failing to observe the divine taboo against their generation of children, planting the seed of Oedipus, who himself will reproduce the parental sign that impairs his body, but with a difference.[19] By blinding himself, Oedipus inscribes on his body the blindness that has dogged his self-knowledge, his failure to have known his origins. His violent inscription is perhaps an act of hubris, since he acts in a godlike manner, and yet it also serves to bring him down to the level of the most humbled men of the city. He is the sovereign exile, the highest and the lowest. Outside the law, above and below, its executor as king, yet at the same time victim of the law that convicts him, Oedipus is the casualty of a familial curse, subject to the law of destiny while subject of the law as king, wielding the law and felled by his own, sovereign hand. In failing to master himself, Oedipus fails to master his kingdom, and in this respect he becomes the mirror image of Creon, who, in failing to master his kingdom, fails to master himself.

Oedipus enters Thebes as if he were a foreigner. It is as a foreigner that he accedes to the throne of Thebes and marries Jocasta, who gives birth to his four children. Yet, his family lineage eventually proves that far from being a foreigner by birth, Oedipus is in fact a member of the royal family into which he has inadvertently married. Having been estranged from his family, put at a distance from them so that he cannot endanger them, he rejoins them, only to unknowingly kill his father and marry his mother, thereby fulfilling the prophecy that Laius and Jocasta had tried to avert, enacting in an extreme, hyperbolic form the recent Athenian turn toward endogamy. Yet, at the same time he enacts, to his knowledge, an exogamous marriage with a woman previously unknown to him, one who is given to him as a gift for his presence of mind (ironically enough) for solving the riddle of the Sphinx. As such, Oedipus comes to stand both for the stranger (*xenos*), the foreigner, the interloper, the other, and at the same time, the familiar, the insider, the one who is not only close by, but intimately related.[20] Through the figure of Oedipus, Sophocles confronts the anxiety about how to recognize a member of one's own family, how to know not only that one's son really is one's son, one's father is really one's father, but even that one's mother is really one's mother.[21] At the same time, he confronts an anxiety about what happens when foreigners (ostensible or otherwise) enter one's homeland, assume rule, and turn out not to be the saviors that they set themselves up to be, or that the citizenry thought or hoped they might be. This is not quite invasion, it is not quite conquering, it is not quite war, but events do unfold as if a foreigner entered the inside of a space and took it over. In this sense, Oedipus is a condensation of the stranger and the blood-relative, the outsider and the insider, the enemy and the friend, all rolled into one, of the dangers inherent in failing to properly distinguish them, yet at the same time of the impossibility and perhaps undesirability of imposing rigid distinctions in law-like ways.[22] Oedipus learns from experience, but he learns too late that intellectual prowess is not enough. Knowing the world requires a certain self-understanding that is elusive because one's feelings, affects, intentions are not clearly reflected in the world, because others intervene, helping to construct situations that are constituted by complex, multiple, and not always self-transparent motives, situations that are produced by and produce material effects, which are more or less opaque.

The effects of the 451BCE law that Pericles introduced in Athens epitomize in many ways the intersecting set of concerns that I suggest informs Sophocles' Oedipal cycle. As a result of the law, when a dispute arose over the distribution of a gift of grain, given to Athenians by the king of Egypt, the claims of many were disqualified because they were determined to be illegitimate by birth and were subsequently sold into slavery.[23] The law is understood to have merely formalized a practice that was already underway, namely that of marrying within, rather than outside, the city.[24] In fact, as Vernant points out, this tendency toward endogamy was taken to an extreme in myth, where we find "many instances . . . of unions within a single family, marriages between close relatives, and exchanges of daughters between brothers."[25] In this context, Oedipus—who marries Jocasta on the assumption that he is a foreigner, but who turns out after all to be a member of her own family, indeed her own son—could have been received by an Athenian audience in 429 BCE both as transgressing the relatively recent law preventing exogamy, and as conforming to the relatively new practice of endogamy. At the same time, Sophocles might be read as drawing attention to the contingency of law, both law in general, and this particular law, which related to foreigners, and resulted in the enslavement of many whose claim to be Athenian had remained previously uncontested.[26] Read as a historical figure of mythical Thebes, Oedipus the foreigner (as far as he knows) would not have been violating any law in marrying Jocasta, but read in terms of the practices contemporary to Sophocles' Athens, he would have been in violation of the law. As the son of Jocasta, Oedipus would have been violating the archaic practice of exogamy, whereas read against the practice that had become conventional in Athens and was enshrined in law by 451 BCE, he would not have been in such clear violation of the law. Nor should the repercussions the law had for determining who would become slaves be forgotten.

The distinction between citizen and foreigner is not the only one that Oedipus's birth and circumstances appear to put into question. Had the circumstances of his literary birth been slightly different, there is a good chance that Oedipus the King might have been a slave. Had his parents been poor, and had they not resorted to abandoning him on Mount Cithaeron, outside the city of Thebes, the infant Oedipus might have been entrusted to magistrates and sold into slavery. A prohibition existed in Thebes against the exposure of infants, so when Jocasta and Laius exposed Oedipus to die, in their attempt to avert the oracle that foretold of Laius's death at the hands of a child to be born to them, they put themselves outside of the Theban law.[27] Transgression of the law and exposure to the elements take on another guise when Oedipus commits incest, and when, in violation of Creon's edict, Antigone buries Polynices. In doing so, of course, Antigone appeals to a higher law, a divine law, and in this sense she does not cast the act of burial as transgression, but rather as an acknowledgment of Polynices' humanity, which, in this context, negatively determined, means his not being a slave, his being part of a legitimate family. As they are so often in the Oedipal cycle, events are doubled, echoing and calling to one another across and within the plays. Oedipus is not the only character for whom the shadow of slavery casts its specter. In reaction to what he sees as Polynices' attempt to enslave Thebes, Creon responds by acting in a way that could itself be construed as slavish. As H. S. Harris puts it, "To leave the dead unburied is unGreek, barbaric."[28] Yet it is his own son, Haemon, whom Creon accuses of being nothing but a woman's slave.[29] For her part, Antigone is invested in ensuring that Polynices is not treated as a slave.

When Antigone stipulates that Polynices is not a slave, but her brother, she is contesting Creon's dishonoring of Polynices in death, but she is also appealing to and reinscribing a distinction between the humanity of the aristocracy to which her family belongs and the inferior status of slaves.[30] Antigone does not want to leave the corpse of Polynices to the birds, but would have no such qualms had he been a slave, rather than her brother.[31] By the same token, since marriage conferred respectability upon women, and Antigone refuses marriage, she is refusing to be respectable in the conventional way.[32] If Antigone identifies herself with her mother in one way—her relation to Jocasta establishes her aristocratic lineage—she distinguishes herself from Jocasta in another way.[33] The act of differentiation is a complex one, which rejects any form of marriage, in order to avert any possibility of repeating the familial pattern of incest, while it also calls attention to the problems inherent in any understanding of marriage in which women are reduced to mere tokens. Antigone will not marry, and she most certainly will not marry someone who turns out to be her own son.

If we take the 451 BCE law into account—a law that discouraged marrying foreigners, and that led to the enslavement of many who were now judged illegitimate—it would seem that a primary concern in Athens was to keep male outsiders out, or rather (and this is crucial) to keep them from legitimately inheriting Athenian wealth. That is, foreigners could become slaves, but they could not amass wealth, or rather they could only do so on their masters' say so. Manumission—sometimes attained through slave earnings, which could accumulate until a slave was able to buy their own freedom, and sometimes written into a will—was at the master's discretion. From the grave, then, the ghostly power of a master could extend across the divide of the dead and the living to free a slave.

As they worked, slaves were contained within the city as inferiors, as subject to those whose wealth became the basis of the slave's subjection. As we have seen, significant numbers of people were relegated to a slave class as a direct result of a law that ostensibly concerned the requirements for Athenian citizenship The inclusion of foreign men within the polis for the purposes of slave labor was thereby deemed acceptable, but their inclusion as fully fledged participants of the practices they supported and afforded the polis (foremost among them the flourishing of the arts, the development of a limited representative democracy, and the concentration of wealth) was unacceptable. Excluded from participatory democracy, foreigners were nevertheless included for the purposes of accruing the benefits of their labor. In controlling the exchange of women, certain boundaries were therefore erected, boundaries which had as much to do with imposing requirements for the acquisition of wealth and selling those whose birth was not deemed pure into slavery, as it did with anything else. In the interests of perpetuating the wealth, culture, and stability of Athens within its city walls, attempts were being made to circumscribe very precisely who could, and who could not enjoy the benefits of fully belonging to the polis, by inheriting its wealth, and by participating in its democratic procedures.

One question that might have arisen for Sophocles, it seems worth wagering, could have been: where would the protective, inward-looking, endogamous practices such as those symbolized in the 451 BCE law lead? My point here is not to pretend to have access to, in the words of Vernant and Vidal-Naquet, "what was going on in Sophocles' head . . . The playwright left us no personal reflections nor any diary: had he done so they would have represented no more than supplementary sources of evidence that we should have had to submit to critical appraisal like any others."[34] Rather, I am offering a hypothesis, which I offer as having explanatory value for the Oedipal cycle, not necessarily based upon what the author intended, but nevertheless reflecting issues that had social and political salience, whether or not they might have constituted part of the author's conscious design. David Konstan points out that tragedians "had to submit their plays to the scrutiny of a public official before they were accepted for sponsorship at a public festival."[35] In the light of this, it might be the case that Sophocles preferred to approach contentious issues concerning foreigners and slavery obliquely. Clearly, like any other critic, my reading will be influenced by the questions I bring to Sophocles, which will inevitably help to frame my reading of the aesthetic and performative dimensions of *Antigone*, its religious, legal, social, and political context, and the anxieties out of which it might have originated, and in terms of which it might have been read.

What might be the end result of a system that consisted in progressively narrowing down the choice of male partners through the exclusion of foreigners, to the point where endogamy could perhaps become a matter of fathers marrying their mothers? After all, this would be only at one remove from the already accepted practice of cousins marrying their first cousins—a practice that Sophocles depicts in Haemon's intention to marry Antigone, for example. In the light of this, one of the crucial issues Antigone poses, though it has not been recognized as such, is the need to formulate, to put into words, to render formal a law that had so far remained unwritten. That law is one that Oedipus's violation had brought into being in a sense, but it was left to Antigone, in retrospect, to attempt to articulate Oedipus's act as a transgression for the first time *in terms of a law*. It is not, as some critics have suggested, that Antigone was recalling, or reinscribing a law, but rather that she was positing it, introducing it, trying to recognize the significance of what Oedipus had done, and in marking it, warning against Oedipal practice becoming accepted practice. One might even say that Sophocles' Antigone is warning against making the Oedipal action exemplary, warning against, perhaps, making Oedipus into the exemplary, literary, and cultural hero that Aristotle made of him, or even making him into the anti-hero that he became for Freud.[36]

Antigone's refusal to marry Haemon, and her mourning of her brother are at the same time a means of reflecting on, and perhaps an attempt to put to rest, the possibility of an extreme version of a practice—endogamy—that was already a general convention. Ismene's recognition of Antigone's act of burial as significant, her acknowledgment of Antigone's introduction of something like a new principle, constitutes a possible site of the conversion of Antigone's solitary act into something like a law. When Ismene changes her mind, having refused initially to help bury Polynices but subsequently wanting to share Antigone's punishment, she sees the logic of Antigone's act of burial. When she expresses her desire to die along with her sister, she interprets Antigone's act as if it had renewed the possibilities of the world, as if it opened up a novel way of looking at things, as if Antigone's were a creative act, which, far from arising, as certain critics have argued, out of a consuming preoccupation with or passion for death, gives birth to a future in which new possibilities come to light.

Against the now conventional wisdom that as an art form tragedy was more democratic than epic poetry, Mark Griffith argues for "another perspective" that is "intertwined" with it: "even as 'democratic' and 'civic' pride are being reinforced, the unique and irreplaceable value of an international network of elite families is simultaneously affirmed."[37] Given that Sophocles is writing at a time when Athenian democracy is still in its nascent state, it would be surprising if the political tensions arising from the gradual shift away from the hegemony of the aristocracy, and toward a more participatory political system were not embedded in his tragedies. As Griffith says, "A contradiction was developing between the new democratic ideology on the one hand, emphasizing equality of all citizens, checks and balances on the exercise of power, and responsibility and loyalty to the *polis* before all else, and, on the other, the old aristocratic ideology of family, entitlement, and competitive display of personal worth and achievement."[38] If it is easy enough to associate Creon with the newly developing democratic ideology in some respects—his emphasis on loyalty to the polis before all else, for example—it is also clear that he is certainly not in accord with the idea that his power should be curtailed in any way.[39] At the same time, his constant suspicions that the only possible motivations anyone might have to question or challenge his authority must involve corruption, betray his overweening and ostentatious concern with protecting his own wealth. He is, after all, a member of the aristocratic ruling class.

That Creon would embody certain democratic values of the polity, while at the same time exhibiting a nostalgic longing for the aristocratic entitlements of the past would be in keeping with the fact that this is a time of political transition, and that despite its democratic impulse—or perhaps precisely because of it—tragedy is wrestling with an elitist political legacy. Griffith observes, "If Greek tragedy is intended to instantiate Athenian civic ideology, then we must acknowledge . . . that even this most authentically democratic ideology . . . still comes with a strongly aristocratic spin."[40] Perhaps it is less a case of instantiation, and more a matter of negotiation. The contradictory elements of Creon's character situate him in terms of his aristocratic roots, which come into conflict with the democratic times in which he finds himself in power.[41] Creon's character embodies the tensions at stake in moving away from the days of aristocratic rule, where powerful families formed alliances with one another across borders through a series of gift-exchanges, culminating in marriage, and the emergence of a more democratic system of law centered on the city of Athens, still dominated by an aristocratic ruling elite, but incorporating to some extent the voices of lower class, free, male citizens. If Creon exhibits the symptoms of a man struggling to come to terms with what it means to be a ruler at a time when the conventions of aristocratic rule are giving way to the emerging institutions of democracy, things are more complex with the character of Antigone.

While both characters are clearly part of the same aristocratic family, the balance of power is equally clearly heavily tipped in Creon's favor, in a number of different ways.[42] As the king, as head of the household, and as her uncle, his position of authority over Antigone is not in question. As female subject, and as a niece subject to her uncle's guardian authority, Antigone has no legitimate political or independent voice. Yet if Creon harbors a certain nostalgia for a political past, where the dominance of aristocratic rule was not yet in question, it is very unclear that Antigone would have had any more say in her fate, had it been possible to unequivocally associate her with the unquestioned privilege and power of the ruling aristocracy to which Creon, despite his allegiance to the limited democracy of the polis, in some ways harks back. Conventionally, women would have been little more than tokens to be passed between one noble family and another, cementing alliances over which they had little control. Thus when the character of Antigone refuses marriage on any terms, whether those of an essentially exogamous or endogamous exchange, hers is a refusal of both the aristocratic system of alliances and the democratic tendency to look inward. Having wandered the countryside for years, guiding her blind father, Antigone is not one to observe convention for convention's sake. She has been both an outcast and a child of freedom, not bound by the rules of any polis, bound only by her love for and loyalty to her father. She and her sister, Ismene, are beloved by their father because of their devotion, in sharp contrast to the harsh treatment Oedipus reserves for Polynices and Eteocles, whom he not only spurns, but curses.

The gradual emergence of democracy in Athens arguably coincided with the increased surveillance and containment of women, while the archaic system over which it took precedence nevertheless depended on the exchange of women between one aristocratic family and another, an exchange in which women constituted objects or gifts, rather than constituting subjects responsible for the symbolic meaning or monetary value of those exchanges. In the archaic system, in which women figured as little more than objects of exchange, the value of which was measured both in terms of wealth and in terms of bonds of friendships and alliances, such exchanges were accomplished between the male guardians of the family who bestowed them as gifts, and those who received the bride in exchange for bride-price.[43] By contrast, the purpose of legitimate marriage in the Athenian polis was directed toward the reproduction of legitimate, male heirs—indeed the very definition of marriage coincided with the procreation of one's own children, according to Demosthenes.[44] When Antigone refuses marriage to Haemon, preferring to honor her brother in death, she is refusing the endogamous exchange from her immediate, birth family to a substitute family, and at the same time she is refusing her socially sanctioned role of reproducing legitimate heirs, which would secure the survival of both the oikos, and the ruling elite of the polis. In both cases, the expectation is that she be exchanged in order to facilitate a symbolic meaning from which she herself is excluded, whether it is the bonds of alliance her exchange accomplishes between the male guardians of aristocratic families, or the system of male inheritance established in order to pass on political succession, citizenship, and wealth.[45] In refusing to facilitate either exchange, Antigone is blocking the inheritance of movable goods, and thereby stopping up a system in which it is difficult, if not impossible, to clearly distinguish her own status from that of the herd of cattle that would have been exchanged for the bride in the archaic system, or from the movable chattels that would have constituted her dowry in classical Athens.[46] Her refusal of any marriage, whether exogamous or endogamous, constitutes a refusal to be merely an object of exchange, in which the terms of that exchange are set in advance and independently of her.

The character of Antigone thus brings into question both the archaic and the classical systems of exchange, while also pointing out that the practice of endogamy, a practice that had not only come to be accepted by Athenian convention, but the legalization of which had reversed the earlier requirements of exogamy, could go too far. Understood as registering the dangers of an excessively endogamous system of exchange, Antigone's distinct lack of interest in her impending marriage to Haemon might be read not simply as a way of protesting the expectation that she marry a first cousin, but more importantly as signaling the continuity between, or proximity of, the apparent excesses of the mythical Oedipus, and the accepted practice already extant in Athens. Consistent with this practice, Creon, as head of the household, would have expected to give Antigone's hand in marriage to Haemon, that is, to marry his niece to his son, an arrangement that would also serve to conveniently consolidate his wealth, and one which was apparently commonplace in Athens.

Whereas archaic, aristocratic convention dictated the exchange of women between one aristocratic family and another, with the intention of establishing, solidifying, or guaranteeing bonds of philia between the male guardians who orchestrated such exchanges, Antigone aligns herself with philia. She thereby refuses to be a merely passive participant in an exchange that is premised on construing her as a mere token, an object to be passed from one man to another, rather than a subject capable of forging a relationship for herself, an active participant establishing her own value. In this regard, Hegel's insistence on construing Antigone's action of burying Polynices on the basis of her natural relationship with her brother, rather than as an act motivated by the philia she herself cites, is at the same time a refusal to grant her an active role in constructing her relationship to Polynices, a refusal to see her as recognizing the importance of philia, and a failure to read Antigone as contesting the idea that she should serve merely as a conduit for circulation among men, rather than as an agent capable of making a natural relationship into a relationship of loyalty. In this context, when Antigone claims that her nature is to love and not to hate, she should be understood as asserting her spiritual capacity, as someone who is making a determination about her right as a subject to recognize other subjects as subjects worthy of love, rather than someone who merely acts unreflectively, and whose act is driven by her status as a blood relative.[47] Nor does Hegel entertain the significance of Antigone's attitude toward her sister, whom Antigone refuses to recognize as worthy of love, once Ismene has refused to help her bury Polynices. If Antigone's bond to her brother is unreflective, how and why is the ostensibly natural bond to her sister differentiated from it? How is Antigone's familial duty to her brother elevated above any relationship she might develop toward her sister? Perhaps Hegel fails to take this difference into account because he assumes Ismene's actions (or lack of them), and Antigone's relationship to her sister, are of little consequence. Such an assumption would be consonant with ancient Greek assumptions about the incongruous fit between women and politics, and the subordinate role of women to men in all aspects of life.

As is well known, the concept of recognition or anagnórisis is central to Aristotle's definition of tragedy in the *Poetics*.[48] Elizabeth Belfiore stresses that recognition in Aristotle's sense, as leading to philia or enmity, is not simply an act of cognition, but is also a matter of acting in such a way as to acknowledge the bonds of philia that tie one family member to another. That is, it is possible for someone who is already known as philos, in the sense of being next of kin, to take on the status of philos in a way that deepens the preexisting kinship relation: "In the paradigmatic cases, 'recognition [leading] to a [state of] *philia* or to [a state of] enmity' is not merely the attainment of cognitive knowledge of the identity of one's biological kin ('to recognize *philia*'), it also involves acting as a *philos* or enemy. Since recognition leading 'to [a state of] *philia*' is the acknowledgement of another as someone toward whom one has obligations of positive reciprocity, people may 'become *philoi*' even when they are already *philoi* in the sense of biological kin."[49] In the cases of Creon and Antigone, the former recognizes Polynices not as philos, but as ekthros, not as a loved one, but as an enemy, while Antigone recognizes him—in the sense of acting toward him in a way that affirms her blood relationship to him (and thereby transforms that relationship into something that goes beyond the merely biological), by burying him—as a *philos*. Antigone's act constitutes a reversal of Creon's judgment of Polynices as an enemy, at the same time as affirming and intensifying his status as philos.

In her opening speech to Ismene, Antigone implicitly identifies Polynices as a friend, but one whom Creon's proclamation designates an enemy. In burying Polynices, in contrast to Ismene, Antigone acts not just in word, but in deed. One could say that she thereby acts in a way that is consonant with Aristotle's later insistence in the *Nicomachean Ethics* against Plato's celebration of intellectual virtue that it is not enough to know the right thing to do, one must also develop the character to be able to act appropriately, when action is called for. One might add that Ismene recognizes the appropriateness of Antigone's action only after the fact, and in this sense, she reverses her earlier forbearance, now expressing the desire to recognize Antigone's affirmation of Polynices' status as philos. The trouble is that once again a gap opens up between her words and her deeds. Whereas before Ismene did not agree to help Antigone, now she wants to claim responsibility for doing so in order to show solidarity with Antigone—and also because she does not want to live a life without her sister—but Antigone taunts her by claiming that not she, but Creon is her friend.[50]

Of course, Aristotle wouldn't have endorsed Antigone's action as significant—which is perhaps why he doesn't comment on it—because he didn't think it was appropriate for women to act courageously, believing rather in women's "inferior class," and regarding slaves as "wholly paltry."[51] Perhaps because he does not construe women as moral agents in the full sense, and because he takes Oedipus, the unwitting actor, as his paradigmatic tragic hero, Aristotle mentions *Antigone* only once in the *Poetics*, and then only to point out that its plot is of the worst type.[52] In accord with this, Belfiore does not consider Antigone's action with regard to Polynices, only Haemon's with regard to Creon.

As a character Antigone exemplifies a moment of transition between conflicting historical, ideological, and identificatory forces. On the one hand (under normal circumstances), as a member of an aristocratic, Theban family, a woman such as Antigone would have been subject to the expectations of the archaic system of the exchange of women, whereby her exogamous marriage might have cemented an alliance between aristocratic families. As such, she would have been married to a foreigner.[53] In this system, the circulation of women was predicated on their exchange for *hedna*, or for its substitutes.[54] On the other hand, with the emergence of the city of Athens with its democratic leanings, a female character such as Antigone would have been read as subject to the practice of consolidating wealth within the family, to the expectation that she perpetuate the family line, and stabilize the security of the city. (After all, the city's existence and stability depended upon its success in war, which in turn depended on the reproduction of loyal, male citizens to protect the city's interests in war.) The expectation that Antigone marry Haemon, the son of her uncle Creon, is clearly in keeping with the idea that the city's permanence be assured by ensuring the continuation of its wealth. As Nancy Sorkin Rabinowitz says, "If a man died leaving a daughter but no sons, the daughter would be married 'with her portion,' *epi-klēros*) to her nearest male relative, thereby keeping the wealth in the family."[55] In this context, when Creon sentences Antigone to death, he refuses to hand her over in marriage to his son, Haemon, marrying her instead to death, a marriage which he understands to be her wish, rather than his. At the same time, Creon's refusal to bury Polynices on the basis of his construal of Polynices not as a member of his family, but as a traitor to the city, is a function of the importance Creon attaches to the value of political loyalty, construed as loyalty to the polis, rather than loyalty to an aristocratic network of alliances that stretched beyond the polis.

Against this background, Antigone's privileging of philia constitutes an elevation and a transformation of the aristocratic network of alliances established through the exchange of women in marriage, while Creon's concerns about corruption constitute a privileging of the monetary benefits of such exchanges, without the corollary ties that bind.[56] Antigone privileges philia, but in a way that departs from convention in that she construes herself as a subject capable of symbolically recognizing the importance of her tie to Polynices—of making him into a brother—rather than being content to occupy the passive position of an object of exchange. She reserves the bonds of philia for her own family, substituting the bond with her father for a bond with her brother, but consecrating this bond only in death. In doing so, Antigone takes up her brother as a loved one, and contests Creon's account of him as enemy and traitor. Yet she does so at the cost of re-inscribing the inferior—and unquestioned—status of slaves.

Thus Antigone can be read as singling out—and, crucially, as claiming it for herself, thereby contesting its restriction to men, and resignifying it—one aspect of the aristocratic system of exchange, namely the way in which it creates friendship across boundaries and forges alliances between foreigners, while Creon can be read as isolating an aspect of the newer, and more endogamous marriage practices, namely the consolidation of wealth within his own family and domain. Of course, Polynices is no foreigner to Antigone, but since he has raised a foreign army against Thebes, attacking the city of his birth, Creon sees him as a foreigner. He is, in a sense, like Oedipus, both insider and outsider. As Griffith says of the archaic system, "Such networks of friendship and alliance may often outweigh loyalties felt towards, and benefits deriving from, the particular local community (*polis*) to which one's family belonged (especially if that community was governed, as Attika was, by a democracy that aimed to minimize opportunities for any one family to accumulate excessive credit and dominate perennially)."[57] It is precisely the issue of conflicting loyalties upon which Creon and Antigone disagree so vehemently. For Creon, Polynices is a traitor, while for Antigone, he is privileged above a potential husband or son—and above a slave. He therefore symbolically usurps the place of a husband or son, at the same time as her loyalty toward him prevents her marriage to Haemon and forecloses the possibility of her giving birth to a legitimate son, an eventuality that brings Creon's oikos to a dead end, since the other son of Creon and Eurydice has already died, and Haemon's suicide results from Antigone's, and in its turn causes the suicide of Eurydice.[58]

The consolidation of wealth that went along with the transition from exogamy to endogamy is accompanied by a tendency to formalize the status of marriage, to purify the circumstances of legitimate birth, and to exclude foreigners, or at least to include them within the confines of the polis only by conferring upon them the status of slaves or *metics*. Clarifying the legal basis for marriage was not merely a matter of controlling the movement of wealth, it was also a matter of excluding foreigners from the benefits of accumulated wealth. One might say that the restriction of wealth—which had been acquired in part through the acquisition of *hedna*—to Athenians ensured both the concentration of wealth within the boundary of the polity and the relegation of foreigners to apolitical positions. Having acquired wealth from foreigners, the Athenians proceeded to change the rules of the exchange game, with the result that they reserved for themselves the assets procured from foreigners, keeping them (along with their women) within the family, behind closed doors. The clarification of legal distinctions, particularly those that solidified the stratification of social levels, would have had several effects, including warding off the unpredictable outcome of war, amongst which would have figured prominently the possibility of enslavement.[59] If laws, rather than wars, became responsible for the legitimization of citizenship, they also portended a system of legalized slavery, divorcing the outcome of war and its attendant spoils from determining the fate of captives vis-à-vis slavery. The more that Athens could secure its wealth, prestige, and cultural hegemony, the more it could assure its continued prominence, and the more effectively it could patrol its borders, the better it could secure itself. Part and parcel of establishing its prominence was the enhanced classification of social roles, backed up by a legal system. Integral to the requirements of citizenship, the status of foreigners, the role of slaves, and gender expectations were discriminations concerning parental rights, obligations to children, and the rights of owners over slaves. Differentiating various roles from one another could not fail to have implications for the level of homogeneity or heterogeneity within the polity. It is within this context that the historical shift from exogamous to endogamous practices of marriage, Antigone's appeal to philia, and her differentiation of Polynices from a slave should be seen. It is also against this context that Aristotle's attempts to distinguish between "natural" and conventional slavery should be seen, particularly his attempt to justify the slavery of barbarians through characterizing them as inferior to Athenians in various ways, while simultaneously emphasizing the contingency of the enslavement of Athenians.[60]

Family, kinship, and sexual difference have constituted the prevailing terms in which Sophocles' *Antigone* has been taken up by a Western philosophical and psychoanalytic tradition that has been heavily overdetermined by Hegel. Derrida, for example, tackles Antigone's place in the Hegelian corpus by situating it within a meditation on the family. Irigaray and Butler, while providing crucial challenges to orthodox Hegelian interpretations from the perspectives of feminist and queer theory, at the same time emphasize the importance of kinship and sexuality, thereby rejoining the Hegelian tradition even as they undermine it in other ways. While Irigaray reads Antigone as symptomatic of a crisis that implicates not only the family and the state, but philosophical thinking itself, Butler inflects this insight in a way that exposes the heteronormative bias not only of Hegel and Lacan, but also of Irigaray. Both Irigaray and Butler, albeit in different ways, read Antigone as an excluded but facilitating other, thereby following up Derrida's discourse in more than one way. Both develop Derrida's reflections in terms of that which is remaindered in Hegel's thought, or the abject in Jean Genet's language, and both make good on Derrida's insertion of a psychoanalytic strand of thinking into his narrative, even as they differentiate themselves, respectively, from its masculinist and heterosexist assumptions.

Antigone makes her first appearance in Irigaray's *Speculum* in her discussion of Freud's fetishism, a critique of which sets up the terms of Irigaray's engagement with Hegel's Antigone. Butler stages her investigation into "kinship trouble" as a debate with Hegel and Lacan, a debate that retains kinship as its central focus, even as it reads Antigone as troubling Hegelian and Lacanian tenets.[61] By the same token, the Eurocentric assumptions in which not only

Hegel and Lacan are embedded, but also the tradition of white feminist theory that this tradition has spawned, remain largely untroubled.

Page DuBois calls for us to understand what she designates the "structuring ubiquity of slaves in ancient society."[62] Arguing that the "invisibility and ubiquity" of slavery and slaves are "mutually constitutive" of one another, DuBois suggests that we engage in various strategies of avoidance and deflection in order to purify our own past. Either we overlook, deny, or disavow the presence or significance of slavery in order to sustain our idealized vision of ancient Greece, to which we trace our own cultural and democratic origins, or we vilify the ancients, projecting onto them our own anxiety about new world slavery.[63] Acknowledging that the "fetishizing of antiquity as a site of origin for Western culture may require the simultaneous recognition and disavowal of such a problematic feature of ancient societies as slavery," DuBois makes a sustained argument for interpreting the "internal logic" of slavery, and for acknowledging it as an "inextricable part of the fabric of everyday life in classical Athens."[64] Given the permanence of war, and the way in which discourse on slavery versus freedom "saturates the political discourse of historians" such as Herodotus, Plutarch, and Thucydides it would be surprising if it did not also infuse the texts of the tragic poets.[65] Thus, Euripides "presents through women characters anxiety about defeat in war, and about the declining political power of the elite."[66] While conventionally the overt concerns of Sophocles might not have been as readily identified with political issues as those of Euripides or Aeschylus, this might well be due to the political and genre assumptions in the disciplinary construction of classical studies, rather than to any inherent characteristic of Sophoclean tragedy, and the Oedipal cycle in particular. If slaves populate the pages of Euripides' plays much more regularly than they do those of Sophocles, and if Aeschylus confronts more directly the status and function of juridical institutions, such as the Aeropogaus in the *Oresteia*, Sophocles' exploration of endogamous family relationships opens up pressing questions about the mutual implications of gender, class, and chattel slavery.

To speak of the mutual implication of these categories in and by one another is to put the point in modern terms. My overarching approach is to situate the issues raised by Sophocles in terms of a discourse in which questions of citizenship, marriage as the gift-exchange of women between differentiated units, and slavery would have been bound up with one another. It is precisely the carving up of gender, race, class, and sexuality into differentiated and separable identity categories that has, perhaps, discouraged feminist theory from taking up the issue of slavery as implicated in Antigone's struggle—and as implicating it. At the same time, it is the insistence with which contemporary feminist theory has interrogated the independence of these categories that makes it possible to look at the reception of *Antigone* and ask, not so much whether we can infer exactly how marriage, citizenship, slavery, and the roles of women might have operated for the social imaginary of ancient Athens, but rather, given the questions that contemporary feminist, race, and class theory has made available, what might traditional interpretations of this social imaginary have overlooked? Any resistance to construing these issues as political is bound up with a reluctance to politicize the classical study of these issues. Even if we can never know with certainty the precise contours of the social imaginary of ancient Athenians—in part because there would have been no single social imaginary—we can at least problematize received ideas about it. We can at least discount views that have passed as authoritative, when those views are shown to be constructed on the basis of glaring omissions. At the same time, we can resist the tendency to reify identity categories by seeing them as implicated in one another. I am suggesting that the fluidity and mutual implication of marriage practices, their impact on lines of genealogy, on legitimating political alliances and determining who had political rights and who were excluded from them, who were slaves and who were citizens, makes it imperative not to isolate questions of gender or sexual difference in interrogating *Antigone*. At issue rather is the determination of whose voices are ascendant, and whose are silenced, whose are heard, and whose are heard only indirectly and by proxy, and whose are heard only at the expense of delegitimating the claims of others.

Even when critics explicitly comment on the language of slavery employed by Sophocles, some of them make no reference to the social institution of slavery, treating the language as if it were divorced from the social reality of slaves. Recounting several examples of Sophocles' utilization of the language of slavery in his exploration of the Sophoclean hero, including Creon's insistence that Antigone is like a "slave" (δουλός) in need of subjection, at *Antigone* 479, Bernard Knox interprets this language as evidence of "the fierce sense of independence of the thorny individual."[67] He assumes that it merely serves as an expression of the discomfort we all feel when we are opposed, but that the hero takes this to extremes. "All of us at times," he surmises, "may find the advice of others or the demands of a situation 'intolerable,' may assert our will in the face of opposition. But the hero does so all the way, to the absolute end of such a defiance, which is death."[68] For Knox, then, Sophoclean heroes "will not be ruled, no one shall have power over them, or treat them as a slave, they are free. . . . The choice, as the hero sees it, is between freedom and slavery."[69] Knox thereby eclipses the difference between the social situation of ancient Greece, which was a slave society, and our own ("all of us" can understand what is at stake here), and reduces any significance that the language of slavery might have to the metaphorical level. While it is well established that the language of slavery can connote subjection in a general sense, and it might well be the case that this is indeed the sense in which Sophocles employs it here, it also seems more than worthwhile to wager that the language of slavery—even when used in this sense—resonated differently for women than it did for men, and for slaves than it did for those who were free.[70] By extension, it seems a safe bet to assume that it resonated differently for a slave culture than it might for us—and that the difficulty we have in recognizing this is bound up with our preference to omit serious reflection about the all too recent history of slavery in the new world.[71]

I want to take seriously DuBois' argument about the difficulty that "readers living in postslave economies" have in seeing slaves, a difficulty compounded, as we shall see, by the fact that the investment in various strategies of avoidance, minimization, or deflection can extend to translators, who write out references to slaves.[72] It is not a question of substituting one focal point—the heteronormativity that Butler allows Antigone to bring into focus, for example—for another. Neither is it a question of arguing that race, rather than family or kinship, is the real abject or unthought that Antigone brings to light. While the issues emphasized by the philosophical and psychoanalytic tradition (Hegel, Derrida, Lacan, Irigaray, and Butler)—family, kinship, and sexual difference—are undoubtedly central to Sophocles' *Antigone*, one of the aims of this book is to broaden the scope of enquiry to include a cluster of themes concerning slavery, outsiders, and foreigners.

Vernant and Vidal-Naquet suggest that tragedy "confronts heroic values and ancient religious representations with the new modes of thought that characterize the advent of law within the city-state. The legends of the heroes are connected with royal lineages, noble *genē* that in terms of values, social practices, forms of religion, and types of human behavior, represent for the city-state the very things that it has had to condemn and reject and against which it has had to fight in order to establish itself. At the same time, however, they are what it developed from and it remains integrally linked with them."[73] While such a view can clearly illuminate *Antigone*, it has been left largely up to other critics such as Charles Segal to develop the general approach of Vernant and Vidal-Naquet in relation to this play.[74] Vernant and Vidal-Naquet attempt to grasp tragedy "as a phenomenon that is indissolubly social, aesthetic, and psychological" yet neither they nor their followers have been immune from reproducing certain blind spots.[75]

One of the ways in which the rethinking of received wisdom concerning the structuring oppositions of *Antigone* will be accomplished is by taking seriously the literary, dramatic, performative, and political tradition that has been inspired by the figure of Antigone, a history in which Antigone has entered into myriad political contexts, serving as an inspiration for those fighting for freedom in the midst of injustice. Thus Antigone demands the attention of Jean Anouilh and Bertolt Brecht in Nazi torn Europe; of Seamus Heaney, Aidan Mathews, Marianne McDonald, Tom Paulin, and Brendan Kennelly in the times of the troubles in Ireland; of Janusz Glowacki in the context of homelessness in New York; of Athol Fugard, Kani, and Ntshona under apartheid in

South Africa; and of Fémi Òsófisan under European imperialism in Nigeria.[76] One could point to many other instances of *Antigone*'s appropriation in contexts of political crises, whether in The Congo (Sylvain Bemba) or Argentina (Gambaro).[77] What would it mean to take such plays as a starting point, and re-read *Antigone* and the tradition of scholarship the play has spawned from the perspectives these plays make available? How might the critical distance such an exercise encourages allow a return to Sophocles, Aristotle, Hegel, Derrida, Lacan, Irigaray, and Butler in such a way as to raise the question of what else might be left unthought by these interventions?

Of course, this tradition is not entirely impervious to the reflections of philosophers, and yet it maps out a rather different trajectory. Here, it is no longer a question of accepting the Hegelian opposition between kinship and state, or the Lacanian distinction between the symbolic and the social order as decisive. The theatrical legacy of Antigone is one that recognizes Antigone as standing up for a principle that a corrupt state has neglected, abandoned, or refused to legitimize. Antigone thus recalls a polity to what should have been its proper function, exposing the corruption or monstrosity of what the state has become. In particular, Antigone has lent her name to racially combustible situations, such as occur under apartheid and in the wake of the legacies of imperialism and colonialism. She recalls the state to its proper function, while also exposing the extent to which the state has deviated from what should have been, but is not yet (or is no longer) its function. She calls for a future that has not arrived, calling out the impropriety of the state insofar as it falls short of a future yet to come. She calls attention to the logic whereby the state depends upon some of its members for certain vital functions, members whom it nonetheless systematically deprives of political rights. This logic, in its most extreme form, brings into question the humanity of those marginally included members, while appropriating from them some of the very assets that translate into the allegedly more secure, less questionable form of humanity that is conferred upon those granted full political rights. The ways in which humanity is parsed out depends crucially on fundamental failures of recognition on the part of those whose power to confer recognition matters. To the extent that the figure of Antigone has itself become embroiled in, and representative of, a Western, hegemonic canon, she too has been appropriated in ways that consolidate, rather than disrupt, a tradition of thought that evades its own implication in slavery and colonialism.

As Derrida intimates when he interrupts his commentary on Hegel's *Phenomenology of Spirit* with a biographical meditation on Hegel's life, Hegel's repressed desire for his sister dictates his insistence on portraying the brother-sister relationship as one of purity in his philosophical tracts. Hegel's philosophy would thereby appear to lay down the law that in his own life he seems to have transgressed. Hegel's reading of Antigone therefore functions as a way of tethering a wayward spirit. The brother-sister relationship must be the purest of all, because Hegel's own relationship to his own sister—an imperative that operates as a fiat—must remain unmixed with desire. The status of this imperative hovers between a retrospective re-installation of a law whose transgression calls for its reassertion, and an attempt to purify, or negate the pollution infecting the Oedipal line. Hegel's theoretical reflections would therefore be an attempt to rectify the contamination of *philia* with *eros* that the relationship between Oedipus and Jocasta had generated, at the same time as amounting to a sublimation of his own instincts, a philosophical attempt to impose order on the disorder that threatens to break out in his own life.

Sexual difference, according to Derrida, is the rock on which the movement of Hegel's dialectical philosophy founders. Spirit is the "ethical life of a people [Volks]," and the family takes its place for Hegel within the "Volksgeist, the spirit of a people."[78] If the family " 'sacrifices itself" for the sake of the people, and if Hegel's "discourse on sexual difference belongs to the philosophy of nature," sexual difference, it seems, is that which is naturalized.[79] Sexual difference appears to be resistant to the otherwise relentless succumbing of nature to spirit in Hegel's dialectical thinking. Antigone, as the sister, and Polynices, as the brother, are allotted their roles on the basis of their sex. In his reading of Hegel in *Glas*, Derrida interrogates this problem. He suggests that sexual difference is "*overcome* when the brother departs, and when the other (sister and wife) remains. There is no more sexual difference *as natural difference.*"[80] Yet to suggest that the other, as both sister and wife *remains*, is to situate Antigone's alterity in a way that resists any resolution.

Glas is devoted to thinking through that which is remaindered by Hegel, "the unthought or the excluded," that which is "inadmissible in the system," or "what cannot be assimilated, the absolute indigestible," "[t]he system's vomit."[81] Given this, Derrida's suggestion that the other, figured indiscriminately as sister and wife, *remains*, should be read with care. Sexual difference is that which remains unsublated in Hegel's system. Antigone is precisely that which cannot be thought, that which cannot be sublated, but she is also that upon which, nevertheless, the system depends. Derrida asks, "Isn't there always an element excluded from the system that assures the system's space of possibility?"[82] For Derrida, Antigone is such an element in Hegel's system.

Antigone makes her entry onto the "scene" of Hegel's philosophical stage in the left-hand column of *Glas*, devoted to Hegel. Her entrance is paralleled with Derrida's commentary in the right-hand column on the appearance of a tube of Vaseline that Genet figures as "the very sign of abjection."[83] Like this object that "falls [*tombe*]," Antigone falls away from the text, dropping out of Hegel's system, like so much "excrement," covered with roses, kisses, and drool.[84] She is hallowed and yet she is the deject of the system. She is elevated, yet she is left behind, a casualty of a system that cannot think her, yet cannot do without her, a system that requires her services, would not have survived without her, would not be what it is without her—at the very least its contours would have been markedly different.

Antigone is thus read, by Derrida, as Hegel's abject other. She is that which cannot be properly incorporated into the system. She offers resistance to it, remaining outside it, at once facilitating it and refusing its terms. She figures that which the system must render disposable, the waste product of his system, that without which Hegel's system would not be what it is, but whose final shape cannot tolerate her inclusion, finding no adequate means of representation for her. Antigone is assigned to the "law of singularity" and thus stands opposed to the "law of universality," an opposition that orders "a whole series of other couples: divine law/human law, family/city, woman/man, night/day, and so on."[85]

Sam Weber has explored the significance of Antigone's appeal to the "law of singularity," arguing that Antigone commemorates the loss of the singular, which is both a condition of the application of the law, and remains excessive to it.[86] Weber introduces his discussion of the "nomos"—which he hesitates to translate as law—of Hegel's Antigone in the context of a discussion of the rule of law in relation to individuality, drawing attention to the juridical tendency of the United States, as opposed to the prevalence of political approaches in Europe, but at the same time alluding to the ease with which international law has been suspended in recent U.S. history, as in its undertaking of preemptive war. In this respect, the rule of law appears to have given way to the rule of rule.

Emphasizing a certain ambiguity in the American tradition of law, Weber points to the tension residing in the celebration of the "individual" on the one hand, and that of the rule of law on the other hand.[87] He finds this tension inscribed in Hegel's dialectic.[88] For Weber, both the state and the family are invested in their own individuality, and insofar as Creon and Antigone can be taken, respectively, to represent these institutions, they mirror one another. Their commitments, however, will also prove to be their inadequacy, since their very partiality will finally be their downfall. Reminding us of the importance of the fact that for Hegel Antigone's truth, no less than Creon's, is one confined to the level of immediacy, Weber concludes that both Creon and Antigone are at fault insofar as they both deny mediation, Antigone treating the family as an end in and of itself, and Creon treating the state qua government as an end in and of itself.[89] Targeting Butler, perhaps, Hegel, Weber tells us, "never 'takes sides' . . . To identify the Hegelian interpretation of Antigone with the position of Creon, for instance, privileging the authority of the state over that of the family, is to ignore the dialectical structure of the Hegelian text." Weber adds that "all the figures that people this [ethical] 'world,' Creon no less than Antigone are equally implicated in its limitations and therefore share its destiny." While Weber is undoubtedly right to remind us that the "ethical spirit of the people" is for Hegel an "immediate truth," and as such it must be surpassed through a resolution of the ethical world into the state of law, I part company with him when he draws the conclusion that *all* the figures of this world are *equally* implicated in its limitations.[90] As we will see in Chapter 2, Antigone is made to stand for an inferior form of self-consciousness in Hegel's account, a liminal consciousness that stands on the cusp of civilization, between the gods of the underworld and the daylight gods, between the state of nature and the social contract, between the realms that Freud has designated pre-Oedipal and Oedipal.

War is the expedient by which the state attempts to secure its individuality.[91] Yet since war elevates death to a heroic principle, the government is implicated in the power of divine law that Creon seeks to deny when he prohibits the burial of Polynices. To understand this implication, we must recall the significance Hegel attaches to burial. For Hegel, the act of burial accomplishes a transformation of the processes of natural degeneration to which the materiality of the corpse renders it susceptible. By taking this act of natural destruction on, through the burial of her brother, Antigone renders Polynices a member of the community, consecrating his memory. In so doing she transforms an act of nature into a conscious, spiritual act. Weber stipulates this in terms of two aspects. First, when Antigone buries Polynices, she acts as a family member who consecrates the memory of Polynices, taking on his death, such that it is not merely a natural act of destruction, but is rather a commemoration of his membership in a community. Through the deed of burial, Antigone transforms her relationship to Polynices such that it is not merely a blood-relationship, which would qualify it as a natural relationship, but it becomes a conscious relationship, mediated, as it is, by Antigone's ministrations. Second, the divine law is tied to the individual as individual, and its power derives from the elemental.[92]

If we ask after the exact nature of this community into which Antigone ushers her dead brother, by transforming his death from a natural event into a conscious, spiritual one, through her recognition of him as a member of her family, two aspects emerge as particularly salient. First, the community into which Antigone seeks to welcome Polynices is the familial community, a community that is thereby irreducible to the blood relationship on which it is nonetheless based. Her bond with Polynices is based not on blood, but on love. Her act of burial testifies to this. In effect, then, Creon seeks to prevent Antigone's transformation of Polynices from a blood relative to a member of a community, where community is understood as family. Yet, is there not a further sense in which Antigone seeks to recognize Polynices as part of a community in burying him, one that comes to the fore once we focus on the fact that she differentiates Polynices from a slave? Antigone recognizes him as human, rather than a mere thing. She embraces him into the fold of humanity, as opposed to the merely inanimate. In order to do so she must make a distinction between the humanity of Polynices and the humanity of a slave: a distinction that works to the detriment of the slave.

The community into which Antigone ushers Polynices through her performance of burial rites, and her absolutely rigid insistence on recognizing her brother's humanity in this way, is, at the same time, a refusal to have her brother assume the status of a slave. For the status of a slave, in Greek society, is precisely debatable, hovering between beast, inanimate tool, and subhumanity. The difference between a thing and a slave does not appear to have constituted a reliable distinction in fifth century BCE Athens, and this instability is perhaps exacerbated in the mythical Thebes staged so regularly by the Greek tragedians, onto which problems about the political, moral, and religious life of Athens are projected.[93] To honor the body in death, is intimately connected to honoring the body in life. If, in life, the bodies of slaves were routinely subjected to beating, on the pretext of the need for discipline, the dishonoring of the body in death—such as the treatment to which Polynices' corpse is subjected—would blur the line between his humanity and that of slaves. Since the humanity of slaves was constantly put in question through attempts to justify slavery, so too the humanity of Polynices would appear to be in doubt. Insofar as Antigone takes for granted the distinction between slaves and free citizens, the blindness of her own motives must also be called into question. By taking seriously the challenges that playwrights such as Ȍsófisan and Fugard et al. issue to the Western tradition of interpreting *Antigone*, by allowing their interrogation and reframing of that tradition not only to compel attention to details of Sophocles' Oedipal cycle that the Western interpretive tradition has so often overlooked, but also to incite vigilant readings of the cultural and political contexts out of which their Nigerian and South African appropriations of *Antigone* arise, the following pages attempt to renew and reinvigorate the debate about Antigone's significance.

2

Antigone's Liminality

Hegel's Racial Purification of Tragedy and the Naturalization of Slavery

If for Friedrich Nietzsche, Plato's Socrates sounds the death knell of tragedy, as he heralds the decisive triumph of scientific rationalism over tragic paradox, what accounts for the apparently obsessive return of German idealism to Greek tragedy? Must Hegel and Friedrich Hölderlin's preoccupation with the tragic be read as a morbid fascination with a bygone age, a melancholic idealization of the poetic idiom of the Greek polis, which amounts to nothing more than a picking over of the corpse of tragedy? Or should the return of German idealists to what Nietzsche regarded as a dead poetic form be read in the register of their efforts to rejuvenate philosophy, which itself had come to suffer from a certain morbidity, after Socrates saw fit to banish Homer and his ilk from the stage of philosophy? Perhaps the return to Greek tragedy effected by Hegel and Hölderlin was a manifestation of their dissatisfaction with the rationalist bent that philosophy had suffered at the hands of Immanuel Kant, whose critical turn bore within it the consummation of a philosophical rigor mortis that had already begun to set in with the triumphal march of Socratic reason. The return to tragedy would then be a means of breathing new life into a stultified body of philosophical doctrines, rendered lifeless precisely by philosophy's ostensible victory over tragedy. Philosophy would be returning to the tragic poets in order to infuse itself with the life that had been sapped out of it by its own relentless prioritizing of logic over passion, reason over affect, mind over body.

The return to tragedy, then, would bring philosophy back to life, enlivening it, after the deadening impact of Kant's bifurcation of nature and necessity from morality and freedom, of pure theoretical from pure practical reason, of the is from the ought. In the paradoxes of Greek tragedy the freedom to choose is not divorced from the realm of necessity; rather the tragic hero is constrained to choose a fate that is orchestrated by forces beyond human control, and in embracing that choice, in fully identifying with the fate thus discovered, there is a going beyond of fate itself, a rediscovery of freedom. When, in *Oedipus at Colonus*, Oedipus accepts responsibility for that which he did without knowing, he takes on the burden of his failure to know, and sacrifices himself for the sake of the city he failed to save as long as he cast himself in the role of the one who knows. If in one sense his failure to recognize his mother and father, the failure of his own self-knowledge—his failure to recognize himself—marked the limits of his ability to understand or control the contingencies of history, at the same time he was able to move beyond the determinacy of history. His ability to embrace his own fate through self-exile marked the capacity of his powers of self-reflection to distinguish himself from a mere plaything of history, and to exercise his freedom once more, even in the face of the realization that his powers were far from absolute.

Or perhaps, rather than reading into Oedipus the freedom of a self-reflexive attitude, we should retain that privilege for the spectator, since it is for the audience, not the participant of Greek tragedy, to judge it as tragic.[1] Perhaps also, rather than requiring of Kant that he stand merely for an overly rigid systemization of thought, we might see the aesthetic judgment of the third critique itself as pointing in the direction of effecting some sort of passage between the claims of pure theoretical and pure practical reason. In this sense, might Kant not have already anticipated Hegel's return to the Greeks? Does not Kant's sublime bear within it the signs of the very paradoxes that Greek tragedy was less interested in resolving than exposing? This is indeed what Miguel de Beistegui and Simon Sparks suggest in their informative reading when they point out that the sublime constitutes "the site of the presentation of the unpresentable," revealing "to the imagination its own limits precisely at the moment when it demands that it go beyond them."[2] The sublime "shakes imagination to its roots" by going "beyond every form." The Kantian formlessness or monstrosity that the sublime introduces, precisely because it is situated at the "very limit of form," is for that very reason "more profound" than the beautiful.[3]

Without detracting from the suggestiveness of this persuasive interpretation, I would like to offer a different trajectory for situating the alleged formlessness that Antigone has been required to inhabit, one that takes seriously the figuring of Antigone as a site of sublimation for a still more pervasive paradox than those excavated within the predominant philosophical and psychoanalytic traditions, within which the reception of the tragic remains ensconced. When Hegel takes up the trope of sublimity to describe Antigone, his association of her with the terrifying but profound monstrosity of formlessness partakes in the ambivalence of holding her up on the one hand as exemplary, as admirable in the extremity and tenacity of her stance, yet on the other hand, if not as a figure of repulsion and disgust, then certainly as staging something incomprehensible, something that stands finally in need of sublation, even as it remains resistant to it. Antigone resists integration into the story that Hegel tells about the necessary raising up of differences into a logic of contradiction that can be cashed out in terms of determinate negation.[4]

While a good deal of scholarly attention has been devoted to the sense in which Sophocles' Antigone claims Polynices is irreplaceable, such that he is distinguished from a future husband or son of Antigone's, there is very little consideration of the fact that Antigone also distinguishes Polynices from a slave, implying that had he been a slave, rather than her brother, she would not have insisted upon burying him.[5] The reference to slavery is no isolated incident. Read against the background of legal measures concerning marriage and citizenship in fifth century BCE Athens, the Oedipal cycle can be shown to be deeply entrenched not only in a discourse about family, kinship, and sexual difference—the concerns that have been prioritized by Hegel and more recently by theorists such as Lacan, Irigaray, and Butler;[6] it is also embedded in what I argue are the equally important, albeit neglected, themes of the legitimacy of male citizens, the purity of lineage, and the identity of slaves.

How, then, is Antigone's effort to discriminate between a slave and a brother to be read and how are we to account for the consistency with which it has not been read, the extent to which an entire tradition of scholarship has been able to read over it? Could it be that the tradition of German idealism that idealized the Greeks, even while it sought to distinguish itself from them, was unable to attend to this reference to slavery because to do so might have led to introspection about its own complicity with New World slavery? Is the failure to notice or attend to the assumptions Antigone imports into her defense of her brother a direct result of the impossibility of a white, European tradition confronting its own failure to see its endorsement of slavery and colonialism as an indictment of its claims to be civilized?

Recently critics have begun to investigate Hegel with a view to addressing his ideas on slavery and colonialism. He justifies the latter, even as he decries slavery. Not all races, according to Hegel, qualify as world historical; Africans suffered from an undeveloped consciousness.[7] Building on the work of such critics, while at the same time taking seriously on the one hand the tradition of postcolonial appropriations of *Antigone*, and on the other hand, the paradox that the Oedipal cycle is written during a period when aristocratic, archaic rule is giving way to democratic rule in Athens, and yet the democracy that was emerging based itself upon a slave society, this chapter seeks to revisit some of the received parameters within which critics have interpreted *Antigone*.

Hegel's Prohibition of Slavery as a Tragic Topic

Hegel's aesthetics has had a determining influence on the critical reception of Greek tragedy, not least his reading of *Antigone*, a play that he considers to be one of the most sublime works of art of all time.[8] From the opening pages of his study, Hegel dismisses the art of "savages" as "effemina[te]" in its indulgence, for failing to accord with "the true ends and aims of life" (I: 3–4; I: 16). He continues his polemics against "provincial females" for being too ready to sympathize with "misfortune" [Unglück] that is merely "external," "finite," and "negative" (II: 1198; III: 525). The philosophical narrative Hegel provides is sustained by a multiplicity of references designed to establish the superior self-consciousness of spirit in the West. His differentiation of nature from spirit, and his accompanying conception of how females differ from males, proceed in terms of a relentlessly racialized discourse, and his aesthetics prove to be no exception. So, for example, in accounting for the development of ancient Greek religion, the transition from the old to the new gods is rendered in terms that privilege spirit over nature, and correspondingly privilege Greece over Asia.[9] Hegel is committed to a nostalgic view of classical Greece, which he construes as the originating force of the modern state, its as yet undeveloped precursor, which lacks the differentiated moral and legal complexity it will come to have in his own time. If Hegel confers upon Greek ethical actors a lack of sophistication, he also admires them for their "unity" (ibid.) and disinclination to evade responsibility for their own actions. The heroic character does not have "recourse to everyone else" or "shuffl[e] guilt off himself so far as possible" (ibid.). Neither is there any distinction between "person and family" (ibid.). The individual takes on the inherited guilt of the family, and enjoys an immediacy in relation to the whole community (see I: 188–9; I: 247–8).[10] In short, the ancient Greeks might have lacked the moral sophistication and self-consciousness of modern subjects, but at the same time they did not share the modern trait of evasiveness.

To gauge the significance of Hegel's view of art, we must take account both of the bifurcation of the passions from reason that Kant made programmatic, but which Plato had already anticipated in requiring desire and passion to submit to the demands of rationality, and of Hegel's ambivalent privileging of the Greeks. On Hegel's account art provided the Greeks with access to the divine in a manner whose immediacy the development of reflective philosophy will put into question, even as the bifurcations of this philosophical development will necessitate a mediation or overcoming that harks back to the tranquility and repose harbored by Greek statues. In the representation of the divine in the human such statues constituted, for Hegel, the pinnacle of art *as art*, rather than art as a conduit of spirit which grants an inferior type of access to truth than philosophy, whose medium is thought.

Although the Greeks had not yet developed a discourse in which "subjective intentions" were separated from the "objective deed and its consequences" (I: 188; I: 247), Hegel nonetheless insists in associating them with freedom. The same ambivalence that situates the ancients in relation to their immediate unity with the substantial whole—which makes them both laudable and morally primitive, in so far as they do not distinguish between acts done unintentionally and in ignorance from those done with full intentionality and knowledge—is characteristic of Hegel's view of the sense in which the Greeks exhibited freedom. In claiming that tragedy began in Greece, Hegel is also importing into his conception of tragedy the burden of requiring it to constitute an earlier version of the fully fledged freedom he sees individuals as taking on in the modern age of the West. Thus for Hegel "truly *tragic* action necessarily presupposes either a live conception of *individual* freedom and independence or at least an individual's determination and willingness to accept freely and on his own account the responsibility for his own act and its consequences" (II: 1205; III: 534). Oedipus takes responsibility for his actions, even though he did not know that it was his father he had killed and his mother he had married. Antigone takes on the burden of being the daughter of Oedipus, laboring under the curse of her family, and inheriting the consequences of her father's acts, even though she had no control over her familial identity.

In locating the true origins of dramatic poetry in ancient Greece, rather than in the East (see II: 1205–6; III: 534–5), Hegel encounters an especially recalcitrant problem. This requires him on the one hand to maintain that the works of the tragic poets embodied a spirit of freedom, and on the other hand to negotiate the fact that the very society that produced the tragic poets, "where the principle of free individuality makes the perfection of the classical form of art possible for the first time" (II: 1206; III: 535), was in fact structured as a slave society. In order to circumvent the blatant lack of freedom that confronting slavery would entail, Hegel is obliged to produce an argument that explains why slavery constitutes an inappropriate topic for tragedy. In doing so, he embraces tragic poetry as an idealized resolution of collisions, to the point of excluding conflicts that would prove to be unaesthetic. Thus Hegel is able to maintain tragedy as a site of reconciliation by admitting only those conflicts that can be said to be ethical as the locus of collision, thereby purifying in advance the contents of tragedy, such that slavery is excluded as a tragic theme. To include slavery within the orbit of tragedy would be to contaminate it with a contradiction that remains unthinkable and irresolvable by Hegelian logic: slavery becomes the excluded, unthought ground of tragedy, and Antigone is decipherable as a figuring of its exclusion.

Ironically, given his ethical ambivalence with regard to the ancients and the moderns—in particular his misgivings about the way in which we moderns shuffle guilt onto others—in determining the scope of tragic content, and thereby identifying which conflicts are appropriate to it, Hegel will engage in some particularly evasive reasoning. In order not to compromise the stability of the state, Hegel finds himself issuing the advice that even though it is unjust, slavery must sometimes be borne. At the same time—in a gesture that, even if it has nothing else to recommend it, at least goes some way toward acknowledging the potential of art to channel political unrest—Hegel advises that tragedy be sanitized of references to slavery, or at least that such references be minimal, that they be fleeting.[11] The grounds on which he makes such a recommendation, however, are internally contradictory. Yet Hegel, the master dialectician, does not prove himself inclined to follow out the consequences of this particular contradiction.

It is well known that Hegel requires of his tragic heroes that their claims are ethically justified, yet at the same time guilty. Less attention has been paid, however, to the convoluted logic that allows Hegel to condemn slavery (while recommending that such admittedly unjust practices must sometimes, of necessity, be borne) and at the same time to exclude such practices as possible topics of tragedy. Hegel restricts the content of tragedy to a range of "substantive and independently justified powers that influence the human will" (II: 1194; III: 521). When such powers come into conflict with one another due to the passionate and single-minded adherence of tragic heroes to a fixed aim with which the characters completely identify themselves, a tragic collision ensues. Hegel regards as the "chief conflict" that which arises between family love and political life, which Sophocles treats the "most beautifully" and which is embodied above all in his *Antigone* (II: 1213; III: 544). In honoring "Zeus alone, the dominating power over public life and social welfare," Creon represents political life or "the state, i.e. ethical life in its *spiritual* universality," while Antigone represents the "family, i.e. *natural* ethical life" (II: 1213; III: 544).

While for Hegel tragic heroes, as ethical actors, by definition—on account of their particularity (see II: 1195–6; III: 522–3 and II: 1205; 535)—represent partial aspects of ethical life, he insists both that they are justified, and that their claims are equal.[12] Slavery is thereby disqualified as a topic for tragedy, since the claims of slave-owners are neither justified, nor equal to the rightful claims of slaves to be free. Yet things are more complicated than this, since to say that tragic heroes are justified is only part of the story; for Hegel the deeds of tragic heroes are "legitimate" on their own terms, but "blameworthy" in terms of the ethical order taken in its totality (II: 1198; III: 526). The guilt of tragic heroes is bound up with their particularity and the opposition into which they are led in actualizing their pathos (II: 1196; III: 523–4). Thus "despite all their justification" (ibid.), tragic heroes are still guilty—indeed it is their honor to be so (see (II: 1215; III: 546). Thus, in contrast to Aristotle, for Hegel, tragic heroes "do not want to arouse sympathy or pity" (II: 1215; III: 546). Such emotions are merely "subjective" rather than "substantive" (II: 1215; III: 546).[13]

This stands in contrast to Hegel's earlier claim, in which he appears to accept Aristotle's dictum that the aim of tragedy should be to elicit fear and pity, but judges that tragedies dealing with slavery fail to achieve this aim. "[W]e entertain neither fear nor awe in the presence of the power of such rights accruing from barbarism and the misfortune [Unglück] of the times, and the pity that we might feel changes at once into repugnance and indignation" (I: 212; I: 277). Instead of characterizing slavery in terms of a clash of rights that accrue from barbarism, and those rights that proceed from human dignity and worth, Hegel glosses the justified rights of slaves to be treated as equal with the phrase "misfortune of the times," a gloss that covers over his equivocation. On the one hand the "legality" of slavery must be "respected and justified" given the "level of civilization" of the times, but on the other hand "for us" it is "without validity or power" (I: 212; I: 276–7). This equivocation will prove to be consistent with his recommendation that, despite its injustice, slavery must sometimes be borne.

Hegel refines his position with regard to Aristotle's theory of tragedy by distinguishing between superficial or subjective feelings and true feelings, and suggesting that "True pity" should not just be sympathy for someone's "misfortune" [Unglück] but equally for the "moral justification" [sittliche Berechtigung] of the sufferer (II: 1198; III: 525). This accords with Hegel's view that "the only important thing for a work of art is to present what corresponds with reason and spiritual truth" (II: 1197; III: 525). By restricting tragedy to ethical subject matter, Hegel thus confirms Aristotle's view insofar as he agrees that tragedy should purify feelings, a process of purification that leads him to admit pity and fear only insofar as they direct us to the ethical justification of tragic heroes. Such justification, because it is partial and one-sided, is at the same time in conflict with another aspect of the ethical order. Accordingly Hegel makes a suggestion that only someone who is not oppressed by an external power, someone who was not a slave for instance, would make: "What a man really has to fear is not an external power and oppression by it, but the might of the ethical order which is one determinant of his own free reason and is at the same time that eternal and inviolable something which he summons up against himself if once he turns against it" (I: 1198; III: 525). Those who fear things that are merely "finite and external" rather than "the power of the Absolute" (II: 1197–8; III: 525) experience, the implication is, merely superficial and subjective fear. By distinguishing between genuine and superficial objects of fear and pity, Hegel thereby dismisses slavery as a worthy subject for tragedy. Due to its injustice, slavery is not a topic that tragedy can purify through its artistic presentation. In effect then, Hegel purifies tragic poetry of the burden of representing the ugliness that would ensue from incorporating into it conflicts based on unjustified beliefs in slavery, yet counsels that such ugliness should be tolerated in life, at least when it appears to be insurmountable. Poetry, it would seem, must be purified of the ugliness, and barbarism that must be tolerated in life.

Even though there is a certain necessity that Hegel acknowledges in the actualization tragedy realizes, and in the dissonance conflict involves when the deed of one tragic hero clashes with another, the Hegelian impulse to reassert the unity that tragic conflict had disturbed is also evident. Above all, it is the reconciliation of conflicting individual aims in which tragedy issues, which reasserts ideality, unity, and eternal justice and which the chorus embodies in its contemplative stance. With regard to its reconciliatory emphasis, Hegel's conception echoes Aristotle's cathartic reading of tragedy. For both of them, tragedy performs a purification of feelings.

It is generally acknowledged that Aristotle's *Poetics* is surely intended, at least in part, as a critical response to Plato's views on poetry. This is no less true for Aristotle's discussion of the tragic emotions of fear and pity than it is for the debate over whether art is to be subordinated to politics, as Plato argued, or whether it has its end in itself, as Aristotle insisted. Aristotle's erasure of politics from the *Poetics* is effected in the service of overcoming Plato's containment of art within the polis. In the words of Charles Segal, "the capacity of poetry to inspire in its audience pity and fear is dangerous" for Plato, who "condemns tragedy" because it "feeds the irrational part of the soul," whereas for Aristotle "the emotions of pity and fear are neutralized, and so rendered beneficial, instead of harmful, whether by purgation, purification, or clarification, or all three together."[14] One of the ways in which Plato expresses his concern about the emotions tragedy invokes, although Segal does not attend to this, is their feminizing influence; it is a concern, as we have seen, that Hegel shares.[15] If Segal calls attention to the opposing effects that the tragic emotions had in Plato's and Aristotle's theories, Edith Hall points to the divergence on the question of whether poetry should be judged according to its political utility. Hall identifies Aristotle's argument that "correctness in the art of poetry is not the same as correctness in the art of politics" as "undoubtedly directed against Plato," for whom "poetry must be judged by the same criteria as political questions," and must be "useful to political communities." By contrast, for Aristotle poetry is "a self-sufficient art whose own correctness or lack of it is immanent, internal to itself, and thus distinct from correctness in any other sphere of human activity."[16]

The debate over whether art is to be subordinated to politics, as Plato argued, or whether it had its end in itself, as Aristotle insisted—and therefore as to whether the standards by which art and politics should be judged differ—is one that informs Hegel's interrogation of aesthetics, and one on which Hegel seems to hedge his bets. He wants to preserve the idea of art having its end in itself, while at the same time embracing a hierarchy between philosophy and art that makes art answerable to philosophy.[17] In deference to the question Hall poses in her article "Is there a polis in Aristotle's *Poetics*?"—which I will follow up momentarily—one might say that Hegel replaces the polis that Aristotle's *Poetics* effaced from tragedy, and that he does so by making good another of its erasures, namely the role of religion.[18] Yet, if in one way Hegel historicizes ancient Greek tragedy, by insisting on its religious significance, in another way he depoliticizes it, not only by casting it as an art that preceded the legality of the state, but also by privileging a particular conception of politics as bound to the state. His understanding of tragic figures as interpretations of Greek gods exempts him from any consideration of tragedy as a site for reflecting on how to construe the political as such, and thus from seeing the contest between Antigone and Creon precisely as a contestation over the meaning of the political.[19] Instead, Hegel takes for granted that the only representation of the political that *Antigone* offers is the one that Creon represents. In so doing he neglects to interrogate both the political significance of Antigone, and the salience of any of the specific measures that were introduced during or preceding the period in which the tragedies were authored.

On the surface, Hegel's aesthetics would appear to be much more in tune with a contextual, historical, and political reading of tragedy than Aristotle's *Poetics*, but Hegel's specification of tragedy as an art form that found its true meaning in relation to Greek religion ensconces it in a particular conception of politics and history that later appropriations of the play have contested. For its part, critics have seen Aristotle's cathartic theory of poetics as conservative, conceiving of tragedy as siphoning off and containing the expression of emotions, including those experienced due to political unrest or discontent, and thereby avoiding potentially disruptive outbreaks of uncontrolled passion. Critics such as Augusto Boal have argued that the cathartic view of tragedy that Aristotle puts forward in the *Poetics* is fundamentally "repressive."[20] In contrast to this, rather than construing the Aristotelian view of tragedy as harnessing emotions in such a way as to ensure their harmless expression, Hall's reading of Aristotle draws out its radical implications.

Remarking upon the fact that for the most part Aristotle situates tragedy and politics in relation to one another, yet in his *Poetics* the civic dimension of poetry is conspicuously lacking, Hall observes that "although he might in theory take the *polis* out of tragic poetry, he could not in practice take tragic poetry out of the *polis*."[21] Hall suggests that "The *Poetics*' near-total displacement of the polis from tragedy" is "an astonishingly original innovation, which adumbrates the incipient and future status of tragedy as an international art-form."[22] She goes on to suggest that Aristotle's *Poetics* "contributed uniquely to the continued rediscovery, reinterpretation, and re-performance of the tragic corpus, and its constant revivification."[23] Hall acknowledges that the impact of Aristotle's "divorce of tragedy from the Athenian democratic polis" in the *Poetics* has been negative as well as positive, in that it has helped to obscure "precisely those local, historical, and ideological specificities of which . . . other contemporaries were so aware."[24] Nevertheless, Aristotle's excision of politics from his *Poetics*, which might at first appear to be merely a weakness of his interpretation, is shown to have positive ramifications. The transposition of tragedy into contemporary social contexts that confer their own, very different, performative conditions is thereby, if not licensed, at least anticipated.

Plenty could be said about the preconceptions Hegel brings to his understanding of *Antigone*, both in terms of his evident attempt to press the play into a mold in which—despite Hegel's claim that the medium of art is not that of philosophy—the claims of the protagonists can be cashed out as oppositional, as logically contradictory, and as therefore susceptible to a form of overcoming or reconciliation that resembles or replicates the model of determinate negation that is the motor of his dialectical logic (see II: 1215; III: 547). Neither is it hard to bring into question the hierarchical and historically successive relationship Hegel sets up between art, religion, and philosophy, which tends to specify art's function as an inferior presentation of the truth that philosophy will eventually deliver as conceptual thinking.

While art as such, considered as an independent domain, retains its own end, considered more broadly, in Hegel's terms, art does not attain the self-reflective rigor of thought that is the proper sphere of philosophy. Thus, while art provides "awareness" (I: 102; I: 141) of true spirit, it does not achieve the self-reflective capacity that thought has. As an expression of spirit, an expression however that has not yet advanced to the truth of thought, art does not unfold as the dialectical resolution of contradiction. Its medium is that of sensuous materiality, not that of logical reason. Yet, Hegel, the philosopher, has no reservations about using the language of *aufhebung* to account for the true meaning of art, which might escape art on its own terms, but does not escape Hegel on his terms.[25] Those terms include a conception of truth and reality as ideal, which privileges ethics understood as divine, and discounts the contingencies and external particularities of the finite world. Hegel includes abuses of power such as slavery in the latter.

To admit slavery as an appropriate topic for tragedy would compromise the implicit faith Hegel attaches to the resolution tragedy brings in its reassertion of the ideality and unity of eternal justice. There can be no preservation (see I: 1215; II: 546), raising up, overcoming, or sublation of the essentially unjustified claim that characterizes those who would uphold slavery. Apparently, then, Hegel sees a need to wait for the logical necessity of history to expunge certain glaring contradictions, a necessity for certain groups of people—slaves among them—to await the freedom promised by the eventual, inevitable working out of differences that prove unsustainable in the particularized real world.

Sculpting Antigone's Ethics from the Gods of "Nature"

Hegel's suggestion that each tragic character identifies solely with such a singular aim is one that critics have disputed, as is Hegel's assumption that each tragic character can be adequately considered to fulfill a representative function. So, too, the mutual exclusivity of the aspects of ethical life that Antigone and Creon are said to represent has been interrogated.[26] Yet, insofar as Hegel acknowledges that the pathos of Antigone (her "interest in the family") and that of Creon (the "welfare of the community" (I: 464; II: 60) are merely aspects of a larger, more complex whole, the ethical and communal fabric of life that the chorus represents, he would be the first to concede that things are more complex than the singular identification of either Antigone or Creon might suggest. In this sense, to insist on the mutual implication of family and state is not so much to challenge Hegel as it is to confirm one of his most important insights into tragedy, namely the one-sidedness and partiality of the tragic heroes, and thus their incompleteness.

It is certainly politically productive to ask whether in fact certain familial forms are not only sanctioned by, but also made possible by the state, and whether in turn certain familial configurations support and legitimize the state. By doing so, the question as to whether the mutually supportive structures of family and state have naturalized heteronormative families has been foregrounded. However, neither objections about the complexity of the tragic characters, nor observations that point to the mutual implication that pertains between family love and state duty challenge the fundamental Hegelian dictum that the chief site of conflict in *Antigone* is that between family and state.

That the state legitimizes a certain representation of the family, while outlawing other representations, is undeniable, as is the fact that Hegel tends to reduce the complex and not necessarily consistent motives and aspects of the character of Antigone, in order to align her both with his reconciliatory vision of the chorus as mediating competing, one-sided, and singular aims, and with his preconceptions about women's proper sphere of action.[27] Still to be interrogated are the purposes such an oversimplification serves, and the extent to which *Antigone* raises questions that go beyond the ways in which circumscribed representations of the family shore up the state, which in turn legitimize a highly particularized and naturalized account of the family. By returning both to the question of representation and to the ways in which familial definitions accord not just with an idealized version of a particular state, but with the very emergence of the state as a state, and its delineation from other states, the various strategies of purification in which Hegel's concept of tragedy is engaged can be traced.[28] So too, we need to consider the various ways in which the concept of the family organizes Hegel's thinking about *Antigone*, and whether the lack of a systematic conceptual genealogy of the family in relation to the historical series out of which the modern concept of the family emerges, including generation (*Geschlecht*), clan and so forth, marks a lacunae that needs to be made good.[29]

If Hegel is forthright in tracking the development of legal thinking and the state as emerging from a more communally based ethics, he is less inclined to attend systematically to the changing shape of kin relations, the modern configuration of which will find its definitive form in the nuclear, patriarchal family.

My speculation is that this lack of concern is bound up with an assumption that the role of women—guardian of the familial—remains in Hegel's mind somewhat static over time. In my reading Hegel imposes a highly particular stasis on Antigone, a stasis that conflates a particular, purified configuration of woman as symbolic of the natural, rather than the contractual, family (the latter being the familial as mediated by marriage) with his more generic conception of tragic figures as interpretations of immobile Greek statues of divinities. Forcing Antigone into the mold of the spiritual actor who cements her familial bond with her brother, Hegel idealizes the brother-sister relation and holds it up as exemplary in a way that capitulates to a particular reading of the myth of the eternal feminine. A different reading, one that is opened up by Hegel's reflections, but not hemmed in by the underlying religious convictions or the naturalized account of gender that Hegel supports by a racializing discourse, is presented here. As the virginal sister, Antigone becomes immobilized: she cannot move within the symbolic economy of exchange that would structure her transition to womanhood, a transition in which she would be the gift that passes from one household to another. Such a passage is thwarted in her case. Her transaction from one *kurios* to another has been blocked by Oedipus' incestual confusion of the symbolic father with the symbolic son, a confusion that would result in Antigone's uncle and *kurios,* Creon (who was responsible for giving away Jocasta to Oedipus as his prize for solving the riddle of the Sphinx), giving Antigone to his own son. Burying Polynices is a way of putting to rest the symbolic confusion generated by Oedipus's incest. Dramatizing this blockage, at the same time Antigone enacts a symbolic revolt against a system in which women can only ever be tokens of exchange in a symbolic system that excludes them from generating meaningful bonds outside this system. Yet Antigone's revolt is one that attempts to shift the rigidity of the bonds that hold women in place only by affirming the bonds that circumscribe slaves. That the blocked passage to which Antigone reacts and that she effects at the same time immobilizes or stultifies the predicament of slaves is not a detail to which many readers of this tragedy have attended.

Nor should we discount Hegel's reluctance to take up the question of what separates one generation from another—even though this distinction is precisely the one that Oedipus had confounded, and is therefore central to Antigone's destiny—from issues of race or slavery. In this regard, it is worth emphasizing that included among the range of connotations that both the terms *Geschlecht* and γένος have is "race." Thus, discussing inherited guilt, Hegel says: "a whole generation [Geschlecht] suffers on account of the original criminal . . . he *is* what his fathers were" (I: 188–9; I: 247). Yet he also uses the term when differentiating between the earlier and later Greek gods: the former are "a raw and savage race [Geschlecht], misshapen, like products of Indian or Egyptian fancy, gigantic and formless" (I: 459; II: 53). When Creon is responding to Haemon, from whom he expects obedience, he says "For if I am to raise my own flesh and blood [to be] unruly, then most certainly [I will raise] those outside my family [to be unruly too]" (Griffith, 326). The word translated as "family" is the genitive form of γένος. Of particular interest is the fact that Creon raises the question of insubordination or unruliness in relation to those inside and those outside the family/race. The borders of the family are to be established, apparently, on the basis of the obedience of its members. Given the views expressed by Aristotle, to be formulated not long after Sophocles composed the Oedipus cycle, concerning the capacity of slaves and women in relation to deliberation and authority, Creon's words take on a special significance.[30]

The cultural requirement that male adults authorize any and every female decision, to the point where women are construed as incapable of taking any important action by or for themselves, is one that plays itself out in the political and ethical philosophies of Plato and Aristotle. *Akyron* means without a guardian.[31] Roger Just points out that, although differently configured, the rule of a free man over a slave, that of a male over female, and that of a man over a boy are all conceived as natural. Aristotle tells us that "the deliberative faculty of the psyche is not present at all in the slave; in a female it is inoperative (*akyron*), in a child, underdeveloped."[32] The difference between the ruler and the ruled is that between the rational and the nonrational.[33] In Antigone's case, Creon is both the *kurios*, the male guardian, the one who expects to give away the bride, and the father of the one who expects to receive her—a doubling of identity that echoes all the other doubled identities that structure the Oedipal myth. For Antigone to be without a guardian [*akyron*] is, then, for her to be unruly—like a slave. For Haemon to follow Antigone's lead is to show the same insubordination as she does. So, too, there is the contaminating influence of Polynices' corpse, which Antigone, seeks to differentiate from a slave by performing burial rites.

Not only is there a purification of emotions at stake in Hegel's reading of tragedy, but also a narrative of racial purification. While Hegel does not take up the issue of slavery in *Antigone* directly, it is deflected in his racially purifying narrative. Antigone occupies a transitional status, in which she serves at one and the same time as a vehicle for Hegel's differentiation of spirit from nature, and as a mechanism that dissociates Athenians—and by implication nineteenth-century European imperial slave-owners—from those whose lineage proves to be less than pure. Admitted into the realm of spirit, Antigone nonetheless occupies its lower echelons, contaminated with nature, as prescribed by her sex. Hegel grants Antigone a marginal spirituality on the basis of his belief that tragic heroes represented gods—but not without making it clear that the particular god that Antigone represents emanates from the old order of gods and as such remains bound to nature. The gods from whom Antigone derives her spirituality are in turn distinguished from the gods of other religions, whose spirituality

Hegel regards as inferior, a view he expresses in racial terms. Yet the distinction leaves a residue: Antigone is closer to these more primitive gods of nature than Creon, who represents rather the newer gods (more advanced, more rational, more masculine, more Greek, more modern, more Christian, more Hegelian).

The essence of tragedy resides, for Hegel, in a conflict between universal, ethical powers and especially in the reconciliation of these opposing powers. Tragic heroes are defined by their complete identification with one such ethical power (understood as a god or a group of gods). In this respect, Hegel compares them to works of sculpture. Tragic heroes "*are* what they will and accomplish" (II: 1214; III: 546). There is no split between the subject and what is willed. The essential pathos of tragic heroes confers on them solidity and steadfastness, which likens them to the statues of Greek gods, while the chorus, for its part, is compared to the temples that house such statues. The chorus is the architectural background against which a drama is played out, a drama constituted by the action of the heroes.

> Just as the Greek theatre itself has its external terrain, its scene, and its surroundings, so the chorus, the people, is as it were the scene of the spirit; it may be compared, in architecture, with a temple surrounding the image of the gods, for here it is an environment of the heroes in the action. (II: 1211; III: 542)

Hegel's employment of this image of a temple containing statues of gods to explain the relationship between the chorus and the tragic heroes is of more than passing interest. The chorus provides a "secure refuge" (II: 1211; III: 541) against the "fearful collisions" which provide the stuff of tragedy, on Hegel's view. In its "equilibrium" the "ethical order appears" (II: 1211; III: 541). If originally in Greek tragedy the relationship between the chorus and the tragic heroes was illuminated by the image of a temple containing statues of gods, the chorus disappears from modern tragedy, which concerns itself with the private, subjective aims of its characters. Hegel links the decline of ancient tragedy to the disappearance of the chorus (II: 1212; III: 542–3). Modern tragedy concerns itself with personal, subjective conflicts. Once the state emerged, it became the objective embodiment of ethics. The emergence and consolidation of the more formal apparatus of the state, which took on the role of rendering rationality "objective" (I: 182; I: 240), and—supplanting the downfall of tragic heroes—the task of punishing infringements (I: 183; II: 241), was accompanied by a transformation in the nature of tragedy. As the "actual substance of the moral life and action of the hero" (II: 1211; III: 541) the chorus provides the security that, according to Hegel, was later to become the preserve of the state. The trouble is, as Hegel acknowledges, the state does not always uphold justice. This accounts in part for the fact that so many poets of the postmodern era have been obliged to break with Hegel's dictum that tragedy in the modern age has become merely subjective. *Antigone* has been taken up in so many diverse political contexts precisely because the state has failed to uphold the rights of some of its members as equal to others, under regimes such as that of apartheid South Africa, for example.[34] Due to such failures, dramatists have turned to *Antigone* as a means of recalling the state to its proper duty, thereby enacting an appropriation that is at once political and ethical, and which also makes an intervention into the narrative of aesthetics, as we will see further.

The fact that Hegel construes tragic heroes as representative not merely of ethical powers, but of divinities, allows him to avert any confrontation both with the rampant inequalities that characterized the lives of slaves in classical Athens, and those characteristic of women's day to day lives. The plasticity he attributes to tragic heroes extends to actual personages of ancient Greece, suggesting that he also sees tragic heroes as representative of historical figures. Yet this inference is indirect enough to prevent Hegel from having to acknowledge the disjunctive relationship between his claim that tragic heroes are equal in their ethical justification and the fact that none of the historical examples he provides of the "actual statesmen and philosophers," or the "poets and thinkers" that populated the "beautiful days of Greece" (II: 719; II: 374), are women. Nor is it easy to see how Hegel could have provided any such examples, given women's second-class status and lack of education in the Periclean age to which Hegel refers. The "men of action" he has in mind are "Pericles himself, Phidias, Plato, Sophocles above all, Thucydides too, Xenophon, Socrates" (II: 719; II: 374). These men are, says Hegel, in a description that unmistakably evokes the idea of Greek statues with which he associates tragic heroes, "great and free . . . ideal artists shaping themselves, individuals of a single cast, works of art standing there like immortal and deathless images of the gods" (II: 719; 374). Hegel's aestheticization of ancient Greece—in its beautiful days—does admit one woman as exemplary of "the same plasticity [that] is characteristic of the works of art which victors in the Olympic games made of their bodies" (II: 720; II: 374). Yet it is neither her ethical actions nor her accomplishments, but rather her naked beauty that gives Phryne the "appearance" (II: 720; II: 374) of plasticity, as she rises from the sea. This association of women with physical, bodily beauty, rather than political or artistic accomplishments, finds its corollary in Hegel's understanding of Sophocles' *Antigone* as answerable to the old order of the gods, rather than the newer order, that is, the order of gods that Hegel construes as akin to nature.[35]

As his concession to Phryne's beauty indicates, women in Hegel's version of ancient Greece are required to play a liminal role. They must be at one and the same time closer to nature and subject to male guidance, and thus capable of a limited spirituality (a view that is uncannily close to Aristotle's view that women, while possessing the faculty of deliberation, lack the authority to properly exercise it). Women are capable of being spiritual actors, of acting on behalf of a certain aspect of the ethical order, as required by Hegel's vision of tragic heroes, but only within certain limits. Their spirituality is circumscribed by their proximity to nature, a characteristic of the old gods, but one which is preserved in the new gods, albeit in a subordinated fashion (see I: 474; II: 73). One of the ways in which women's liminal spirituality is etched out in the contours of Hegel's thought is through his differentiation of the gods of ancient Greece from those of other countries. The ideal of beauty with which he associates Phryne or Artemis is infused with unstated assumptions about chastity and modesty. By implication the excessive, unchaste, immodest, ungovernable goddesses of the East are impure, and incapable of purification, just as they are incapable of governance.[36]

The dual demand that women be closer to nature than men, yet capable of a limited display of spirituality is, indeed, exactly the situation that defines Hegel's assessment of Antigone, who represents the old order of ancient gods. In contrast, Creon (on Hegel's reading) represents Zeus, a god of the new order. The group of gods that includes Dike—on whom Antigone calls—"borders on what is inherently ideal, universal, and spiritual" but lacks "spiritual individuality," so that these gods "retain a closer bearing to what is necessary and essential in nature" (I: 462; II: 57). In this liminal or borderline spirituality, "the categories of right and justice already obtrude" (I: 462; II: 58), but they veer toward "abstraction" or toward nature. As Hegel puts it—and the formulation accords well with Antigone's devotion to Polynices—at stake here is an "obscure right of the natural element within spiritual relationships, e.g. love of kindred and its right" (I: 462; II: 58). In fact, as Hegel continues his thought, although this was certainly not his intention, he expresses the limitations that ancient Greece would have imposed on women's freedom to perfection: "This does not belong to the spirit which is conscious of itself in its clear freedom and therefore it does not appear as a legal right" (I: 462; II: 58).[37] Dike is associated with "natural needs and their satisfaction" (I: 467; II: 64); the right it represents is not "specified in laws deriving their origin from the self-conscious spirit" (I: 467; II: 64). The distinction between the immediacy of need on the one hand and "political organization which makes its aim the spiritual realm" (I: 461; II: 56–7) on the other hand, governs Hegel's account of the gods, whom he views as becoming progressively more capable of imparting "ethics, law, property rights, freedom and community" (I: 461; II: 57) and less bound by the immediacy of need, as they advance from nature to spirit. By associating Antigone with Dike and Creon with Zeus, Hegel thereby associates Antigone, the woman, with immediate needs, and Creon, the man, with the political realm, in which spirit has advanced to a higher level of self-consciousness. Crucially, by associating Antigone with the earlier Greek gods, rather than the later, Hegel thereby aligns Antigone with the savagery those gods of Eastern heritage—those misshapen, formless gods of another race.

It is important to point out that, far from associating Antigone with woman-in-general, Hegel associates Antigone with the natural, rather than the contractual, family.[38] Specifically, Hegel emphasizes Antigone's identification with her sisterly bond to her brother, a relation that Hegel distinguishes from the husband-wife relation, since he discerns in marriage the beginnings of a political bond.[39] For Hegel, therefore, Antigone's prioritizing of Polynices over her future husband is entirely consistent with her attachment to blood kindred, to the older gods, who are associated more directly with nature than are the newer ones, and with the immediacy of need rather than the bonds of community. In this respect, Antigone's claim that Polynices is irreplaceable, in a passage that has proved so controversial for some commentators, poses no problem at all for Hegel. At the same time, Antigone's attachment to her natural family, rather than to her future husband or to a future son, confirms that Hegel' reading appeals to Antigone's liminal spirituality. As a tragic hero, and as emblematic of ancient Greece, Antigone is inscribed within the orbit of spirit's self-progressive realization, yet her inscription, for Hegel, is such that she hovers on the edge of a world in which the ethical order is about to be submitted to legal formulae guaranteed and underwritten by the state, an ethical order no longer subsisting simply in the life of the community.

The Simplicity, Solidity, and Plasticity of Tragic Heroes in a Pre-Legal Era

Hegel's attitude toward this shift is distinctly ambiguous, as we have already begun to discern. On the one hand he extols the virtues of classical Athens, in which ethics is not yet tied down to legislation, but is precisely communal, but on the other hand, the informality of ethics, the fact that it is so embedded in the community, signals a lack of determinacy. In this respect, the function of tragedy is precisely to confer individuality on particular ethical commitments, a conferral that renders such claims particular, substantive, and concrete, by tying them down to actual deeds, and associating them with particular characters.[40] By the same token, it is the solidity that Hegel so admires in tragic heroes, the fact that they do not deviate or hesitate, but they are what they are through and through. Hegel casts this in a negative light insofar as it reflects a state of affairs prior to the emergence of a fully-fledged social contract, and all the legal apparatus that supports the state, while at the same time it testifies to a lack of inner complexity.[41] Yet there remains something impressive and admirable about the moral fortitude of tragic heroes. Moreover, Hegel sees in their fixity a certain necessity, as if it is precisely their refusal to be anything other than what they are that carves out the conceptual space for the religious and legal principles that will later settle in their place. It is precisely her unyielding, inflexible grasp of her position that renders Antigone so significant for contemporary dramatists. As a tragic hero, standing firm, like a statue, she is unmovable. Her statuesque immovability (one thinks of the civil rights movement, of Martin Luther King's occupation of a prison cell, of Rosa Parks' refusal to vacate her bus seat, of the suffragettes chaining themselves to the railings outside parliament, of the imprisonment of anti-apartheid activists) constitutes a mimetic, transformative performance of the immobilizing exclusions perpetrated in the name of race and gender, visited on those excluded from the social pact by dint of their race or gender, those whose stance already situates them outside the social contract that their protest seeks to radicalize. Remaining firm in one's beliefs, refusing to be condemned for what one is, calling on the state to observe a higher form of justice than that which its exclusionary, parasitical, and contradictory policies permit by excluding some of its members from the full political rights of citizens while also constituting them as an underclass, demanding of the polity an ethical accountability, refusing to be swayed in one's call for justice—this is what Antigone stands for. In such standing firm, the shifting representational content of her ethicality is not nature, family, or religion, but a dynamic demonstration of the contradictory logic subtending a polity that depends materially, psychically, or spiritually on those it symbolically and politically excludes. Whereas Hegel conflates Antigone's forthright ethical stance with a naturalized, eternal ethic that entombs her within a particular conception of purified womanhood, woman as virginal, unmarried sister, woman as emblematic of the natural family of blood relatives, those dramatists that appropriate Antigone as a vehicle for exposing the illogicality of a state premised upon an unacknowledged dependence on those it symbolically excludes, read Antigone's refusal to move in a more vital way. Her refusal to compromise, her standing firm becomes the pivot that disrupts the particular conception of politics that has congealed into a racist or an apartheid state. Her immobility becomes the locus for rethinking the principles that have petrified the state, ossifying beliefs into exclusionary laws. Her immobility, her refusal to mold herself according to the polity's expectations, becomes a force that challenges the state to mobilize its rigid laws into laws that answer to a justice that those very laws have come to occlude. Antigone's statuesque refusal to compromise becomes a force for political change.

Essential to Hegel's conception of Attic tragedy as a form of art is its historical emergence at a time during which legal and moral principles are still in the process of being formulated, when ethics have not yet been institutionalized in legal or moral precepts, but remain communal. The ethical order, which the chorus articulates, is understood precisely as a communal ethics, which the poets themselves play an important part in formulating, in an age that is "pre-legal" (I: 185; I: 244), where morality is not yet institutionalized in universal legislation and maxims. In such a situation tragic heroes confer upon the ethical force with which they coalesce a solidity that precedes any stability that could derive from the permanence of legislation or the fixity of moral imperatives. Prior to a time at which the state confers security and stability on the life of a nation, the dramatic poetry of Athens played a decisive role in formulating ethically justified and stable characters, each of which brought to life and actualized through their pathos one of the Greek gods (see I: 102; I: 141). While the chorus articulated the ethical substance of the community, the tragic heroes represented partial claims of the whole fabric of the ethical order, which would later be formalized as moral and legal principles (see I: 194; I: 255). Hegel says "the chorus is essentially appropriate in an age where moral complications cannot yet be met by specific valid and just laws and firm religious dogmas, but where the ethical order appears only in its direct and living actuality" (II: 1211; III: 541). In the heroic age (depicted in tragedy) "the universal ethical powers have not been explicitly fixed as either the law of the land or as moral precepts and duties" (II: 1208; III: 539). In the absence of the fixity of such institutions, a "fixed aim" is provided by the " 'pathos' and power" of the tragic hero (II: 1214; III: 546), where there is no separation or cleavage between subject and object: "the bond between the subject and what he wills as his object remains indissoluble" (II: 1214; III: 546). In this regard it is worth recalling that the art of sculpture, for Hegel, is "objective," whereas the art of poetry is "subjective" (I: 89; I: 123). Sculpture—by reference to which Hegel understands tragic heroes, which are poetic interpretations of statues—constitutes the "unqualified realization of the *classical form*" of art (I: 90; I: 123). It is in the context of this claim that Hegel's insistence upon the plasticity of tragic heroes, which he understands as interpretations of Greek statues of divinities, should be read.

Woven into Hegel's narrative of the progressive self-realization of spirit as self-consciousness is a commitment to Christianity, through the lens of which he views the religion of ancient Greece, and in distinction from which he makes pronouncements about the inadequacies of Islam. Indeed it is precisely on the grounds that Mohammaden poetry lacks a sufficiently developed sense of individual freedom vis-à-vis the individual's "subjection to the will of God" (II: 1205; III: 535) that Hegel dismisses the possibility of it meeting his criteria for dramatic poetry. The balance is too much in favor of the "abstractly universal" and not tipped enough in the direction of particularity (II: 1205; III: 535). If the Islamic God is too powerful, the gods of India and Egypt are not powerful enough. They are too "savage," too "raw," and thus "ungovernable" (II: 459; II: 53). In China and India, we might say, there is too much particularity and not enough universality, for there is "no accomplishment of a free individual action" (II: 1206; III: 535). What is given life is merely "events and feelings," with no ethical principle or aim at stake.

Hegel is invested in positing ancient Greece as the origin of civilized western Europe—and therefore as a culture based on free human individuality—yet as still undeveloped in relation to his own time. As such, the freedom he associates with ancient Greece, and more specifically with the tragic drama of fifth century BCE Athens, is a freedom that is not as reflective as it will become in the modern era (see II: 1219; III: 551), but which already shows such potential. Thus Oedipus almost qualifies as a modern hero, in that he embodies the signs of subjectivity, by developing the capacity for self-knowledge, thereby becoming a vehicle for the expression of an inner reconciliation, or of the split between subjectivity and objectivity that will not emerge fully until later (see I: 213–4; I: 279–90).

At the same time as identifying ancient Greece, as distinct from the East, including China and India, as the origin of dramatic art, Hegel also sees ancient tragedy as reflective of a transition from a state of nature (see I: 466; II: 62) to a more highly developed form of political society, in which the state has established a measure of stability that was previously lacking. On the one hand, then, ancient tragedy becomes emblematic of a time that preceded the Western, Christian state, a time in which morality had not yet been fixed, either by legislation or by Christianity, while on the other hand it is celebrated for having provided a measure of fixity through its representations of tragic heroes, whose passionate attachment to particular aspects of Greek ethical life brought to life their divinities. It is hard not to speculate that Hegel's conception of Greek tragic heroes as bringing to life the gods of ancient Greek religion is indebted to his Christian allegiance to spiritual incarnation.

Art Must Be Purer than Life

As we have seen, some conflicts, among them slavery, are grounded in such barbarism that they must be excluded from dramatic poetry, which would otherwise lose its beauty. In this respect, Hegel demands a higher standard of purity from art than he does from life: in life, slavery must sometimes be borne, whereas in tragedy it is impermissible to represent it thematically. On the basis of the fact that the claims of tragic heroes must be ethically justified, and that slavery is an unjustified practice, Hegel excludes slavery as a proper subject for tragedy. He requires that the work of art satisfy his criterion of beauty, while at the same time designating certain conflicts as unsuitable topics for tragedy on the grounds that they are based on nature (rather than spirit). It turns out, however, as Hegel himself specifies, that such barbarism is not due to any conflict proceeding from nature, but is rather due to the habit of attributing to nature what is in fact the result of convention. If, as Hegel says, some natural accident of birth is endowed by "custom or law" with the power of an insuperable barrier, so that it deprives an individual of those rights which "belong to him by the nature of man," then "that individual is from the beginning to be relegated not by his own doing, but by the accident of nature, to some class or caste irrevocably" (I: 208–9; I: 272). In such cases, a wrong that has been inflicted through convention or legality is naturalized. It "appear[s] as a wrong that has become natural, as it were" (I: 208; II: 272). It does not occur to Hegel that it is precisely such a process of naturalization in his own reading of Sophocles that aligns Antigone with the family and deprives her of political rights. It is conspicuous, for example, that when Hegel discusses the right of succession, a right that is linked to nature through kinship, and one that is disputed in the collision between Polynices and Eteocles, and treated by Sophocles in the Theban cycle, he fails to notice that the right of succession for Antigone and Ismene is excluded from his own consideration due to an accident of birth. Antigone and Ismene are not considered to have any rights to succession, for no other reason than that, unlike their brothers, they were not born men, and as such are not considered suitable political leaders.

While Hegel acknowledges that "differences of castes, classes, privileges, etc., may have arisen from differences of nation and race," he dismisses this as of "no consequence," insisting rather that "the chief point lies only in the fact that such relationships of life, regulating the whole being of man, are supposed to derive their origin from nature and birth" (I: 209; I: 273). Among the effects of Hegel outlawing slavery, and other practices allegedly based on natural differences, as legitimate subjects for tragedy is the perhaps surprising outcome that melancholy collisions are not the proper subject of tragedy. While Hegel advocates that "true free art" should not "respect" such "melancholy and unfortunate" collisions as stem from conflicts arising between "the position assigned to a man by his birth" and "his different measure of spiritual education and its just demands" (I: 209; I: 273), he nonetheless advises that men must "sacrifice" their interests when barriers prove to be "insuperable" (I: 211; II: 275).

Hegel's restriction of tragedy to specific types of action that render it exclusive of slavery has a dual impact. On the one hand it preempts any attention to extant references to slavery in Greek tragedy, erasing the significance of such references, and on the other hand it operates prescriptively to discourage the exploration of such themes in the modern era. We might even read Hegel's erasure of the thematic treatment of slavery as implicated in his championing of Sophocles as having produced *Antigone*, the tragedy that (on his reading) deals with the most important conflict, and his corresponding denigration of Euripides—whose plays attend to slavery more than those of both Aeschylus and Sophocles—for falling prey to the depiction of emotions and attempting to elicit pity (see II: 1215; III: 546).[42] Notwithstanding Hegel, and making good on Hall's observation about the incipient future of international tragedy announced by Aristotle's *Poetics*, there has been a return to Greek tragedy; in particular, appropriations of *Antigone* have flourished, in which the questions that Hegel argued were not the proper content of tragedy have become thematic. Rather than following Hegel's advice to the "reasonable man" to "bear the inevitable calmly and patiently" and "at least withdraw into the *formal* independence of subjective freedom" (I: 211; I: 275), contemporary dramatists have turned to *Antigone* as a resource for illuminating the conflicts inherent in colonialism and slavery, which arise on the basis of the type of collisions that Hegel excludes from aesthetics. In doing so they challenge the content Hegel ascribes to rationality, and contest the significance he attributes to a merely formal freedom, as well as resisting his advice for forbearance. They thereby offer a dual challenge to Hegel: on the one hand they hold tragedy accountable as an aesthetic form that is implicated in a history of imperialism that the discourse of Western aesthetics has justified, and on the other hand they take both that history and the ethico-political theory that has accompanied it as themes to be interrogated. At the same time these plays transform the tragic genre itself, renewing the question of what the tragic form has become.

By transgressing the formal requirements Hegel imposed upon works of art, by introducing the ugliness of slavery and colonialism into the work of art, contemporary appropriations of *Antigone* also offer resources for an alternative aesthetics, one that does not accept that the end of art is dictated by the contemplative ideal of tranquility, repose and unity required by Hegel. Neither does it accept that art must be purified of conflicts that must be borne in life. No longer—not that it was ever only this—a vehicle for religious representation, the tragic genre has been transformed into an art that explores such human conflicts as arise from religious and racial discrimination. This aesthetic is one that confronts the ugliness of conflicts that have led to discrimination on the basis of hegemonic conceptions of gender, race, and class, inviting us to explore the implications of the fact that such ugliness is an invention of humanity, rather than passing it off as a conflict proceeding from nature.

These plays transform the tragic genre by reflecting on its literary accomplishments in the light of the historical conditions of its production—including the social and political exclusions that both tragedy itself and aesthetics naturalize even while calling them into question. They thus take as a theme for investigation the successes and failures of tragedy and its reception, the elisions and erasures of theories of tragedy, and the role of tragedy and aesthetics in elaborating ideologies of religious chauvinism, nationalism, and empire. These plays subject the themes of imperialism, colonialism, and racism to ethical and political critique, and in this sense they contest the Hegelian dictum that tragedy concerns the conflict of equally justified ethical claims, maintaining rather, the complicity not so much of tragedy as of its theorists with nationalist and imperialist ideals, and their tendency to legitimate both the political claims of one protagonist at the expense of the other, and the model of the political Creon espouses. In this sense, contemporary political appropriations of *Antigone* expose Creon's claim to be concerned about the welfare of the community as a whole as disingenuous, assuming, as it does, the subordination of both women and slaves. Fémi Òsófisan, for example, transposes the figure of Creon into a British colonial governor, thereby drawing attention to the colonial exploits undertaken in the name of empires that trace their legacy back to classical Athens, whose celebrated art trades in compromised claims. At the same time, Òsófisan explores the way in which Antigone's legacy is compromised, not only foregrounding gender conflicts but also acknowledging the history of slavery that helped to shape his country, and in which Antigone remains complicit.[43]

Considered strictly within the logic of his analysis of tragedy, Hegel aligns himself with the chorus, which accords "equal honor to all the gods" (II: 1215; III: 547), and in doing so apportions equal justification and blame to both Antigone and Creon. From a broader perspective, Hegel's tendency to construe the tragic claims of Antigone and Creon as equally justified, and at the same time to see them as equally blameworthy or guilty, is fraught with difficulty because it stands in tension with the indisputable priority Hegel accords to the state over the family in his political philosophy. Yet it is precisely the equality Hegel accords to tragic heroes that gives his reading of *Antigone* a potentially radical edge. In this respect Hegel's reading of tragedy, and of *Antigone* in particular, might be said to be ahead of its time precisely insofar as it insists in construing Antigone's and Creon's claims as ethically equal to one another. In contrast both to the mores of ancient Greece—articulated and justified by its philosophers—and to those of his day, Hegel confers on a female character—albeit a tragic female character—the capacity to be ethical. Hegel thereby joins Sophocles in treating Antigone's ethical claims as worthy of being heard. Indeed he not only gives them credibility, he confers on the piety and holiness of Antigone's attachment to religion and her familial obligations a certain ideality and purity. However, I have sought to show that this purity is attained at a price. Hegel's purification of Antigone is effected by means of a discourse that indulges the racial disparagement of foreign gods, that corroborates Antigone's assumption that slaves are not human in the same way that her royal brother is, that naturalizes Antigone's gender in relation to her attachment to family as blood kin, and that associates the ethics she embodies with the older, primitive, order of gods, who are closer to nature than the newer gods. Not coincidentally, those newer gods of ancient Greece, with whom Hegel identifies Creon, exhibit traits that approximate more closely to a more modern, more "civilized" conception of ethics and the divine, one that Hegel articulates in part through racial denigration of other religions. Antigone's defiance, her refusal to bend to Creon's will, her wild, savage, untamable nature, her unruliness, precisely her *formlessness,* is accomplished in Hegel's reading as her failure to conform to an edict that is marked in Hegel's discourse as the product of a masculinized expression of concern for the welfare of the community, a community that is shaped through the exclusion of women and of slaves as political subjects. Hegel's reiteration of Antigone's wild, savage nature—which is one with which Lacan also toys—capitalizes on Aristotle's belief that women were incapable of governing themselves, and renders explicit the inconsistent assumptions that characterize social contract theorists, who on the one hand uphold the equality of individuals as central to their theories, and on the other hand fail to recognize certain humans—women and raced subjects prominent among them—as individuals.[44]

Antigone's liminality is severely overdetermined in Hegel's account. As a Greek mythical figure, she represents the consummate hero, and yet she represents a religion that has given way to Christianity, and an ethical world that has been superseded. As an artistic figure, she represents the pinnacle of (Greek religious) art, the true meaning of which has now, however, been revealed as (Christian) philosophy. As an ethical actor whose deed is her own, she is distinct from those whose misfortunes are brought about simply through accidents of birth, yet her fate is inseparable from that of her family. As a tragic hero, her representational status is obfuscated; she represents a god, a god who is more spiritual, more beautiful than the gods of Asia, and yet more natural than the Greek gods of the newer order, whom Creon represents. She represents devotion to her natural family and piety to the gods, and yet the ethical, spiritual sensibility she embodies is considered primitive and natural in contrast to Creon's commitment to the welfare of the community, which will be supplanted by the state in the progression of history. As a mythical figure of the past, she is by definition universal, and as such shorn of particularity, and yet understood as an ethical character, whose fixed aim is a precursor to modern moral principles, she is determinate. In this very determinacy, she stands for a partial view that is susceptible to sublation, the terms of which are dictated by a conception of politics that privileges the authority of the modern state even while acknowledging that the state can fail to uphold justice, as when it legalizes slavery. As a female character, Antigone is made to stand for the state of nature that both precedes and threatens to disrupt the contractual obligations with which Hegel associates his masculinist account of the social contract.[45] As sublime, Antigone is formless—like foreign gods—that is, she lacks the form of politics that Hegel attributes to Creon and his ilk.

If Antigone's liminality is overdetermined, so too is the rationale for why slavery cannot be a proper subject for tragedy for Hegel. Tragic heroes must be of a princely or royal class; otherwise their deeds will not be free or independent. Their misfortunes must not derive from contingent circumstances, which for Hegel include abuses of power such as slavery. Precisely because such abuses of power are unjustified, they cannot constitute the kind of deed characteristic of a tragic hero, whose act must be both ethically justified and equal to the contested, but equally ethical claim to which Hegel opposes it, an opposition that results in a collision that leads to the reconciliation Hegel sees as the proper outcome of tragic conflicts, an outcome that privileges the state over familial claims.

Hegel's theory of tragedy, which privileges *Antigone* as exemplary, proceeds by way of intersecting discourses concerning racialized and feminized others. It is the intertwining of these motifs that, I have been concerned to demonstrate, structures Hegel's reading of *Antigone*. Yet even to speak of intertwining is not quite correct, since it implies assumptions about the discrete existence of race and gender, which I have been at pains to resist.[46] The point is rather that circulating within a nexus of ideas about marriage, stock, generation, and exchange are mores that we might crystallize around the concepts of race and gender, but that the language of Sophocles articulates in more mobile terms. For his part, Hegel's discrimination between the old order or race [*Geschlecht*] of the gods and the new order serves to sublimate the distinction between the familial, spiritual, unconscious, chthonic ethics incarnated by Antigone and those espoused by Creon which he couches in terms of a conscious but perilously narrow concern for welfare of the ship of state.[47] This discrimination assumes a continuity between Hegel's racially disparaging account of Eastern gods, and the gods of whom he takes Antigone to be representative, while the new gods are construed as precursors to a Christian ethics, and Creon is construed as a statesmanlike figure whose concern for the state, albeit it overweening, anticipates the more rational expression of the polity that will take shape as a social contract and which will be hedged with guarantees, should the sovereign overstep his mark.[48] The legal apparatus of government will supplant Creon's overbearing claims to power, and will contain and channel any sentiment that threatens to counter it, formalizing the hierarchy between a feminized, domestic space and a masculinized public space.

Hegel's suspicion of mere feelings is coded as a rejection of the feminine. Feelings must be purified of their contingency and negativity, and raised up to the level of spirit, which is thereby masculinized. The grounds on which Hegel excludes slavery as a proper theme for tragedy are bound up with the purification of spirit, from which all traces of the feminine must be expunged. Glossing slavery as the misfortune of the times, Hegel distinguishes true pity from the sympathy elicited by the accidental, human abuses of power that he characterizes in terms of external, finite circumstances, thereby distancing himself from such feminized tendencies. To put it simply, to sympathize with slaves is degrading.[49] In defying Creon, in claiming the authority to bury her brother, not only does Antigone attempt to performatively distinguish the death of Polynices from that of a slave; she also lays claim to her status as royalty, and in so doing she attempts to distinguish herself from a slave, from someone who has no authority to speak or do things for herself, in her own name, as a person to be accorded legal rights. She seeks to lay claim to her royal prerogative, a prerogative of which her status as a woman and as a non-citizen if not deprives her, certainly puts into question. How far Antigone's attempt to speak for herself, and to distinguish her brother from a slave, relies on, affirms, preserves, buttresses, and petrifies the institution of slavery remains a question that deserves further interrogation, but one that I suggest should give us considerable pause.

Just as Hegel distances himself from the sympathy elicited by the "misfortune" of the times by marking it as feminine, so he specifies Antigone in racialized terms. The race [Geschlecht] of the Eastern gods with whom Hegel associates Antigone establishes her as more savage, more akin to nature than those with whom he associates Creon. Her association with "the gods of Hades," those "inner gods of feeling, love and kinship, not the daylight gods of free self-conscious national and political life" (I: 464; II: 60), is delineated in relation to foreign gods, whose chief content is nature. These gods come from a wilder, more primitive time and are associated with a non-Greek geographical location. They have not yet developed the more "civilized" discourse of ethics and laws that characterizes more ideal, Christian times, where an inner depth facilitates indifference to external circumstances (see I: 191; I: 251). Hence Hegel can counsel that when the barriers to overcoming injustice—slavery, for example—are insurmountable, the injustice must be borne. "Where battle is of no avail, a reasonable man is quit of it so that he can at least withdraw into the *formal* independence of subjective freedom" (I: 211; I: 276). The plasticity of tragic heroes would prevent such a withdrawal to the inner recesses of subjectivity. And, in any case, since slavery might not have been brought about by the slave's own deed, and since it does not rest upon a justified ethical claim, the art of dramatic poetry cannot purify the sympathy that might be felt for slaves—whose subjection and lack of freedom would disqualify in advance any representation. Since tragedy is exemplary of a free society, only those, such as royalty, can constitute tragic heroes, so that they can be truly free and independent in their acts. That such freedom and independence is premised on the subjection of others, whose labor facilitates their freedom—whether in ancient Greece or in new world slavery—is not a complication Hegel is prepared to take on.

One final note is called for.[50] Received wisdom has it that Hegel's famous master-slave dialectic is not about slavery as such. It is about anything but. We are taught that the master-slave dialectic is probably reflective of feudal relationships (see Bull 1998, 103), or, as Susan Buck-Morss observes, that it has its origins in Fichte, or Aristotle, or Plato (2000, 843).[51] As Malcolm Bull says, in relation to C. Arthur's argument, commentators distance "Hegel's dialectic from classical and colonial slavery on the basis that Hegel's terms for master and slave, *Herr* and *Knecht*, are more appropriate to the feudal relation of lord and serf, or master and servant. But this is a false distinction" (103). He goes on to observe that the word Aristotle uses for slave, *doulos*, is translated both as *Sklave* and *Knecht* in an authoritative German translation of Aristotle's *Politics*, but that "where the slave is directly juxtaposed with the master—rather than discussed in general—the two are almost invariably described as *Knecht* and *Herr*" (104). Yet, Bull comments, the scholarly notes undermine any suggestion of a rigorous distinction between *Sklave* and *Knecht*. Commenting upon the diligence with which the Hegel establishment has invested itself in arguing that Hegel's master-slave dialectic has nothing to do with actual slavery, Buck-Morss maintains on the contrary that Hegel was reacting to the slave revolt that has come to be known as the Haitian Revolution. "No one has dared to suggest that the idea for the dialectic of lordship and bondage came to Hegel in Jena in the years 1803–5 from reading the press-journals and newspapers . . . about real slaves revolting successfully against real masters" (843–4).

So where does this leave us? If Bull is right that attempts to establish the rigidity of etymological distinctions between *Sklave* and *Knecht*—whether in German translations of Aristotle, or in Hegel's works—founder, and if Buck-Morss is correct in arguing that the master-slave dialectic finds a historical reference point in the Haitian slave revolt, of which Hegel was fully aware, then it seems that Hegel's master-slave relation has everything to do with the actual slaves. While Hegel might have privileged the term *Knecht* rather *Sklave* in his elaboration of the master-slave dialectic as a tactic of misdirection intended to deflect the true object of his consideration—new world slavery—the fact remains that whether he is discussing the famous master-slave dialectic, or slavery [*Sklaverie*] in the classical context, the same structural contours of his argument assert themselves. The death or servitude of the slave is not of any real import to Hegel. What is important is that if the slave chooses life—chooses servitude—over death (understanding that freedom is nothing without life), the dialectic can continue, premised upon the slave's subjugation. The slave resigns himself to his fate, but, crucially, is also enlightened through confronting his own finitude. The slave learns to plough the land, or harvest the crop and in doing so is involved in a productive negation . . . the story is familiar enough. The slave remains a slave until such time as the historical truth reveals itself. The historical lesson that is narrated, the truth arising from the conflict of the master-slave dialectic, in other words, is the same as the advice Hegel dispenses in the *Aesthetics*: enlightened resignation. Or, less politely, he advocates the continuation of slavery until the time is ripe for its overcoming. And when will the motor of history dictate that the time is right? Not yet, is Hegel's answer, in the age of New World slavery.[52]

3

The Performative Politics and Rebirth of *Antigone* in Ancient Greece and Modern South Africa

The Island

If the death of tragedy can be asserted with confidence from the perspective of German idealism, for which art tends to remain in the service of the stability and preservation of the state, not everybody was invited to the funeral: Antigone, for instance. Antigone has taken on a life of her own. Or rather, she has taken on multiple lives in multiple epochs, political contexts, and performative conditions. Having died so many deaths, Antigone seems to refuse to die definitively. As many times as she dies, she comes alive, reborn time and again, born anew each time she enters the theatrical stage, inserting herself into a new political history, providing a commentary on the history of a people, embodying the hopes for the rebirth of a nation. The energy of the play would seem to be conducted through the figure of Antigone, transmitting itself from age to age, from continent to continent, from one political struggle to another.[1] What accounts for this incessant rebirth of Antigone in widely divergent, international, political contexts, and how might it inflect the Western philosophical tendency to imagine tragedy as dead, superseded, relegated to a past that bequeaths us only tragi-comedy?

The Incessant Renaissance of Antigone

Antigone's "excessive" character, her excess of love for her brother, her refusal to be circumscribed by Creon's law has been explained in terms of the appeal her character makes to unchanging, timeless, eternal laws, in an Hegelian invocation of her sublimity, a gesture that succumbs to his taming of the terrifying visage of Antigone's extremity, surrendering her spirit to the ostensibly reasonable demands of the state. Perhaps Antigone's excess lies rather in her strategic reemergence at times of political crises, which tells a different story.[2] If so it is precisely the contingency of the lines demarcating Antigone's exclusion that marks out her story, a contingency that becomes all the more pronounced with each rebirth of the play, as each new political context continues to plot out a history of the unstable content of excluded yet constitutive others, a history that proves to be variegated over time and across cultures. Perhaps also, if there is a sense in which excess should be associated with the name of Antigone, what is excessive should be thought in another register. The logic of the excluded other is reiterated by Antigone herself. The gestures her character commits in the attempt she makes to have her voice count, in her effort to include herself in a system that relies on her exclusion, amount to another kind of excess. The ways in which Antigone appeals to and deepens a discourse that underwrites and justifies a system of slavery have exceeded the orbit of most critical commentaries.

The incessant, theatrical rebirth of Antigones in diverse political contexts opens up the possibility of interrogating conventions that have consolidated themselves as political necessities, which might take shape as enshrining the need for apartheid, and the dangers of dismantling it—or might require numerous other boundaries of containment. By interrogating not only the specificity of the excluded other that Antigone comes to represent in new appropriations of her tragedy, but also the particular political configurations that demand such exclusions, whether these comprise a limited democracy such as that of ancient Athens or an exclusionary racial politic such as apartheid in South Africa, I begin to delineate the political logic according to which the tragedy of *Antigone* can participate in a regeneration of the political. I point not only to the contingency of Antigone's position as excluded, but also thereby to the contingency of a political system of domination that excludes her, even as it implicates her in its own mechanisms of power. The extent to which a polity affords its excluded others the possibility of self-representation, and the precise ways in which it sanctions or prohibits such representation, constitute the sites of negotiation between the tragedy of *Antigone* and politics of its interpretation. How particular traditions of interpretation render certain exclusions legible, while requiring others to remain illegible, is indicative of cultural impasses that have yet to be fully articulated, and which are reflected in the limits of such interpretations.

If tragedy is not what it used to be, this is in part because the political function of theatre has changed: modern appropriations of the tragic tend not to be officially legitimated, as was the case for the Greeks. If in the guise of *Antigone* the tragic has come to embody a means of resisting oppression in the name of restoring, for example, a democracy that has been violated, the different logics according to which this resistance takes place and how these logics are specified by and implicated in the relationship that pertains between politics and the art forms that tragedy becomes can be parsed out. These logics will be reiterated in ways that sometimes replicate the logic of constitutive exclusion in more or less self-conscious ways, and will sometimes be interrogated even by texts that utilize such logics. Each new iteration of *Antigone* helps to specify the history of Antigones, and in so doing, Antigone is reinvented in a way that both resembles Sophocles' Antigone, and departs from her. Each new departure contributes to the replication of Antigone, taking its place in a mimetic history that refigures Sophocles' Antigone, reenacting her drama in new ways, making of Antigone something new, addressing a new set of political constraints.

If tragedy attests to a certain "absence of significance" or "meaninglessness," (Reiss 3) and does so precisely in calling for a discursive shift, if it arises at moments of "epistemic change," flowering in a particularly virulent form in fifth century BCE Athens and again in sixteenth and seventeenth century Europe, perhaps its resurgence at moments of crisis signals the attempt to render visible suffering that is in danger of remaining invisible, or insignificant.[3] Perhaps the many instances of turning to Antigone signal in their own way a call for an epistemic shift, by registering the meaninglessness of suffering under prevailing regimes of representation, and thereby rendering it meaningful, calling for its alleviation. In such instances, a performance of Antigone articulates the failure of dominant regimes to make visible, or acknowledge suffering, a failure that occurs even as the continued existence of such regimes as dominant requires that others suffer. Suffering is both constitutive of, and refused representation by, hegemony. In this sense, the rebirth of *Antigone* effects a critique of the conditions that perpetuate such systematic blindness—calling for a future that does not allow suffering to continue as the unabated and unacknowledged condition of prevailing regimes of representation.

If there is a sense in which Antigone exceeds any attempt to reduce her to the politics and ideology of the classical era, in which it would have been enough to be a woman to suffer a politics of exclusion, I also want to resist the abstract gesture that is content to construe Antigone merely as a figure of excess, as if she merely marked the limits of the articulate, serving as a placeholder to designate that which is outside discourse. As if her multiple dramatic rebirths did not itself etch out a political genealogy of multiple occupancy, a continual renaissance of that which is said to be excessive for each new political staging of Antigone's rebirth. As if the literary and political machine of tragedy did not inculcate Antigone herself into reproducing anew cultural gestures of exclusion of which she herself is a symptom. The sense in which Antigone would constitute a figure of excess for a given interpretation informs us about that which a given political culture finds intolerable in its understanding of itself, that which it finds impossible to represent without either embracing self-contradiction or resorting to fetishization. At the same time, if Antigone stands as excessive in some ways, in other ways she serves to exemplify the standards of humanity from which certain others are excluded—or at least within which slaves are at best dubiously included.

I argue against a Lacanian and Žižekian tendency to fetishize the figure of Antigone, in favor of a reading of Antigone that sees her excess as symptomatic of a society that cannot tolerate integrating her into its sanctioned self-representations.[4] Unlike the Hegelian, the fetishist has no trouble at all in simultaneously sustaining positions that, if cashed out logically, would yield contradiction. The fetishization of Antigone oscillates between glorifying Antigone as enigmatic savior and denigrating her as unnatural or uncanny, without compromising the integrity of either position. I read the figure of Antigone as making an intervention into the reifying and stabilizing logic of fetishistic disavowal, as drawing attention to the politics of its excluded but constitutive other, even if, at the very same time as drawing attention to this logic, she also participates in it, reproducing it in another way. Her intervention is not one of purity.

One of the ways in which the fetishization of Antigone plays itself out is in the political imperative stipulating the performative conditions of Greek tragedy in fifth century BCE Athens, which dictated that male actors perform female roles to an all-male audience. This exclusion is accomplished in fifth century BCE Athens by means of a porous boundary, which operates to include the representation of women in a limited, controlled, and very specific way, even as it prohibits their bodily presence.

Critics such as J. Peter Euben argue that tragedy calls into question the silencing of women, and others such as David Halperin point out that the silencing of actual women in Greek political life was but the necessary corollary of the volubility of fictional women in tragic drama.[5] Yet little attention has been paid to the peculiar relationship obtaining between the political imperatives informing the performative conditions of ancient Greek tragedy—as opposed to the performative conditions of modern appropriations of the tragic—and the resulting constraints upon how tragic drama might impact the idea that a citizenry has of itself. Where dramatic performances were sanctioned by the state, the attendance of a male citizenry was mandated, and women were excluded from the political processes of self-representation and self-reflection afforded by such performances, this relationship would have played out with largely predictable results.

By contrast, in *The Island*, a South African play within a play, which reinvents *Antigone* in the political context of the racial oppression of colonialism and apartheid, a context in which (depending on the color of one's skin and the township in which one lived) to perform a play was to risk arrest—the results are far from predictable. In *The Island*, by Athol Fugard, John Kani, and Winston Ntshona (1974), two Robben Island prison inmates perform a version of *Antigone*, in which the prisoner playing the role of Antigone, who must dress as a woman, becomes an object of ridicule. The play thus destabilizes the cross-dressing of Greek drama that Kirk Ormand has argued would have operated neither as "drag" nor "as a kind of flirting with an alternate gender identity" but rather in terms of a strategy of containment.[6] This destabilization occurs in the wider context of political resistance to a system that legitimates racial inequality. The legitimated sexual inequality of ancient Greece that constituted the background of tragic drama is transposed into a political legal system that uses racial identity to legislate inferiority. Yet this transposition leaves a residue.

Not only does Antigone's legacy lend itself to commentary on racial issues of postcolonial identity, but it also points out how exclusionary logics reiterate themselves. *The Island* both explores and protests an unjust racial politic, and draws attention to the performative constraints dictated by apartheid South Africa. It does so in a way that reconfigures the exclusionary conditions pertaining to the performance of Greek tragedy in Athens, transposing the logic into one that can be thematized within the theatrics of the performance itself, and serving to interrogate the exclusionary politic that dictates apartheid. If in one way it usurps Antigone's outsider status for its own ends, in a literature of resistance that reinvents the gendered exclusionary terms that others have contested in Antigone's name, in another way it thereby spells out the procedure by which the logic of the excluded other replicates itself, even within progressively political texts. Before turning to *The Island*, I reflect upon the performative conditions of Greek tragedy, and of *Antigone* in particular.

Performative and Political Reflections on Greek Tragedy

We should not imagine that the significance and meaning of the original production of *Antigone* is easily deciphered. Although we are dealing with a play penned by a male dramatist, acted by an all-male cast for what was almost certainly an all-male audience, in a society in which women occupied a marginal role, we cannot assume that a performance of *Antigone* would have operated solely in the service of patriarchal ideals, simply through the suppression of women.[7] Politically, women were confined to the private realm and excluded from the public—yet the play itself concerns how to negotiate the boundary between public and private, of where and how to draw the line.[8] Any interpretation of the impact of tragic theatrical performance in fifth century BCE Athens will depend both on what we take to be the political function of tragedy—the subject matter of which, in the case of *Antigone*, includes contesting the confinement of women to the private realm—and on how the performance itself enacts, even as it disavows, its own critique, recreating the very conditions of exclusion it scrutinizes.

If tragedy itself partakes in a process of meaningful political critique, we cannot assume that tragic drama merely confirms the sociopolitical privileges that dictate male privilege.[9] While Euben's claim that "Tragedy called into question the dominance of *polis* over household, the enforced silence of women, the traditional masculine drive for glory and power, and the division of public and private in terms of rigid gender distinctions" is borne out by *Antigone*, it is also clear that the material conditions of its performance reenacted the very disavowal that it theoretically put into question.[10] If women are confined to the *oikos*, excluded from political participation and also from the theatre of Dionysus, it was their exclusion that made possible the process of critical reflection enabled by the performance of tragic drama. Without the contributions of women and slaves, without their work behind the scenes—a phrase that can be read here more literally than usual—men would not have been free to pursue political debate, including that in which dramatic performances were implicated. Structurally the freedom of free citizens was dependent upon the manual labor of slaves including housework, in the same way that "[c]itizenship was dependent on family lines."[11] Halperin suggests that "the silence of actual women in Greek public life and the volubility of fictional 'women' (invented by male authors) in Greek cultural expression do not represent opposed, contradictory, or paradoxical features of classical Greek society but, on the contrary, are connected to one another by a strict logical necessity. Greek men effectively silenced women by speaking for them on those occasions when men chose to address significant words to one another in public, and they required the silence of women in public in order to be able to employ this mode of displaced speech—in order to impersonate women—without impediment."[12] If the silence of women was required, so too was their physical seclusion; they occupied separate living quarters, a separation that was at least in part a function of the need to assert control over lines of inheritance.[13] Women were to be contained and controlled not least because they were needed to ensure the continuation of the polis through the reproduction of citizens, hence Solon's restrictive legislation concerning not only, in Anne Carson's words, "the walks, feasts, trousseaux, mourning, food, [and] drink" but also the "sexual activity of women."[14] Secluded in the house for the most part, even within the house women were confined to certain rooms. In the words of Anne Carson, while men "habitually . . . le[ft] the house to confront the outdoors in war, commerce, political life, the fields, the sea, the *agora,*" a woman's life was typically "closed upon itself in its own domestic space," said to have been, according to Pomeroy, "dark and insanitary."[15] Pomeroy suggests that, "Women of all social classes worked mainly indoors," concerning themselves "with the care of young children . . . fabrication of clothing, and the preparation of food." While "[p] oorer women . . . went out to work . . . as washerwomen, as woolworkers [and] as vendors, selling food or what they had spun or woven at home" they mostly "pursu[ued] occupations that were an extension of women's work in the home."[16] How far the tendency to construe all women's activity as an extension of women's activity within the home is itself reflective of an ideology that privileges gender over class, and that is embedded in an understanding of the private versus the public realm that was formulated during an era of feminism that viewed gender as foundational, and other factors such as class and race as secondary, must remain an open question.

So too, the politics of how to read women's formal exclusion from the polis is worth reflecting upon. The political and legal inferiority of women in fifth century BCE Athens is well established. Yet how far this legitimates the view that women were totally excluded from making any significant contribution to the polis is a matter of dispute. According to Helen Foley, women "play virtually no public role other than a religious one in the political and social life of ancient Greece."[17] Since religion, as Sarah Pomeroy points out, "was subordinate to and an integral part of the state, and the state . . . was in the hands of men," even women's religious role was circumscribed.[18] Pomeroy observes that "[d]irect participation in the affairs of government—including holding public office, voting, and serving as jurors and as soldiers—was possible only for male citizens" and that "Athenian law of all periods tended to regard the wife as a veritable child, having the legal status of a minor in comparison to her husband."[19] Women's work, says Pomeroy "was not highly valued . . . and their lives were not dissimilar" from those of slaves.[20] Again, there is reason to question this elision of the difference between women's lives and those of slaves.

The expectation, according to Pomeroy, was that women produce "legitimate heirs to the *oikoi* . . . whose aggregate composed the citizenry."[21] Marriage, with the aim of procreation, was therefore considered the principal duty of females, a duty that took on particular importance due to the scarcity of males as a result of frequent war. Women were not citizens and yet were strictly necessary in their reproductive status. As Nicole Loraux says, "As progenitor of male children, woman provided her husband with sons, perpetuating his family, and the polis with citizens, for its own posterity. Without this other, this woman, there was no polis . . . And yet in the Greek imaginary she was still an extra."[22]

A principal reason for requiring that women's speech and movement be curtailed was the need for the polity of fifth century BCE Athens to control what was deemed to be women's otherwise uncontrollable eros. For the Greeks, Carson suggests, women are associated with

> formlessness and the unbounded in their alliance with the wet, the wild, and raw nature. They are, as individuals, comparatively formless themselves, without firm control of personal boundaries. They are, as social entities, units of danger, moving across boundaries of family and *oikos*, in marriage, prostitution, or adultery. They are, as psychological entities, unstable compounds of deceit and desire, prone to leakage.

> In sum, the female body, the female psyche, the female social life, and the female moral life are penetrable, porous, mutable, and subject to defilement all the time. . . . It is in her erotic life that woman most vividly lacks completion . . . This porous sexuality is a floodgate of social pollution, for it is the gate of entry to *oikos* and *polis*.[23]

The demand for the policing of women's sexuality resided in the importance of establishing clear lines of inheritance, which could only be achieved through the surveillance of women's reproductive power.

If this was an era in which "[c]lear lines of reproduction were vital to the polis," it was also an era in which the nature and clarity of those lines was put on trial in Aeshcylus's *Oresteia* and in Sophocles' Oedipal cycle.[24] Yet we should not imagine that the capacity of tragedy to constitute critique had uniform effects for all its subjects, any more than we should assume that women's silence was absolute.[25] As Euben says, "By putting recognizable actions onstage and so on trial before the citizenry who had decided upon them but were now reconstituted as an audience reflecting on what they had done, tragedy contributed to the democratic tradition of self-critique."[26] Of course, what needs to be emphasized is that in so far as this citizenry was exclusive of the active political participation of women and slaves the scope and implications of self-critique were always already susceptible to compromise. At the same time, just as sanctioned forms of the public expression of women's voices, such as ritualized mourning, were subject to both delimitation and transgression, so the officially sanctioned public representations of femininity that theatre constituted could not control the meanings performances might take on. Laura Mclure points out that in tragedy "most of the extant plays situate the action at the house door, a realm that is both a private domestic context and a public platform, where women's presence was considered a potentially disruptive and dangerous intrusion into public space." She draws the following conclusion: "For this reason, tragedy tirelessly enumerates the importance of remaining within the house for both women and girls."[27] One might equally read tragedy as challenging the enforcement of boundaries that keep women behind closed doors, as pointing out the liminal character of women's position, poised on the threshold.

In remarking on the fact that dramatic performances both exceed, and are subject to re-inscription by authoritative convention, it is worth reminding ourselves—and it does seem to be necessary to keep bringing it up, such is the frequency with which it disappears from view—that as far as we know the character of Antigone would have been acted by a male for an all-male audience.[28] What is usually dismissed as Ismene's conventional feminine obedience, or heralded as Antigone's courageous stand against such conventionality, would have been presented by a male actor to what we assume to have been an all-male audience (although there is still some controversy about this).[29] The fact that a male actor would have performed Antigone's part means that a play that examines as a major theme the political exclusion of women reenacts this exclusion as a condition of staging its interrogation. A politics of exclusion thus redoubles itself, even as it creates a space in which the performance of Antigone exceeds the political requirement that dictates women's silence in the public sphere.

In the performance of Greek tragedies the set of conventional corporeal codes intended to mark a character as a woman would have operated in such a way as to bracket the presence of a male body onstage, allowing the audience to read the performance of the character as a woman. The confinement of free women within the house was such a mainstay of Athenian life that one of the performance features indicating to the audience that a character was female rather than male was a lighter skin color (since women would not have been tanned, given their confinement indoors), an effect that could be produced, if necessary, by the use of white lead.[30] Other indicators included tunics that were shorter than those worn by male characters, masks with long hair and "body padding . . . if the evidence of vase painting" is to be taken at face value.[31] These performance codes operated in a manner that, rather than being disruptive of gendered roles, kept them safely in their place. As Kirk Ormand says, "Such conventions—body padding being the most obvious example—serve a double function: they allow the audience to suspend judgment on the sex of the actor, and they allow the actor to portray the female sex without fully taking the risk of adopting the other gender."[32] Accordingly, in contrast to Sue Ellen Case, Ormand concludes that far from seeing the "theatrical transvestism" of Greek drama as "drag" or "as a kind of flirting with an alternate gender identity" we should read it in terms of a strategy of containment.[33] "The formalized conventions used to portray women on the Athenian stage . . . effectively served to insulate the actors from any risk of a conversion that might carry over, dangerously, into real life."[34] If male actors were insulated from the risk of adopting the other gender, is it also the case that their performance of female gender would fail to jeopardize the clear lines of demarcation requiring women's seclusion, silence, and subordination to an essentially reproductive function? Would the performance codes of Greek tragedy simply reenforce the silencing of women, even if they sometimes became the subject of contestation within a particular play? Or should we imagine a more complex and conflictual series of dramatic effects?

A masked actor performing a female role produces a performance that on the one hand provides the ancient Athenian audience with the assurance that the conventions demanding the successful containment of women were not being violated, and on the other hand provided for a controlled range of representations of femininity, the terms of which were dictated (but not entirely contained) by those in power. A double condition must be thought through.

For the Greeks, tragedy explores and contests the political requirement (among other things) that women remain subordinate, even as it controls the danger women are taken to represent by enacting onstage their transgression of socially condoned limits. It does so in a performance that reproduces women's exclusion from political processes by removing women's bodies from public view, and having men speak their parts. This situation mimics women's actual marginality, and the fact that they were under the guardianship of men, who did their public speaking for them.

It has been acknowledged more than once that female characters play "double duty," that they serve as a "location from which to explore a series of problematic issues that men prefer to explore indirectly and certainly not through their own persons."[35] At the same time, it has been claimed that due to their very marginality, tragic female characters are more revealing; glossing Zeitlin, Foley says that "they represent a more complex perspective than male characters."[36] If male citizens indirectly explore their own social tensions and anxieties through female characters, surely there is more to be said of the marginality and consequent complexity of the representation (or even the lack thereof) of slaves?

Intervening in Fetishistic Readings of *Antigone*

By now it has become commonplace to remind ourselves that the project of defining the political itself necessarily involves political judgments, yet the application of this observation will not cease to yield new insights, as long as politics remains a contested field—that is, as long as the political retains its character as political. If theoretically this point is familiar enough, the practice of politics and the assumptions of theory do not cease to find new ways of cordoning off certain beliefs as if they were inviolable, offering them up as sacrosanct and incontestable, hermetically sealed from any conceivable challenge.[37] One might almost say that social history marches on in the name of progress precisely by rendering evident "facts" that will come to be disputed by certain interest groups. In the process of protesting the apparently impervious character of a particular state of affairs, protestors as often as not, and usually inadvertently, find themselves enshrining new grounds as unassailably true, thereby setting off a new series of disputes, which in turn reveal the contingency of the adduced grounds, even as they proceed to hypostasize differently articulated grounds which will themselves come to be treated as hallowed—until challenged. And so on, ad infinitum.

Marx illuminated the mystification that occurs in processes of reification, whereby historical forces represent themselves as indisputable and implacable, standing over against the would-be freedom of its subjects. The magical allure of the fetish, be it of the commodity or psychic variety, resides in its appearance of necessity. We do not seem to be able to circumvent it—so compelling is its attraction. Whether the fetish imposes itself as irresistible in the sense of erotically desirable, or in the shape of an apparently self-evident, transcendent truth, it presents itself as inescapable. For Marx, only the emergence of a new form of production can dispel the illusion of the implacability of the commodity form. What psychoanalysis has illuminated in the dynamic of fetishism are the lengths to which we are prepared to go in order to maintain our imaginary beliefs, even in the face of evidence that belies them. Even with the benefit of an intellectual analysis that maps out the illusory nature of a belief, the pull it exerts need not falter. The truth or falsity of an idea does nothing to interfere with the dynamic of fetishism, the solution of which is not to acquiesce to the falsity of an idea once it is revealed, but to disavow it, whether it is true or false. Accordingly, the revelation of falsity does not succeed in dispelling the affective power of the fetish, precisely because the fetishist has found a way of entertaining two contradictory truths without compromising the integrity of either of them, by oscillating between them. One might even say that the compulsion of fetishism concerns the incommensurability between logic and the affective investment in the fetish. A token that condenses meaning into a hieroglyphic and idiosyncratic language, the fetish is intended to keep at bay—without removing—a belief that has captured our imagination. In this sense, fetishism constitutes a strategy of avoidance.

Any attempt to engage with the logic of fetishism cannot afford to abstract itself from the history of particular fetishes, so that there can be no pure meta-narrative of fetishism. One might think that the critical value of debunking theories of fetishism lies in clarifying how particular figures have come to signify as fetishistic. And yet, the logic of fetishism consists precisely in a refusal to draw the Hegelian conclusion that derives from the application of reason, canceling out and surpassing a previously persuasive truth, which now betrays itself as one-sided and incomplete. Far from negating a previously held truth, by incorporating this negation in order to go beyond it in a way that reaches toward a more adequate account of reality, the fetishist has no trouble at all in simultaneously sustaining positions that, if cashed out logically, would yield contradictory positions. As such, fetishism proves to be peculiarly resilient when it comes to sustaining a belief in a world, the internal dynamics of which are logically inconsistent. This would suggest that no attempt to unpack the logic of the fetish by pointing out its false assumptions will manage to undo its psychic investments. The falsity of premises holds no interest for the fetishist, whose compulsion is the fetish in which affect is invested. It is important then to unfold the specific dynamic according to which a fetish compels the interest of the fetishist, and the particular ways in which this affective investment precludes investigation of that which is disavowed, as prefatory to mapping out the contours of its excluded ground.

If one of the lessons of fetishism is that mere logic will not suffice to remove an affective investment, one of the more striking aspects of psychoanalysis is how it sustains its retreat from the logic of determinate negation in and through its appeal to fetishistic disavowal, allowing it to refrain from interrogating the adequacy of its own premises.[38] One can know perfectly well that woman is castrated, while at the same time maintain one's investment in a fetish that compensates for her castration, without ever stopping to question the assumptions informing the mythical character of one's belief in castration theory. Even when the fictional character of the castration myth is articulated—there never was a penis in the first place, and the assumption that there was derives from the masculine expectation that female morphology should be homologous with male morphology—there is no compunction to give up, or withdraw one's affective investment from, the fetish. Indeed the fetish distracts from the fictional status of castration theory, making not only "the truth" but also the discrepancy between one myth and another irrelevant. Psychoanalysis is therefore able to affirm the authority of its own mythical origins without contest. There is no reason to interrogate a myth that is disavowed, especially when the fetish has been fabricated in the service of the pleasure drive. No reason at all—unless of course one is a casualty of that disavowal.

This presents a problem for the theoretician. Assuming there is a certain affective investment in maintaining the invisibility or irrelevance of issues of slavery, no amount of theorizing or evidence will suffice to dislodge such an investment. Assuming also that Antigone has been invested as an ethical hero of sorts, a figure who has been championed by feminist accounts of the play, there will be considerable resistance to conceding that this figure might be compromised in any way, tainted by colonial or racist legacies. Even if plays succeed in mobilizing affective investments in ways that encourage or enable identification and sympathy with characters who challenge Antigone's complicity with colonial history (as *Tègònni* does explicitly, as we'll see further in the next chapter) or even if they succeed in challenging the presuppositions of a framework that makes it intelligible for Antigone to plead guilty (as Winston does in *The Island*) there are no guarantees that such affective investment will translate into theoretical insight. And nor should there be. The moment at which affect translates into intellectual understanding must remain inexplicable. The most one can do, perhaps, is to render articulable certain sites of investment, thereby making them available for reflection, without in any way being able to ensure that such reflection, if it occurs, will have any intellectual or political consequences.

One of the functions of theatre is to recreate the affective pull of the ideological in all its particularity, as well as to scrutinize its politics. Yet the logic of the fetish reasserts itself with peculiar virulence in critical analyses of Sophocles' *Antigone*. It would seem that critics have been seduced by the allure of the fetish, even as they have attempted to analyze it. In an almost slavish devotion to the figure of Antigone, commentators have been blinded to the political logic that attends her dramatic positioning, dazzled by a highly eroticized vision of the purity of her devotion, fascinated by her demonic extremity, awed by her "unnatural" death wish, whether in praise or condemnation. Swept away by the passion of such a vision, they have neglected the thoroughgoing political critique in which Antigone is implicated, even as she seduces readers of Sophocles. Critics have often failed to exercise reflective caution about their own ideological commitments, so that even those who argue, with some justification, that the figure of Antigone becomes an occasion if not to reshape the political, certainly to consider what should constitute the political, often fall back on unexamined political assumptions about the possibility or desirability of eliminating disorder from the political order. These assumptions take various shapes, including a refusal to entertain the question of gender as a political question, to confront the multiple registers in terms of which exclusion is explored in *Antigone* (including the mechanisms of exclusion invoked by Antigone herself), or to consider the variable political circumstances of performance, which are not only worthy of consideration but central to the dramatic importance and longevity of Sophocles' play.[39]

It turns out, then, that the reign of fetishism has every reason to continue its refusal to question its assumptions when it comes to Greek tragedy. The missing penis, which for Freud was a product of the masculine imaginary, turns out to have been there all along in the case of Antigone—albeit veiled![40] Or perhaps we should say, given the profound ways in which Greek myth, not least the dramatic fate of Oedipus, has shaped the masculine imaginary—and Freud's theoretical apparatus is exemplary in this regard—that the presence of male bodies in the theatre of Dionysus will turn out to have everything to do with the subtext of the theory of fetishism. After all, as I argue elsewhere (and this will come as no surprise to anyone who has spent time trying to decipher the convoluted defenses Freud constructs with his infuriatingly yet deliciously tortuous intellectual maneuvers), fetishism reveals itself to be a strategy for men to avoid homosexuality![41] In effect, fetishism allows men to engage in relationships with women to whom they accord the phallus, which prevents them from having to confront what is read as the horror of women's mutilation, the "nothing to see" of castration anxiety, while also "saving" them from engaging in relationships with other men. On this scenario, male actors provide the missing female phallus, thereby themselves performing a fetishistic function.

To read the character of Antigone—or any other female character of Greek tragedy for that matter—as a woman fails to challenge the rules of conduct governing performances of women by male actors, performances that would have occurred within fictional scenarios that would only have been sustained as long as the audience agreed to acquiesce to a general suspension of knowledge:

male actors always play female characters. This is the classic fetishist scenario, but with a twist: I know very well (that the actor is male), but all the same (I agree to read the character as female). Depending on the stability and uniformity with which this fiction is maintained, the very appearance of female characters could serve either as a reminder that no female actors are allowed onstage (in which case the exceptional mimetic "presence" of female characters becomes the exception that proves the rule), or it could serve to obfuscate this fact. Presumably, the more successful the performance of the actor playing the role of a female, the more one could forget the actual exclusion of women from the stage. The more a male actor passes for a female, the less one remembers that the actor is male and not female.

What happens, then, in the case of a female character, such as Antigone, whose characterization in and of itself is presented in such a way as to draw attention to the fact that her actions and words do not conform to those to which women were expected to conform? In not only disobeying Creon's prohibition, but exhibiting pride in having done so, even proclaiming herself to be in the right, Antigone is met with Creon's concerted resistance to her having flouted his authority. If she has overstepped the bounds of acceptable feminine conduct, this excess lies not only in her failure to obey Creon, but in the manner that she refuses to acknowledge that her act of defiance constitutes a failure, in her claim, instead, to be in the right. *Antigone* could thus be said to stage the oscillation of the fetishistic scenario, so that the audience alternates between reading Antigone as a woman by following the conventions of the performative cues in play, and recalling that a male actor plays Antigone. From Creon's point of view, Antigone is, by definition, guilty—that is, she is guilty of having acted inappropriately as a woman. Yet if she is guilty of disobeying him, she is also guilty of failing to recognize her disobedience as inappropriate. As such, she is guilty of acting *as if she were a man*—that is, as if she had the right to act on principle, for the sake of a principle, as if she had the right to stand up for, to articulate, a principle that is disputed by Creon. In fact, the words of Antigone's character would have been legitimated by, albeit via a circuitous route, the presence of a male body onstage, within a plot originating from a male playwright whose views on women are generally recognized to have been conservative. The condition that demanded the exclusion of female actors from the stage, paradoxically, is also one that brings a peculiar verisimilitude to Antigone's manly demeanor, providing a fleshy materiality to her having taken up a masculine stance. The performative conditions of Antigone ensure that her aberrational behavior is brought into line with the normative expectations requiring any challenge to political authority to be underwritten by the presence of a male body. Yet would the performance of Antigone not also have had ramifications beyond the legitimating male body onstage? Would it not have taken part in a fetishistic oscillation between knowledge and belief, reminding the audience of the political conditions that exclude a woman from performing the part of Antigone? Would Antigone not have also drawn attention to the political subordination of women that leads to their exclusion from the performance of their roles, thereby rendering visible the political boundary that operated both to prevent women's entry into the theatre and to allow their theatrical representation? In order to follow through two possible ways in which Antigone's performance might have been read (for surely it would have been read in more than one way), let me first present a reading that remains within the confines of the oscillation played out by fetishistic disavowal (I know that the actor is male, but all the same I agree to read Antigone's character as female), and a second reading that sees Antigone as intervening in the logic of disavowal, pointing to the discarded ground on the basis of which the fetishistic fiction is maintained—namely the political conditions of exclusion that require that men stand in for women in the first place. This second reading, in which women's political exclusion from a theatrical space in which they are nevertheless represented by male performers suggests that the motif of abjection might be appropriately applied to Antigone's capacity to draw attention to the excluded other, the exclusion of which is accomplished by means of a porous boundary, one that operates to include women in a limited, controlled, and very specific way even as it prohibits their bodily presence.

In the first register, Antigone's act can be read as restorative, as an act that puts women back in their proper place, secures their subordinate roles, and affirms the need for the family to be loyal to and answerable to the polis. Read in this way, Antigone acts to restore the kinship laws that Oedipus had violated. She becomes a memorial to that loss, a means of bringing back an old order that had been transgressed. In attending to the corpse of Polynices, Antigone's act puts to rest the aberration of a norm, restoring the proper order. Such a reading is consistent with the fact that the dramatic performance of Antigone would have taken place at a public festival sanctioned by the state, a celebration that either materially or notionally would have been aimed at a male audience.[42] The life and death of Antigone would have confirmed the need to uphold the incest prohibition, the need for men to control women's reproductive activity with the interests of the state in mind, and the sacrificial imperative—the need to eliminate the threat of disorder that Antigone, the product of incest, constitutes in her very existence.

To read Antigone as positively affirming the established order to such an extent that she is willing to die for it—while it may well have served the purposes of those seeking to perpetuate the structures of power already at work in Athens—is to reduce her to a conduit for Athenian society to produce an image of itself that reestablishes the need for a preexisting order that would keep women in check. Even if women had the freedom to be heard, the power to think and act for themselves, the message seems to be, they would affirm the order more or less in place. Were women capable of the best kind of political deliberation (something doubted by Aristotle), they would merely invoke the boundaries that they were considered to endanger, reaffirming these boundaries in the face of their violation, and at the same time justifying male authority.[43] Similarly, to celebrate Antigone for standing up against Creon, for being able to discern the dependence of the polis on the family with greater insight than he can, is merely another way of putting women back in their place. It is to affirm the political order that Creon tries, and fails, to protect, rather than to follow through the principle to which Antigone draws attention—or rather initiates. In short, such a reading runs the risk of once again fetishizing Antigone, who becomes merely a decorative ornament in a system that attempts to confirm its status as necessary.[44] The tendency to fetishize the figure of Antigone operates within the confines of sanctioning women's seclusion, failing to question the contours by which the political constitutes eros as subordinate to the aims of a polity that benefits from the contributions of women and slaves but in which full political participation is restricted to men.

While there are certainly grounds to suppose that a performance of *Antigone* would have condoned the need to confine women to highly circumscribed and subordinate roles, I am suggesting that such interpretations might coexist with alternative readings of the Sophoclean figure of Antigone, which contest, rather than confirm, the view that women are in need of confinement, to be restrained by the guardianship of men.[45] In one of its registers the performance of Antigone would have thereby confirmed the need for women's containment, even as in another register it interrogated any idea of the *oikos* as a space bounded by pre-political rules, by drawing attention to the politicized character of the boundary separating the *oikos* from the *polis* and the ways in which this boundary operated in the service of attempts to assure the stability of the *polis*, suggesting it could be otherwise.[46] It is worth hypothesizing that those members of the Athenian audience in whose interests it was to control women's allegedly unruly eros might have found the first reading amenable, while those at the receiving end of exclusionary political measures (even if their access to theatrical performances was mediated by the reports of others) might have found the second reading more amenable. Read in this second register, Antigone exhibits leadership in her reconceived relationship to eros, calling for a new political order—not one that consists in tyrannical rule and uncompromising orders, but one that calls attention to the excluded other of the polis, its necessary remainder.[47] Far from merely corroborating the idea that women were especially susceptible to unruly eros that runs roughshod over boundaries and distinctions, and are therefore in need of the constraint of marriage and the subjugation of a husband, Antigone presents an alternative view of eros. She does not merely subject herself to the kinship strictures of patriarchy, she also points beyond them, disrupting the certainty and self-assurance of its claims.

In attending to this second register, I want to outline the political logic according to which Antigone lends herself to myriad political struggles. By figuring the excluded constitutive ground of the polity, Antigone illuminates the processes according to which any contingent fact (not just gender or sexuality, but also race, class, nationality, religion, or some other contingency) can become a ground for an exclusionary politics. In this sense, it is not a question of Antigone acting as a woman—or in any other specifically gendered way. Rather it is a question of her acting in such a way as to rewrite or transform the grounds on which her exclusion from the system is written off as both inevitable and at the same time unintelligible to it. Antigone calls herself into intelligibility by challenging the grounds on which the polity writes her as unintelligible, unreadable, unsignifiable within its terms.[48] In doing so, she opens up to interrogation the condition that the polis, as represented by Creon, has written off as beyond the bounds of interrogation, as beyond the bounds of signification. Were her exclusion to have become capable of representation within the set of significations that requires it, then that system itself must have undergone transformation. Antigone calls for a redrawing of the lines of the polity, such that it is no longer possible to figure her only as its excluded outside—that is, to refuse her "proper" representation—while at the same time drawing on her resources for its own purposes. In this sense Antigone calls for a future polity that does not rely on the political exclusion of some of its members, and then legislate that exclusion as unthinkable, or render it non-negotiable. She draws attention to political gestures that rely on casting as unintelligible those on whom it depends materially and psychically, but whom the state systematically excludes from legitimate symbolic representation. Antigone is a figure who can only ever be represented improperly within the terms dictated by the politics of Greek tragedy.

As such she becomes a site for the reworking of the distinction between improper and proper, between that which is cast outside a system of intelligibility as unimaginable within its current configuration, and that according to which something is cast out as impermissible and unacceptable: she calls into question the very terms that render an order proper by designating something other than it as improper. She insinuates herself into a system that is sealed off from her proper representation. At the same time, she calls attention to the impossibility of her proper representation within the system that excludes her. This is not to say that she makes clear that her representation is impossible per se, only that it is impossible within the terms of representation as currently conceived. She calls, then, for a transformation of the politics that endorses her exclusion as a necessary condition of any proper representation—both the actual representation of those legitimated by it, and the potential representation of those excluded by it.

Yet there is one more twist. Not only does Antigone make available for interrogation the logic of exclusion by challenging the political system that excludes her at the same time as depending upon her, thereby calling for a renewal of that system. In her very attempt to render her claim intelligible, in her demand to be heard, which is also a demand that challenges the rules of intelligibility, she also participates in and perpetuates a logic of exclusion. In asserting her own claims as a subject, and in seeking to gain recognition for her brother as someone worthy of burial, Antigone has no qualms about confirming the unworthiness of slaves. Her attempt to write herself into history, to speak in a way that challenges her own exclusion, is articulated in such a way as to require the exclusion of slaves from the standards of humanity to which she demands access.

An erotic fetishization of Antigone's sacrifice fails to think through the ramifications of Antigone's redirection of eros, which acknowledges the dependence of *philia*—and therefore, by extension, the reliance of the ordering of the *polis*—on the control of eros. The incessant rebirth of Antigones opens up the possibility of reshaping conventions that have consolidated themselves as political necessities, which might enshrine the need for apartheid, and the dangers of dismantling it, or the need for British imperialism to express itself in a colonial relationship to the Irish, who are figured as otherwise wild and untamable—or the need for numerous other boundaries of containment.[49] In order to begin to take seriously not only the politics of exclusion practiced in fifth century BCE Athens, and its impact on the performance of roles such as that of Antigone, but also *Antigone*'s multiple political legacies and the multiple political exclusions about which her performance has come to speak, I will not restrict my interrogation of *Antigone* to fifth century BCE Athens. Let me turn, then, to *The Island*. Given the fact that pointing out the inconsistent grounds that inform fetishistic oscillation between two contradictory beliefs does nothing to lessen affective investment in them, following out the implications of such inconsistency will do nothing to relieve their hold on us. Dramatic performances that succeed in eliciting sympathetic identification with the predicament of characters who operate as excluded yet constitutive others can, however, create alternative sites of affective investment. Whether or not such affects will lead to political change is impossible to predict, but the role that drama can play in the psychic survival of those who suffer political exclusion can be vital, as the historical circumstances surrounding the inception of the play *The Island*, as I discuss below, show.

Antigone's "False Titties": *The Island*

In *The Island*, Antigone is used as a vehicle to speak out against apartheid laws, including those prohibiting marriage between whites and blacks. Of particular interest here is the way in which homophobic and gendered anxiety serves as a metaphor to explore the racial divisions of apartheid. The play compares the intensity of the bond that has developed between John and Winston to that of a marriage (I 65), a comparison that is evoked because they spend so much time together that they might as well be husband and wife, and since they are so often handcuffed to one another. The forced proximity of prisoners sharing a cell with one another develops into a mutual dependency that is threatened when John unexpectedly hears that his sentence has been reduced from ten to three years, as a result of an appeal filed by his lawyer on his behalf. Winston must confront the fact that he will be left in prison in three months time, while his cellmate is set free. He will have to learn to share his days with new cellmates, to develop new strategies for survival, to let go of the old habits that he and John have devised in order to get through their days—recalling the plots of favorite movies, imagining phone calls to mutual friends on the outside, remembering happier times in days gone by.

At John's instigation, Winston has agreed to take part in an abbreviated version of *Antigone*, in a performance that will constitute the finale of the annual prison concert. As *The Island* begins, the performance is scheduled to take place in six days' time, and John wants to rehearse Winston on the details of the plot. Having been subjected by the prison guard Hodoshe—a character named for and based on a notorious guard at Robben Island—to the grueling, "back-breaking" (I 49), dehumanizing, and futile labor of shoveling sand from one pile to another, Winston is exhausted and has trouble remembering that Antigone is not the mother, but the sister of Polynices (see I 51), or that it was not Eteocles, but Polynices whom she buried against Creon's orders (see I 52).[50] For those in the know, Winston's confusion on both points reflects the uncertainty that has been generated on the one hand around the systemic confusion that afflicts the symbolic familial roles that afflicts the Oedipal familial line, and on the other hand the question as to how identifiable the corpses of Polynices and Eteocles would have been. The latter is a question that Anouilh's appropriation of *Antigone* plays on. In terms of the reading I am developing here, the potential substitutability of the bodies of Polynices and Eteocles reflects the fragility of the boundary separating slaves from non-slaves, a boundary that stands in need of being enforced hyperbolically precisely because it is so tenuous. Winston's refusal to accept Antigone's guilt also raises fundamental questions about who determines guilt and innocence. Of course, the ease with which any distinction between guilt and innocence can be made has been put into question by Hegel's conception of tragic heroes; it is put into question in yet another way by an apartheid state, which punishes individuals on the basis of the color of their skin. When it comes to whether Antigone pleads guilty or not guilty, Winston cannot make sense of why Antigone would plead guilty. John tries to reason with him:

> JOHN: Now look, Winston, we're not going to argue. Between me and you, in this cell, we know she's Not Guilty. But in the play she pleads Guilty.
>
> WINSTON: No, man, John! Antigone is Not Guilty . . .
>
> JOHN: In the play . . .
>
> WINSTON [*losing his temper*]: To hell with the play! Antigone had every right to bury her brother. (I 52–3)

While John insists on Winston getting the plot right, he agrees with Winston that Antigone had every right to bury Polynices; this is precisely why the dispute between Antigone and Creon is so resonant for him, and why he insists on putting on an abbreviated version of *Antigone*. In the words of Winston—the final words of the play—like Antigone, he too "honoured those things to which honour belongs" (I 77). We learn that the reason Winston is in prison, condemned to a life sentence, is because of his involvement in a protest, in which he burned his passbook in front of a police station (see I 63). As Errol Durbach says, the "pass-law system [gave] the state the right to control the movement of Blacks in South Africa, which [could] compel them to work in a specific area under penalty of being deported to one of the Bantustans, which ha[d] the effect of enslaving the worker to his permit, destroying families, and depriving the Black man [sic] of mobility, self-determination, and freedom."[51] In the gloss that John provides, Winston put his "head on the block for others" (I 72). He stood up for the rights that were being systematically denied to some South Africans on the basis of their skin color under the system of apartheid. Winston honored his race, a thing to which honor belongs, in the face of the dishonor accorded it by apartheid.

It is against this background that we should read Winston's emphatic insistence upon distinguishing between history—a history that has imprisoned him for being in the right, and for upholding a principle of justice against a corrupt state—and legends. Winston says:

> Only last night you tell me that this Antigone is a bloody . . . what you call it . . . legend! A Greek one at that. Bloody thing never happened. Not even history! Look, Brother, I got no time for bullshit. Fuck legends. Me? . . . I live my life here! I know why I'm here, and it's history, not legends (I 62).

Of course, the irony underlying Winston's insistence upon the historical cause of the events that have led up to his imprisonment is that the history of racism, as we have learned from Frantz Fanon among others, has everything to do with myths and legends—and Greek legends at that.

At first glance, it might appear that *The Island* transposes the issues Sophocles explores when Antigone contests her exclusion from a polity that refuses to grant her a public voice on the grounds that she is a woman into the racial issues of exclusion raised by apartheid. Yet *The Island* does not merely transpose Antigone's demand to be honored for her beliefs and judgment in a political context that does not regard a woman's beliefs as worthy into John and Winston's demand to be honored in a polity that deprives subjects of basic political rights on account of their race. It also takes up the issue of gender in a way that exposes the mechanisms of exclusion in which Sophocles' Antigone participates. As the actor playing Antigone, Winston must give the appearance of being a woman. The play stages the constraints under which this performance takes place, bringing to light in the process the tension it produces for Winston's character, who must perform a woman's role in woman's clothes.

While Winston is concentrating on memorizing the plot of *Antigone*, a device that also serves to provide a contemporary audience with the basic plot of *Antigone*, John has been scheming to find ways of improvising costumes for Creon and Antigone, and has found a way to fabricate "false 'titties' " (I 61) for Antigone. The perfunctory costume afforded him as a prison inmate also includes the head of a mop, worn as a wig. John has persuaded Winston to play Antigone, but cannot resist laughing at his expense. When Winston tries them on, with only one more day to go before the performance, John teases him mercilessly, circling him in mock admiration, fondling Antigone's breasts, and removing his own trousers, implying that he finds the figure that Winston cuts, dressed up as Antigone, sexually irresistible. John's relentless laughter and sexual innuendo finally proves too much for Winston. Humiliated by his cellmate's laughter and anticipating further humiliation from a prison audience, Winston rips off the costume, and tells John: "Take your Antigone and shove it up your arse! . . . I'm not doing Antigone. . . . I'm a man, not a bloody woman" (I 56–7). When John's laughter subsides, and he tries to backtrack, not wanting to lose Winston's commitment to playing the role of Antigone, Winston retorts that he would rather endure the humiliation of the prison guard than John's: "I am not doing your Antigone! I would rather run the whole day for Hodoshe. At least I know where I stand with him. All *he* wants is to make me a 'boy' . . . not a bloody woman" (I 60). Winston's claim to prefer the treatment he suffers at the hands of the prison guard than to perform Antigone is a striking one. We have witnessed the acute humiliation, including physical abuse, to which Winston has been subjected by Hodoshe, we know that it enrages him, and yet he professes to prefer such treatment to the ridicule to which his cellmate subjects him. Such a profession is a measure of how unnerved Winston is by John's sexual taunting. The terms in which Winston expresses his preference are indicative of his anxiety about his sexual identity. He would rather tolerate Hodoshe because the prison guard only wants to make Winston into a "boy," not into a "woman." Winston would rather be infantilized, he attests, he would rather suffer a retardation of his manhood than be made into a woman by his cellmate, becoming the butt of John's sexual jokes.

Being made into a woman here functions as so undesirable that even the inhumane behavior to which Winston is subjected on a daily basis by his sadistic overseer is seen as preferable. An echo of the untenable, unthinkable position occupied by slaves in Sophocles' *Antigone* is found in the way that women function in *The Island,* where fear of being made into a woman figures in relation to the theme of apartheid that informs the text at every level. Winston would prefer to be made into a boy than into a woman. Can his humanity be more easily recuperated in one case than in another, and if so why? How does his preference play out in terms of the effeminizing trope deployed by racist strategies? In what ways is Winston's acute anxiety about impersonating a female exacerbated or shaped by the fact that as a prison inmate he is thrown together with another man in highly confined quarters, forced into an intense and prolonged physical and emotional intimacy?

Toward the beginning of the play, which opens with the prisoners being subjected to the Sisyphean labor of moving sand from one pile, then moving it back to another, John had felt the need to reaffirm to his cellmate the adult masculinity that Hodoshe, the prison guard, is trying to undermine. He affirms to Winston "I'm a man, brother, A man!" (I 49) but confesses that if Hodoshe had kept them to the "back-breaking and grotesquely futile labour" (I 47) for "five minutes longer" (I 49) he would have become a "baby." "I nearly cried" says Winston (I 49). The stage directions at the beginning of the play clearly recall Oedipus and the riddle of the Sphinx, as John and Winston are shackled together, forced to run to their cell "three-legged" (I 47), but fail to run fast enough to avoid being beaten by Hodoshe, whose offstage presence is figured as the curse under which the Oedipal family labors. The beatings John and Winston sustain, which recall the routine beating slaves received in fifth century BCE Athens, as much as they do the treatment of black South Africans under apartheid, leave Winston with "a bad blow to the eye" and John with a sprained ankle (I 47). Both of them are reduced to crawling across the cell—John because of his injured foot, and Winston because he is "blind with rage and pain" (I 47). Crawling on all fours, running "three-legged," asserting their manhood in trying to stand on their own two feet, sustaining foot and eye injuries, Winston and John embody the various stages of man that Oedipus deciphers in the Sphinx's riddle.[52] At the same time they reflect the injury inflicted on Oedipus as an infant that resulted in his name, and the injury he inflicts on himself, when he blinds himself, casting out his eyes.

If at the beginning and end of the play—when Winston and John resume their three-legged run (I 77)—the Sphinx's riddle is recalled, in the middle of the play the feminization Oedipus suffers at the hands of the Sphinx is also explored.[53] At John's hands, not only Winston's sex, but also his sexuality, is put into question. Winston can apparently abide being made into an immature male—treated as a boy—by the prison guard, but he cannot put up with having his sexual identity put in question by his cellmate. He cannot tolerate having his sexuality challenged. He is, he insists, a man, not a woman. But what makes him capable of abiding the treatment to which Hodoshe subjects him is precisely the intimate relationship that he maintains with John, a relationship that the play figures in myriad ways in terms of a symbolic marriage.

Despite his vociferous protests, Winston ends up playing the role of Antigone after all. In this sense his repudiation of being "made into a woman" is recuperated. Yet at what cost is this recuperation effected? Friendship is elevated above Winston's anxiety about his sexual identity, but in the process, is an appeal to a universal humanism that transcends all differences invoked? The audience is not privy to Winston's change of heart, but we gather that his friendship and loyalty to John, with whom, he has learnt, his shared time in prison is finite—given the reduction of John's sentence—trumps his disinclination to risk the ridicule of his cellmates. Winston's commitment to John overcomes his distaste at being made into the butt of John's sexual jokes. When, in the final scene, Winston appears as Antigone, standing up for her rights against Creon, there is no hint of ridicule. So too, when the performance that inspired *The Island* actually took place in the prison at Robben Island, there was no sign of the laughter that Winston fears.[54]

What, then, do we make of Winston's reluctance to deal with John's ridicule of him? And what is the significance of the fact that he manages to overcome his aversion to playing Antigone? Clearly the fact that as cellmates Winston and John must, of necessity, deal with the pressure of each other's constant company needs to be taken into account. Winston's sensitivity to John's sexual innuendos is due in no small part to the constraints of a situation in which the two men are required to be one another's companions, day in and day out. Privacy is nonexistent. John and Winston clean each other's wounds, tell one another stories, work, sleep, eat, and wash together, in the same confined space. John tries to clean the wound to Winston's eye with his own urine (see I 47), a gesture whose intimacy conveys at once the depth of their bond and the constraints of their forced bodily and psychic proximity. When John makes fun of Winston's attire, his laughter might well be a means of relieving the pressure that builds up in such a situation. It might also be a defense, a means of distancing himself from any sexual tension that has built up between the two of them. To act as if he is enamored of Winston, but to do so in such a way as to induce humor, both allows John to express sexual feelings toward his cellmate and yet at the same time to disavow them. To understand the complexity of this situation is to understand both that John is availing himself of a generic cultural ethos of homophobia—taking advantage of the available social text of homophobia—while at the same time manipulating the situation to render it safe for him to express a sexual desire for Winston that is tightly circumscribed within the bounds of humor. When Winston aggressively deflects John's sexual reaction to him in the guise of Antigone, his response must also be read against the intense relationship that has been established between the two cellmates. "Take your Antigone and shove it up your arse!" exclaims Winston to John, in a line laden with innuendo.

When John, in a desperate attempt to convince Winston to agree to wear the makeshift costume of Antigone after all, adorns himself with the wig and false breasts, inviting Winston to laugh at him, the appeal he makes to Winston appears to be simple and direct: "behind all this rubbish is me, and you know it's me" (I 62). Just as Winston can see beyond the façade of his costume to John, so the other prisoners will see through the costume; they will know that the person underneath is really Winston. At the same time, Sophocles' Antigone shares something in common with Winston, that which makes it so hard for John, and ultimately for Winston too, to give up the idea of performing a version of *Antigone*: they are both being punished for what they know to be right. Neither of them is prepared to compromise the principle in which they believe. In this sense John's suggestion takes on another, more profound meaning. The prisoners will know that Winston has an affinity with Antigone that is deeper than any hilarity his costume might occasion. They will recognize his refusal to give up his conviction that he is right to honor "those things to which honour belongs" (I 77). The boundaries of sexual dimorphism are safely reinstalled, after their temporary destabilization, as are those of the heteronormative order. Against the background of the performative constraints of Greek tragedy, where male actors played female roles, this scene takes on a peculiar importance. *The Island* is a play inspired by the female character Antigone, a figure that has stood the test of time, standing up for justice in an unflinching way. It is also a play that takes up and explores the symbolic importance of gender in a way that reflects on, rather than repudiates, the performative constraints that would have informed the dramatic production of the play in fifth century BCE Athens. In the performance of *The Island* by the Remy Bumppo at the Greenhouse Theatre in Chicago in 2010, the exchange between Winston and John around the appearance of Winston's costume of a mop and "false titties" served as a vehicle to prepare a contemporary audience to take Winston's performance of Antigone seriously. The scene functioned as comic relief, and as an escape valve for the audience's anxiety around sexuality. When Winston played the role of Antigone at the end of *The Island*, there was no laughter to be heard. The audience had been brought to understand what the prisoners who witnessed the play in Robben Island had understood: the voice of Antigone had become Winston's voice, empowering and inspiring him, providing him with the strength to face the future without John. Far from constituting an object of ridicule, the guise of Antigone confers on Winston a strength and fortitude on which he draws.

John's assurance to Winston that his audience will know it is really him rings true, as the heteronormative order and the demarcation between female and male are back in place. Any deviation is just that, and we can all rest easy. While *The Island* effects a partial recuperation of the abject figuring of homosexuality, then, insofar as Winston takes on the risk of playing Antigone, there is also an implicit appeal to abstract humanist values, which tend to be modeled on the idealized features of specific citizens. We are all fundamentally the same; we all deserve equal rights. It's just that some are more equal than others, and that rights discourse tends to proceed by requiring those to which equality is formally extended to resemble those who enjoy rights by fiat—and what this tends to mean is that recognition of otherness in fact proceeds according to the capacity of others to be represented as if they were not in fact other, but rather the same.

The Island recasts the performative and gendered questions inherent in the performance of ancient Greek tragedy. Here Antigone is played by a woman not, as in fifth century BCE Athens, because women in general were not allowed to act female parts, but because blacks in general were subject to unjust and harsh treatment in twentieth century South Africa, as a result of which Winston is imprisoned. The situation that results is one in which John and Winston find themselves thrown together in the confined space of an all-male prison, where if a play is to be performed, it is to be performed by an all-male cast. In his desperate attempt to retain his sanity under the brutal conditions of Robben Island, Winston claims to prefer his treatment at the hands of Hodoshe, declaring his preference to be treated as a boy rather than as a woman. What happens, then, when Winston relents, agreeing to play the role of Antigone, agreeing to perform the role of a woman after all?

Winston's decision to take on Antigone's role occurs within a play that is inspired not only by *Antigone*, but also more immediately by another play, the version of *Antigone* that took place in Robben Island. That performance too has a history that can be traced back to the performance of *Antigone* by a black drama group that was initiated when four people approached Athol Fugard to ask for his help. The story of Antigone's "lone voice raised in protest against what was considered an unjust law" had spoken to the drama group from the Eastern Cape Province of South Africa, the Serpent Players.[55] Made up initially of "four black men and one woman (Norman Ntshinga, Welcome Duru, Fats Bokhilane, Mike Ngxcolo, and Mabel Magada)," these founding members were soon to be joined by others.[56] Such was the significance to these actors of performing *Antigone* that when the actor scheduled to play Haemon, Sharkie (Sipho Mguqulwa), was summarily arrested on trumped-up charges—as was common under apartheid in the "black townships in and around Port Elizabeth"—the denial of the opportunity to play Haemon weighed more heavily on him than the prison sentence meted out to him.[57] Fugard reports: "The fact that he had been robbed of a chance to go on stage as Haemon and argue with his father for the life of someone he loved, and for her right to act in accordance with her conscience, was . . . an even greater blow than the sentence of twenty years that had been imposed on him."[58] In prison, Sharkie found a way to stage a "pocket version" of *Antigone*, relying on memory to distill the play into a fifteen-minute performance that could be fitted into the rubric of the annual concert granted prisoners on Robben Island.[59] Sharkie reduced the drama to the "final confrontation between Creon and Antigone."[60] In the play that was to become *The Island*, Fugard, Kani, and Ntshona, based their story on "Sharkie's extraordinary fifteen-minute *Antigone* in the prison concert on Robben Island."[61] Fugard goes on to compare the reception of the play to that of

> Anouilh's *Antigone* in Paris during the German occupation. The front row of German army officers had thought they were enjoying French culture, while behind them Parisians received a political message of hope and defiance. So too on Robben Island, the South African warders sat in front of the audience of prisoners, and really admired these Bantus for what they had cooked up for their entertainment.

Fugard offers the following comment: "I like to think of that moment of Sharkie's triumph as possibly the greatest fulfillment of this magnificent play's message since Sophocles first staged his *Antigone* in Athens in about 440 BC."[62]

The Robben Island performance of *Antigone* thus provided the context for a play in which the living death Creon plans for Antigone parallels the living hell faced by incarcerated prison inmates.[63] Antigone's premature entombment in a cave for a crime that is not a crime serves as a metaphor for Winston's incarceration in a prison for a crime that was not a crime. Sophocles' Antigone is imprisoned as much for being a woman who dares to oppose Creon as she is for burying Polynices; in apartheid South Africa it was enough to be black to be treated as a criminal. For all his reluctance, Winston ultimately chooses to risk performing Antigone, and in doing so, paradoxically, there is a sense in which he risks being himself. He takes on the role from which he had distanced himself so vehemently, to the point of proclaiming his preference for the cruelty of a prison guard. The words that John uses in order to persuade him to take this risk resonate in more than one way.[64] "They will know it's really you." The audience of prison inmates—with whom audiences of *The Island* are required to identify—will recognize that behind the façade of a woman is a man, but they will agree to suspend this recognition, an agreement that might well be informed by a political insight that allows a reading of Antigone's contest with Creon to reflect a black South African's struggle with apartheid. To see in Antigone's plight that of a black South African, is to see someone imprisoned for being who she or he is, imprisoned for being born a woman in fifth century BCE Athens, or for being born black in apartheid South Africa, or for any other contingency of birth. The audience will recognize themselves, and the contingency of the political conditions that dictate, or offer relief from, their own imprisonment.

If the performance of drama in Athens constituted an occasion for political critique, crucial for the political consciousness of the audience, such occasions were sanctioned in a way that can hardly be said for performances of *Antigone* in South Africa, where black actors risked arrest. If such performances embodied, in Fugard's words, "one of theatre's major responsibilities in an oppressive society: to break the conspiracy of silence that always attends an unjust social system," we are led to wonder what impact the demand that men—and only men—speak for women might have had on the limitations of Athenian democracy.[65] For the actors themselves, the performance of such plays constituted a matter of survival, rather than a duty to the polis. To anticipate the discussion of Agamben in Chapter 5, survival here connotes a life that refuses to be confined to life in the sense of *zoē*, a life that is construed as *bios*, a life that survives psychically, not merely biologically, retaining hope for the future that consists in construing a polity that does not adhere to the regime of apartheid. In the contexts of oppressive regimes, theater becomes a means of psychic survival, and at the same time a means of envisioning a future not determined by the prevailing political conditions. It becomes a way of reimagining the life that has come to pass for the proper form of life, of refusing the propriety of oppression.

Concluding Remarks

I have tried to elucidate how the conditions of performativity might have played out in relation to the political impact of tragedy in two different registers. In Athens, in a society in which women played no visible, political role, the female as well as the male parts in *Antigone*—a play that brings into question the separation of public and private, and how this lines up with male/female—would have been acted by male actors. In one register Antigone would have been fetishized by readings that disavow the legitimating male bodies that constitute a condition of performing tragic drama: I know that the actor is male, but all the same I read the character as consistently female. On such a reading, a successful performance will consist of a male actor passing as a female, and will tend to minimize any oscillation between knowledge and belief. An erotic fetishization of Antigone succumbs to the allure of a character in love with the death drive, and dedicated to the preservation of the new laws of the socio-symbolic realm, which exclude women from the political and require the subordination of their erotic drive to the polity. In a second register, Antigone can be read as figuring the excluded, constitutive remainder that is disavowed. Here the challenge she presents to the social convention dictating women's silence is read not as a nostalgic memorial to the past, to the lost/missing/mythical object, but as a call to the future, for an expanded notion of democracy, one that is not premised on the silencing of women. This future democracy brings into question the narrow definition of the political construed by Creon, as order for the sake of order, a political order that would try to eliminate any risk or disorder by fiat. By refiguring the relation between *philia* and *eros*, Antigone acknowledges the symbolic importance of restoring the distinctions Oedipus had confused. Yet her act is not merely restorative of an order that had been violated. To restrict the meaning of Antigone's insistence upon burying Polynices to the restoration of the incest taboo is to read the tragic effect as a reining in of *eros*, consistent with the assumption that the political function of tragedy is entirely controlled by its sanctioning as a state performance. Antigone's sacrificial death would be in the service of the ordering of the polis; the meaning of her act of burial would be harnessed to the purpose of stabilizing a state that excludes women from full participation. Antigone's erotic aims would be subordinate to order and stability, as if the political meaning of the play could be reduced to the recognition of the importance of the discrimination of various filial relations for the sake of initiating erotic relations appropriate to the preservation of a polity that persists in its subordination of women's erotic desires to its own ends.

To read the character of Antigone as one whose action calls attention to—rather than disavowing—the political conditions that exclude women from the public sphere, dictating that her role can only be performed by a man, is not to see the political function of tragedy as confined to the subjugation of women to the status quo. It is also to see tragic drama as performing a critique of political exclusion, a critique that calls for a version of democracy that does not survive by disavowing as excluded others members who are constitutive of its preservation. Antigone makes an intervention into the logic of fetishism by drawing attention to that which is disavowed, and as such her legacy is taken up beyond the logic of sexual difference. In *The Island*, the dynamic of abjection is explored in a way that does not merely condone a chain of abjection, but explores the reiteration of dejects (or those who suffer abjection) within a play that takes the risk of showing how racial exclusions can devolve into the abjection of women, while also recuperating that abjection. When Winston overcomes his fear and plays Antigone, replete with his ridiculous wig and false titties—the only costume his incarceration affords him—his audience does not ridicule him, because they see the profundity of the relationship between apartheid and Creon's version of tyranny.

While there are grounds for reading *The Island* as a play that appeals to a kind of universalism, celebrating the call for justice in all its multivalent guises, I have offered a different reading, one that draws attention to the not necessarily benign reiteration of the logic of exclusion that it both exposes and recuperates to some extent. I am suggesting that the dynamics that pertain between sexuality, sexual difference and race in *The Island* help to shed light on the dynamics that structure the relationship between the status of women, slaves, and outsiders in Sophocles' *Antigone*. In *The Island* the sense in which Antigone's plight parallels that of Winston and John is explored, at the same time as the disjunction between their situations is exploited. A structuring theme in Sophocles' Antigone, but one that has been allowed to fly under the interpretive radar, is the way in which slavery becomes a foil both to Antigone's effort to establish her voice as legitimate in the public realm, and to those who would try to contain, quell, and repress the legitimacy of that voice.

The history of appropriations of *Antigone*—more than the "original" play—calls for a polity premised not on excluded but constitutive others, but rather one in which the possibilities of political representation are transformed, so that the polity no longer relies upon stipulating certain subjects as unthinkable within its terms, while continuing to benefit from its appropriation of the material contributions of these non-subjects, contributions that are nonetheless deprived of equal representation by the symbolic systems of signification in place. The history that refigures Antigone calls for a polity that does not insist upon creating its own enemy within the city walls, relegating some of its subjects to a mythical state of nature, as if they were not civilized enough to fully participate in the democracy they nonetheless help to sustain. This history calls for a polity in which women are no longer the eternal irony of the community. It calls for a polity in which not only do women vacate this role, but where no one is made to take their place.

The chapter, then, is an attempt to outline the political logic according to which Antigone lends herself to myriad political struggles by figuring the excluded yet constitutive ground of a polity. If in some cases this logic is reiterated at one register, even it as it is questioned at another, in other cases the mythological reiteration of Antigone throughout various epochs, becomes a theme for investigation within the play itself.[66] The history that rewrites *Antigone* illuminates the processes according to which any contingent fact (not just gender or sexuality, but also race, class, nationality, religion, or some other contingency) can become a ground for an exclusionary politics—even if Antigone herself is enlisted in the very exclusionary logic she exposes at another level. In this sense, it is not a question of Antigone acting as a woman—or in any other specifically gendered way. Rather it is a question of her acting in such a way as to rewrite or transform the grounds on which her exclusion from the system is written off as unintelligible to it. Whether or not Antigone is rendered intelligible only at the cost of rendering some newly othered group unintelligible is a question that must be negotiated by each new rendering of *Antigone*. Antigone calls herself into intelligibility by challenging the grounds on which the polity writes her as unintelligible, unreadable, unsignifiable within its terms. Were her exclusion to have become capable of representation within the set of significations that requires it, then that system itself must have undergone transformation. Antigone calls for a redrawing of the lines of the polity, such that it is no longer able to cast her out as its excluded outsider—that is, to refuse her "proper" representation—while simultaneously drawing on her resources for its own purposes. In this sense Antigone calls into being a future polity that does not rely on the political exclusion of some of its members, while legislating that exclusion as unthinkable, or rendering it non-negotiable. She draws attention to political gestures that rely on casting as unintelligible those on whom it depends materially and psychically, but whom it systematically excludes from legitimate, symbolic representation. Antigone becomes a site for the reworking of the distinction between improper and proper, between that which is cast outside a system of intelligibility as impermissible within its current configuration, and that according to which something is cast out as unacceptable: she calls into question the very terms that render an order proper by designating something other than it as improper. Her own impropriety, in this process, must also become a theme for investigation, for she is not the pure, unspoilt hero that Hegel would have her be.

4

Exempting Antigone from Ancient Greece

Multiplying and Racializing Genealogies in *Tègònni: An African Antigone*

If Hölderlin and Hegel, in different ways, saw tragedy as signaling epochal shifts, recent appropriations of Antigone have focused upon conflicting interpretations of such shifts. Paradoxically, then, the tragedy of *Antigone* has come to embody the hopes of those who appear to be hemmed in by implacable forces, who turn to Antigone, again and again, as a way of renewing their hope precisely when injustice might seem to have won the day.[1] If, as Reiss says, tragedy "fulfills the role of making a new class of discourse possible," and if its appearance as a literary form occurs "at the moment of a shift in the discursive order that rules a society," perhaps we must say not merely that we no longer have any need for tragedy, having hypostasized it into the tragic where it has come to refer to those events that do not consort with everyday realities, but which disrupt the humdrum existence that tends to characterize the flow of everyday life.[2] Perhaps we should say, at least in the case of *Antigone*, rather that tragedy has been transformed into a vehicle of protest for those whose interpretation of everyday life as tragic is systematically delegitimated, or not given a proper hearing. When the banalities of what has come to appear as the everyday for some rest upon systematic racial injustices for others, when business as usual for the white ruling classes of South Africa is premised upon apartheid, or when postcolonial, imperial practices of European powers exploit the natural resources of Nigeria through their support of multinational conglomerates, is it accidental that the casualties of those practices have found literary dramatists who have turned to *Antigone* to expose the injustices to which those who justify the systems of oppression from which they benefit can remain, if not oblivious, at least defensive and uncaring?

Perhaps dramatists have turned to *Antigone* again and again because it explores so effectively not only the impact of systemic blindness, how competing value systems can come to operate as absolute grounds, so that individuals become inured to acknowledging or being able to see any other meaning than their own, but also how such grounds acquire authority. When competing views point out that the absolutism of these grounds is premised on the dual condition of usurping others at the same time as systematically failing to acknowledge this usurpation, these views fall on deaf ears.

The literary, dramatic, performative, and political tradition that has been inspired by the figure of Antigone is a history in which Antigone has entered into myriad political contexts, serving as an inspiration for those fighting for freedom in the midst of injustice. As Òsófisan says, "Each Antigone at a specific time in history, where there is oppression, injustice, or tyranny."[3] The theatrical legacy of Antigone is one that recognizes Antigone as standing up for a principle that a corrupt state has neglected, abandoned, or refused to legitimize. Antigone thus recalls a polity to what should have been its proper function, exposing the corruption or monstrosity of what the state has become. In particular, Antigone has lent her name to racially combustible situations, such as occur under apartheid and in the wake of the legacies of imperialism and colonialism. She recalls the state to its proper function, while also exposing the extent to which the state has deviated from what should have been, but is not yet (or is no longer) its function. She calls for a future that has not arrived, calling out the impropriety of the state insofar as it falls short of a future yet to come. And yet there is more to be said.

"It was a brother, not a slave [δουλος], who died" Antigone says to Creon in Sophocles' *Antigone* (517).[4] While a good deal of scholarly attention has been devoted to the sense in which Antigone claims Polynices is irreplaceable, such that he is distinguished from a future husband or son of Antigone's, there is very little consideration of the ease with which Antigone dismisses slaves.[5] It would seem that what is decisive for Antigone is not Polynices' act, not any significance, political or otherwise, attached to what he has or has not done in life, but rather the importance of acknowledging his blood relationship to her—or, more specifically, the fact that he is born of the same mother [μητρὸς].[6] In specifying Polynices as a son born of a mother she shares in common with him, Antigone is distancing herself from Creon's judgment of Polynices in more ways than one. In contrast to Antigone, Creon emphasizes the lineage from her father, rather than stipulating Polynices as her mother's son, and construes Polynices as an enemy, a traitor to the state, rather than a friend or family member.[7] At the same time, however, as Antigone aligns herself with *philia*, Antigone appears to be endorsing a problematic view of slaves, apparently writing them off as not worthy of burial.

Earlier in the play Creon had suggested that Polynices had tried to "enslave" [δουλώσας] the Thebans (202) by attacking the city, and later he will call Haemon a woman's "slave" [δούλευμα].[8] By insisting that Polynices is not a slave, Antigone is repudiating Creon's association of him with slavery. Yet Antigone does not bring into question the status of slaves as inferior anymore than Creon does. Critics have observed the extent to which Creon associates Polynices, Antigone, Ismene, and Haemon with "slaves and animals" but have not problematized Antigone's own implicit assumption that had Polynices been a slave, he would have been unworthy of burial.[9] O'Brien cites Goheen as having explored the extent to which Creon labels others as slaves and animals, but does not put into question the assumption that Antigone and Creon appear to share, namely that the House of Labdacus is human in some way that slaves and animals are not.[10] The closest O'Brien comes to confronting this issue is when she observes that Creon treats Ismene and Antigone as "less than slaves" (531–33), as females not allowed to "range abroad" (579).[11] The reference is to Creon's simile comparing Ismene to a "viper."[12]

The unstated presupposition here is that while slaves are still recognizably human, animals are not. The question arises then as to what precisely differentiates Polynices from a slave. Is the humanity of slaves questionable in a way that is not reducible to their animality? Is it the deprivation of their freedom that brings into question their humanity? Is there not a sense, then, in which treating them as if they lacked humanity, rather than putting them on a par with animals, in fact brings into question the humanity of those who enslave them? In this sense, perhaps there is a way in which those who refuse to question enslavement fail to match up to animals, since at least animals do not deprive some humans of their freedom, while retaining for themselves the right to freedom. Of course, crucial questions have been raised about the ease with which humanist discourse appeals to animality, as if the animal were a coherent concept, one that could be unproblematically distinguished from humanity (as if not only all animals were animal in the same way, and all humans were human in the same way, but also the humanity of the latter were somehow established in relation to a boundary or divide such that all animals line up on one side, and all humans line up on the other).[13] Could it be that those who have insisted upon associating Antigone with monstrosity have fallen prey to some of the metaphysical misconceptions Derrida and others have brought into question, not the least of which is the reduction of multiple animals to an animality, the construction of which serves to contain many a human anxiety about how questionable our own humanity might be?[14]

By distinguishing between the kinship bonds that link her to her brother, and the ties that link her to objects and to slaves that also constitute the oikos or household, is Antigone attempting to establish the right to bury Polynices, and at the same time her own right to be included within the polis, her right to be considered human? Is she trying to demarcate those who are included within the oikos because of family ties from those included as possessions? Does her reference to slavery serve to demarcate those who do not share in common with Antigone bonds of kinship from those who do? Perhaps the status of a slave serves not only to distinguish Antigone's kinship relation to her brother, but also to mark Polynices' freedom as decisive for his humanity? If Polynices is human as a free man in a way that a slave, by definition, would not be, doesn't slavery become the unthought ground on the basis of which Antigone rests her claim to enact the bonds of humanity, to recognize her brother as human by consecrating his memory as such?

How would sustained attention to the dynamic of slavery in *Antigone* have altered the reception of *Antigone*, for which Hegel's reading has been decisive, and how would the tradition that has celebrated Antigone have been altered by it? What would that tradition have looked like, had it been capable of attending to Antigone's apparently unproblematic endorsement of slavery? How do plays that take up *Antigone* in a postcolonial context allow us to renew the philosophical and psychoanalytic tradition that has taken up *Antigone*? How do plays such as Òsófisan's *Tègònni* complicate Antigone's legacy as a freedom fighter, by implicating her in colonialism, even as she embodies a certain spirit of defiance? How does Òsófisan allow us to problematize the Western legacy of *Antigone*, rather than to repeat, its blind spots? How might such a problematization ramify throughout this tradition of tragic interpretation, and how might it intervene in this history, even to the point of recasting it, revising it, or rewriting it?

In what follows I propose a reading of an African version of Antigone, *Tègònni: an African Antigone*, a Nigerian play that transposes the concerns of Sophocles' *Antigone* into a colonial context. Instead of Polynices' burial being prohibited by King Creon, it is the burial of Tègònni's brother that is banned by the colonial regime, and it is Tègònni, rather than Antigone, who flouts the prohibition. Òsófisan also introduces the issue of interracial marriage into the plot, at the same time as he confronts the complex and problematic ways in which the mythological figure of Antigone has held sway over the philosophical, literary, and psychoanalytic imagination of the West through the ages. In attending to the articulations of this play, which responds to a complex, racially divisive situation, I shall build on, modify, and amplify certain insights contributed by Judith Butler and Mary Beth Mader, in an attempt to expand the salience of familial kinship structures. Far from maintaining a narrow focus on the kinship arrangements that might seem to dominate interpretations of the original play, the history of Antigones has in fact spoken to a wide range of contemporary political situations, not least those that are specified in terms of racially informed prohibitions. In doing so, this history also opens up the original play to be read in ways that dominant philosophical and psychoanalytic interpretations have tended to eclipse.

Butler and Mader: Making Polynices Only a Brother

In her important discussion, Judith Butler argues that Antigone "exposes the socially contingent character of kinship."[15] There are plenty of reasons not only to take Butler's argument seriously, but to consider it as crucially important. First, and perhaps, most obviously, there is no question that the issue of kinship, the prohibition of incest, and its transgression, is central to the Oedipal cycle itself. Secondly, and no less importantly, Butler's questioning of who Antigone is, and what kind of example she might provide, enables her to draw attention to the way in which structures of kinship and the state are deeply implicated in one another.[16] Butler is able to raise significant political questions about the investment of the state in maintaining the stability and fixity of normative familial configurations, while outlawing those configurations that threaten its legitimacy. She is also able to comment on the investment of Lacanians in distancing themselves from the proliferation and instability of the symbolic maternal and paternal positions that are currently operative. By pointing to the instability of maternal and paternal positions, Butler suggests that the symbolic and the social are not as easy to separate as Lacan suggests. Where "more than one woman . . . operates as the mother" or "more than one man . . . operates as the father," Butler suggests, "the place of the father [or mother] is dispersed."[17] For Butler, the Lacanian symbolic, as the structure of intelligibility, idealizes certain kinship structures at the expense of others, but Lacanians make this idealization unavailable for questioning, in severing the symbolic from the social, and attributing a universality to the former.[18] For Lacan, the symbolic renders itself immune from interrogation; his very distinction between the symbolic and the social covers over the fact that the symbolic borrows certain features from a normative interpretation of the social, disavowing its normative dimension, failing to notice that it is derivative of heteronormative kinship structures. Lacan's symbolic thus barricades itself against critique. The symbolic comes to function as a law, yet any questioning of its legality is considered out of bounds. For Butler, it is impossible to definitively purify the symbolic, as a formal requirement, from normative social arrangements.[19] In contrast to Lacan, Butler sees the symbolic not as an idealized precondition of the social, but as itself constituted in and through the various sediments that make up the spectrum of social relations. "My view," says Butler, "is that the distinction between symbolic and social law cannot finally hold, that not only is the symbolic itself the sedimentation of social practices but that radical alterations in kinship demand a rearticulation of the structuralist presuppositions of psychoanalysis and, hence, of contemporary gender and social theory."[20]

Butler's argument that the distinction between the symbolic and the social is not as easily maintained as Lacanians tend to insist is one with which I concur. Yet I wonder whether there is a sense in which Butler herself allows her own investigation into Antigone to be circumscribed by the particular way in which psychoanalysis conceives of kinship structures as foundational for culture, even as she seeks to put into question other psychoanalytic tenets.[21] Butler questions the rigidity of both Hegel's distinction between kinship and the state and Lacan's distinction between the symbolic and the social. Yet in doing so, there is a sense in which Butler allows her privileging of Hegel, and particularly of Lacan, to limit her purview, so that she emphasizes kinship at the expense, for example, of race. Although Butler raises the question of race briefly, she does so only insofar as it relates to the question of kinship.[22] In this respect she allows her analysis to be limited to the questions that Lacanian psychoanalysis, indebted as it is to a Hegelian legacy, has highlighted.

Without detracting from the significance of the effort to resist attempts to render Antigone as representative in any straightforward sense of either the ethical claims of the heteronormative family (as Hegel tends to do) or the claims to extend political rights to women (as some feminist interpretations have done), I suggest that *Antigone* raises a range of issues that dominant theoretical interpretations have neglected. Butler provocatively and brilliantly takes up the aberrant status of Antigone both to challenge the rigidity of contemporary legal systems whose recognition of kinship forms is highly circumscribed, and to illustrate how the legitimacy of kinship forms and state sanctioned laws are mutually implicated in one another. In doing so, Butler formulates a crucial critique of Lacan, yet at the same time I suggest she capitulates to some basic assumptions that characterize the shared tradition that defines Hegel and Lacan's interest in *Antigone*. A European, colonialist framework continues to drive Western, philosophically and psychoanalytically inspired readings of the Oedipal cycle, invested in retaining the invisibility of the founding paradox upon which I suggest a good number of post-Hegelian interpretations are premised.

A good deal of the power and radicality of Butler's argument seems to rest on her interrogation of Lacan's effort to sever the symbolic from the social. In locating the aberration of the Oedipal family in Oedipus, and not in Antigone, Mary Beth Mader might appear to deprive Butler's argument of one of its most politically productive moments. By identifying the aberration in kinship relations that plagues the Oedipal family with Oedipus's incest, and refusing Butler's suggestion that Antigone's relation to Polynices is incestuous, Mader seems to distance herself from an important aspect of Butler's argument. One of Butler's main points of contention with Lacan is that the distinction between the symbolic and the social is ultimately untenable. For Lacan to insist that the symbolic position of the father remains the same, no matter who fulfils that function at the level of the social, amounts to an assertion of the force of law, according to Butler. This law rings hollow; the very attempt to preserve the formality of the empty categories "mother" and "father" as distinct from the human beings who actually perform paternal and maternal roles is susceptible to critique in

Butler's view. Butler's point here is that it is impossible to maintain that the symbolic operates at a transcendental level, which endows the status of pure or empty signifier on positions that are purely structural. If those who function as mothers or fathers differ from those who have been traditionally sanctioned to do so, such functions renew the very categories themselves, breathing new life into them, changing the meaning and function of the symbolic positions themselves, which do not operate in abstraction from the performative, but are rather constituted in and through the practices that renew and contest them. For a norm to be a norm is for there to be cases that deviate from the norm; but it is also to be susceptible to challenge and reconfiguration.[23]

While accepting Butler's suggestion that Antigone "exposes the socially contingent character of kinship," Mader sets out to explain Antigone's enigmatic claim that "she would not have deliberately violated Creon's command, would not have intentionally broken his law or edict, had this edict barred her from burying a child or a husband of hers."[24] By emphasizing that Antigone's claim relates not to all brothers, but to Polynices, the son of an incestuous union, Mader shows that commentators go astray when they fail to understand Antigone's claim to relate to this very specific case. Here is the principle according to which Antigone acts, as Mader sees it: "she is establishing (or attempting to establish) her brother as *only* her brother by symbolically refusing a family precedent, namely that of *generating one's own sibling*."[25] The law according to which Antigone acts, according to Mader, is "recognize your parents as they who can generate those who you can, though must not, generate. The crucial causal corollary is: it is precisely by this recognition that such beings as parents, children, and siblings are made as such in this particular kinship order."[26]

If, as on Mader's reading, Antigone in effect reinstates the incest prohibition that Oedipus had violated, she seems to throw her lot in with the law, coming to stand for, even reerect, the law. Of course Antigone reenacts the law only after having deviated from it, only by being outside the law (as a child of incest), even if she symbolically invokes or appeals to the law that she herself had displaced. Through her act of burying her brother, through what she does, she distinguishes herself from her identity as the daughter of an incestuous union. Antigone becomes something other than what she was in and through her act of burial. Antigone does not merely repeat an Oedipal pattern, but rather acts in order to restore that which Oedipus had violated. Part of the strength of Mader's argument is that it emphasizes the capacity of Antigone to act in her own right, and in doing so to acknowledge the deed of Oedipus, to differentiate herself from her father, his deed, and its effects. I would also say that Antigone does not merely reverse Oedipus's transgression, she does not simply restore the law transgressed by Oedipus, but she also acts in such a way as to open up new possibilities that go beyond any impact Oedipus might have had. She acts in her own right, and she acts on the basis of a principle that refuses to apply royal prerogative selectively according to gender differentiations. By acting in a sovereign way in her own right, she contests the practice of excluding women, by definition, from political action. Yet if in one way this Theban princess acts to differentiate herself from the inferiority that Athenian society ascribes to her, in another way she reinscribes the distinction between slaves and freemen, both in her attempt to differentiate her brother from a slave, and in her effort to distinguish herself from the reputation of a slavish mentality with which fifth century BCE women of Athens would have been tarnished. If Antigone seeks to lay claim to an aristocratic privilege that is Creon's by right of his gender, and thereby to contest the political silence that is imposed on her, she does so by leveraging an unquestioned distinction between those who are free and those who are not, as if that distinction remained intact and were perfectly natural, beyond question. Antigone acts, but her act is compromised by a failure to interrogate another blatant denial of freedom, a denial that is used to substantiate her own claim to be heard.

In burying Polynices, Antigone is no longer merely the product of an incestuous marriage, no longer merely the daughter of Oedipus; not only does Antigone's act effect a change in Polynices' identity, it also changes Antigone herself, enabling Antigone to effect change. As she confers on Polynices the singular status of a brother, Antigone becomes the agent who reenforces the prohibition that Oedipus had violated. For Mader, Antigone seems to be made into a representative of the law precisely in contesting her status as an aberration to the prohibition of incest; she makes herself into such a representative by clarifying that her brother is only her brother. So the question remains as to whether Mader's argument has the effect of taming the radical edge of Butler's. Does Antigone, on Mader's argument, merely become one who transgresses the law in her very existence, but whose transgression of the law becomes the occasion for its reinforcement? Or does Mader's analysis actually open the way for a still more radical interpretation than that which Butler provides? I suggest that Mader's focus on the implications of the particular law according to which Sophocles' Antigone undertakes the act of burial can be extended in a productive way that helps uncover the multifarious practices that Antgione comes to signify in various political appropriations of the play. Rather than reading Antigone as resurrecting a law that Oedipus had transgressed, and thereby restricting the impact of her act to its restorative effect, I suggest that Antigone's act is in fact also directed toward the future. In this interpretation, Antigone does not so much reinstall a law that had been violated as write into law a principle that had been transgressed (and in that transgression appeared as a law), calling for a future that does not repeat the old principle but cites it in one respect only to deviate from it in another respect. Even as Antigone invokes the incest prohibition, thereby restoring that which Oedipus had violated, even as she sanctions the very brother-sister bond between Creon and Jocasta that recognizes Creon as king, she questions the political assumption that only a male line of inheritance is qualified to take on the role of a king. She presumes to speak on an equal footing with him, and in doing so she contests the unwritten kinship laws that specify that only the male line of filiation legitimates a claim to sovereignty. Even as Antigone observes Creon's rightful claim according to the laws of kinship she seeks to restore, she disrupts his claim according to another claim that those laws do not respect, namely the rights of women. That is, she refuses to accept her second-class status as a woman. Secondly, she contests the content of the proclamation Creon issues when he prohibits the burial of Polynices. In doing so, she consecrates in general Creon's particular claim to be king, while contesting the particularity of the configuration of these specific kinship laws. Insisting on the burial of Polynices is, then, paradoxically, a way of upholding Creon's claim to kingship in one way, even as it undercuts his authority in two other ways. On the one hand Antigone refuses Creon's absolute claim to authority, by violating his edict, but on the other hand in doing so, she shows herself to be more cognizant of the mutual implication of kinship and state than Creon himself. At the same time she contests the particular way in which the kinship lines are construed, such that they sanction the claims of male kin to be king, while excluding any claim that female kin might have as part of the royal line.

While Mader is absolutely right to emphasize the singularity of Polynices as brother and Antigone as sister, the implication of taking seriously this singularity as explanatory of Antigone's insistence on burying this brother, born of Oedipus, is also the annulment of its singularity. That is, if Mader is right, Antigone's act of burial is directed toward making her bond to Polynices a bond that particularizes him as exemplary of the universal brother-sister bond that Oedipus had put into question. Having resurrected the kinship bonds that happen to pertain in ancient Greece, Antigone's political judgment proves to be superior to that of Creon's; she understands that the rule of law is dependent on, and not merely superior to, the bonds of *philia* Creon repudiates, and in that understanding proves herself capable of the judgment of which her exclusion from the royal line of inheritance on the basis of her gender fails to recognize her as capable.

As excluded from the political realm, Antigone insists on burying her brother. In doing so, she observes the bonds of *philia* that unite her to her brother, underwriting the difference between *eros* and *philia* by disentangling bonds that Oedipus had mingled. She thereby enacts the familial bonds on which Creon depends as ruler of Thebes, bonds that Creon repudiates rather than acknowledging. In observing the importance of burial rites Antigone is acknowledging that which Creon is unable to see: the dependence of his idea of the polity on precisely that which he refuses to acknowledge, and the importance of the distinctiveness of the brother-sister bond, on which depends

Creon's inheritance of the title royal king of Thebes. Were his relationship to Jocasta not what it was—were it in danger of being contaminated, entangled with, or doubled by some other familial relationship, his claim of inheritance might be contestable.[27]

Building on Mader's argument about the nature of the law that articulates the principle of Antigone's act, and extrapolating from the debate concerning the significance attaching to Antigone's determination of Polynices as *philos*, I argue that when Antigone chooses to die for the love (*philia*) of Polynices, rather than living for the (erotic) love of Haemon, she redirects eros away from its subordination to the reproductive telos governed by the polis. Through this redirection of eros, she resurrects the distinction between brother and son that Oedipus had violated, renewing the possibilities of *philia* in a way that acknowledges the sustaining role it plays not just for the ordering of *oikos*, but also for that of the *polis*. In this sense, Antigone acts for the preservation of the *polis*, and not for its destruction. Yet at the same time, her act constitutes an intervention into the logic of exclusion that configures her relationship to the idea of the polis upheld by Creon. One might be tempted to say that she acts as a woman, whose insight into the meta-logic of the state's dependence on the family is superior to that of Creon's, proving her political capacity to be more profound than his, despite her exclusion, as a woman, from the public realm of politics. No sooner has a phrase such as "she acts as a woman" been articulated than the performative conditions that would have pertained in the original production of Antigone throw into question the intelligibility or legibility of such a claim. Nor does Antigone's character allow these performative conditions to fade into the background: there is an insistence on thematizing Antigone's refusal to adhere to the accepted boundaries of conventional femininity. The implications of Antigone's act—in so far as she is read as a female character, played by a male—bring into question the preservation of the actual political contours of the polis, calling for a polity in which the lines of inheritance that qualify heirs as royal leaders would not be restricted to men, but would extend to women, a polity in which women would be allowed to represent themselves both as political citizens and in theatrical performances. In this sense, Antigone calls into question what it might mean to act as a woman, or to act as a man for that matter, by drawing attention to the way in which her character disrupts conventional gendered assumptions that require certain bodies, and certain body parts, to represent femininity, while others are required to represent masculinity. It is not that she acts as a woman (nor that she acts as a man, nor as androgynous, nor as one whose sexuality is undecidable), rather she acts in such a way as to draw attention to the illegibility of her act as one that is authored by an excluded other, to the impossibility of it signifying as politically meaningful in a polis that is structured so as to exclude the very possibility of it becoming meaningful as a political act.

As we have seen, basing her argument on Antigone's effort to treat Polynices as a brother, as distinct from a nephew or an uncle—familial roles that Oedipus's incest with Jocasta had confounded—Mader understands Antigone's argument about irreplaceability to mean that she herself should not replace her brother. That is, Antigone should not beget another brother, by committing incest.[28] Antigone's insistence derives from her attempt to rectify the confusion caused by her father's failure to recognize Jocasta as his mother, and Jocasta's failure to recognize Oedipus as her son. Mader's argument has the considerable merit of taking seriously the words that Antigone herself uses to explain her deed, rather than accepting Creon's condemnation of Antigone's act as endangering the polis. What, then, would it mean, to both take Mader's argument about the irreplaceability of Polynices seriously, and inflect it in a more political direction than she herself does?[29] By building on Mader's argument about irreplaceabilty in the context of other contemporary readings of *Antigone*, I both want to reconstitute and recontextualize the political, philosophical, and dramatic revisions that Antigone has undergone, and to broaden Mader's argument about the law that Antigone specifies.

As the maternal uncle of Antigone, according to the laws of inheritance of ancient Greece, Creon has a legitimate claim to be heir to the throne.[30] As the brother of Oedipus's wife (rather than as the brother of Oedipus's mother) Creon would have no such claim.[31] Symbolically, then, in denying Antigone the right to bury Polynices, Creon is undercutting his own claim to be king, since, if Mader is right, in burying her brother, Antigone is both clarifying that Polynices is her brother—and *only* her brother (rather than her nephew or her uncle)—and at the same time she is conferring upon Oedipus the symbolic status of father, *and nothing else* (not also the brother that Oedipus's marriage to his mother had made of him to Antigone). In failing to recognize that Antigone's act symbolically affirms his right to be king, Creon would seem to be unwittingly undermining his own claim to be king by persevering in his absolute prohibition against Antigone's burial of Polynices.

If we follow through the political implications of Mader's argument for Creon's claim (true to his name, which means ruler in Greek) to be the ruler of Thebes, we are confronted with a further set of questions regarding the impact of Antigone's restorative act on Creon's authority as king. Antigone's restoration of the incest prohibition violated by Oedipus also contests Creon's right to be king. To reinstate the claim that Polynices has on her as a brother, and only as a brother, is to undercut the legitimating claim of the kinship ties that prevail. Given the death of Polynices and Eteocles, as brother of Jocasta, Creon is next in line to inherit the throne. Insofar as Creon's claim to be king rests upon his kinship to Jocasta, as her brother, Antigone's act of disambiguating Polynices' relation to herself, clarifying his status as brother, might seem to sanction Creon's claim to be king. Yet if Creon is the brother of Jocasta, his inheritance also issues from the incestuous union between Oedipus and Jocasta, a union that Antigone's act of burying Polynices renders symbolically illegitimate. In this sense Antigone undercuts Creon's claim to be king. By emphasizing that Polynices shared the same womb as her, that is, that he qualifies as her brother because he shares her maternal lineage, Antigone draws attention to the maternal genealogy that unites her to Polynices.[32] She does so at the expense of the kinship line she shares with Polynices due to their common father, Oedipus. Had Oedipus not married Jocasta, Creon would have no claim to be king. So by emphasizing maternal, rather than paternal genealogy, Antigone might be said to be severing the legitimacy of Creon's claim to be king while at the same time underlining the fact that the bloodlines that establish Creon's claim to be king are the very same bloodlines that establish her as part of the royal family—bloodlines that proceed from an incestuous union.[33] If Antigone's very existence as a child of incest is read as horrific, then so too is the nature of Creon's claim to rule Thebes, since it is based upon the same incestuous union that Antigone seeks to repudiate.[34]

Instead of appreciating Antigone's attempts to repair the lines of kinship that ensure his claim to be king, Creon inadvertently destroys the continuation of his own *oikos*. Creon's insistence on putting Antigone to death results in his bringing his *oikos* to an end, without any male issue to continue his familial line, since Antigone, who was to have married Haemon, instead becomes the catalyst for his death. As Antigone's death is also the cause of Haemon's death, it becomes in turn the cause of Eurydice's death, while Creon's other son has already died in battle. No son will be born, therefore, who can inherit either Creon's property or his royal lineage.[35] In his failure to recognize Antigone's attempt to distinguish between the familial positions of her immediate kin, rectifying the conflation that Oedipus had effected, Creon brings his own family line to an abrupt end.

Where Oedipus had mingled *eros* with *philia* in such a way as to make of Jocasta a loved one in two divergent and incompatible respects, as both mother and wife, redoubling the bonds of *philia*, Antigone disambiguates *philia* from *eros*, not only putting her blood relationship with Polynices before her erotic bond with Haemon, but in doing so specifying and delimiting the sense in which Polynices is a loved one, *philos*. He is a brother, and must not be a potential lover, but beyond this, he is a brother, and not also an uncle (as the half brother of Oedipus via Jocasta, who is not only wife but also mother of Oedipus).

If Antigone insists on clarifying her relation to Polynices, making him a brother and nothing else, what impact does her disambiguating act of burial have on her own kinship status? She becomes nothing but a sister, distinguishing herself from the self-generating mother that her incestuous line had made of her. Symbolically, as a result of Oedipal incest, Antigone is already the next generation. As both daughter and granddaughter of Jocasta, she is, one might say, her own daughter; she is mother to herself. She herself must grieve for her impending death not only because Jocasta is dead, but also because there is a sense in which she herself is the granddaughter Jocasta will never have. Antigone is her own child.[36] From this point of view, Antigone's lament for her own death is not inconsistent with her forthright character, as it has sometimes been read, but rather the result of her taking on the multiple roles that Oedipus's incest has forced her to occupy. She is both the daughter and granddaughter of Jocasta, since Jocasta is not only her mother, but also (as mother of Oedipus) her grandmother. She grieves then for a lost opportunity, for a child that will never be, for a generation that cannot be generated, for a generation that has been generated already. She grieves, one might say, for the child that she herself is, as mother and child rolled into one. This confusion of roles might account both for her lament, and for her identification of herself with Niobe, Kore, and Demeter, which would not be merely contradictory.[37] Each of these figures represents one of the multiple roles that Antigone must inhabit. Antigone will die a virgin, Creon's imprisonment of banishing her to a cave, thereby petrifying her fertility—although her suicide subverts his end insofar as she herself takes control of her capacity to give (or not to give) life—just as Niobe is enclosed in stone, punished for boasting of her maternal skills.[38] Antigone, then, like Niobe, is a woman whose fertility is cut off in her prime—she is turned to, or encased in, stone.[39] Demeter, a maternal figure of mourning, but one who is eventually reconciled with her lost daughter, Kore, serves to parallel the loss of the child Antigone will never have, and (if we follow Tyrrell and Bennett's reading in this respect), the symbolic transition Antigone effects, from virgin to bride, in her marriage with Hades.[40] The parallel with Kore serves to underline the sense in which Antigone becomes her own daughter: she must give birth to herself. Antigone's reconciliation with death makes her a bride, of sorts, and the fruits of her act of defiance in burying her brother take the shape of the legacy she bequeaths. The multiple rebirths that Antigone has undergone, in different times and in different places, by various scribes, mark the fertility of this legacy.

This multiplicity, Antigone's split identity, has been taken up and rewritten in the legacy Antigone has bequeathed, in which Antigone has come to occupy multiple symbolic roles, each role constituting a position that is written off as incomprehensible, intolerable, or unacceptable to a political order that refuses to recognize it as coherent or permissible, yet continues to usurp or exploit it in some way it renders unsignifiable. In attempting to render signifiable a position written off as incomprehensible, oppositional logics often participate in dynamics that replicate the logic of the excluded other, displacing it onto another identity, requiring some other to become other in order for the subject to become a subject. Antigone's split generational identity accords her multiple identities; perhaps this is why her character resists any easy resolution of subjectivity, whereby a subject shores up its identity by requiring the subjectivity of others to become unintelligible, in order to make intelligible its own claim as a subject. The political inheritance of *Antigone* is one that resists such a resolution; it is not a history in which one group's struggle for political representation succeeds at the expense of the marginalization or unintelligibility of another group, but rather one in which the successful articulation of one claim for political inclusion infuses life into the political struggle of another group, even as it mimics the abjection of dejects, while at the same time offering a recuperation of abjection. The regenerating energy of *Antigone*'s inspiration is geographically and historically dispersed, its dislocations facilitating metaphorical displacements that illuminate one political struggle from the perspective of another.

The political renews itself in Antigone's reconstitution of *philia* as central to the polis in such a way as to confirm the need to oversee the lines of inheritance, even as Antigone contests the very definition of the political as masculine. She thereby gives rise to a new way of conceptualizing women's relationship to eros at the same time as she both broadens the meaning of the political beyond Creon's narrow conception of it, and contests what it might mean to be a woman. Unlike Creon, Antigone does not want order for the sake of order, and neither does she act in such a way as to merely confirm or disrupt the prevailing conventions of femininity. If she works to reinstate distinctions that are vital to both familial and political life, this work does not merely eliminate the disorder that women's association with eros was conventionally taken to embody, nor does it merely introduce disorder into the political order. It opens up to interrogation that which Creon tries to define as civil order by decree. Antigone is said by her sister, Ismene, to be "in love with the impossible" and yet in her insistence on burying Polynices she brings to light a new possibility, the significance of which Ismene ultimately recognizes. That which was said to be impossible according to the limitations of Creon's order, proves to be possible in view of the new political order that Antigone could be said to call for.

Where Oedipus had mingled *eros* with *philia*, making of Jocasta a loved one in two divergent and incompatible respects, as both mother and wife, redoubling the bonds of *philia*, Antigone "disambiguates" *philia* from *eros*, putting not only her blood relationship with Polynices before her erotic bond with Haemon, but in doing so specifying and delimiting the sense in which Polynices is a loved one, *philos*.[41]

Let us grant, for now, the plausibility of Lacan's assumption that the very possibility of linguistic communities is bound up with the prohibition of incest, and that therefore any meaningful exchange—including the exchange of marriage vows—must take place in a context that presupposes the inauguration of the symbolic order, or perhaps, is synonymous with it. Even on its own terms, Lacan's account of the symbolic could be rewritten to take account of the sense in which not only sexual but also racial categories might be infused into the very possibilities of recognition it facilitates. If there is a sense in which the kind of recognition at stake in kinship laws presupposes a prior recognition of an other as human (rather than nonhuman), and if there are some cases in which the humanity of some racialized group is rendered dubious in advance, by some feature that would seem to mark it out as less than human, wouldn't this more primordial sense of recognition operate at a level that is even more fundamental than—or at least as fundamental as—kinship?[42] When certain groups, classified according to the color of their skin, are denied basic human rights, when laws are erected in order to prevent them enjoying the protection of those laws from which other racially classified groups benefit due to the color of their skin, this deprivation of human rights signals a failure to recognize both groups as equally deserving of legal rights. Racial taboos that rest upon neglecting to concede that certain individuals qualify as properly human, taboos that acquire legal authority under certain conditions, such as apartheid, do not afford those individuals protection under laws that other groups can assume, including the right to marry regardless of skin color. If there are certain humans whose humanity is in question, humans who do not unequivocally signify, for those in whose hands lie the power of definition, as human, and if their failure to qualify as unambiguously human puts them off limits as sexual/marriage partners, this would appear to prescribe that only those whose humanity is not in question are acceptable sexual partners.[43] If skin color becomes a mark of race, and race becomes a way of distinguishing between those who qualify unproblematically as human, and those who barely qualify as human, then racial taboos would seem to function as inarticulate conditions, invisibly built into the incest prohibition.

Racial taboos limit the potential pool of marriage partners by imposing an endogamous rule that constitutes whiteness as the criterion for inclusion within the group. Whereas incest prohibitions specify particular individuals as out of bounds, racial taboos specify entire groups as out of bounds. In doing so, racial taboos operate to designate racially homogenous groups as permissible candidates for marriage, while incest prohibitions create an exception to the general rule articulated by racial taboos. Racial taboos, in effect, specify a pool of potential marriage partners as those worthy of being considered, those whose humanity is not rendered questionable by their race. They function as positive incitements to marry, as injunctions to marry within this group, rather than another. From this perspective, incest prohibitions can be construed as endorsing the racial incitement to marry within a group that constitutes itself as not racially contaminated, but specifying certain exceptions within that group. Not only is there a taboo against homosexuality built into kinship structures; the symbolic is infused with kinship structures that assume both heteronormative and miscegenating biases.

Citizens, Substitutes, and Slaves

In the context of the 450/1 Periclean law, which establishes the requirement that both parents be Athenian as the criterion for Athenian citizenship, the pool of future Atheninan citizens is purged of the contaminating influence of slavery. No longer would the common practice of recognizing children conceived by slaves and male citizens satisfy the requirements for citizenship. Is Antigone not only intent upon clarifying the status of Polynices as a brother, but also in clarifying his status as a free man? By implication, does she not also, retrospectively, eliminate any ambiguity surrounding the status of Oedipus, her father (and only her father) in this regard? Does she not attempt to put to rest the questions that his exposure on Mount Cithareon raised, and the doubts that plague the mind of Jocasta?

Drawing on Sheila Murnaghan, Tyrrell and Bennett explain Antigone's assertion that husbands are replaceable with reference to the Periclean law requiring that both parents be Athenian.[44] Tyrrell and Bennett suggest that Antigone is responding to the argument between Haemon and Creon, in which Creon asserts to his son, in a remark that is demeaning to Antigone, that there are other fields to plow (RS 114). The idea that Antigone is merely a field to plow posits her as nothing but a reproductive vessel, and suggests that another woman's reproductive capacity would be just as good. The remark is callous, to say the least, given that Haemon is betrothed to Antigone, who accordingly draws attention to the logic that reduces her to a replaceable furrow to be sown.[45] The image, which conjures up myths of autochthony, is not uncommon. As Loraux notes, "in marriage as on the tragic stage, woman is a field to be worked, a furrow to be sown."[46] Antigone's argument responds in a way that distinguishes her from a mere "furrow," a mere channel of earth, essentially identical to any other furrow. Her argument, and the fact that she makes one in and of itself distinguishes her from a furrow, drawing out the implicit logic behind the assumption Creon makes. That is, she draws attention to the replaceability of the men who, according to the image, sow the seeds. If it is demeaning to reduce women to potential wives who can be sown with male seeds, and to thereby eclipse their individuality, it is also problematic to reduce men to the sowers of such seeds. Yet this is precisely what Pericles' law does.

If we read Antigone's definition of a husband as consonant with this, as Murnaghan does when she points out that Antigone defines a husband "not as the unchanging identity of a specific individual but as an abstract role that could be played by several different men," then it is not Antigone who is callous (as she is sometimes interpreted), but the prevailing view embedded in the acceptance of the Periclean law outlining the requirements for citizenship.[47] Creon echoes this view, combining it with his deliberate occlusion of any affective bond that might tie Haemon, his son, to Antigone, his niece, to one another. The

Periclean law treats both men and women as bearers of Athenian heritage, and nothing else. As Tyrrell and Bennett observe: "From the viewpoint of marriage as an institution, one husband is as satisfactory as another. This is a rationale behind Pericles' law on citizenship of 451 B.C.: the *dêmos* cares nothing for the emotional bonds in marriage but only that the man and the woman be Athenians" (RS 114). Still drawing on Murnaghan, Tyrrell and Bennett go on to cite Pericles' Thucydidean funeral oration, which they identify as expressing the same idea. If this is the "rationale behind Pericles' law on citizenship of 451 B.C.," Tyrrell and Bennett remark, it also expresses the "conception of marriage in the Thucydidean funeral oration" (RS 114). Glossing Murnaghan, Tyrrell and Bennett show how the Periclean law posits husbands as substitutable for one another. As long as they are Athenian, the specificity of individuals is unimportant: "[P]arents do not have children solely for their own benefit; from the viewpoint of the *polis* and its orator, they have them for the city's salvation. The *polis* needs warriors for its defense; in this respect, individuals are interchangeable, replaceable" (RS 114). This idea of interchangeable warriors reflects the ideal of a uniform wall of soldiers, in which a wall of shields makes it difficult, if not impossible, to distinguish one soldier from another, one individual from another. If one soldier falls in the line of battle, another one steps up to replace him. In the words of Tyrrell and Bennett, "one hoplite is as good as another as long as the city has hoplites to defend it" (RS 115). The idea of warriors defending the city as being interchangeable is also maintained in burial practices for soldiers. On "the third day of the public funeral . . . the individual dead lost their separate identities to be buried together in chests organized by the tribes of the city whose interests they died aiding" (RS 115). Both Pericles' law and burial practices reflect the indistinguishability of warriors. If Antigone's burial of her brother works to subvert this indistinguishability, her refusal to marry Haemon works to subvert the indistinguishability of women as furrows. Given the peculiarity of her situation, however, it does more than that. It also subverts the expectation that she transfer her dead father's property to her nearest male relative.

As Ormand observes that "the *epiklēros* was a woman whose father died without male heirs. According to Athenian law, such a woman was required to marry her nearest male relative beginning with her father's side, to whom she would then transfer her father's property . . . the law defined a basic patriarchal principle: when no male heirs exist, the woman preserves the paternal line of her original *oikos*. . . . the paternal line is preserved through the daughter. . . . The married woman lives under a divided *kurieia*."[48] Antigone's public defiance of Creon, in the wake of the death of her father and two brothers, and her suicide, constitute a refusal of this divided loyalty. Antigone will submit to no one's authority but her own. She will not be permanently transferred to Creon's household. Given Oedipus's stateless, vagabond state, it is doubtful that she would have been guardian of any property in any case. In the light of Mader's reading, Antigone works to distinguish Polynices from a potential marriage partner (her rationale for burying her brother as brother, and nothing else, distinguishes him from any other symbolic function that he might have occupied due to Oedipus's incest). In turn, her burial of Polynices puts her in the position of both flouting Creon's authority as her *kurios*, and refusing to marry Haemon, now the closest remaining male relative.

In specifying the importance of burying her brother as a brother, not only as a unique individual, but as a philos, as a member of her own family, Antigone is reclaiming the individuality of her brother as one who died defending his right to rule Thebes—as a member of the Oedipal family, that is, as the son of a father whose actions have inadvertently thrown into confusion the logic of inheritance that pertain in this particular family. There are several levels at which Antigone's attempt to assert the uniqueness of her brother operates. Polynices is not merely a military actor acting on a political belief, he is also a philos. He might be construed by Creon as a traitor (although that judgment is debateable, given that Eteocles has violated the agreement the two brothers had made to share leadership of Thebes), but he is also Antigone's brother. That is, he is a member of her family, and as such, Antigone is exercising her right, as a familial member, as Tyrrell and Bennett express it, to bury her brother, even if the judgment that he is a traitor were to be accepted. The right, Tyrrell and Bennett suggest, is one that Athenians would have accepted.

As Mader points out, Antigone is also resurrecting the symbolic familial functions that Oedipus has confused. At the same time Antigone asserts her right as philos to bury her brother no matter how his attack on his brother is construed, or how disloyal his actions might prove to be with regard to Thebes, the symbolic other/mirror image of Athens. Moreover, Antigone's act of burial also raises an unstated question about the logic according to which slaves can defend a city as soldiers, from whom they are excluded at the level of political participation. Are warriors, as warriors, truly interchangeable? How far does their interchangeability extend, if they can substitute for one another on the battlefield, but not as actors in the political demos?[49] The fact that Creon accuses Haemon of being "a woman's slave" indicates not only, as Ormand suggests, that he is reiterating his denial of "Antigone's sexual dominion over his son," nor can its significance necessarily be reduced to "a stock characterization."[50] Even if it qualifies as stock characterization, it is surely worth asking how it attained such popularity, and what its underlying significance is. If the Periclean law concerning citizenship is understood in the context of its impact in defining who was a slave and who was not, and if Creon's reference to Antigone's replaceability, as just one among many furrows to be plowed, is read as a reference to Pericles' law, his reference to Haemon acting as a slave of Antigone might also be read as a reference to the ramifications of that law, which directly impacted the determination of who was designated a slave and who was not.

If Tyrrell and Bennett's illuminating reading not only establishes the sense in which Sophocles' representation of Antigone can be read as a response to Pericles' law on citizenship (though it does not elaborate how this scene has implications for slavery), it is also helpful in pointing to how *Antigone* stages the transition that virgin women, on marrying, would have been expected to effect into womanhood, since the young Antigone's symbolic marriage to Hades is not a transition to a new life, a new future, but cuts off her life as it couples her with death. Antigone, as Tyrrell and Bennett put it, "has undergone a transition, dying as her old self as Jocasta's daughter to be reborn as a new self as Hades' bride. The virgin daughter and the married woman have different perspectives" (RS 115).[51] However, as I have suggested, Antigone's marriage to death might extinguish her own life, her own future, but it also embodies a political principle, the legacy of which future generations have inherited, as when Antigone is reborn in a new context that transposes her challenge to Creon in a way that enables her legacy to live on.[52] Playwrights have taken up the inspiration of Antigone, not as unambiguously liberatory, but in a way that attends to some of the complexities that define her position in relation to slavery and colonialism, even as they take up these questions in another historical context—or in multiple historical contexts.

What happens, then, if we expand Mader's approach to a play in which the contest between Antigone and Creon is reborn, where the contested terms of their dispute no longer adhere to those specified by Hegel (kinship or family versus state) or Lacan (symbolic realm versus social order), a context in which Antigone's protest acquires a metaphorical resonance for those fighting racial oppression, one that brings to light the issues surrounding slavery that have lain dormant, for the most part, in interpretations of Sophocles' text? Taking into account Tyrrell and Bennett's understanding of Antigone's burial of Polynices as a refusal of the interchangeability embedded in both Pericles' citizenship law and in the burial practices pertaining to soldiers, her act becomes legible not only as disambiguating the symbolic, familial functions that Oedipus had conflated, but also as insisting on the uniqueness and irreplaceability of Polynices in another sense. Polynices is not just one citizen of many, he is not just one soldier of many; his role is irreducible to the duty expected of male citizens to defend the city. He is also a brother to Antigone, and in his capacity as such, a bearer of kinship ties, which themselves must be observed in support of the very political structures that Creon seeks to defend. By failing to acknowledge the importance of the disambiguation Antigone seeks to perform, and the dependence of the shape of the polis on the bonds of philia that she enacts, Creon undercuts his own claim to act with authority as king, and in doing so ultimately destroys his own family, his own kin, bringing his familial line to an end.[53]

In construing Jones as a marriage partner, Tègònni calls into question the racial taboo that mandates against interracial marriage. In doing so she calls for a future in which the legacy of colonial history is overcome. To marry outside one's race is to call for a future where skin color is not determined by history. Of course, the call will fall on deaf ears, in one sense, as the play culminates in violence; and yet this mythical future remains in tact in another sense, signaled by the dreamlike departure of Tègònni, Antigone, and Yemoja. In Òsófisan's play Tègònni brings into question the racial taboo that prohibits black, Nigerian colonial subjects marrying white British colonizing subjects. Is there a law that Antigone might be said to insist upon in this dramatic political context? Is it a law that Antigone enunciates or represents, or is it rather a practice that she incites? Is it a relation that she embodies to the state, a relation of renewal and rejuvenation, of hope?

I suggest that Antigone's impact is not limited to exposing "the socially contingent character of kinship" but that the history of appropriations of *Antigone* also exposes the socially contingent character of laws under apartheid, or that of postcolonial practices. If Sophocles' Antigone conspires with the commonplace Athenian denigration of slaves, Osófisan holds her accountable for such denigration, as he raises the question of her complicity in European colonial legacies. In calling for a renewal of the political that is not premised on apartheid, or for a future that is not determined by the history of colonialism and imperialism in plays such as *The Island* or *Tègònni*, Antigone precisely throws into crisis, in Butler's words, the "reigning regimes of representation," but such regimes are not limited to prevailing kinship structures.[54] Rather, they extend to the racially inflected regimes that inform postcolonial relations or the hierarchies that structure apartheid regimes. Both Butler and Lacan tend to conflate the legitimacy of the symbolic with the existence of the incest prohibition—or with its violation. Yet what if the origin/possibility of the symbolic is bound up with racial taboos?

A Story to Pass On? Antigone's Mythological African Sister, Tègònni

In violating a racist taboo against miscegenation, a taboo that has all the trappings of colonial ideology, Tègònni (Antigone's double) disrupts two very different traditions, both of which oppose her marriage to Captain Allan Jones (the metaphorical equivalent of Sophocles' Haemon). On the one hand there is the tradition to which Isokun refers, and on the other hand there is that to which Governor Carter-Ross (the metaphorical equivalent of Sophocles' Creon) appeals. Isokun thinks Tègònni will be making a "tragic error" (T 22) in marrying the District Officer, and wants Tègònni to find a husband "among us, among her own people" (T 20). He points out that "It's never been heard of, that a woman of our land, and a princess at that, would go and marry one of those ghosts from across the seas (T 21), and that "No one here accepts it, except . . . her friends" (T 22). In terms of kinship lines, Isokun represents a traditional view, advocating racial closure. At the same time, he supports Tègònni in her quest to become the first female carver, and encourages her to petition Jones. Isokun wants to preserve the racial homogeneity of his own people as a basis for a cultural identity, which, however, is not based on an atavistic ideal, but which is rather open to progressive influences. His reason for wanting Tègònni to marry among her own has to do with carving (excuse the pun) out a cultural identity that submits neither to colonialism, nor to an allegedly pure, idealized cultural tradition that preceded colonial oppression.

If Isokun wants Tègònni to remain among her own, rather than marrying a foreign invader, Governor Carter-Ross sees Jones's act as an inappropriate act of insubordination that flies in the face of everything he has been working for. Here is what he says to Jones: "You thought you were being a fucking hero, didn't you! You'll marry a nigger woman and show us all! Teach us a lesson perhaps on the equality of races! Rebuild the world with your penis! . . . You want to undo, in one single day, the work it took me years to accomplish here! Undermine our authority! And you think I'd let you!" (T 120–21). Accordingly, Carter-Ross arranges for the corpse of Tègònni's brother to block the path of the wedding celebrants, who are prevented from reaching the palace, where they intended to honor the grave of Tègònni's late father, Oba (Oedipus), as was the custom (see T 45). As a result, Tègònni's wedding day is cursed. Prince Oyekunle (Haemon), who was killed in battle defending his people against the British, must remain unburied by order of the Governor. Just as Sophocles' Antigone buries Polynices, so Tègònni insists on burying her brother, and is arrested for doing so. Her wedding is thereby effectively disrupted.

In putting her love for Jones above her loyalty to her own people—or perhaps in looking to a future that sees beyond racial divisiveness—and in putting aside any misgivings she might have about marrying a "ghost from across the seas," Tègònni acts on her belief, in Yemisi's words, that "he was always different" (T 46) from other white men. As Kunbi says, he "decided to do what other white men have never done—he went and paid the dowry!" (T 45–6). Unlike others "who fought their wars in the beds of our women," he "was polite and gentle" (T 46); he respected the traditions of the people in whose country he was living.

In her desire to see beyond the racial divisions created by colonialism, Tègònni decides to marry Jones; her desire is also a desire for peace, for an end to the war; for the "whiteman" in Kunbi's words to be an "ally" rather than an "invader" and "antagonist" (T 22). If the aggression of colonialism was justified by the assumption that the British knew what was in the best interests of the Nigerians better than they did themselves, it was also buttressed by the assumption of the inherent inferiority of black-skinned peoples. Hence the racial taboos against whites marrying blacks. When Tègònni decides to marry

Jones, she brings into question the validity of such racial taboos, and at the same time affirms herself as equal to Jones. In effect, she contests the law that dictates that neither whites nor blacks should marry outside their race, but only inside, positing a new law that affirms the right to marry across racial boundaries, irrespective of skin color. Rather than reaffirming a prohibition that had been violated, as is the case with Sophocles' Antigone, when, on Mader's reading, she invokes the law that Oedipus had transgressed, Tègònni brings into question the validity of a racial taboo that prohibits marriage across racial lines. She acts in such a way as to discredit such racial prohibitions, and the social hierarchies from which they stem, hierarchies that might originate from British colonialism, but which African tribal leaders have exploited.

In the program notes to the 1994 production of *Tègònni* at Emory University in Atlanta, Georgia, Òsófisan highlights the way in which the apartheid regime in South Africa was used by the political leadership of other African nations as a diversion to mask the corruption of their own regimes. He observes that the "struggle against South Africa's apartheid" served as a "smokescreen to mask th[e] . . . villainies" of African leadership, which, he says, "kept our people in abject misery, easy prey to diseases and natural disasters, while, without compunction, they sent ambassadors everywhere to beg for aid" (T 8). Citing the influence of "foreign multinational business interests" (T 8), and widespread corruption of democratic processes, Òsófisan states that "the fight for freedom remains a concrete, and burning, issue for our deprived populations" and he calls on "the world to listen" (T 9). Òsófisan wants to add his voice "to the millions of other small voices in Africa, all shouting unheard and pleading to be set free—voices that are waiting desperately for help from friends in the free world" (T 10). *Tègònni* is written, then, as an appeal to "friends," those in the international community in a position to listen and respond to the plight of the poverty-stricken people of Nigeria. It is worth remembering, in the context of this appeal, the Sophoclean Antigone's appeal to *philia*, an appeal that has stepped beyond the pages of the ancient Greek tragedy that Sophocles named *Antigone*, to reach, among others, African dramatists and their audiences in the late twentieth century. In the absence of democracy and in the presence of corrupt military regimes that threaten the viability of his country in the 1990s, Òsófisan turns for inspiration to the "story of Antigone" (T 10).

When Antigone arrives on the scene in Òsófisan's *Tègònni*, she is late. Having traveled "a very long way, through the channels of history," traversing a road that "at many points is unsafe" (T 25), she arrives with bodyguards, and asks, "Has the play started? . . . we hurried as fast as we could. We wanted to catch the beginning" (T 25). While the play appears to have begun without her, the form that it takes is in fact predicated on her very existence as a literary figure who refuses to be confined to the annals of history. In one sense, the story that is told in *Tègònni* is one more variation of Antigone's myth, and in this sense, it owes its shape to the lasting impact her character has had in its multiple "incarnations" (T 26).[55] Yet *Tègònni* is neither reducible to Sophocles' *Antigone*—"a story goes on, no matter when one arrives in it" (T 28)—nor to its rich historical and performative legacy. If *Tègònni* takes its place in a long tradition of interpretative drama that has turned for inspiration to ancient Greek tragedy, and to *Antigone* in particular, it is at the same time just as firmly embedded in the history of British colonialism and European imperialism, which prepared the ground for the series of military dictatorships that dominated the political landscape of Nigeria at the end of the twentieth century. Of course, insofar as the champions of colonialism are convinced of their inherent superiority to the natives they conquer, and are thus able to rationalize their actions by reference to their civilizing influence, they are content to emphasize the continuity between the achievements of the golden age of fifth century BCE Athens, and their own cultural supremacy. As the British Governor puts it,

> I grew up in an age when certain things were taken for granted. We did not need to write the rules down, everybody knew what you had to do, and the options were simple. You came with the gun in one hand, and the whip in the other. You barked out orders, and you punished summarily. You knew you were right, because you were white, and you believed in the Cross and in the Empire. You hammered the Union Jack down their throats, and made them sing "God Save the Queen"! For if you didn't do that, they would quickly resort to barbarism, to cannibalism, to living like apes. (T 133)

Bayo, a colonial priest, sees things rather differently, pointing out that the implacable belief of the British in their civilization is undermined by their means of securing power: "Yes, you've built an Empire, as you boast to us. You've conquered our people. But so what? That's the power of guns not of civilization. Any brute with a gun can give orders!" (T 55).

Òsófisan employs a framing device at the opening of the play in order to introduce one of the mainstays structuring the colonial history of Africa, namely the question of race relations. The question arises in terms of which actors are available to play the parts of certain characters in the ensuing drama, the beginning of which has been delayed due to the fact that the director has been unable to find any white actors for the roles of the British Governor Carter-Ross, his Aide-de-camp (ADC), and his district officer or DO, Allan Jones. Impatient to have the play underway, an actor volunteers his services, only to be rejected by the director because he doesn't have a white skin. Using the occasion as an opportunity to introduce a question about the status of theatre vis-à-vis realism, Òsófisan has the actor retort to the director, "But use your imagination, man! Theatre is all about illusion, isn't it?" (T 14). When the director acquiesces to this idea, the actor presses his advantage, and Òsófisan makes the actor complicit in his solicitation of the audience's cooperation: "All is illusion here, and everyone in the audience has come to play his or her own part in a dream. And dreams are where anything can happen. So give me a costume, anything to mark me out from the others, and this evening's dream begins" (T 14). At the same time as thematizing the illusory, dreamlike, utopian quality of theatre—a quality that the political realities of Nigeria's colonial legacy that Òsófisan sets out to explore belie, even as the play sounds a note of resistance to this legacy—the actor's observation draws attention to the arbitrary status of skin color as a signifier of racial oppression. If "anything"—a costume, a wig—can serve to "mark" him off from the others, so that the costume or wig becomes a symbol signifying his race, then skin color no longer seems to retain its over-determined significance in relation to racial signification. If racial signification can be displaced from the skin onto a wig in a play, then perhaps a similar displacement can occur in "real life." While the displacement of racial signifiers in and of itself does not necessarily dislodge the power of racial discrimination, it does make it much more difficult to attribute racial signification to inherent traits, by suggesting that race is a phenomenon that becomes attached to socially agreed-upon conventions. Yet the over-determination of race by skin color proves not to be as easy to dislodge as the actor might have hoped. Accordingly, myths of racial disparities, such as the one Tègònni invokes when she ironically exclaims to the governor "How can I be black and intelligent! You're slipping?" (T 81) are not as easily dispelled as we might have hoped, resting, as they tend to do, on deeply embedded assumptions about the natural inferiority of some races in relations to others.

Once the costumes manager has handed wigs to the actors who are to play the white characters, the governor, the ADC, and the DO, the dream can begin to unfold, but not before another actor receives her wig: Antigone. Òsófisan thus sets up the encounter between Antigone and the friends and sisters of *Tègònni* as one in which their expectation that the color of Antigone's skin be white can be thwarted. In a moment that conforms to the historical over-determination of race by skin color—a moment that will, however, once again be deflected, Kunbi exclaims to Antigone "But you . . . you're black!" (T 26). Having been prepared in advance by Òsófisan's framing device, the audience is already in on the secret, as it were. On cue, then, Antigone laughingly reacts to the suggestion that she must be an "imposter" because she is black (T 26) by posing the question, "What colour is mythology?" (T 27). Harking back to the opening scene of the play, in which a black actor has insisted on the need to use your imagination in the theatre, Antigone's crew chimes in, "We always come in the colour and the shape of your imagination" (T 27). As the play proceeds it becomes clear that Antigone and her entourage have taken part in many other plays, also inspired by Sophocles' Antigone: they have taken on many different hues throughout the ages. Having transcended the particulars of Sophocles' play, Antigone and her crew thus come to take part in a script that is "well rehearsed . . . the story we rehearsed, as it's happened at other times, in other places" (T 29).

Taking advantage of her status as both inside and outside of the play, as a mythological figure who comes from elsewhere, and yet one who has come to take part in Tègònni's story, Antigone plays the role of director at times, moving in and out of her part.[56] She tells her bodyguards that they may as well play the soldiers of the Hausa constabulary, since they are already dressed for the part, and anyway they've been well rehearsed. For the most part, the soldiers obediently play the roles assigned to them, adopting a characterization reminiscent of the metaphorical stand-ins for Nazi guards in Anouilh's *Antigone*, repeatedly uttering the refrain that "orders are orders." Yet if the soldiers in Anouilh's *Antigone*, in Ismene's words, "do exactly as they've been told, without caring about right or wrong," the bodyguards playing the solidiers in *Tègònni* object to playing soldiers, as the following exchange reveals:[57]

> 2ND SOL: You've got to find us another role. This one's no fun at all!
>
> ANTIGONE: You're tired of being soldiers?
>
> 4TH SOL: Demoralised. All we do is carry corpses.
>
> 2ND SOL: Or build execution platforms—
>
> 4TH SOL: Or terrorise people—
>
> 2ND SOL: Burn and plunder houses—
>
> 4TH SOL: Collect bribes!
>
> 3RD SOL: We're so ashamed! Is this all that soldiers do in this country?
>
> 2ND SOL: Not even one act you could call humane?

Unlike Anouilh, whose portrait of the soldiers remains true to Arendt's well-known analysis of Eichmann as succumbing to the "banality of evil," Òsófisan uses Antigone's crew to pass judgment on the excesses and injustices of colonial rule.[58] Yet at the same time, since Jones and Carter-Ross are played by black actors, the audience is encouraged to see the African leaders of the 1990s as mimicking the abuses of colonialism.

Òsófisan's Antigone becomes a critical commentator on the impact that her mythological character has had throughout the ages. In her meta-theatrical role, she takes it upon herself to test the mettle of Tègònni. The exchange that follows articulates one of the central issues at stake in this work, namely how and whether those who have suffered injustices can avoid perpetrating new injustices in their own turn, thereby perpetuating a cycle of oppression. In suggesting that even if Sophocles' Antigone condones slavery, the history of appropriations of *Antigone*, including Òsófisan's, interrogates such complicity, I am calling for this history to be read as one that brings into question and reworks both Antigone's abject status, and her abjection of slavery. The history of appropriations of *Antigone* calls for a freedom that is not premised on the subjugation of others. Similarly, Òsófisan's play celebrates Antigone as a figure whose rebirth throughout the ages keeps alive the hope of freedom, even in the face of implacable obstacles. Antigone declares that "Freedom is a myth," insisting that "Human beings throw off their yokes, only for themselves to turn into oppressors" (T 125). Tègònni retorts: You say freedom is a myth. But where do you think we'd be without such myths? . . . Freedom is an undying faith, the force which underwrites our presence here on earth, as human beings. When we lose that faith, we die!" (T 125). To this, Antigone responds: "Come, my sister, embrace me! I was testing you. And now I find you're a true believer, like me! Yes, it is true that many tyrants have marched through history. That for a while, people have been deprived of their freedom. But oppression can never last. Again and again it will be overthrown, and people will reclaim their right to be free!" (T 125). This assertion will itself be tested when at the end of the play shots ring out, and the violence of force appears to win the day against freedom. Yet the bond that unites Antigone and Tègònni, making of them sisters across the ages of history, is one that ensures that Antigone and Tègònni will "rise again" (see T 127 and 147), and that the spirit of freedom, on which neither of them—despite being tested—will renege, lives on. Even if Antigone dies each time she enters the stage, her story lives on.[59] In the epilogue of the play, despite the fact that Tègònni has been shot, both Tègònni and Antigone sail off with the Yoruba water goddess, Yemoja—with whom Antigone had arrived at the beginning of the play. We are reminded of the dreamlike quality of theatre to which our attention had been drawn at the beginning of the play, and in which we had become complicitous. Anything can happen in a play.

Antigone attests that "There's only one Antigone," only to concede a couple of lines later that "Antigone belongs to several incarnations" (T 26). As the play proceeds, we are offered a way of understanding the tension involved in sustaining these two claims, as the singular spirit of freedom Antigone embodies refuses to be quelled, and is rather reincarnated with each rebirth of the play, including Òsófisan's *Tègònni*. As a character in a story that is both her own, and not her own, Òsófisan's Antigone is able to reflect on how and why Sophocles' Antigone has lent her name to so many struggles, in so many epochs. The promise that both her character and that of Tègònni's hold out is that many more Antigones are to come. Of course, this also implies that there will be many more threats to freedom. Yet each time an oppressive regime comes to power, an Antigone—whether it is under her own name or under another name—will rise again to call its abuses into question.

Tègònni engages at least three different time frames, that of Sophocles' "story of Antigone," the "British colonization of Nigeria and the defeat of [Òsófisan's] ancestors" in the late nineteenth century, and finally the imperialist exploitation of late twentieth-century Nigeria by Western powers such as Britain, Germany, and France, who "lend support to military dictatorship, just as long as their vast economic interest in oil exploration, telecommunications, the construction industry, and so forth are protected" (T 10). While Òsófisan sets the play in colonial Nigeria, drawing on the "well-known format of Sophocles' *Antigone*," his main concern is the "problem of political freedom" in Nigeria at the time he writes the play, in the 1990s (T 11). Straddling twentieth-century and nineteenth-century Nigeria, *Tègònni* comments on the abuses of power committed by imperial Britain on the one hand and those of African leaders on the other hand. The play contrasts the assumption of rights by British subjects with the complete absence of rights for colonial subjects (see T 120). At the same time it decries the maltreatment of its own people by corrupt, military regimes. Isokun, the official town poet in *Tègònni*, exclaims "Tell me, what cruelties have we not inflicted on ourselves, we black people, as agents in service of others!" (T 108).

The triple referentiality of the play's historical frames allows Òsófisan to engage the figure of Antigone in their interplay. When Antigone suggests that it is her story that is being told, Yemisi responds, "Your story! Sorry, you're mistaken. This is the story of *Tègònni*, our sister. Funny, the names sound almost the same . . ." (T 25). Neither *Tègònni* nor Antigone is Sophocles' Antigone, but both of them are inspired by her, a fact that Òsófisan problematizes even as he draws on the Antigone of Greek mythology. As Yemisi contests Antigone's assumption that it is her story, insisting that it is in fact *Tègònni*'s story, Òsófisan confronts the question of how a postcolonial nation fosters a culture that is neither a mere repetition of its colonial heritage, nor merely a reactive rejection of it. The story is familiar enough—theorists such as Homi Bhabha and Frantz Fanon are among those to have exposed the dangers of anticolonialism, when it appeals to an inert, fossilized, atavistic politics in an attempt to resist the excesses of colonialism. While colonial powers justify their subordination and exploitation of colonies by maintaining that they represent a civilizing influence (a view that can only be maintained on the basis of a highly selective account of its own dynamic), there is a tendency for anticolonial forces to formulate versions of their national identity that require less privileged members of the polity to play the role of stabilizing forces of purity. As often as not, as Uma Narayan and Gayatri Chakravorty Spivak, among others, have shown, this burden falls disproportionately on women, who are expected to safeguard mythical, imaginary versions of a national culture that are themselves called into being largely in reaction to Western imperialism, but which are celebrated as if they represented a return to some pristine, authentic, precolonial national identity, which was violated and disrupted by the invasion of colonial powers.

In these terms, the attempts by the elders, including Bayo and Isokun, to persuade Tègònni to apologize for defying orders by burying her brother, Oyekunle (symbolic equivalent of Polynices), against the orders of Carter-Jones, the British colonial Governor, can be seen as a measure of their successful inculcation of colonial ideology. The efforts of the elders to bring Tègònni and her supporters back into line are met with the following refusal by her sister, Kunbi: "After surrendering our land, they want us to surrender our spirit too into the bargain" (T 90). Inasmuch as Butler interrogates the assumptions that tend to operate as necessary prerequisites in Hegel or Lacan's schemata, she takes up the challenge Antigone effects in her refusal to be circumscribed by any Hegelian or Lacanian grid. Even as Butler seeks to bring into question attempts to explain *Antigone* that adhere to the oppositional terms kinship/state, or symbolic/social, she nonetheless accords a certain privilege to these terms—and therefore to the philosophical and psychoanalytic Western tradition from which she draws them—in her very insistence that Antigone raises the question of their adequacy. In exposing the limits of the systematic theories Hegel and Lacan erect, Antigone also calls for a renewal, or a rethinking of the political assumptions that have consolidated themselves in such a way as to inform these theories as necessary points of departure, and in doing so have made themselves unavailable for questioning. Yet there remains the question of what is foreclosed by Hegel, Lacan, and—insofar as she adheres to their terms of reference—even Butler.

As excluded from, but necessitated by, the regime of colonialism, Tègònni rises up to change her status, and in doing so, she challenges and rewrites the law that prohibits her marriage to Jones. As such she calls for a future not specified by racial taboos, not determined by a conflictual racial past, a future in which the invisible racial taboos that structure incest taboos comes to the fore, which is a condition for their overcoming. As long as they remain tacit, unspoken, invisible, and as long as the suffering they promote remains unseen, such racial taboos remain resistant to change, as the hidden condition of incest prohibitions, and the hidden condition of the kind of (white) psychoanalytic theory that writes them out of its technical apparatus, while secretly appealing to them.

Tègònni explores the way in which women are caught up on the one hand in the traditional expectations of their culture, and on the other hand in the burdens of colonialism: "To slave for husbands—is our fate! Their burdens—are ours too! If you accept—it's trouble! If you refuse—it's trouble!" (T 71) In this context, the fact that Tègònni is the first woman to have joined the guild of casters takes on a great deal of significance. She has led the way, and encouraged other women to follow in her footsteps. The masks that she and her fellow carvers produce play a crucial role in the action; Tègònni's sisters, and friends, Kunbi, Yemisi, and Faderera disguise themselves behind bronze masks, confusing and frightening the soldiers, who try to dismiss their "juju" (T 109). The masks have a particular significance, since Tègònni was the "first woman to join guild of bronze casters" (T 39), at a time where to be a "Caster of Bronze" was "a trade formerly unknown to women" (T 42). As Faderera says, Tègònni had "helped train other women, so that we now have our own Women's Guild of Carvers and Casters" (T 78). The relationship between Tègònni and her sisters is therefore established as one of trust and solidarity, Tègònni having broken tradition by learning the craft of casting in bronze, and having passed on her craft to other women. Metaphorically, the kind of relationship Tègònni has with her female sisters and friends is echoed by the relationship that develops between Antigone and Tègònni. Unlike the relationship between Ismene and Antigone in Sophocles' *Antigone*, Tègònni's sisters and friends are unhesitating in their support of Tègònni from the beginning. It is as if they have the benefit of having learned from Ismene's change of heart.

Tègònni is punished for burying her brother against the orders of the British colonial Governor, while the character named Antigone, having transcended the particulars of Sophocles' play, comes to take part in a script that, "is the story we rehearsed, as it's happened at other times, in other places" (T 29).[60]

It is not enough to observe that Antigone marks the limits of intelligibility of a particular system that would seek to contain her; in marking those limits, she exposes the system itself as unintelligible. Her very unintelligibility for the system becomes a signal that demands a rethinking of the system itself. Taken to its limits, an analysis of that which is cast out of a system as unthinkable within its current topos, that from which the system nonetheless profits, even as it refuses proper, symbolic representation to that which it casts out, must address the ways in which a system, a text, or a theatrical performance inscribes within it certain reference points that function as inscrutable, unreadable signs from the perspective of the system or text itself. Yet when read as a symptom of precisely what such systems or texts render illegible within their own terms, these signs are no longer illegible, opaque stumbling blocks; they become legible as they open up new vantage points from which to read the text, which now appears to be orchestrated in terms of a series of foreclosures, repudiations, or disavowals that preempt the meaningful protestation of that which is foreclosed or disavowed. If certain forms of kinship relations are repudiated in advance through the positing of a hierarchical relationship that must of necessity obtain, an ordering that assumes the authority of the state over not just any family but a family configured in a particular way, one which is organized according to a heteronormative and reproductive imperative, and if Antigone must be excised because she does not answer to the requirements of that system, Antigone becomes a site of tension and instability for the system. As such she can be taken up as a device for unsettling distinctions and hierarchies that tragic theory has tended to treat as invulnerable, as inscribed in the very nature of things. In this way Antigone serves as a revolutionary figure.

While kinship remains an important reference point for Sophocles' Antigone, and for many of his prominent Western commentators, not the least of whom is Hegel, it has not always been the focal point for dramatists who have found inspiration in the figure of Antigone. Or rather the ways in which kinship has raised questions around race, and what Orlando Patterson has called social death—the erasure of the existing kinship ties of slaves. Antigone rises again and again, in different contexts, in diverse guises, often embodying an irrepressible spirit of freedom. Indeed, we might say that in recent times whenever and wherever a political regime threatens the obliteration of freedom, there, as often as not, a dramatist or poet will turn to Antigone for inspiration. I say in recent times, because at least up until the seventeenth century, tragedy was taken not just as a representation of nature, but as nature itself, insofar as, in the words of Reiss, "the proper order of tragedy, of mind, and of the world" is assumed to be one and the same.[61] If tragedy has been transformed into a literature of resistance in its modernist guise, this was far from being the case for Dryden, for whom it provided a model, an ideal for social order, and who therefore conferred upon the tragedian the task of heightening the beauty of nature, while hiding its "deformities"—such was the educational function of tragedy, the purpose of which was to maintain proper order.[62] Of course, as Reiss points out, "The 'real situations' of which we take tragedy" to make sense "do not precede tragedy: they come into existence with it."[63] There is no preexisting order in itself: in its referentiality each tragedy represents a particular historical and political moment, and in doing so it might impart a certain necessity to the interpretation of the situation it explores through the syntax of tragedy—especially if it partakes in a realist aesthetic. Yet it remains an interpretation, albeit a realist one. In this sense Reiss can claim that "*Tragedy is a discursive process that creates order and makes it possible to ascribe meaning to that order.*"[64]

What then becomes of the tragic form once, as Reiss puts it, "there is no more *need* for tragedy?"[65] Reiss suggests that tragedy is no longer needed because for us, inheritors of modernity that we are, the tragic has been transformed from the realm of the discursive, where it constituted one literary means, among others, of making sense of things, to the realm of "everyday parlance," where "To say something is 'tragic' is a means of recuperating a situation that would otherwise remain unaccountable, of relating it to the known. We have transferred the idea of the tragic from the realm of discourse into that of the real. We have made the tragic a piece of reality."[66] To invoke the tragic as descriptive of events such as Columbine, 9/11, Katrina, or the BP oil spill in the gulf of Mexico, is to acknowledge them as catastrophic in some sense, but at the same time it can be a way of situating these events in such a way as to render them anodyne, precisely by clarifying that they are out of the ordinary, that they are exceptions to the normal run of things, and that therefore we can be justified in our everyday expectations that events like this will not usually happen. It can be a means of rendering them explicable precisely by situating them as inexplicable, in a way that obfuscates responsibility for them, as if there were not decisions and policies in place that led up to and contributed to these "tragedies" (lax gun laws, a long history of irresponsible and unjust foreign policy, a failure to properly oversee the erection of levy walls, a completely inept federal response in the wake of Katrina, a lack of safety precautions in oil drilling).[67] This latter use of the term tragedy suggests that its hypostasization in the realm of the everyday is less an indication that tragedy has become known to us in the form of the tragic, and that therefore we have no further need of it as an art form, than a sign that that which takes some of us by surprise is the result of all-too-predictable events for others. The tragedy, then, lies, not only in the event named tragic itself, but also in the failures of responsibility that have led up to it, failures that result not so much from aberrations as they do from permanent features of social structures and institutionalized attitudes about how valuable the lives of some people are in relation to the worth of others.

5

Agamben, Antigone, Irigaray

The Fetishistic Ruses of Sovereignty in Contemporary Politics

> What Antigone supports, shores up, is the operation of the law . . . by confronting the discourse that lays down the law she makes manifest that subterranean supporting structure that she is preserving, that other "face" of discourse that causes a crisis, when it appears in broad daylight. Whence her being sent off to death, her "burial" . . . Must one see in that penalty the effects of a historical era? Or the *constituent necessities of rationality?* In what respect are these latter causing a problem at the present time, and even provoking a crisis?[1]

If, as Michel Foucault suggests, the operation of power should no longer be framed in terms of state, sovereignty, and the law, but rather in terms of biopolitics and technologies of the self, Antigone's conflict with Creon might seem to have lost its relevance to the modern democratic state.[2] Yet if Giorgio Agamben is right to suggest that "the juridico-institutional and the biopolitical models of power . . . cannot be separated" and if "the inclusion of bare life in the political realm constitutes the original—if concealed—nucleus of sovereign power," we cannot afford to neglect the processes by which sovereignty seeks to maintain itself, as illusory as the fictions of sovereignty might prove to be.[3] Neither has it escaped notice that the progressive abandonment of the rule of law in the United States under George Bush's presidency was accompanied by an extraordinary concentration of executive power, to the point where the safeguards intended to be guaranteed by constitutional separation of powers, like so much else under his administration, no longer seemed to retain their efficacy. This consolidation of power, while not perhaps identical with sovereign power, begins to look an awful lot like it. This in turn suggests an amendment to Agamben's rejoinder to Foucault.

Agamben cites Aristotle's distinction between the head of an estate (*oikonomos*) and the head of the family (*despotēs*) on the one hand, and the politician on the other hand.[4] This is the very distinction that Creon's relation to Antigone puts into question, since he is both her *kurios*, or guardian, and her king. It is the rigidity of this distinction between ruler of the household, or estate—which includes not only goods but also slaves—and the ruler of the polis that Agamben displaces when he locates in the differentiation between the two the hidden origin of the logic according to which those who are excluded from the polis and consigned to bare life are in a certain sense also incorporated into or included within the political.[5] Such a logic anticipates the transformation of politics into biopolitics, where the bare life of the subject comes to be administered not by the state, but by subjects themselves, through subjectivation.

By making the concentration camp the "hidden matrix," the "nomos" of the political space in which we are still living (HS 166), Agamben both remains beholden to narratives that insist on identifying Europe as the originating locus of our political and philosophical paradigms—as if Europe's trauma must be the foundational, orchestrating trauma—and at the same time declines any serious consideration of the gendered dynamics that underlie the separation of bare life from the proper forms of life as politically and ethically defined by Aristotle. This is despite the fact that the hallmark of the "simple natural life" that is "excluded from the *polis* in the strict sense" and "confined" to the "oikos, home" is reproduction (HS 2). Given that reproductive life is definitive of life understood as *zoē*, that is, "the simple fact of living common to all living beings (animals, men, or gods)," rather than life understood as "*bios*, which indicated the form or way of being proper to an individual or group" (HS 2) and given how crucial this differentiation becomes for understanding bare life, one might have expected the presuppositions that designated some individuals as only suitable for the administration of life in the home, while others were designated as suited for the political life of the community, to become a matter of interrogation. That is, one might have expected the assumptions about women and slaves that informed their confinement to the private sphere of the household, and their exclusion from participation in political life, to become a theme for investigation. One might have hoped for a critical interrogation of exactly why women and slaves were considered only fit for those aspects of life concerned with reproduction and subsistence, and unfit for political life. Yet no such interrogation is forthcoming from Agamben, who might appear to preclude such critical examination, precisely insofar as he constitutes bare life as that which is equated to animality, to the repetitive, cyclical, reproductive level of subsistence life, which is thus consigned to silence, of which there is nothing more to be said. Yet it is one thing to assign these characteristics to the private sphere of the oikos and quite another to refuse to interrogate the mechanisms by which some individuals are, by definition, consigned to this sphere of life, and some are—precisely in and through the confinement of some to it—freed from it. Indeed it might be said that the very "structure of the exception" that Agamben delineates, and the question he poses as to "why Western politics first constitutes itself through an exclusion (which is simultaneously an inclusion) of bare life" (HS 7) calls for and necessitates the interrogation of such mechanisms and assumptions.

The fact that those consigned to bare life, in ancient Greece women and more particularly slaves, left no written record of such life, renders all the more important Sophocles' inscription of the character Antigone and her public differentiation of her brother from a slave—a declaration that also differentiates herself from slaves. The lasting power of the figure of Antigone, a figure whose extraordinary inspiration lives on, lies not only in her own insistence upon being heard, but also in her failure to indict slavery, and in her implicit endorsement of it.

Insofar as Agamben acquiesces to the unquestioned centrality of Europe—and of the critically unexamined version of ancient Athens that is taken to be its precursor—as the originating matrix of conceptual and cultural meaning, Agamben joins in the uncritical glorification of the philosophical masterpieces of ancient Athens, construed as the crucible of European culture, but fails to confront the significance of the system of chattel slavery that afforded the philosophers and tragic poets the leisure to create their philosophical treatises and theatrical masterpieces, which nonetheless owe their existence to the system of slavery. Agamben thereby perpetuates a Eurocentric discourse of race, based on an idealized version of ancient Greece that plays down the gendered implications of his own intervention, even as his focus on race in the modern state (albeit a Eurocentric account of race) provides a necessary corrective to Irigaray's equally problematic and Eurocentric account of sexual difference as foundational. At the same time, Irigaray's focus on sexual difference serves as a corrective to Agamben's exclusive focus on race.

Agamben advances the "idea of an inner solidarity between democracy and totalitarianism" (HS 10). The tyrannical aspects of Bush's reign were not lost on Seamus Heaney, who points out in the appendix to his poetic interpretation of *Antigone* that Bush's notorious declaration that you are either "with us or against us" is reminiscent of Creon.[6] Just as Creon makes it clear that anyone who supports Antigone's belief in her right to bury Polynices, whom Creon regards as a traitor, will be tarred with the same brush, so Bush fostered an atmosphere in which those of us who opposed the war in Iraq were made to feel that we were unpatriotic (despite the fact that we were ostensibly going to war in order to defend, among other things, freedom of speech). *Antigone* takes on a renewed relevance, appearing, as new versions of *Antigone* tend to do, at a time when an unjust system is in danger of becoming the norm. Now, more than ever, Agamben tells us, in the "urgency of catastrophe" (HS 12), the exception seems to have become the rule (see HS 9). Post 9/11, the rhetoric of an apparently—although oxymoronic—permanent emergency has been fuelled by the constant appeal to the need to be vigilant in the form of what was designated the "war on terror." The threat to peace and security and the climate of fear that accompanies it, has, in the popular imaginary, become the norm, and has in turn been used to justify the suspension of rights that had previously been considered central to the fabric of democracy.

In her reflections on the infamous Adolf Eichmann trial, Hannah Arendt states the following: "Eichmann was indeed normal insofar as he was 'no exception within the Nazi regime.' However, under conditions of the Third Reich only 'exceptions' could be expected to react 'normally.' "[7] Arendt is thus the philosopher to have anticipated Agamben's association of the state of exception with the concentration camp (see HS 20), although it is Carl Schmidt, rather than Arendt, whom Agamben cites in his discussion of the state of exception. Agamben construes the camp "as the pure, absolute, and impassable biopolitical space (insofar as it is founded solely on the state of exception)." Accordingly he sees the camp "as the hidden paradigm of the political space of modernity whose metamorphoses and disguises we will have to learn to recognize" (HS 123). Given his analysis in *Homo Sacer* of the writ of *habeas corpus* as an implicit "first recording of bare life as the new political subject" (HS 123), it was not surprising that critics were quick to take up Agamben's analysis in applying it to the suspension of *habeas corpus* at Guantánamo an application later endorsed by Agamben (2008, 4).[8]

Nor is it entirely surprising to find that Agamben's analysis—despite the anachronism of the Roman figure of *homo sacer*—can be mapped on to the dilemma of *Antigone*. Agamben draws attention to the dynamic of the sovereign exception, invoking the distinction between "*zoē*, which expressed the simple fact of living common to all living beings (animals, men, or gods), and *bios*, which indicated the form or way of living proper to an individual or a group" (HS 1). As Clifton Spargo puts it, "Especially in times of crisis, sovereignty reverts to its constitutive principle of power as a capacity to enact such determinations, and this is the role Creon would reserve for himself as king."[9] Creon interprets his mandate as sovereign in the light of the crisis that has befallen Thebes. Not only is there the immediate crisis precipitated by the civil war in which Eteocles and Polynices have killed one another.[10] There is also the more pervasive crisis, which extends to a crisis in the legitimation of sovereignty itself, a crisis brought on by the curse under which the family of Oedipus and Antigone labors.[11] Given the ways in which political boundaries are drawn, for the Greek polis, Antigone is always already in a state of exemption, by virtue of her disenfranchised position as a woman. As Spargo says,

> Among the crucial markers of sovereignty is the crude power it exhibits in determining which human lives are included in law, which unprotected by it—or in deciding who will be protectively subjected to the State's constitutive violence, who relinquished again to the violence of the so-called natural world. In acting against Creon's law Antigone not only imaginatively places herself outside of law, but by anticipating and embracing the violence Creon might exercise against the bare life which has been devoted to him as political life (*zoon politkon*), she arrogates to herself the very function of sovereign. This may be her greatest offense against her uncle, who believes himself the proper vehicle for sovereignty in Thebes.[12]

In committing suicide, and thereby denying Creon the right he assumes as his prerogative either to take her life or grant her a reprieve, Antigone usurps the right that Creon assumes as sovereign at the same time as she contests his idea of politics. While I do not question the relevance and importance of applying Agamben's analysis to *Antigone*, I want to suggest that there are slippages in Agamben's own analysis that need addressing, and that the reading of *Antigone* I develop here can help to illuminate these slippages. In particular, the state of exception is in need of a more variegated and nuanced treatment than Agamben himself extends to it. I do not think adequate attention is paid to the gendered dynamics underlying the state of exception. In this respect, I am in agreement with both Andrew Benjamin and Ewa Ziarek, who develop such critiques, albeit in different idioms.[13]

If I am, on balance, persuaded that Agamben offers a useful corrective to Foucault on the issue of the stances of sovereignty being less separable from the biopolitical than Foucault might have imagined, I am less than persuaded that sacrificial logics have been as thoroughly supplanted by the logic of *homo sacer* as Agamben maintains.[14] For Agamben, "In modernity, the principle of the sacredness of life is . . . completely emancipated from sacrificial ideology" (HS 114). I would argue, however, that he is too quick to suggest that "we are all virtually *homines sacri*" (HS 115), and that his analysis suffers from a certain leveling out that ignores precisely the continuing ruses by which sovereignty continues to assert itself, to which his own analysis points, but which he does not develop. Agamben sees a proliferation of zones of indistinction, yet his pronouncements on this issue are made not from the point of view of those who have carried the burdens of bare life. I am concerned that Agamben allows his view that "the exception everywhere becomes the rule" (HS 9) to slide into an assumption that everyone is in the same boat with regard to the state of exception, and that there are no significant differentiations between nations, or sectors of national populations. If, as Penelope Deutscher has shown persuasively, there are various legal bases upon which states of exception are construed, so too there are various socially determined sediments that stratify populations in such a way as to constitute some as more liable to exceptionality than others.[15]

I suggest that his appeal to a vocabulary of revelation, while it needs to be problematized on one level, in fact points to an issue that Agamben's own analysis forecloses, one that constitutes its condition, and one that Irigaray's analysis of Antigone helps to elaborate.[16] As part of his attempt to correct or complete Foucault, Agamben claims to have discovered that which escaped Foucault (HS 9). Invoking the language of concealment, secrecy, and hiddenness, Agamben appeals to the "*concealed* nucleus of sovereign power," to the "*hidden* foundation on which the entire political system rested," and to the "*secret tie* uniting power and bare life," which is "the inclusion of bare life in the political realm [my italics]" (HS 6). "At once excluding bare life from and capturing it within the political order, the state of exception actually constituted, in its very separateness, the *hidden* foundation on which the entire political system rested [my italics]" (HS 9). The secret link between bare life and politics is what renders indiscernible the difference between right/left, private/public, absolutism/democracy (see HS 4), and unlocking this secret will even enable us to bring "the political out of its concealment" (HS 5). This rhetoric of revelation is bound up with Agamben's claim to go beyond a blind spot in Foucault, who failed to discern the "*hidden* point of intersection between the juridico-institutional and the biopolitical models of power [my italics]" (HS 6).

Skepticism has been expressed about what Paul Patton calls Agamben's "conceptual fundamentalism," or what Ernesto Laclau identifies as his legitimation of "the *genealogy* of a term, a concept or an institution."[17] In effect, as Laclau puts it, Agamben "jumps too quickly" from such a genealogy "to determine its actual working in a contemporary context;" for Agamben "in some sense the *origin* has a secret determining priority over what follows from it."[18] While I share this suspicion, I want to develop it in another direction, one that gives some historical specificity and substance to Agamben's claims of secrecy and concealment, but which in doing so also alters them, by acknowledging the political exclusions on which rests the viability of the distinction from which Agamben takes his bearings, namely that of *zoē* and *bios*.[19] While Agamben never attends to it, there is of course a politicized subtext to the separation of *oikos* and *polis*, spheres that Arendt thematized in terms of private and public, the arenas in which biological life on the one hand and the pursuit of an individual or collective form of life on the other are respectively undertaken.[20]

Excluded from participation in the political realm, an array of animalistic others have populated the realm that Arendt conceived as that of necessity, as distinct from the political sphere of freedom, the *oikos* as opposed to the *polis*. If slaves and women were required to meet the repetitive, cyclical daily needs of free citizens who were destined for higher things than that of the *animal*, or if you prefer *homo laborans* in ancient Greece, in the contemporary times of the western world, the life of the mind or the *vita activa* is reserved for those of us who benefit from multinational outsourcing in a global economy that depends upon an international division of labor, which is both racialized and feminizing. Such exploitation of human labor has long been accompanied by exploitation of raw materials, such as oil reserves, by imperial powers. Perhaps it could have been foreseen that one more step would be taken in this direction, in the form of the wholesale military invasion of Iraq. If in one sense the forces determining such a step were already well ensconced, in another sense, this step nonetheless amounted to a decisive and qualitative leap in cynical exploitation.

The point I wish to emphasize is that if, in Agamben's words, "Western politics first constitutes itself through an exclusion (which is simultaneously an inclusion) of bare life," it does so—and this is what Agamben fails to thematize—by exploiting and resignifying the gendering of women, or the racializing of Iraqis, whose lives are already marked as insignificant politically by hegemonic, Western ideology.[21] There is, in the words of Irigaray, "an absorption of other into self."[22] What this absorption facilitates is nothing other than the operation of the law—which includes the right of sovereign exception, the right to suspend the law. The stories that both Foucault and Agamben tell about the biopolitical stand in need of a crucial supplement.[23] If the biopolitical became the focal point of the modern administrative and bureaucratic state, so that reproductive processes, levels of fertility, and a host of measures germane to population control, and the administration of life itself proliferated, with the result that bodies were subjected, and subjects subjected themselves, to ever more minute regulation, this does not mean that there was no control of such processes hitherto. Rather, the agencies and location of that control were differently specified. Previous strategies of control might not have been biopolitical—but there is no doubt that they existed.

Take the polis of ancient Greece, for example—the background against which the original performance of Sophocles' *Antigone* was staged—where such strategies might not have taken place in the full light of day, and might have been far more crude insofar as they coalesced with the boundary separating the political from the nonpolitical as such. Women's movements were carefully curtailed by the ingeniously simple expedient of keeping them indoors. Indeed—to draw on the conventional codes of theatrical performance in fifth century BCE Athens, in which the first staging of *Antigone* took place, being indoors and being female were practically synonymous with one another. A fair or untanned skin was one of the codes that signaled to audiences at the festival of Dionysus that a given character was a woman; if necessary, the actors—all male—used white lead to give their skin the appropriate appearance.[24] One need not speculate long in order to arrive at the reason women were largely confined to indoor spaces, which was not merely so that they could oversee the smooth running of the *oikos*, but rather precisely in order to ensure strict supervision of, and knowledge of, their reproductive activities.

We should not underestimate the enormous significance that overseeing the reproductive activity of women must have had for the *polis*. We might even surmise that it was the greatest barrier preventing women from partaking in political life. How could the necessary measures of control over women's sexual activity be maintained, if women had the freedom to come and go as they pleased, as did men? In short, I am suggesting that the reason that the biopolitical emerges as a uniquely modern form of power is intimately connected with the redrawing of political boundaries that organized the freedom of women's movement and speech, boundaries that at the same time controlled reproductive freedom. The control of women's reproductive freedom, in turn, was intimately connected in fifth century BCE Athens with preserving the purity of genealogy and heredity, such that, for example, aristocratic lineage could be clearly distinguished from any contamination with slavishness. The historical trend away from exogamy and toward endogamy that characterizes Sophocles' Athens is bound up with the symbolic importance of establishing the legitimacy of one's genealogy. These issues permeate the Oedipal quest to reconstruct the events of his life in order to understand his familial origins, and they infuse Antigone's insistence upon distinguishing her brother from a slave.

If, prior to modernity, the state did not exert biopolitical control, in the case of reproductive processes, this was not only because the state itself was still emergent, still nascent, but also because there was no need for it to do so explicitly, since it could rely on the gendered conventions that were already in place to accomplish its work, without having to regulate such conventions. Ostensibly concerned with the cultural virtues of chastity and modesty, the confinement of women within the home, and the restriction of women's movement this imposed, had everything to do with controlling women's reproductive activity, and with ensuring the purity of male lines of inheritance. In effect, the complete exclusion of women from the life of the political was the corollary of their containment within the walls of the *oikos*. At the same time, the spatial inclusion of these contained, domestic spaces within the physical boundary of the polis, together with the political exclusion of the inhabitants thus contained, amounted to a system of domination that on the one hand can be described as a variation of Agamben's exclusion that is also an inclusion. On the other hand, there is more to be said: this geographical inclusion and confinement, hand in hand with a political exclusion/dominance accomplished a usurpation, appropriation, or re-signification of that which the polis found productive, and a simultaneous casting out, banishing as unsignifiable or unrepresentable that which it encountered as dangerous. The only representation granted women's sexuality was, needless to say, that which made it productive for the polity, namely its reproductive power, a power that had to be harnessed to the name of the father. That which is productive is the clarity of lines of inheritance. What is dangerous is anything that threatens such clarity: women's freedom of movement and speech, for example, women's inclusion in the political system (which might result, among other things, in the contesting of restrictions placed on women's movement, challenging the limitations of their capacity to be heard). The very organization of political space as exclusive of women sufficed to exert control over women's reproduction, and moreover it did so almost as a side effect.

Assumptions about the sexuality of women, and the need to contain their apparently ravenous sexual appetite, derived—it is not hard to see—not so much from any traits women might have exhibited, but rather from the tremendous fear men must have had about their inability to determine their own progeny, without meticulous oversight of their wives or sexual partners.[25] Hence, the polis necessitated that women should be cast out of the political realm and banned from public debate, precisely because of the importance of overseeing their reproductive capacity, which assured the continuation and longevity both of wealth in the form of goods within the *oikos* and of power in form of the lines of kinship and descent assuring royal lineage. Uninterrupted and unproblematic generation of the family or *genos* assured both the identity of the family as a unit, and the stability of the rule of law, by establishing clear lines of inheritance. The events that unfold in the Oedipus cycle put into crisis the claims of inheritance based on generation both at the level of the family and that of political leadership. This is, after all, not just a family, not just any family, but the Oedipal family, an incestuous, patricidal, royal family. Any crisis in distinguishing the familial positions of mother from wife (Oedipus's wife, Joacasta), or brother from uncle or nephew (Polynices), or sister from aunt or niece (Antigone), also constituted a crisis of political authority. The fact that it is Antigone who brings to light this crisis by her insistence on burying Polynices *as a brother and nothing else*, means that the questions posed by *Antigone* are not restricted to the order of: what does it mean to be a brother as distinct from a father?—or for any familial position to be distinct from any other—but also extend to the legitimacy of political claims to be ruler.[26] If the freedom of women was feared because a failure to contain them, to have their physical whereabouts known at all times, amounted to a failure to know for sure the identity—the name—of the father, the chaos that threatened to break out in the Oedipal cycle was not confined to a crisis in private inheritance, but rather extended to a crisis of political leadership.[27]

It is against this heteronormative background with its reproductive logic, I suggest, that Sophocles' Theban dramas must be read, and it is in this context that Irigaray's account of Antigone as an excluded yet facilitating other both has such pertinence, and stands in need of supplement. Irigaray's initial reference to Antigone in *Speculum* is not in relation to Hegel, but in her discussion of Freud, specifically in relation to fetishism. In fact the entire "*Hegelian dream*" of Antigone can be read in terms of the fetishistic logic of compensation: it is "already the effect of a dialectic produced by the discourse of patriarchy. It is a consoling fancy."[28] As Irigaray points out, fetishism involves an overvaluation and a corresponding veiling of that which is made to occupy the role of a lesser value: the value associated with conception, for instance.[29] Fetishism involves a compensatory mechanism, fuelled by a threat of otherness that cannot be integrated into one's preconceptions without altering those preconceptions. It is in discussing the importance of venerating the phallus that Antigone enters the scene for Irigaray: "Preserving it from derision, insignificance, and devaluation. Even if woman must die in the attempt, she will carry out her mission. Virgin? Her deed will be all the more exemplary. Condemned by the king? She will have shown all the more clearly the contradictions in the system. As the ruler's unworthy anger shows . . . the patriarchal regime could scarcely be expected to tolerate Antigone's loud assertions."[30] It is thus a consideration of the "fetishistic economy" that sets the context for Irigaray's analysis of *Antigone*, who "remains the very ground in which manifest mind secretly sets its roots and draws its strength," as the excluded yet facilitating other.[31] Through "assimilating the external other into and for the self . . . man absorbs the other into himself." Due to "its desire to return to sameness," difference has already been excluded.[32]

Quoting Freud, Irigaray says, "We know how children react to their first impressions of the absence of the penis. They disavow the fact and believe that they *do* [*SE*, italics] see a penis, all the same. *They gloss over the contradiction between observation and preconception.*"[33] Irigaray comments, "Almost imperceptibly . . . Nature and her work" is brought "into the fetishistic economy by hiding all she is capable of producing and preventing us from appreciating it. Beliefs and preconceptions, from now on, are supported. And kept away from the contradiction of observation" (116).

Bearing this fetishistic economy in mind, let me return to one of the most important political sleights of hand to have been committed in recent history. I want to sketch what I take to be a pervasive political strategy of political self-representation in the United States of its own policy under the Bush administration, which I think can usefully be conceptualized in terms of the structure of fetishistic disavowal. U.S. politicians are still invested in certain mythical preconceptions about what the United States must be, despite all the evidence to the contrary. On the one hand they insist on seeing America as a country that upholds the law, a country that does not merely participate in international law, but is exemplary in its moral standing and leadership. The United States sees itself as a beacon of justice, one that respects the rights of sovereign nations, embodies the ideals of true democracy, and fosters free speech, a country in which everyone has the right to due process including a fair trial, and the rights entailed by the writ of *habeas corpus*, a country that is in fact distinguished by the fact that it extends such rights, rather than endorsing the barbaric practices of allegedly less civilized nations such as Iraq, countries which—precisely because of the extent of their so-called barbarism—require us to suspend the usual rules of engagement.

On the other hand, we were ruled by a president who lied to the citizens to whom he was beholden, not about an event that happened in his private life concerning consensual extra-marital sex, but about the political justification for taking the United States to war, which is probably the most serious lie a president—as a president—can tell. When the United States declared war on Iraq, it violated the sovereignty of a secular country, and when even the most diehard supporters of the war could no longer maintain that weapons of mass destruction existed, it justified this preemptive war by pointing to Iraq's abuses of human rights, such as torture, which, it turns out, the U.S. government routinely sanctions, as became painfully clear first when the photographs of Abu Ghraib finally surfaced, and again with revelations about waterboarding. (That torture is a common practice by the U.S. government was already clear for those who wished to know). Not only did the U.S. government see fit to suspend the writ of *habeas corpus* at Guantanámo Bay, but it also pushed through the surveillance bill, which, among other things, retroactively changed the law so that leading telecommunications companies were absolved for capitulating to the government's demand that it facilitate routine and pervasive spying on its own citizens.

The fact that somehow the belief that the United States stands for freedom, democracy, and benevolence sustains itself in the face of all the evidence to the contrary, suggests not so much that the myth of the superiority of the West outweighs the facts on the ground, but rather that that there is something about the myth of American superiority that makes what has been called the "fact based community" simply irrelevant. Whatever evidence could be adduced to the contrary, the belief in the superiority of the United States remains untouched, since the facts are beside the point. What is important is that we maintain the preconception of the United States as unassailable and unimpeachable. If the facts get in the way, the easiest way to proceed is to destroy the evidence. Given this investment in the benevolence and good intentions of U.S. supremacy, evidence to the contrary seems to be simply beside the point. The casualties of this irrelevance continue to mount, as political instability and continued violence haunts Iraq.

The lesson here, like that of fetishism, seems to be clear enough. If the facts on the ground don't match up with our preconceptions, we remake history to make it fit, and this substitute reality suffices. (If there is no penis, as we had expected there to be, fabricate a substitute one—hence the fetish). If the mirroring function of the world around us doesn't reflect our own idea of what it should be, we manipulate the reflection until it accords to this idea. If evidence begins to get in the way, it can be disappeared, and a new reality erected in its stead. If we don't control the resources we want, we simply get rid of those who do, by declaring war on them and establishing bases in their country, under the pretense of exporting democracy—as if we still knew what that might mean. There seems to be something important to us in the maintenance of the fiction of the goodness and purity of our intentions in all of this—something crucial in evoking the democratic myth. It is not enough to have declared a permanent war on terror as a way of justifying the suspension of law; at the same time, there is a robust investment in the denial of this state of affairs, a denial that displaces the blame for the state of exception. A double exemption is at work here, one that invokes a perfect future in which we will no longer be forced by the terrorists to abandon democratic principles—and Derrida's discourse on the autoimmunity of democracy comes into its own here.[34] This future, however, depends on the terrorists' suspension of terrorism—and one cannot prove definitively that the amorphous threat of terrorism will ever be in abeyance.

The strategy of overvaluing the power of the phallus and its fetishistic substitutes functions as an undervaluing of the powers of conception, suggesting that the gendering and racializing processes that perform the subtext of that which has been theorized under the heading of the state of exception require our attention. Equally demanding of our attention is the dynamic underlying the invasion of Iraq, an insidious confluence of racism and the U.S. belief in its sovereign right to control the terms on which the earth's resources are extracted in support of consumerist lifestyles that proceed in oblivion to environmental concerns. The hubris that Creon exhibits in his belief that his power over his dominion is absolute, and his downfall is bound up with the fact that it extends even to what Hegel calls the elemental.[35] Creon has no respect for the earth to which Antigone wants to return the body of Polynices, just as the Bush administration maintained a cavalier attitude toward the environment, whether it was a question of extracting oil or refusing to sign the Kyoto agreement.

In concluding, I suggest that the continued relevance of *Antigone* can be productively analyzed as symptomatic of hegemonic regimes of race and gender in which the nexus of sovereignty, state, and law on the one hand and biopolitics on the other hand are brought together. Antigone's incessant reemergence derives in part from the fictions of sovereignty that continue to unfold. I have also suggested that, for all his purchase, the recent surge of interest in Agamben needs to be supplemented by careful attention to the gendered dynamics underlying the state of exception, and that these dynamics should not allow us to resolve too quickly by affirming that "we are all virtually *homines sacri*" (HS 115), or that "the exception everywhere becomes the rule"—we are not all in the same boat with regard to the state of exception, and Irigaray's account of fetishism allows us to see that there are significantly differential gendered dynamics that make it more legitimate for some of us to inhabit states of exception differently from others.

If Irigaray's exposure of the dynamic of fetishism in *Antigone*, and her insistence on the motif of the assimilation of the excluded but constitutive other that underlies it, provides an interpretive device that is more sensitive to the gendered dynamics of the state of exception—one that also helps shed light on the current political state of affairs, which is characterized not only by the declaration of emergency, but equally by its rhetorical denial, and in this sense by a strategy that might be identified as meta-fetishistic—I also want to indicate the danger of making sexual difference into a new foundational ground.

Agamben does not specify the dynamic according to which the exclusion that is already an inclusion follows a politicized logic, in which not only are certain lives more expendable than others, but their expendability at one level is premised on their incorporation or appropriation at another level. In a sense, his insistence upon "zones of indistinction" prevents him from doing so. This prompts the question of whether the articulations that become indistinct are not worth specifying because they are not of interest to him, or because he believes there is something that makes it inherently unhelpful to specify them. Or again, do the articulations I am pointing to precisely become unreadable in a way that is politically salutary? After all, there is a risk in reifying certain claims of discrimination, so that one form of marginality, such as sexual difference, becomes foundational, thereby both eclipsing the ways in which other forms of marginality feed into and constitute the marginality of sexual difference, and at the same time denying the importance of those other forms of marginality in their own right.[36] What needs to be thought through is the proclivity with which fetishistic economies produce phallus substitutes, which only serve to extend, rather than to undermine, the fabrication of new realities, premised on newly abjected others. My own view is that the risks of marking, articulating, and yes, even perhaps reifying certain economies of difference must be undertaken, so that the abject grounds on which such reifications rely can be exposed. At the same time, these reifications themselves need to be called to account. Accordingly, the model of the excluded but constitutive other, which Irigaray and others have elaborated in their readings of Antigone, stands in need of further elaboration. The work that Irigaray performs in excavating the ways in which Antigone comes to stand as the unacknowledged ground of a polity that she sustains yet from which she is excluded needs to be complicated. For even as Antigone attempts to write herself back into the political structures that have produced her excluded status, she herself confirms and reproduces the structure of slavery that subtends her own claim to be heard. Standing on the shoulders of those whose subhumanity she thereby colludes in enforcing, she specifies her brother as a member of a community worthy of recognition by distinguishing him from those who are not. And so the pattern of the excluded other, of which Antigone has become symbolic, reiterates itself in a new guise. Those of us who celebrate Antigone's resistance to a polis that formally excludes her from political participation, without noticing the way Antigone colludes with a system of chattel slavery, reproduce that collusion.

6

Concluding Reflections

What If Oedipus or Polynices Had Been Slaves?

The Oedipal cycle can be read as a hyperbolic parable about the difficulty, perhaps impossibility, of preserving the sanctity of boundaries. The boundaries in question are not just concerned with those that Oedipus transgresses when he marries his mother, or murders his father. Just as important are the boundaries conferring the privileges of freedom and full political participation on some members of the polity, but not on others, boundaries that were invoked in Athens to qualify some as free citizens, while disqualifying others. Distinguishing between citizens and non-citizens, between free adult males and slaves, women and metics, is, I suggest, more than a peripheral issue in the Oedipus cycle. Indeed it is a central and structuring, albeit neglected, theme. A tale that begins with shepherds meandering into neighboring provinces, violating orders to kill the infant Oedipus, ends by revealing the terrible consequences of what happens when the attempt to keep outsiders out becomes so pronounced that it turns into incest.[1]

Could it be that the Oedipal cycle should be read just as much as a warning against the culturally incestuous gesture of exclusivity as a commentary on actual kinship practices? Whether we consider the shepherd violating his orders, facilitating a crossing of boundaries that results in Oedipus passing so successfully for a stranger to his native land that he is crowned its king, or whether we dwell on the bodily scarring with which Oedipus afflicts himself, as he casts out his eyes, the difficulty of clearly establishing one's identity as an outsider or an insider, as a king or an outcast, as a member of the royal family or as a foundling fit to be sold into slavery, is exacerbated throughout Sophocles' interrogation of compounded and fraught identities.[2] Whether we consider Antigone's differentiation of her brother from a slave in justifying her burial of Polynices, or Creon's efforts to insult and dismiss Antigone by identifying her with slavery, Sophocles' attention to the importance of clarifying a boundary that was in fact under constant threat suggests a pervasive anxiety amongst those who could be counted as free to maintain intact the boundary separating them from those who could not assume freedom. Against the context of the Zoroastrian ritual, observed by some ancient Iranians (although assuming mythological proportions in the Greeks' representation of their "others"), of exposing corpses to be picked over by carrion birds, Antigone's insistence upon burying her brother takes on a peculiar urgency, one that highlights her anxiety to usher Polynices into a common humanity through religious rituals defined in distinction from other, non-Greek religions.[3] Antigone's insistence in defying Creon in her specification of Polynices as worthy of burial appeals to a distinction that aligns slaves with those not worthy of a burial that is marked as specifically Athenian, thereby underlining the desire of Athenians to envisage slavery as something that happens to barbarians, but which should not happen to them. In this regard, recall Aristotle's tortuous attempts to explain the difference between those who are naturally suited to slavery and those who are not. As Peter Hunt puts it, "In his defense of slavery, Aristotle assumes the slavishness of 'barbarians.' It is only the enslavement of Greek prisoners of war that gives him pause: such slaves were often not natural slaves."[4]

Is there a sense in which Sophocles' preoccupation with the Athenian need to articulate boundaries that distinguish themselves from those who do not deserve or merit a proper burial, to constantly attend to the threatened and precarious differentiation between the free and the unfree, has been eclipsed by recent interventions to reorient readings of *Antigone* around sexual difference, which generally assume, without marking them, particular conceptions of family and kinship? Have the issues of slavery and citizenship, what it means to be an insider or an outsider, been allowed to fade into the background of scholarship on *Antigone*, and the Oedipal cycle more generally?[5] A more thorough investigation of Sophocles' explorations—which this book seeks to open up—would demand a consideration of these issues, the avoidance of which, I have suggested, is bound up with the implication of the proponents of tragic theory in the construction of narratives that function to protect themselves from confronting the threats to empire and colonialism in their own era. Interrogating the reception of Greek tragedy through the lens of Hegel's German idealism, we find that its overdetermining impact on tragic theory has inflected the critical discourse in such a way as to detract from the issues of slavery and citizenship and the difficulty of neatly separating slaves from those who enjoy freedom, or citizens from non-citizens.

Taking stock of the current state of the literature on *Antigone*, we see that a good deal of important recent work has been done on *Antigone* around the themes of burial, marriage, reproduction, and kinship as social institutions that defined women's roles in fifth century BCE Athens. A recent shift can be marked away from interpreting the importance attaching to burial in *Antigone* exclusively in terms of religion, toward readings that emphasize questions of social attrition.[6] Recently critics have approached Antigone's insistence upon burying her brother by focusing, for example, on the relevance of attempts to restrict the scope of mourning, and specifically women's participation in funereal lament.[7] Solon introduced a reform, for example, which restricted the rituals of mourning and lamentation at funerals, and which thus helps to constitute the political backdrop against which much of the more interesting recent work on *Antigone* has been played out. As Olga Taxidou observes, Plutarch reports that Solon's sixth century legislation prohibited "everything disorderly and excessive in women's festivals . . . and funeral rites."[8] Explanations for these restrictions have highlighted the democratically inspired wish to curb lavish and ostentatious displays of aristocratic wealth at funerals and the political attempt to control women's influence.[9] Even the limited sphere of women's influence in religious ritual was under erosion. The single important exception to the general rule of women's exclusion from public, civic duties was religion. As Cartledge says,

> Athenian women, in the sense of the mothers, sisters, wives, and daughters of Athenian citizen men, were 'citizens' only by courtesy, in all respects but one—religion. . . . [which] was the one public activity in which Athenian women might achieve parity or even superiority of esteem *vis-à-vis* their menfolk . . . [I]n the sphere of death, burial and mourning the women of Greece had traditionally taken the more active and more publicly demonstrative religious role. Correspondingly, the one civic function approximating to the holding of public political office by men that Greek citizen women might legitimately perform, indeed were required to perform, was to serve as priestess of an officially recognised city cult, usually of a female divinity.[10]

Since women's influence was limited to religion, in particular to burial rites, any restriction of their religious observance, such as that of Solon, would have represented an incursion into the one sphere in which women exercised some responsibility and authority.

At the same time critics have rightly striven to construe tragedy as not merely reflective of prohibitions outlawing the excess of emotion in female lamentation and mourning, but also as a site of struggle, which reworks tensions in mourning rituals, and thus resists laws that outlaw female expressions of grief as much as it mirrors oppressive and restrictive legislation.[11] Creon's prohibition of Polynices' burial, and Antigone's transgression of it, can be seen as just such a site of reworking.

Just as Antigone's tragic insistence upon burying her brother has been read as challenging the prevailing trend to curtail women's right to funereal lamentation, so Antigone's determination to die an unwed virgin has been understood to protest the matrimonial system of women's exchange.[12] The social and political context that has been emphasized is the need to control female reproduction, kinship lines, and the inheritance of wealth. The importance of reproducing male heirs to legitimate inheritance was definitive of women's function for the Athenian polis. Women's exclusion from political life went hand in hand with the firm expectation that they agree to a marriage arranged by their male guardians, and produce heirs to continue the familial line and facilitate the inheritance of the wealth that Athens had amassed.[13] The social tensions this produced were among the structuring themes explored by tragedy. As Hall puts it, "The tragic household is obsessed with its own perpetuation through legitimate male heirs . . . and it is a constant theme of tragic lamentation that the crises enacted will result in the extirpation of a family line. Childlessness itself is a concern of men in tragedy . . . The destruction of the kinship line is a major theme in tragedy."[14] The necessity of women for a body politic that denied them political rights constituted a strange logic of dependence, whereby women were figured by political and ethical thought on the one hand as apolitical, as outside the polis, but on the other hand as essential for its continuation. Roger Just points out that

> women's membership of the Athenian *polis* was always derivative, dependent on their associations with the men through whom they gained their status and their rights. Like other non-citizen groups of the Athenian population their presence was necessary for the existence of that state—vitally so, since they bore its progeny and transmitted political rights among them—but they were not in their own right members of the *polis* which remained '*un club d'hommes.*' They were members of the *oikoi* of those who were members of the state. Their position was, as it were, marginal. They existed on the peripheries of political life—necessary for its maintenance, excluded from its activities. . . . They were endowed with those characteristics of sensuality, irrationality, emotionality which, though recognized as always present in and even necessary to human existence, had to be restrained, controlled, and subjugated if civilized life was to be maintained. Women's natural characteristics were those which were peripheral to the character of free, self-governing, and autonomous men. Just as women were in an important sense outside the *polis*, so the characteristics which they possessed were in an equally important sense outside the nature of its *politai.*[15]

Women were required to be repositories of passion, to be ready and available for reproductive purposes, and at the same time condemned for precisely these characteristics, as incapable of self-control, as unable to exert authority over themselves.

Critics have often remarked that while women were barely present in public life, they feature prominently in tragedy.[16] In explanation of the paradox that while women's public roles in Athens were severely restricted, female characters nonetheless frequently populated the tragedy of the Athenian poets, Hall observes that since "[d]eath and killing are so central to tragedy," burial rituals and the lamentation and grief that accompanied them—and hence women—were also bound to be commonly treated by tragedy.[17]

Notwithstanding the importance of recent work surrounding the socio-symbolic significance of female mourning and lamentation, and the importance of work on the exchange of women in marriage, my effort is to insist on understanding this work as significant in terms of a larger frame of reference. The relegation of not only women but also slaves, male and female, to the care of the bodily, material aspects of life, while the care of the soul was the exclusive preserve of free, male citizens, articulates a logic that demands attention. Not only women, but also slaves and barbarians were associated with excessive emotion, and lacking in control over such excess, and as such construed as unfit for political life. The circumscription of hired mourners and women at funerals was part of the attempt to define mourning no longer as the province of the family, but under civic jurisdiction. Similarly, the expectation that women produce male heirs, thereby facilitating a line of male citizenry from which they themselves were excluded, also implicated them in excluding slaves from that line of inheritance.

At one level, in relation to *Antigone*, it is perhaps not surprising that the question of slavery and the implication that Pericles' reform carried with it for excluding foreigners, have not been followed up for the most part, given that there are few slaves in the tragedy. As Hall points out, not much work has been done in general on the significance of slaves in Greek tragedy, and what little has been done has tended to focus on Euripides.[18] Yet at another level, the systematic omission or erasure of slavery from the critical study of tragedy itself calls out for interpretation. *Antigone* can be read as drawing attention to the dangers inherent in a system that emphasizes endogamous marriage practices. We have seen that Zeitlin draws attention to the sense in which tragedy figures Thebes as a closed society, imagining Athens, by contrast, to be open. In *Antigone* tragic Thebes could also be understood as a dystopia that underlines the dangers of endogamy, which, in its extreme form, leads to incest. As Hall points out, *Antigone* is unique in that it includes only Thebans, while every other extant tragedy—with the exception of Aeschylus' *Persians*, in which everyone is Persian—is more ethnically diverse.[19] By reading this hyperbolic representation of endogamy as implicating ideas about slavery and barbarians, by asking after the significance of the slave who, along with Laius, was killed at the crossroads, but is rarely mentioned, by insisting upon construing the significance of slavery as integrally bound up with the Oedipal plot, I have sought to redraw the boundaries of the usual interpretive configurations.

Thus, at the same time as insisting upon the significance of Antigone's disambiguation of Polynices not only from a potential son or husband, but also from a slave, I point to how this disambiguation echoes a thematic concern that, once one begins to look for it, shows up throughout the Oedipal cycle. Sophocles' conern with *genos* is not restricted to a narrow understanding of kinship, but extends to the differentiation of citizens from non-citizens, freemen from slaves, and Greeks from barbarians. The very clarity that Antigone seeks in ensuring that her brother is recognized as her brother, precisely her anxiety in preserving or reinstating the difference between brother and uncle, is also a way of distinguishing between her family lineage and the deracination of slaves, or what Orlando Patterson refers to as "social death," a fate that Oedipus himself narrowly avoided.

I have suggested that among the events informing Sophocles' conception of the Oedipal cycle is Pericles' citizenship law, a law that directly impacted Sophocles' family.[20] While this latter detail is hardly decisive on its own, in conjunction with the textual details amassed, along with other contextual, historical considerations concerning citizenship and slavery, it does indicate that the debate between Antigone and Creon over the authority and nature of *nomos* has implications not overtly addressed by Hegel or his critics. As Adele C. Scafuro points out, "According to [Pericles' law] as cited by [Aristotle] *AP 26.4* 'whoever has not been born of two *astoi* parents has no share in the polis.' Plutarch refers to the same legislation as a *nomos* (law) about *nothoi* (bastards) and reports that in accordance with it 'only those born from two Athenians were Athenians.' "[21] Scafuro goes on to clarify the effect of the law on citizenship and kinship when she says that "children born of mixed unions would lack both *politeia* (citizenship) and *ankhisteia* (membership in the group of *ankhisteis* or kinsmen)."[22]

Despite legal attempts to restrict citizenship, such as Pericles' 450/1 law, which, as W. Robert Connor observes, "has plausibly been seen as a reaction against . . . inclusiveness," the definition of citizenship remained a contested issue in Athens.[23] Given the nascent state of the legal system in classical Greece, to what extent it is legitimate to approach citizenship as a legal concept, rather than as a social question, is itself at issue—indeed it is a question that the character of Antigone addresses in her appeal to an unwritten, religious law as more important than any human law that could be legislated. As Philip Brook Manville suggests, in an observation that is especially pertinent in a context where the very nature and character of law itself is under contest, "law itself becomes less significant than the thought processes of the citizens that would lead to its being enforced or ignored."[24] Such thought processes are under interrogation in the confrontation Sophocles stages between Creon and Antigone, where what is at stake is the very definition, nature, and authority of law, whether law is taken to be secular or religious, constructed or natural, contingent or timeless.

If the symbolic divide between slaves and non-slaves, citizens and non-citizens is enforced dramatically by the social imaginary of Athens, in practice, these boundaries were precarious. Thus while Hunt can view the social distinction between slaves and citizens as all but "impermeable," since "the foreign extraction of most slaves led to the feeling that they were completely and naturally different from and inferior to citizens," Connor construes the boundary separating citizens and non-citizens as in all likelihood "permeable."[25] There is a sense in which both Hunt and Connor are right: the boundaries separating citizens, non-citizens, and slaves from one another were both permeable and impermeable. As Hunt goes on to observe,

> To some extent the polarity of slave and citizens was so important and sharp because the contrast between actual slaves and citizens was so important and sharp. . . . [Yet there is] a certain excess in the way the Athenians emphasized the distinction. In vase paintings, in comic masks, in the law courts, the Athenians were not merely depicting the difference between slaves and citizens. They insist upon and mark out the opposition. . . . [T]he absolute distinction between slave and citizen provided an imaginary resolution of real social tensions.[26]

It was precisely the precariousness with which these boundaries obtained in the social sphere that required their enforcement, including their hyperbolic and excessive representation in the form of exaggeration and caricature in the slave masks worn in ancient comedic drama. The tenuous nature of the boundary between citizens and slaves was due, at least in part, to the fact that anyone who became a victim of war was liable to become as slave. As Hunt says, "wartime events and circumstances undermined in practice the boundary between citizen and outsider. Athenians could fall out of the category of citizen."[27] The more tenuous the justification for the distinction in the social sphere, the greater the requirement that the distinction appear writ large in the form, for example, of comic dramatic masks, or in the form of a law such as that of Pericles. Moreover, Antigone's anxiety to distinguish Polynices from a slave reflects the implication in Creon's refusal to have him buried; as a traitor to Athens, Creon sees Polynices as nothing more than a slave. After all, had Polynices been captured by a victorious brother, instead of Eteocles and Polynices killing each other in mutual combat, Polynices would have become a slave. As Hunt suggests, "The ideological insistence on the dichotomy of slave and citizen suggests anxiety both about the boundary between slave and free and about the unity of the citizens."[28]

Such anxiety, I suggest, informs Antigone's attempt to differentiate Polynices from a slave. Some critics have depicted women as the excluded other of the polis, and have read Antigone as representative of a figure of exclusion.[29] Josiah Ober expresses the excluded status of certain others in the following way: "The

Athenians . . . limited citizenship rights to freeborn males of Athenian ancestry. Women, slaves, and resident aliens, a majority of the total adult population, were excluded from participation in political life."[30] He goes on to suggest that women perform a place-holding function, serving the vital role of cementing the citizenship from which they themselves are excluded, holding the generational place between the father and the son.[31] Ober says, "women [are considered] as place-holders of citizenship, that is, of citizen blood, though barred by their gender from political rights," observing that "Exclusion of 'others' from the political sphere was . . . a very important factor in the coalescence of the political society."[32] While it is no doubt true that there are certain parallels to be drawn between women, slaves, and resident aliens, as Ober implies, it is also true that the status of women who are not slaves, for example, would differ significantly from that of slaves. It is such a disjunction that Cynthia Patterson captures when, in contrast to Ober, she suggests that it is not a question of reading "women as an excluded 'other,' " nor should female citizenship be understood as "mere place-holding or reflection of male relatives' authentic citizen status."[33] Both Manville and Patterson argue that while women are formally excluded from citizenship, they nonetheless contribute significantly to the public life of the polis. Brook Manville comments that "Although the 'true citizens' are the adult Athenian males, their political life is constantly shadowed by their networks of associations."[34] For Patterson too, "women's involvement in, and commitment to, the public life of the polis (whether we choose to call it 'citizenship') [is] both significant and substantial."[35] Patterson specifies that if some Athenian women performed the role of excluded other, the more privileged Athenian women—of which Antigone as a member of the royal family is in some sense representative—helped to shape and sustain a society whose free members had a vested interest in enforcing the boundaries between themselves and slaves. While the work that Antigone accomplishes does not qualify as biopolitical, since, as we saw in the previous chapter, biopolitics emerges with the modern state, this does not mean that certain measures were not in play, even if they did not take shape as formal regulations. Just as gender conventions dictated the restriction of women's movement in the service of safeguarding pure lines of inheritance, so certain conventions, in which tragic drama participates, served to keep slaves in their place. In the play named for her, Antigone does her part to ensure that slaves adhere to the roles that were carefully prescribed for them.[36] Perhaps, then, the work of Antigone's loyal interpreters can be construed as legitimizing and upholding biopolitical techniques. By continuing to interpret Antigone as a character whose exclusion from public life defines the resistance she displays to Creon's rule, without regard to how this resistance upholds the institution of ancient slavery, critics remain in thrall to arguments that are embroiled in implicit support of a literary tradition inherited from and formulated by a colonial empire that ritually cites as its origin a version of ancient Athens that isolates Greece from the influence of other cultures.[37]

In this sense, the interpreters that read over or condone Antigone's differentiation of her brother from a slave continue to marginalize those modern and contemporary others who have stepped into the shoes of the non-Athenian and the non-free that Patterson invokes when she says of ancient Athens, "the context in which child-bearing took place—for example, an Athenian *oikia* as opposed to a public brothel—would decisively distinguish one woman from another. If we say that as members of Athenian households, Athenian women were 'exploited,' we need to recognize also that they were themselves 'exploiters' of the non-Athenian and the nonfree."[38]

I have suggested that the strategies Antigone employs in order to resist the terms on which she is excluded from political life implicate her in the maintenance of the institution of slavery in a way that reflects the productive roles that free women in Athens would have played in sanctifying the boundary distinguishing slaves from free men and women. In attempting to resist her own relegation to the peripheral and subordinate roles to which Creon would consign her, Antigone's character allows herself to be enlisted in a sustained effort to establish her own status, and that of her brother, as superior to that of slaves. In doing so, her character is made to both reflect and fortify the efforts in which the free members of Athenian audiences of tragic drama would themselves have been engaged. At the same time, I have suggested, by expanding Mader's argument, Antigone's justification of her actions can be read as reflecting the 450/1 Periclean law, one effect of which is to purify the pool of legitimate Athenian citizenry and kinship lines of the contaminating influence of slavery. If, as I have suggested, Sophocles' staging of the figure of Oedipus foregrounds an anxiety about his origins that does not merely revolve around the name of his father or the identity of his mother, but also extends to the fragility of the boundary separating his destiny from that of a slave, then Antigone's burial of her brother should be read not only as her effort to disambiguate her brother Polynices from her father; it should also be read as Antigone's insistence on violating the law in order to usher her brother into a community whose humanity is underwritten by the implicit denial of humanity to those slaves for whom Antigone would not have transgressed the law in order to bury. In demanding, in the action of burial that she performs, that she be taken seriously as an ethical subject, in her demand not to be relegated to the shadowy, indistinct realm of slavish women to which Creon wants to abandon her, Antigone asserts her non-slavish status only by reconfirming the inferior/inhuman status of those who (the implication is) are really slaves. The burial is as much a performative recognition that Polynices is not a slave (while others are) as it is a corroborating differentiation of Antigone herself from the slavery to which Creon attempts to consign her.

We have seen that Antigone's ethical heroism, and Hegel's attempt to purify it, become symptomatic of the crisis into which the relationship between the state and family is about to be thrown in the nineteenth century, a crisis that Hegel attempts to resolve in a predictable way, by reasserting the natural alignment of women with the family. The family, Hegel assumes, is answerable to the natural authority of a state whose power is vested in male leaders. I have suggested that there is another crisis that Hegel's argument as to why slavery must be excluded as a topic for tragedy signals. Hegel's insistence on the purity of Antigone's ultimately limited ethicality not only serves to contain a femininity that threatens to break out of the role within which Hegel's ethical discourse would confine it; in his assignment of Antigone's primitive ethical mentality to her allegiance to the old order of Greek gods, those gods who are closer to nature than the gods of the newer order, and in his anxiety to establish the superiority of Greek religion—as a precursor to Christianity—over other religions, Hegel manages to discipline Antigone's unruliness in a way that participates in and contributes to a racial denigration of foreign gods. He thereby barricades himself against any direct confrontation with new world slavery and colonialism, while simultaneously indirectly indicating the continuity between his ideas about the backwardness of African and Asian cultures. As Caroline Rooney puts it, "Africa is foreclosed from history in Hegel's thought"; his need both to discipline Antigone in the way that he does, and to foreclose slavery as a legitimate topic for tragedy are of a piece with his view of African culture.[39]

If feminist interpretations of *Antigone* have sought to question the limitations that Hegel imposes on Antigone when his inscription of her ethical status also serves to underwrite the subservience of the private, familial realm that he requires her to occupy in the service of the state, feminist challenges to Hegel have also tended to operate in ways that sanction Antigone's apparent acquiescence to the system of slavery that she enlists as one of the grounds on the basis of which her own claim, in establishing the importance of burying Polynices, is heard. There is a sense in which such challenges, while departing from Hegel in one way, accept the terms of his enquiry in another way, and thereby repeat a blind acquiescence to the history that occludes the ethical claims of slaves, and in this way continue to sanitize the tragedy of *Antigone*, by writing out the relevance of slavery. One might even say that to the extent that feminist interpretations have failed to address the arguments that Hegel feels it incumbent upon him to articulate, in order to justify the exclusion of slavery as an appropriate topic of tragedy—albeit that these arguments are highly convoluted and self-contradictory—such interpretations have proved themselves to be still less willing to approach the issue of slavery in tragedy than was Hegel himself.

Whether it is a matter of mobilizing Antigone's appeal to a higher justice in whose name we can challenge state sanctioned discrimination, as in *The Island*, or whether it is a matter of transposing and exacerbating some of the tensions that are embedded in Sophocles' *Antigone*, around the issues of colonialism, slavery, and a taboo marriage, as in *Tègònni*, Antigone's appropriation in multiple, international, political contexts opens up questions of interpretation that have been buried by Hegelian—or post-Hegelian—obfuscation. *The Island* re-signifies the performative constraints imposed by Athenian theatrical mores by calling attention to them, as when Winston is ridiculed for impersonating a woman as he prepares to act the role of Antigone. If in *The Island* cross-dressing becomes an occasion for ridicule, in Sophocles' *Antigone*, slavery serves as the denigrated ground on which Antigone stands in order to argue the case for the recognition of her brother's humanity. At the same time, *The Island* ingeniously makes available for theoretical interrogation and reflection a neglected aspect of tragic performances, namely the performative codes of Attic drama, especially the convention whereby female characters would have been played by male actors. While Winston's eventual decision to follow through on his commitment to act the part of Antigone recuperates, without obliterating, the abjection of cross-dressing that the play exposes, the denigration of slaves performed by Sophocles' Antigone, the complicity it signals with the institution of slavery, and its attendant motifs, I have suggested, have not been paid the attention they deserve.

It turns out that the issues raised by Òsófisan and Fugard, Ntshona and Kani, far from being tangential to those of Sophocles, are inscribed at the very heart of the Oedipal cycle. Yet their inscription has proved difficult to read by interpreters of *Antigone* who have inherited ways of reading inflected by philosophical and psychoanalytic legacies, which are themselves implicated in imperialism, bolstered by new world slavery. The exposure of the infant Oedipus on Mount Cithaeron at birth is mirrored by the exposure of Polynices' corpse by Creon, and in both cases, the implication that can be inferred from a little textual and historical digging—even exhumation or disinterment—is that the skeletal structure of slavery is very much at issue. Had Oedipus not been exposed on the hills outside Thebes as an infant, he might well have been sold into slavery. Had Antigone not buried Polynices, whose attack on Thebes is read by Creon as the attack of a foreigner, he too might well have suffered a fate akin to that of a slave, or a non-Greek. Dramatizing the contingencies and accidents of such literary fates, attending to how precariously the boundaries separating free citizens from enslaved foreigners were sustained, Sophocles' *Antigone*, I have sought to show, explores fundamental but unresolved social tensions permeating Athenian society. How deliberate Sophocles was in attending to these themes, or whether or not this was Sophocles' conscious intention is not, perhaps, the most interesting question. It might have been—but whether conscious or unconscious, and whether these questions seem urgent today will depend on which interpretive tradition one grants authority. I have sought to make a case for an interpretation that takes its cue from the appropriations of *Antigone* that transpose the play into apartheid South Africa and postcolonial Nigeria, arguing that the issues at stake in Sophocles' "original" play—as if the original were not always already mediated by interpretive assumptions that postdate it—call for such appropriations. The point is that what is at stake in defining the "others of Athens" circulates in Sophocles' *Antigone* in ways that demand attention.

I hope it is clear that my effort here is not to produce a universal narrative in which the truth about *Antigone* turns out to be that it is really about slavery, and thus modern, literary appropriations of *Antigone* succeed in recognizing this truth that has been obfuscated through the denial, aversion, or repression of the philosophical and psychoanalytic traditions of the West. The emergence of race as a modern concept, among many other factors, militates against such a suggestion.[40] My effort has been directed, rather, toward taking seriously the specific configurations in which Antigone is born anew—and goes to her death—each time she enters the stage of literary, dramatic history, and in thinking through the way she exposes the limits of what a given society finds it tolerable to represent to itself. To take this history seriously is also to suggest that the ways in which what might have been figured as the necessary limits of representation for a particular form of political organization have been refigured by subsequent eras, and thereby rendered contingent limitations. It is also to suggest that the history of appropriations and interpretations of *Antigone* has itself played a part in this refiguring, at the same time as it might have enshrined as incontestable certain grounds that themselves need to be brought into question.

If Hegel outlawed slavery as a topic for tragedy, arguing that it was too ugly to admit of the beautiful resolution that the conflict of competing tragic aims called for, there is a sense in which Hegel's master-slave dialectic domesticates and tames the ugliness of slavery. True to Edward Said's argument, a sanitized, mediated version of slavery is thus admitted into Hegel's philosophical corpus, while its true horror is foreclosed from philosophy, and written out of tragedy.[41] If we take seriously Susan-Buck Morss's argument about Hegel sublimating his response to the Haitian slave revolt in the master-slave dialectic, we should read this account—and the white-washing of it that Hegel's commentators accomplish—as a means of defusing the politically and ethically charged tragedy with which slavery would otherwise confront us.

While it is true that I want to affirm a sense in which the character of Antigone—in her multiple incarnations—transcends the boundaries of the historical epoch of her dramatic inception, that her influence continues to be felt beyond the bounds of the era in which she was conceived, the argument is less about celebrating a transhistorical figure than it is about taking seriously the widely divergent political and dramatic conditions in which she has been appropriated, thinking through the different ways in which the apparently boundless and irrepressible energy of Antigone is transmitted from age to age as she is reborn in each new appropriation, and yet how her intransigence leads to her inevitable death. Antigone becomes, for each epoch in which she is reborn, a token of excess, a reservoir of that which a given polity cannot resolve or think through, without revising its prevailing symbolic—without putting her to death—a figure whose internal contradictions or impasses are not always made available for questioning. Antigone has served to condense the tensions of an age, tensions that have not always been unpacked, let alone resolved, but which have remained compacted and condensed, as the enigma of Antigone still requires to be read. Her apparent endorsement, in her "original" incarnation, of the necessity of slavery, and the ways in which critics have so often complied with that endorsement, help to constitute, I have suggested, this enigma that stands in need of unraveling.

Who owns Antigone? The answer, clearly, is that, despite her multifarious rebirths, she resists definitive appropriation. Yet it remains instructive to delineate the various, conflicting ways in which she has been pressed into service, appropriated by Western philosophy as a disciplining mechanism for nineteenth-century notions of domesticated femininity, serving double duty as a poster child for the religious piety and ethical duty Hegel advocated for women, and as emblematic of a more refined version of femininity than that evidenced in what he regarded as more primitive cultures. Her appropriation as an ethical hero has veiled and repressed the work she performs to keep slaves in check. Her ambiguous role is exposed by Òsófisan, who draws attention to her complicity with colonial agendas and the New World slavery that supported them, at the same time as he nods in the direction of her legacy as inspirational for freedom fighters. She has been taken up, by Fugard and others, as an inspirational figure in struggles for civil rights, although for them too, her legacy is not unambiguously liberatory. The name of Antigone is enlisted in a play that protests apartheid, even as her gender becomes a site of expression for the transgendered/homophobic anxiety that is fuelled by the forced confinement of Winston and John in an all-male prison. Philosophy, psychoanalysis, and imperialism have initiated competing claims for Antigone, yet her spirit remains irrepressible. With each rebirth of Antigone, every time Antigone goes to her death her legacy lives on, and she is configured anew.[42] No one owns her; Antigone rises again and again. Antigone's rising is not attributable to some universal appeal that a play about fundamental, competing visions of justice has for all time; Antigone's continual re-inscription articulates the ever-changing fears of each epoch, and her reconfiguration in racially combustible scenarios by poet-dramatists such as Òsófisan redresses the obfuscation of a tradition that had perhaps been too hyperbolic in its recuperation of Antigone as an uncomplicated freedom fighter, who could be championed with too much ease as a hero of sexual difference—or even as an aberrant, transgressive, figure (despite all the caveats resisting any straightforward representative function Antigone might have), who lent herself to the project of regenerating familial kinship groups not postulated on the heteronormative ideal.

Synopses of *The Island* and *Tègònni*

I provide, below, brief summaries of the *The Island* and *Tègònni, an African Antigone*, in case the reader finds it helpful to refer to them. I do not provide a synopsis of Sophocles' *Antigone*. One aspect of my argument is that the "original" play no longer stands intact as easily separable from the history of appropriations that has come to define it. I prefer to allow the text of this book to stand as my reading of *Antgione*, a text that is concerned as much with the philosophical reception of *Antigone* as it is with an interpretation of *Antigone*.

The Island

Winston and John are cellmates in Robben Island prison. The play opens with a long Sisyphean sequence in which they toil under the hot South African sun. Wordless, they endure the back-breaking labor of moving sand from one pile to another and back again, apparently endlessly. Eventually they are herded by their abusive jailor, Hodoshe, back to their cell, where they attend to one another's wounds, sustained under the blows of the prison guard. As they share a washcloth, they also share with one another how they came to hate one another, as each one approached with another wheelbarrow of sand. The genius of the hard-labor characteristic of this prison system is that it turns political prisoners against one another.

John has persuaded Winston to play the role of Antigone in a performance that will take place at the annual prison concert. John rehearses the plot for Winston, which Winston has trouble remembering, objecting frequently—not least to the idea that Antigone pleads guilty. John has improvised costumes for Antigone and Creon (to be played by John himself); for Antigone, a necklace made of nails, a mop as a wig, and "false titties." When Winston adorns himself in Antigone's attire, John cannot contain his laughter (although it is unclear how much his lack of restraint is motivated, as he will claim, by an effort to prepare Winston for the reaction of the prisoners). In any case, it proves too much for Winston, who refuses to play the role of Antigone as a result of John's hilarity and ridicule.

John is called away and unexpectedly hears of his early release. On his return to the cell, he and Winston anticipate his release, until John, unable to imagine that he will really be free, calls a stop to their reveries; eventually they both fall asleep, but not before Winston has pushed to the limit John's capacity to withstand the mixed emotions he is undergoing.

The play ends with John's and Winston's rendition of an exchange between Creon and Antigone, an exchange that resonates powerfully as symbolic of their own situation, as prisoners under the apartheid regime. Winston wears the attire he had earlier sworn he would not, and he does so proudly, as Antigone's words transform into a vehicle for his own commitment to the truth.

Tègònni, an African Antigone

Tègònni is set in the imaginary town of Oke-Osun, in Yorubaland, Nigeria, where a wedding is planned between Tègònni, princess of Oke-Osun, and Captain Allan Jones. Jones is a white officer, who is posted to the town. The play begins with an exchange between the play's director and those who will act in it, as to the availability of appropriate actors. Antigone is a character in the play, who arrives late on stage, and who is a "metaphor" in a story in which history "repeat[s] itself." She plays the role of a mythical figure, who has traveled through history, and who hails from Greek and other mythologies. Her bodyguards play the role of soldiers in the story that is both hers and not hers, but in whose general contours she appears to be well versed.

Tègònni's sisters are ready to support her, and to celebrate her wedding. But the wedding procession is interrupted when the road is closed due to the presence of soldiers, who are guarding the unburied corpse of Tègònni's brother, Prince Oyekunle, which Lt. General Carter-Ross refuses to have buried. Oyekunle took part in a revolt against British rule, and is thus considered a traitor. Carter-Ross has become a symbolic father of sorts to Jones, and in this sense also he parallels Creon. His disapproval of the impending wedding is responsible for the blockage of the celebrations. Tègònni and her sisters are arrested when they violate the soldiers' orders to leave the corpse of Tègònni's brother unburied. They escape, after some harsh exchanges between Tègònni and Carter-Ross.

The deaths of Tègònni and Jones at the end of the play are shrouded in mystery (as are those of their Sophoclean counterparts, Antigone and Haemon), and the final, dreamlike sequence includes an image of Antigone and Tègònni sailing off together in a boat—presumably to prepare for their next mythopolitical intervention. Just as Antigone's tragic end has not prevented her from rising again, neither has Tègònni's.

The play is situated in Nigeria at the end of the nineteenth century, but also resonates with Nigeria of the 1990s, the period of its creation, and at the same time it self-consciously situates itself in relation to the era of Antigone's birth, that of a previous colonial empire, classical Athens. In addition to thereby exploring its own relationship to the cultural legacy of colonial rule, it self-consciously situates itself in relation to Yoruba tradition and culture. The question of gender features prominently, most obviously through the exploration of what expectations Tègònni has of marriage, and through reflections on her role as a caster, a craft in which she has attained some prominence, as the first woman to achieve such a status. The question of slavery is also referenced, through the figure of Reverend Bayo Campbell, a Church Missionary. The clash between British imperial traditions and Yoruba traditions is one that is explored throughout the play. The mythological significance of the figure of Antigone, who serves both as an inspiration for Tègònni and as figure who is emblematic of European, colonial oppression, allows Òsófisan to situate her in the context of European colonial history, and to highlight its imperial ambitions. Equally in evidence is his effort to address the corrupt regimes of contemporary Nigeria, which have capitulated to the exploitation of European multinational corporations.

Notes

Preface

1. In this regard Gregory Vlastos's argument that there is an analogy between the relation of mind to body and master to slave in Plato is worthy of note. See Vlastos, "Slavery in Plato's Thought," in *Platonic Studies* (Princeton: Princeton University Press, 1981), 154. Vlastos also points out that for both Aristotle and Plato "there is no difference . . . between the relation of a master to his slave and of a sovereign to his subjects" (151).

2. While Wm. Blake Tyrrell and Larry J. Bennett, in *Recapturing Sophocles' Antigone* (Lanham: Rowman and Littlefield, 1998) have made a connection between the Periclean law and Antigone's argument about the replaceability of a potential husband or son, they have not drawn out this connection in terms of the larger argument I am making about the structuring role of slavery in the Athenian (un)conscious/imaginary. I located Tyrrell and Bennett's argument late in the writing of this book. I thank Ali Beheler for drawing their work to my attention. Hereafter cited in the text as RS, followed by page numbers.

3. Dietrich Huff, "Archaeological Evidence of Zoroastrian Funerary Practices," in *Zorastrian Rituals in Context*, ed. Michael Stausberg (Boston: Brill, 2004), 593–630. See also Robert W. Habenstein and William M. Lamers, *Funeral Customs the World Over* (Milwaukee: Bulfin Printers, 1960), 181.

4. In an important, recent book, Barbara Goff and Michael Simpson, acknowledging their debt to Paul Gilroy, stipulate their effort to explore the dynamic of cultural transmission at stake in a series of more or less contemporaneous appropriations of Greek tragedy by transposing Gilroy's motif of the "Black Atlantic" into that of the "Black Aegean," by which the authors designate "Africa and the diaspora, ancient Greece and contemporary Europe," *Crossroads at the Black Aegean: Oedipus, Antigone and Dramas of the African Diaspora* (Oxford: Oxford University Press, 2007), 34 and 8. Yet even as they go some way toward offering this new and suggestive conceptual framework, Goff and Simpson tend to assume the terms in which the Oedipal complex has itself assumed under the pens of Sigmund Freud and Jacques Lacan, as if it provided an appropriate framework within which to consider African appropriations of *Antigone*, plays such as *The Island* and *Tègònni*. While I share their commitment to according these plays the serious scholarly attention they deserve, I think that the questions at stake in these

plays, questions arising out of the histories of apartheid, slavery, and colonialism also require an interrogation of the terms of inheritance that have shaped our reception of the Oedipal myth. While psychoanalysis remains important—I would say crucial—as a means of theoretical and affective excavation, its inception and history is one that is steeped in problematic assumptions and systematic erasures, not the least of which are implicated in its own repression of colonial imperialism.

5. The importance of Anne McClintock's *Imperial Leather: Race, Gender, and Sexuality in the Colonial Contest* (New York: Routledge, 1995), especially the light it sheds on the extent to which the category of gender, in Freud and others, is "articulated . . . *through and by class*" (94), should not be underestimated. In the Victorian period, McClintock suggests, class was managed by projecting the "ideology of race" onto working class women" (95). While I question the exact terms McClintock employs in laying out this suggestion, especially in terms of a kind of slippage that occurs both between class and race, and between highly specific psychoanalytic terms—a problem that is hardly unique to McClintock, I think her excavation of the critical but neglected role that governesses, nurses, and other ostensibly marginal figures play in Freud's case studies is crucial.

6. I use the term postcolonial here with some qualification, given Gayatri Chakravorty Spivak's interrogation of the term in *Critique of Postcolonial Reason: Toward a History of the Vanishing Present* (Cambridge: Harvard University Press, 1999), and given Òsófisan's own misgivings about reducing his plays to a "postcolonial" context. Spivak's concerns about the cooptation and ghettoization of "postcolonial/colonial discourse studies" and the danger of postcolonial studies "unwittingly commemorating a lost object" (1) is consonant with concerns that Òsófisan has also expressed about the theoretical frameworks critics use to interpret his plays. Whether the "production of current neocolonial knowledge" places "colonialism/imperialism securely in the past" or suggests "a continuous line from that past to our present" (1) it is in danger of eclipsing important questions. For Òsófisan, one of his concerns about the term postcolonial is that it continues to posit the West as the center, and, according to this view, Africa would be the Other of the West. Instead, Òsófisan posits himself firmly in Africa, from which standpoint the West, not Africa, is the Other. Òsófisan is concerned about the reduction of African literature to a "writing back" to "Empire," and prefers the term "post-Negritude," which he construes not as rejecting "wholesale the use of the inherited colonial language as a language of national communication and of artistic creation; but . . . also [as] recognize[ing] the validity of our local languages, and advocate[ing] the promotion of all of these," "Theatre and the Rites of 'Post-negritude' Remembering," *Research in African Literatures* 30 (1999): 3, 11.

7. Fémi Òsófisan, *Tègònni, an African Antigone* (Ibadan, Nigeria: Kenbim Press 1999). Hereafter cited in text as T, followed by page numbers.

8. Athol Fugard, John Kani, and Winston Ntshona. *The Island*. In *Statements: two workshop productions. Sizwe Bansi is Dead*, and *The Island*; and a new play, *Statements after an arrest under the Immorality Act* (London: Oxford University Press, 1974). Hereafter cited in the text as I, followed by page numbers.

9. The play was also performed, among many other venues, in New York, 2003, performed by the Royal National Theatre and the Market Theatre of Johannesburg. I was able to view the digital recording of this performance at the New York Public Library for

the Performing Arts, Dorothy and Lewis B. Cullman Center. I was also able to attend the production by the Remy Bumppo Theatre Company at the Greenhouse Theatre in Chicago 2010, directed by James Bohnen, a production whose stage setting was clearly influenced by the New York production.

10. Edith Hall, "When is a Myth Not a Myth? Bernal's 'Ancient Model,' " in *Greeks and the Barbarians*, ed. Thomas Harrison (New York: Routledge, 2002), 134.

11. While not necessarily appealing to any conscious design on the part of Sophocles, my argument is that the issues of defining slaves, barbarians, and outsiders, precisely to the extent these were determinative of the fabric of daily life in Athens, also help to configure the climate in which Sophocles was creating his tragedies.

12. It is, perhaps, worth clarifying, for example, that I agree with both the appreciation Hall expresses concerning the intervention of Martin Bernal, *Black Athena: The Afroasiatic Roots of Classical Civilization*, vol. 1 of *The Fabrication of Ancient Greece 1785–1985* (New Brunswick, New Jersey: Rutgers University Press, 1987), and the caution she advocates concerning the status of myth in his work. In "When is a Myth Not a Myth? Bernal's 'Ancient Model,'" in *Greeks and the Barbarians*, ed. Thomas Harrison. (New York: Routledge, 2002), Hall acknowledges that Bernal's argument in *Black Athena* is an "important one" (134) but criticizes him for implying that Greek myth contains "unmediated literal, historical truths" (148). Bernal, says Hall, "sets up two rival models of Greek prehistory" (133), the one that he advances, which "sees ancient Greece as essentially a Levantine culture, on the periphery of the Egyptian and Semitic spheres of influence," and the one he contests, which he calls "the extreme Aryan Model" (133). This latter view "was invented . . . in the early nineteenth century" and "saw the Greeks as Indo-European speaking invaders from the north" by those who were loathe to admit "any Semitic or African influence on the 'pure childhood' of Europe" (133–4). Hall concludes that Bernal deserves credit to the extent that he has helped us "reject forever the 'Aryan Model' and leave the question of who the Greeks actually were, biologically at least, buried with a proper degree of contempt." She goes on, however, to suggest that "in altogether abandoning the 'Aryan Model,' the nineteenth century's Myth of the Northern Origin of the Greeks, we ought not simply substitute another myth, the Myth of the Egyptian and Phoenician Takeover of Pre-Greece. What we must do is reject the historical validity of both myths" (149). The problem with Bernal's position, according to Hall, is that "he wants the Greek myths to contain historical truth" (139) and in doing so he implicitly treats them as if they revealed an objective reality, while failing to account for the fact that "the ruling families in every polis defined their subjective ethnicity by tracing their forefathers' genealogies in different ways" (142). For a useful discussion of historiography in relation to the important questions and challenges raised by Bernal's work, see also, Mario Liverani, "The Bathwater and the Baby," in *Black Athena Revisited*, ed. Mary R. Lefkowitz and Guy Mclean Rogers (Chapel Hill: The University of North Carolina, 1996), 421–427.

13. Having said that the issues surrounding race in the twentieth century plays I discuss are not of a piece with the issues surrounding barbarians or slaves in Greek tragedy, no doubt Hall is right when she observes that "the complex system of signifiers denoting the ethnically, psychologically and politically 'other' " in the "Panhellenic ideology which the poets both produced and reflected . . . were to be of lasting influence on western views of foreign cultures, especially the portrait of Asiatic peoples as

effeminate, despotic and cruel" *Inventing the Barbarian: Greek Self-Definition through Tragedy* (Oxford: Clarendon Press, 1989) 2. I thank both Lynne Huffer and Mary Beth Mader for pushing me on this question in different ways.

14. Nonetheless, racialized characterizations of certain people play into Aristotle's thinking about who conforms, allegedly naturally, to slavery, as we shall see.

15. The problem is a particularly vexed one since the issue of change—which is bound up with ideas of what is under individual control and what it not—is sometimes used in differentiating between racism and other forms of prejudice. Benjamin Isaac says, for example, "The major difference between racism and ethnic and other group prejudices is that such prejudices do not deny the possibility of change at an individual or collective level in principle. . . . Both racist attitudes and ethnic prejudice treat a whole nation or other group as a single group or as a single individual with a single personality." *The invention of Racism in Classical Antiquity* (New Jersey: Princeton University Press, 2004), 24. Hereafter cited in the text as IR.

16. Hall, "When is a Myth Not a Myth? Bernal's 'Ancient Model,' " in *Greeks and the Barbarians*, ed. Thomas Harrison (New York: Routledge, 2002), 136.

17. Paul Cartledge, *The Greeks: A Portrait of Self and Others* (Oxford: Oxford University Press, 2002), 125–6. Hereafter cited in the text as GP, followed by page numbers.

18. Edward Said, *Orientalism* (New York: Vintage Books, 1979).

19. Benjamin Isaac, *The Invention of Racism in Classical Antiquity* (New Jersey: Princeton University Press, 2004), 9. Hereafter cited in the text as IR, followed by page numbers.

20. See, for example, Michael Omi and Howard Winant, *Racial Formation in the United States: From the 1960s to the 1990s* (New York: Routledge, 1994).

21. E. R. Dodds, *The Greeks and the Irrational* (Berkeley: University of California Press, 1951).

22. Cynthia Willet, The *Soul of Justice: Social Bonds and Racial Hubris* (Ithaca: Cornell University Press, 2001), is noteworthy in this respect.

23. Shahrokh Razmjou, "Religion and Burial Customs," in *Forgotten Empire: The World of Ancient Persia*, ed. John Curtis and Nigel Tallis (Berkeley: University of California, 2005), 154.

24. Shahrokh Razmjou, "Religion and Burial Customs," in *Forgotten Empire: The World of Ancient Persia*, ed. John Curtis and Nigel Tallis (Berkeley: University of California, 2005), 154.

25. See *Antigone* 205–6. Creon says, in Storr's translation, "For Polyneices 'tis ordained that none / Shall give him burial or make mourn for him, / But leave his corpse unburied, to be meat / For dogs and carrion crows, a ghastly sight," *Sophocles in two volumes*, vol. 1, *The Loeb classical library* (Cambridge, Massachusetts: Harvard University Press, 1981).

26. See Nicole Loraux, *The Experiences of Tiresisas: the Feminine and the Greek Man*, trans. Paula Wissig (Princeton: Princeton University Press, 1995).

27. Hall, *Inventing the Barbarian: Greek Self-Definition through Tragedy* (Oxford: Clarendon Press, 1989), 179. Hall cites Sophocles, *Antigone* 1002.

28. If my suggestion that the oracle that Oedipus tries unsuccessfully to evade—that a son born to Jocasta and Lauis will murder his father—might itself reference ancient Greek beliefs in the heritability of slavery, it might also refer to the idea that slavery

is natural (articulated by Aristotle), that it is dependent upon the passing down of a particular type of soul from one generation to another.

29. See Carol Jacobs, "Dusting Antigone," *MLN* 111 (1996): 898. See also Butler, *Antigone's Claim: Kinship Between Life & Death* (New York: Columbia University Press, 2000), 7.

30. Tyrrell and Bennett cite Robert Parker, *Miasma: Pollution and Purification in Early Greek Religion* (Oxford: Clarendon Press, 1983), 44.

31. My suggestion here is not that Aristotle literally thought of slaves as animals or tools, but he does employ these analogies in a way that degrades the humanity of slaves.

32. Nicole Loraux, *Born of the Earth: Myth and Politics in Athens*, trans. Selina Stewart (Ithaca: Cornell University Press, 2000), 14.

33. Loraux, *Born of the Earth: Myth and Politics in Athens*, trans. Selina Stewart (Ithaca: Cornell University Press, 2000), 14.

34. Loraux, *Born of the Earth: Myth and Politics in Athens*, trans. Selina Stewart (Ithaca: Cornell University Press, 2000), 14.

35. Loraux, *Born of the Earth: Myth and Politics in Athens*, trans. Selina Stewart (Ithaca: Cornell University Press, 2000), 9.

36. Loraux, *Born of the Earth: Myth and Politics in Athens*, trans. Selina Stewart (Ithaca: Cornell University Press, 2000), 9–10.

37. Hall, "When is a Myth Not a Myth? Bernal's 'Ancient Model,' " in *Greeks and the Barbarians*, ed. Thomas Harrison (New York: Routledge, 2002), 144. Hall's reference is to Froma I. Zeitlin, "Thebes, Theater of Self and Society in Athenian Drama," in *Greek Tragedy and Political Theory*, ed. J. Peter Euben (Berkeley and Los Angeles: University of California, 1986), 101–141.

38. N. R. E. Fisher, *Slavery in Classical Greece* (London: Bristol Classical Press), 1993.

39. Peter Garnsey, *Ideas of Slavery from Aristotle to Augustine* (Cambridge: Cambridge University Press, 1999), 6–7.

40. Aristotle, *Nicomachean Ethics*, trans. H. Rackham, vol. 19 *The Loeb Classical Library*, Aristotle in twenty-three volumes (Cambridge, Mass.: Harvard University Press, 1975). Cartledge takes Aristotle's "iron commitment to the natural necessity of slaves for the living of the good life in the *polis* by non-slaves" as an indication of the importance of slaves for Classical Greek civilization (GP 137).

41. Cartledge is citing Charles Segal, "Afterword: J.-P. Vernant and the Study of Ancient Greece," *Arethusa* 15 (1982): 232.

42. Cartledge was not the first to say this. See also, for example, to Edith Hall *Inventing the Barbarian: Greek Self-Definition through Tragedy* (Oxford: Clarendon Press, 1989), 2.

43. For a discussion of the differences between *astoi*, *politai*, and *xenoi* in relation to Pericles' law, see Cynthia Patterson, *Pericles' Citizenship Law of 451–50 BC. Monographs in Classical Studies.* (Ayer Company: Salem, New Hampshire, 1988), 151–167.

44. At the end of *Antigone*, Antigone refers to herself twice as a metic, as an "alien midst the living and the dead" (851), and as "an alien" who goes to meet her dead father and mother "there below" (869). She thus evokes the idea of being between the living and the dead, between, perhaps, the full life of the adult male citizen, and the bare life of slaves.

45. See Cartledge, GS 105–32.

46. Aristotle, *Politics*, trans. H. Rackham. *Loeb Classical Library*, Aristotle, vol. 21. (Cambridge: Harvard University Press, 2005), 1252b and 1252b5–7. Like so many of Aristotle's assertions regarding slavery and women, this assertion proves to be untenable in the light of other views he holds. If women and slaves hold the same rank among barbarians, a postulation that is used to discredit barbarian males, and yet barbarian men are said to be effeminate—in part because they lack control over barbarian women—then women are implicitly regarded as holding a higher rank than slaves. Given the elision of the difference between barbarians and slaves in the popular Greek imaginary, barbarians as a whole are regarded as slavish, and this presents further problems for what Aristotle is asserting here.

47. See Bernard Williams' discussion of women and slaves in Aristotle, *Shame and Necessity* (University of California Press: Berkeley, 1993), esp. 118.

48. Again, Cartledge is not the first to have observed the way in which the convergence of the idea of barbarians and slaves for the Greeks. See Hall *Inventing the Barbarian: Greek Self-Definition through Tragedy* (Oxford: Clarendon Press, 1989), 2, for example.

49. Although Aristotle does not confront this question directly, the convoluted reasoning in which he engages concerning stooping bodies and souls might be taken as a sign that he obliquely addresses it. See Cartledge GP 140.

50. Fisher is generous when he characterizes Aristotle's attempt to provide a theory of natural slavery as "complex and thoughtful," though "flawed by fundamental contradictions and illogicalities," *Slavery in Classical Greece* (London: Bristol Classical Press, 1993) 94. Paul Cartledge is closer to the truth when he calls it "ethically retrograde" and "flawed by its unexamined presuppositions" (GP 141) and Bernard Williams is also on the money when he judges it simply "incoherent," *Shame and Necessity* (University of California Press: Berkeley, 1993), 111.

51. Also see Wilfred Nippel, "The Construction of the 'Other.' " *Greeks and the Barbarians*, trans. Antonia Neville, ed. Thomas Harrison (New York: Routledge, 2002), 292.

52. A complex relation pertains between the alleged despotism of those construed as slavish barbarians, and Athenian consciousness. This complexity begins to emerge in considering the fact that the term *despotēs* was the usual Greek term to designate, as Cartledge says, the "master of slaves" (GP, 112). At the same time the term connotes the "head of the family," as Giorgio Agamben renders it, *Homo Sacer: Sovereign Power and Bare Life*, trans. Daniel Heller-Roazen (Stanford: Stanford University Press, 1998), 2. The attempt of a newly democratic Athens (with all the caveats that need to be added to specify that this form of democracy excluded women and slaves) to differentiate itself from other cities and peoples, and especially from the Persians, was conducted in part through specifying Athens as democratic. The rule of male Athenian citizens over women and slaves was of a piece, then, with the Athenian empire, and the way it positioned itself in relation to non-Greeks, as well as over other Greek poleis. Questions of tyranny and despotism are at the heart of Creon's dispute with Antigone, a dispute implicated in debates over the status of barbarians as much as in debates regarding female or male traits. For a discussion of the term *despotēs* in the Corinthian's exchange with the slave in *Oedipus Rex*, see Frederick Ahl, *Sophocles' Oedipus: Evidence and Self-Conviction* (Ithaca: Cornell University Press, 1991), 200.

53. Giorgio Agamben, *Homo Sacer: Sovereign Power and Bare Life*, trans. Daniel Heller-Roazen (Stanford: Stanford University Press, 1998), 7.

54. Moira Fradinger, "Violent Boundaries: Antigone's Political Imagination," *theory@buffalo* 10 (2005): 103–128. The option, as Creon figures it here, is that either the Thebans are enslaved, or they enslave their attacker, their enemy. Polynices tried to enslave Thebes, and so he should be treated in death as a slave.

55. In this respect it is worth recalling that Sophocles has Creon compare Antigone to a horse, a steed, who must be broken in (*Antigone*, 476). See Fisher on various terms used for slaves, and for elaboration on meaning of *andrapodon*, *Slavery in Classical Greece* (London: Bristol Classical Press, 1993), 7. On the question of whether or not there was a "continuum," which more accurately describes the relation of free to slave than an antithesis, see Cartledge's reference to Finley (GP 144). See M. I. Finley, *Ancient Slavery and Modern Ideology* (London: Chatto & Windus, 1980).

56. See Frederick Ahl, *Two Faces of Oedipus: Sophocles'* Oedipus Tyrannus *and Seneca's* Oedipus, trans. with an introduction (Ithaca: Cornell University Press, 2008), 1–2.

57. In Chapter 3 we will see how *The Island* takes up the Sphinx's riddle, dramatizing a creature on four feet, when Winston, having been injured by a prison guard, crawls around his prison cell on all fours, a creature on three legs when John and Winston are forced to run in a three-legged formation.

58. Frederick Ahl, *Sophocles' Oedipus: Evidence and Self-Conviction* (Ithaca: Cornell University Press, 1991), 201–5.

59. Frederick Ahl, *Sophocles' Oedipus: Evidence and Self-Conviction* (Ithaca: Cornell University Press, 1991), 201–5. The word, from *Oedipus the King* 1168, translated here as "blood" is genos; F. Storr translates it as "race." See Storr, *Sophocles in two volumes*, vol. 1, *The Loeb classical library* (Cambridge, Massachusetts: Harvard University Press, 1981).

60. On the exposure of infants see Fisher, *Slavery in Classical Greece* (London: Bristol Classical Press, 1993), 36. See also Cynthia Patterson " 'Not Worth the Rearing:' The Causes of Infant Exposure in Ancient Greece," *Transactions of the American Philological Association* 115 (1985): 103–23.

61. Frederick Ahl, *Sophocles' Oedipus: Evidence and Self-Conviction* (Ithaca: Cornell University Press, 1991), 12.

62. Ahl argues that the origins of Oedipus are never satisfactorily cleared up, and that Sophocles leaves his audience to draw their own inferences. Oedipus convicts himself on the basis of flimsy evidence. This argument accords with my own sense that Sophocles's Oedipal cycle does all it can to complicate the question of legitimacy and origins, and that one of the issues at the center of these questions is the legitimacy of slavery. See *Sophocles' Oedipus: Evidence and Self-Conviction* (Ithaca: Cornell University Press, 1991), 11–12.

63. Cartledge cites Finley, who says, "everyone was agreed that the institution should be preserved" (GP121–2).

64. Williams, *Shame and Necessity* (University of California Press: Berkeley, 1993), 112.

65. Williams, *Shame and Necessity* (University of California Press: Berkeley, 1993), 113. See also Cartledge, who observes, "The initial postulate, that the good life for mankind can be lived only within the framework of the *polis*, is crucial for Aristotle. . . . Aristotle's

gloss on the ordinary free Greek's view of slavery could be woven seamlessly into his anti-conventionalist, teleological view of the good life for mankind within the *polis*. For, aside from purely notional automation, he could imagine no alternative to slavery as a means of providing the privileged Greek citizens with the necessary leisure (*skholē*) for their *praxis* of politics and philosophical contemplation" (GP137–142).

66. Williams, *Shame and Necessity* (University of California Press: Berkeley, 1993), 114.

67. Aristotle, *Politics*, trans. H. Rackham. *Loeb Classical Library*, Aristotle, vol. 21 (Cambridge: Harvard University Press, 2005), 1285a22–3.

68. Williams characterizes Aristotle's argument vis-à-vis tools in a particularly telling way when he says, "if there were self-propelling tools that could perform the tasks, 'either at our bidding or itself perceiving the need,' there would be no need of slaves," *Shame and Necessity* (University of California Press: Berkeley, 1993), 112. For a discussion of Aristotle's comparison of slaves with animals (as well as with savages, women, and children), see Garnsey, *Ideas of Slavery from Aristotle to Augustine* (Cambridge: Cambridge University Press, 1999), 110–115.

69. As Cartledge formulates it, "although the natural slave has a share in reason, it is only a partial share: though sufficient reason ought to be obeyed, it is completely incapable of independent reasoning on its own behalf" (GP 140). See also Garnsey, *Ideas of Slavery from Aristotle to Augustine* (Cambridge: Cambridge University Press, 1999), 13 and109. As Cartledge observes (GP 137) Aristotle is following the lead of Plato here. See also Fisher, *Slavery in Classical Greece* (London: Bristol Classical Press, 1993) and Garnsey, *Ideas of Slavery from Aristotle to Augustine* (Cambridge: Cambridge University Press, 1999) on the relation between Plato and Aristotle with regard to their views on slavery.

70. Aristotle, *Politics*, trans. H. Rackham. *Loeb Classical Library*, Aristotle, vol. 21 (Cambridge: Harvard University Press, 2005), 1254b23–4.

71. Fisher *Slavery in Classical Greece* (London: Bristol Classical Press, 1993), 93. See Aristotle, *Politics*, trans. H. Rackham. *Loeb Classical Library*, Aristotle, vol. 21 (Cambridge: Harvard University Press, 2005), 1327b29 and 1285a20. See also Plato, who comments in *The Republic* on the "element of high spirit" in the "populations of the Thracian and Scythian lands and generally of northern regions," *Republic I,* trans. Paul Shorey. *Loeb Classical Library* (Harvard University Press: William Heinemann, 1978), 435E.

72. Aristotle, *Politics*, trans. H. Rackham. *Loeb Classical Library*, Aristotle, vol. 21 (Cambridge: Harvard University Press, 2005), 1327b31–33.

73. Fisher, *Slavery in Classical Greece* (London: Bristol Classical Press, 1993), 96.

74. Aristotle, *Politics*, trans. H. Rackham. *Loeb Classical Library*, Aristotle, vol. 21 (Cambridge: Harvard University Press, 2005), 1327b33–34.

75. Hall says, "The barbarian world of the tragic stage had come to serve as an expression of what structuralists call *l'Autre*, everything that Hellas, and in particular the male 'club' which constituted the Athenian citizenry, was not, for the Greeks' culture was now defined by comparison with and negative," *Inventing the Barbarian: Greek Self-Definition through Tragedy* (Oxford: Clarendon Press, 1989), 162. Hall goes on to say that the "Athenian City Dionysia," where most of the Attic tragedies were performed, "presented, of course, an opportunity to vaunt Athenian ascendancy over the other Hellenic states" (162).

76. Hall argues that "Greek writing about barbarians is usually an exercise in self-definition, for the barbarian is often portrayed as the opposite of the ideal Greek," and suggests that "the polarization of Hellene and barbarian was invented in specific historical circumstances during the early years of the fifth century BC, partly as a result of the combined Greek military efforts against the Persians. The notions of Panhellenism and its corollary, all non-Greeks as a collective genus, were however more particularly elements of the Athenian ideology which buttressed first the Delian league, the alliance against the Persians formed in the years immediately after the wars, and subsequently the Athenian empire. The image of an enemy extraneous to Hellas helped to foster a sense of community between the allied states. The Athenian empire was . . . a democratic constitution. . . . The most important distinction Athenian writers draw between themselves and barbarians is therefore political. Greeks are democratic and egalitarian; the barbarians are tyrannical and hierarchical. But the economic basis of the Athenian empire was slavery, and most of the large number of slaves in fifth-century Athens were not Greek. The class division along ethnic lines provided further stimulus for the generation of arguments which supported the belief that barbarians were generically inferior, even slavish by nature," *Inventing the Barbarian: Greek Self-Definition through Tragedy* (Oxford: Clarendon Press, 1989), 1–2.

77. Hall, *Inventing the Barbarian: Greek Self-Definition through Tragedy* (Oxford: Clarendon Press, 1989), 161.

78. See Nippel, "The Construction of the 'Other.' " *Greeks and the Barbarians*, trans. Antonia Neville, ed. Thomas Harrison (New York: Routledge, 2002), 291.

79. Aristotle, *Politics*, trans. H. Rackham. *Loeb Classical Library*, Aristotle, vol. 21 (Cambridge: Harvard University Press, 2005), 1252a.

80. It is worth noting that Aristotle was not a citizen of Athens, but lived there for most of his life as a resident alien (metic). See Cartledge GP 125.

81. Garnsey, *Ideas of Slavery from Aristotle to Augustine* (Cambridge: Cambridge University Press, 1999), 108. See also Williams, *Shame and Necessity* (University of California Press: Berkeley, 1993), 114–5.

82. Aristotle, *Politics*, trans. H. Rackham. *Loeb Classical Library*, Aristotle, vol. 21. Cambridge: Harvard University Press, 2005, 1255a.

83. Aristotle identified with the ruling class of Athens, although not a citizen himself (see Cartledge, GP 164–5).

84. See Williams, *Shame and Necessity* (University of California Press: Berkeley, 1993), 106.

85. Williams, *Shame and Necessity* (University of California Press: Berkeley, 1993), 118. Williams cites Loraux, *The Children of Athena: Athenian Ideas about Citizenship and the Division between the Sexes*, trans. Caroline Levine (Princeton: Princeton University Press), 1993; the reference Loraux gives is to Aristotle's *Athenian Constitution*. For a compilation of other original sources referencing Pericles' law, see Cynthia Patterson, *Pericles' Citizenship Law of 451–50 BC. Monographs in Classical Studies* (Ayer Company: Salem, New Hampshire, 1988).

86. It is unclear how far Pericles' law concerned marriage as such (although it has been sometimes taken to do so), and how far it simply mandated that henceforth those who qualified as citizens must be born of Athenian fathers and mothers.

87. Patterson, *Pericles' Citizenship Law of 451–50 BC. Monographs in Classical Studies* (Ayer Company: Salem, New Hampshire, 1988), 130.

88. Patterson, *Pericles' Citizenship Law of 451–50 BC. Monographs in Classical Studies* (Ayer Company: Salem, New Hampshire, 1988), 130–132.

89. Williams, *Shame and Necessity* (University of California Press: Berkeley, 1993), 125.

90. M. I. Finley, *Ancient Slavery and Modern Ideology* (London: Chatto & Windus, 1980), 86.

91. Finley, *Ancient Slavery and Modern Ideology* (London: Chatto & Windus, 1980), 89–90.

92. Garnsey, *Ideas of Slavery from Aristotle to Augustine* (Cambridge: Cambridge University Press, 1999), 4.

93. Fisher on various terms used for slaves, and for elaboration on meaning of *andrapodon*, *Slavery in Classical Greece* (London: Bristol Classical Press, 1993), 16.

94. Finley, *Ancient Slavery and Modern Ideology* (London: Chatto & Windus, 1980), 75.

95. Fisher, *Slavery in Classical Greece* (London: Bristol Classical Press, 1993), 6. Fisher's reference is to Orlando Patterson, who explores what he calls social death in *Slavery and Social Death: A Comparative Study* (Cambridge: Harvard University Press, 1982).

96. Garnsey, *Ideas of Slavery from Aristotle to Augustine* (Cambridge: Cambridge University Press, 1999), 1.

97. Garnsey, *Ideas of Slavery from Aristotle to Augustine* (Cambridge: Cambridge University Press, 1999), 6. See also Williams, *Shame and Necessity* (University of California Press: Berkeley, 1993), 107.

98. Finley, *Ancient Slavery and Modern Ideology* (London: Chatto & Windus, 1980), 85.

99. Finley, *Ancient Slavery and Modern Ideology* (London: Chatto & Windus, 1980), 68. As Garnsey puts it "A slave was property. The slaveowner's rights over his slave-property were total, covering the person as well as the labour of the slave," *Ideas of Slavery from Aristotle to Augustine* (Cambridge: Cambridge University Press, 1999), 1.

100. Finley, *Ancient Slavery and Modern Ideology* (London: Chatto & Windus, 1980), 74. Finley is quoting Orlando Patterson, "The Study of Slavery," *Annual Review of Sociology* III, 1977: 407–49.

101. Finley, *Ancient Slavery and Modern Ideology* (London: Chatto & Windus, 1980), 97.

102. Finley, *Ancient Slavery and Modern Ideology* (London: Chatto & Windus, 1980), 95.

103. Fisher, *Slavery in Classical Greece* (London: Bristol Classical Press, 1993), 95.

104. Bonnie Honig, "Antigone's Laments, Creon's Grief: Mourning, Membership, and the Politics of Exception," *Political Theory*, February 2009 37: 5-43. I thank Bonnie Honig for our exchanges on Antigone during the period in which I was writing this book.

Chapter 1

1. Rabinowitz suggests that the "resistance to seeing Greek society as a 'slave society' " in the nineteenth century was linked to the abolitionist movement, while the Cold War provided the context "for more recent discussions," "Slaves with Slaves: Women and Class in Euripidean Tragedy," in *Women and Slaves in Greco-Roman Culture: Differential Equations*, ed. Sandra R. Joshel and Sheila Murnaghan (New York: Routledge, 1998), 56. Finley quotes Arnold Heeren, writing at the beginning of the nineteenth century, as follows: "everything that moderns have said about and against slavery may also be applied to the Greeks. . . . But one should not try to deny the truth that, without the instrument of slavery, the culture of the ruling class in Greece could in no way have become what it did. If the fruits which the latter bore have a value for the whole of civilized mankind, *then it may at least be allowed to express doubt whether it was bought at too high a price in the introduction of slavery*," Finley, *Ancient Slavery and Modern Ideology* (London: Chatto & Windus, 1980), 12. Finley goes on to summarize Heeren's view in this way: "slavery, though an evil, was not too great a price to pay for the supreme cultural achievement (and legacy) of the Greeks" (14). It is worth noting Finley's own elision of the sense in which women and children's labor has traditionally been construed as unproblematically subservient to the family—the head of which has traditionally been construed as unproblematically male. In defining slavery, he distinguishes "labour for oneself and labour for others" Finley notes that he is "aware" that he faces "objections from several directions" when he says that: " 'Oneself' is to be understood not in a narrow individualistic sense but as embracing the family . . . That is to say, the work of the women and children within the family, no matter how authoritarian or patriarchal its structure, is not subsumed under this category of labor for others" (67). One direction from which one would expect objections is a feminist one. In the context of *Antgione*, where Antigone's own insistence upon burying her brother, and her refusal to deny that she has done so, not only (as it is usually taken to do) performs the work of distinguishing her right as a member of Polynices' family to bury his corpse from the authority of the state as enshrined in Creon's prohibition against the burial. Antigone's act and her defense of it also performs the work of distinguishing such a right from its subsumption within the family, since Antigone claims to be the author of this act, and will not allow Ismene, who did not perform the act, to lay claim to it. At the same time, in asserting her right to act on her own behalf, and in asserting the rationale for her act, she lays claim to a public voice, contesting her exclusion from the political, and thereby not only distinguishes the body of Polynices from a slave, but also establishes the difference between her action and that of a slave.

2. Yvon Garlan, *Slavery in Ancient Greece*. Revised and Expanded Edition, trans. Janet Lloyd (Ithaca: Cornell University Press, 1988), 144.

3. Gregory Vlastos, "Slavery in Plato's Thought," in *Platonic Studies*, 147–63 (Princeton: Princeton University Press, 1981), 153 and 162.

4. Page duBois, *Slaves and Other Objects* (Chicago: University of Chicago Press, 2003), 166.

5. Gayle Rubin, "The Traffic in Women: Notes on the 'Political Economy' of Sex" in *Toward an Anthropology of Women*, ed. Rayna R. Reiter (New York: Monthly Review Press, 1975).

6. As Fisher says, Athenian men imposed on women "strict codes of chastity and marital fidelity in order to preserve the reputation of the family, and to prevent there being any hint of doubt about the parentage of children. . . . a respectable woman had to have a male relative in authority over her as her legal guardian (kyrios) throughout her life. . . . Women were thought to derive more pleasure from sex than men, and be more lacking in moral self-control . . . Equally, women were widely supposed to be more likely than men to be 'enslaved' to the pleasures of food and especially drink, to be excessively emotional, to be weak, cowardly and fearful, and to be unable to develop rational arguments," *Slavery in Classical Greece* (London: Bristol Classical Press, 1993), 105–6.

7. Since Dionysos is the god of fertility, Antigone flouts both of the gods to whom the chorus of *Antigone* appeals (the other being the god of Eros).

8. As Froma Zeitlin says, in *Oedipus at Colonus*, the daughters of Oedipus tend him "despite the social conventions that would keep them safely at home," "Thebes: Theater of Self and Society in Athenian Drama" in *Nothing to do with Dionysos? Athenian Drama in its Social Context*, ed. John J. Winkler and Froma I. Zeitlin (Princeton, New Jersey: Princeton University Press, 1990), 159.

9. Derrida, *Glas*, trans. John P. Leavey and Richard Rand (Lincoln: University of Nebraska Press, 1986).

10. In her important article, "Antigone's Line," Mary Beth Mader suggests that Antigone's insistence upon burying Polynices should be read as an effort to disambiguate the symbolic order of the father from the son, an order that Oedipus had conflated through incest. I am suggesting that the ramifications of Antigone's burial of her brother not only asserts the importance of differentiating between the familial roles of father and son, but also implicates her both in an attempt to articulate the significance of the fact that Polynices is a free man, rather a slave, and in clarifying the conditions under which women are exchanged through marriage, for the sake of male inheritance. In distinguishing her brother from a slave, Antigone is at the same time distinguishing herself from a slave, claiming a voice in order to assert the bonds of philia between women, rather than between men. Although Ismene at first refuses to join Antigone in her act of defiance against Creon, she later wants to share in Antigone's death, yet is prevented from doing so by Antigone, who asserts the imperative need to observe the relation between deeds and words, and to be consistent in one's affect. In pointing to the affect that marks the impossibility of her exchange from her uncle/king to her affianced cousin, Antigone refuses not merely her particular marriage to Haemon. She refuses any marriage in which women are reduced to objects of exchange. More pertinently, she refuses the endogamous system of marriage of which Oedipus' incest has becomes a hyperbolic instantiation, exemplary of the more pervasive tendency of endogamy from which Antigone marks her distance. See "Antigone's Line," *Bulletin de la société Américaine de philosophie de langue Francaise*, 14: 2 (2005): 18–40.

11. Whether the exchange of women was intended to consolidate relationships between powerful families, or to perpetuate the households that constituted the city by legitimating male inheritance, the marriage of women was a matter of cementing a system of socio-symbolic alliances that excluded women while at the same time depending on women to facilitate such alliances. See Jean-Pierre Vernant, *Myth and Society in Ancient Greece*, trans. Janet Lloyd (New York: Zone Books, 1990), 51.

12. There was one important exception to the general rule of women's exclusion from public, civic duties. The sphere of women's influence was limited to religion, in particular to burial rites. As Cartledge says, "Athenian women, in the sense of the mothers, sisters, wives, and daughters of Athenian citizen men, were 'citizens' only by courtesy, in all respects but one—religion. . . . In the real world, religion was the one public activity in which Athenian women might achieve parity or even superiority of esteem *vis-à-vis* their menfolk. . . . [I]n the sphere of death, burial and mourning the women of Greece had traditionally taken the more active and more publicly demonstrative religious role. Correspondingly, the one civic function approximating to the holding of public political office by men that Greek citizen women might legitimately perform, indeed were required to perform, was to serve as priestess of an officially recognised city cult, usually of a female divinity," " 'Deep Plays': Theatre as Process in Greek Civil Life" in *The Cambridge Companion to Greek Tragedy*, ed. P. E. Easterling (Cambridge: Cambridge University Press, 1997), 27. Antigone appeals to Dike, to Justice, in the words of Griffith, "conventionally imagined as Zeus's daughter," "The Subject of Desire in Sophocles' Antigone" in *The Soul of Tragedy: Essays on Athenian Drama*, ed. Victoria Pedrick and Steven M. Oberhelman (Chicago: The University of Chicago Press, 2005), 111.

13. We might add that part of the genius of Derrida's reading of *Antigone,* Hegel and Genet in *Glas*, trans. John P. Leavey and Richard Rand (Lincoln: University of Nebraska Press, 1986) is his focus on the symbolic role of the sister both in Sophocles' text, and in Hegel's text.

14. See Zeitlin "Thebes: Theater of Self and Society in Athenian Drama" in *Nothing to do with Dionysos? Athenian Drama in its Social Context*, ed. John J. Winkler and Froma I. Zeitlin (Princeton, New Jersey: Princeton University Press, 1990), 131, 138, and 158).

15. Fisher says, "To work for another was what slaves did . . . Athenians wished to avoid seeming 'slavish' through being too dependent on their own desires and passions, particularly those associated with the body," *Slavery in Classical Greece* (London: Bristol Classical Press, 1993), 101–3.

16. Fisher, *Slavery in Classical Greece* (London: Bristol Classical Press, 1993), 56.

17. See Vernant and Vidal-Naquet, *Myth and Tragedy in Ancient Greece*, trans. Janet Lloyd (New York: Zone Books, 1990), 107.

18. Ahl points out that "in his description of the piercing of Oedipus's feet in 10.5.3" Pausanius "recalls almost *verbatim* Euripides' *Phoenician Women* 25–26," *Sophocles' Oedipus: Evidence and Self-Conviction* (Ithaca: Cornell University Press, 1991), 12.

19. The ambiguity as to whether the marking or branding of his body is a result of divine intervention or rather due to Oedipus's own efforts could be read as a commentary on whether slaves were born to slavery or whether they suffered slavery as their just desert. As Williams says, "Public slaves, at least, were marked with a brand, which, as Xenophon observed, made them harder to steal than money," Williams, *Shame and Necessity* (University of California Press: Berkeley, 1993), 108.

20. While there is a rich scholarly tradition that takes up the theme of *deinos*, and the uncanny, this tradition has not pursued the social and political implications of the status of strangers in ancient Greece.

21. While establishing the true identity of one's children might seem to be a peculiarly male anxiety, in the light of the fact that adoption was an accepted practice in fifth century BCE Athens, in addition to the widespread existence of slavery, and given the common practice of Athenian citizens mating with slaves, it should not perhaps be seen as the exclusive preserve of men.

22. In some ways Oedipus embodies the same trope explored by Homer in the figure of Odysseus, who also returns home after a long absence, provoking ambiguity around the question of familial recognition, an ambiguity that is finally resolved through bodily scarring, but whereas Homer's *Odyssey* entertains the tension between foreign suitors and Odysseus, and the dangers confronted by Penelope and Telemachos, so that Odysseus feels it incumbent upon him to return in disguise, Sophocles employs the mechanism of having Oedipus's parents send him away so that he himself is ignorant of his identity. Not only does his family fail to recognize him, but he fails to recognize them, and it is this mutual failure of recognition that throws into crisis the normative familial boundaries that might have obtained otherwise. Sophocles' uses the failure of both self-knowledge and knowledge of the other to comment on, and perhaps warn against the growing tendency to marry one's own, a tendency that is liable to become culturally incestuous, in addition to its more overt dangers. The irony of the somewhat inward-looking traits of Sophocles' interpreters is that the cultural narcissism against which Sophocles can be read as warning appears to have been lost on an entire interpretive Western tradition, so much so that some of those who champion above all else reading the canon—and Sophocles is nothing if not canonical—align themselves with ideologies of exclusivity intent on keeping out the foreigners, as it were.

For a different, but compelling reading, see Zeitlin, who develops the relationship between autochthony and incest, and who suggests that Oedipus "qualifies himself for the role of an adopted stranger who will henceforth protect the city, one who will in the future distinguish between insiders and outsiders on the basis, not of any given status, but of actions and intentions," "Thebes: Theater of Self and Society in Athenian Drama" in *Nothing to do with Dionysos? Athenian Drama in its Social Context*, ed. John J. Winkler and Froma I. Zeitlin (Princeton, New Jersey: Princeton University Press, 1990), 161.

23. Plutarch, Pericles 37, *The Rise and Fall of Athena: Nine Greek Lives* (London: Penguin, 1960), 203–4. See also Rabinowitz, *Anxiety Veiled: Euripides and the Traffic in Women* (Ithaca: Cornell University Press, 1993), 3.

24. Vernant, *Myth and Society in Ancient Greece*, trans. Janet Lloyd (New York: Zone Books, 1990), 57 and 67.

25. Vernant, *Myth and Society in Ancient Greece*, trans. Janet Lloyd (New York: Zone Books, 1990), 70.

26. Vernant and Vidal-Naquet point out that Sophocles himself was affected by this law. See *Myth and Tragedy in Ancient Greece*, trans. Janet Lloyd (New York: Zone Books, 1990), 303.

27. I extrapolate this scenario from observations made by Yvon Garlan, who points to an exception to the general rule that a "slave could not be a former member of the civic body," namely that "newborn infants" could be handed over by poor citizens to "magistrates, who then sold them as slaves." This was the alternative to the "exposure of

infants" which "was forbidden—in Thebes for instance," *Slavery in Ancient Greece*. Revised and Expanded Edition, trans. Janet Lloyd (Ithaca: Cornell University Press, 1988), 45. See also Fisher, who says of fifth century BCE Athens, "Some infants of Greek birth may have been exposed because of their parents' poverty or because they were unwanted bastards, and then found and sold to be slaves. How often this happened is unknown; but the chances of any such slaves being 'recognised' by their original families and restored to freedom were minimal, despite the prevalence of this pattern in the plots of Greek plays," *Slavery in Classical Greece* (London: Bristol Classical Press, 1993), 36. See also Vernant and Vidal-Naquet, *Myth and Tragedy in Ancient Greece*, trans. Janet Lloyd (New York: Zone Books, 1990), 127.

28. H. S. Harris, *Hegel's Ladder*. vol. 2: The Odyssey of Spirit (Indianapolis: Hackett Publishing Company, 1997), 223.

29. Sophocles, *Antigone* 756.

30. To the extent that anxiety was prevalent due to the possibility that anyone might become a slave due to capture as a result of war, one might read the amassing of wealth and culture within the polity of Athens as a defense against slavery. The fact that the aristocratic, free way of life depended upon the perpetuation of slavery within Athens only serves to reinforce the distinction between those who were enslaved, and those who were not, a distinction that Antigone also seeks to reinforce in order to make the case to bury her brother.

31. Vernant points out that the distinction "between the *nothos* and the *gnēsios* is in no way an absolute one," and shows that illegitimate offspring were frequently held in high regard, *Myth and Society in Ancient Greece*, trans. Janet Lloyd (New York: Zone Books 1990), 63.

32. As Antigone's *kurios* by proxy (after Oedipus' death), Creon has authority to arrange her marriage. Antigone's refusal to follow Creon's edict banning Polynices' burial is at the same time, in effect, a refusal to abide by the authority of her *kurios*, whose prohibition turns out to prohibit her marriage too, insofar as it mandates the death of anyone who flouts the edict. See Rabinowitz, *Anxiety Veiled: Euripides and the Traffic in Women* (Ithaca: Cornell University Press, 1993), 4.

33. Antigone's identification with her mother is symbolized by her suicide: as many critics have noted, she will eventually hang herself, like her mother.

34. Vernant and Vidal-Naquet, *Myth and Tragedy in Ancient Greece*, trans. Janet Lloyd (New York: Zone Books, 1990), 8.

35. David Konstan, "The Classics and Class Conflict," *Arethusa* 27 (1994): 47–70.

36. Karen Bassi remarks that "[T]he persistent return to and authorization of the *Poetics* is indicative of the modern critic's desire to comprehend Greek drama from the privileged point of view of an elite Athenian, like Aristotle . . . the return to Aristotle's aesthetic principles is part of a larger project of valorizing and reanimating (as it were) a normative and universalized masculine subject—as ritual initiate, tragic sufferer, soldier-citizen, and literary critic or philosopher—who plays his role in the unique cultural and political destiny of ancient Athens," *Acting Like Men: Gender, Drama and Nostalgia in Ancient Greece* (Ann Arbor: University of Michigan Press, 1998), 3.

37. Griffith, "Brilliant Dynasts: Power and Politics in the *Oresteia*," *Classical Antiquity*, 14 (1995): 64.

38. Griffith, "Brilliant Dynasts: Power and Politics in the *Oresteia*," *Classical Antiquity*, 14 (1995): 66.

39. Zeitlin makes the interesting point not only that Creon's predicament is a more general one, but also that it puts into question the ability not only to rule the city, but to rule the self: "A typical Theban scenario shows us a king who at first governs, as he imagines, wholly in the city's interests, relying solely on his powers of reason and judgment to maintain civic order. But the pressure of events reveals him as one who has confused the relationship between ruler and city, identifying the state, in fact, with himself. In each case, the true imperative is the desire to rule, to exercise single hegemony over others and to claim all power for himself. Yet once confronted with the limitations he has never acknowledged, this ruler discovers that he cannot rule himself, cannot maintain an unequivocal identity," "Thebes: Theater of Self and Society in Athenian Drama" in *Nothing to do with Dionysos? Athenian Drama in its Social Context*, ed. John J. Winkler and Froma I. Zeitlin (Princeton, New Jersey: Princeton University Press, 1990), 149.

40. Griffith, "Brilliant Dynasts: Power and Politics in the *Oresteia*," *Classical Antiquity*, 14 (1995): 123.

41. Vernant and Vidal-Naquet point out that "it is misguided to inquire into the greater or lesser unit of the character of the tragic protagonists, as some modern critics do," and suggests that "the tension . . . between past and present, between the world of myth and that of the city, is to be found again within each protagonist. At one moment the same tragic character appears projected into a far distant mythical past, the hero of another age, imbued with a daunting religious power and embodying all the excesses of the ancient king of legend. At the next, he seems to speak, think, live in the very same age as the city, like a 'bourgeois citizen' of Athens amid his fellows," *Myth and Tragedy in Ancient Greece*, trans. Janet Lloyd (New York: Zone Books, 1990), 34.

42. In a nuanced and compelling, but ultimately, I argue, problematic, reading of *Antigone*, Patchen Markell suggests that interpreters of *Antigone* have gone astray in emphasizing the characters of Antigone and Creon at the expense of the plot of the play. Markell's fundamental point—and it is one with which I agree, at least in a qualified way—is that the tragedy of *Antigone* reveals that the aspiration for sovereign mastery not only reaches for an untenable ideal, but that the illusion that one could ever be completely in control of the meaning of one's actions amounts to a fundamental misconception. Here I want to register a difference concerning his attribution of symmetry to Antigone and Creon. Although Markell acknowledges that the symmetry between Antigone and Creon is "partial" due to the fact that Antigone dies but Creon does not, due to the "profound social and political inequality" between men and women, and due to the "relative ease" with which some occupy their kinship positions as compared to others, there is, throughout his discussion, a strong tendency to treat Antigone as if, like Creon, she mistakenly pursues sovereignty and recognition; see *Bound by Recognition* (Princeton and Oxford: Princeton University Press, 2003), 68. Yet this seems to ignore both the radically different circumstances of Antigone's and Creon's situations, and the fact that right from the beginning, Antigone accepts the fact that she is doomed to die because of her decision to bury Polynices. Although she crosses over into the public realm just by virtue of her defiance of Creon's edict, and (as Butler has emphasized), due to her insistent publicity of that defiance, she knows that by doing so she has no future. She seems to accept her finitude from the beginning. Unlike Creon, she doesn't

seem to be caught up in any illusion that she could control her own fate. Rather, she shows herself, from the opening exchange with Ismene, keenly aware of the suffering of her family, and the extent to which her options are limited by the contingencies of her situation, including—and perhaps especially—her finitude.

Is there not a sense in which, on Markell's own reading, Antigone's and Creon's situations could be read, then, as approximating to the difference Markell points to when he stipulates that there are structures that organize the world "in ways that make it possible for *certain people to enjoy an imperfect simulation of the invulnerability they desire, leaving others to bear a disproportionate share of the costs and burdens involved in social life*" (22, my emphasis)? Couldn't Creon be read (at least until the denouement) as exemplary of those who "enjoy an imperfect simulation of the invulnerability the desire," while Antigone bears "a disproportionate share of the costs and burdens involved in social life?" In other words, I am suggesting that, rather than reading the positions of Antigone and Creon as if they were more or less symmetrical with one another, there are good reasons to read them as radically asymmetrical. After all, as Markell acknowledges, the play takes place against a background of "profound social and political inequality" (88) that would seem to disqualify in advance any aspiration Antigone might have for sovereignty. Despite her status as a member of the aristocratic, royal family, as a woman deprived of political rights and public voice she acts from a position of powerlessness. Wouldn't stressing the asymmetry of Antigone's and Creon's position, rather than their symmetry, therefore, bear more fruit in terms of Markell's own analysis? Isn't there a sense in which Antigone understands any aspiration she has for sovereignty to be severely compromised? If she nevertheless is characterized by an apparent conviction that she must act, and act alone, this is perhaps not so much because she believes in self-mastery and isolation, but rather because her attempts to solicit Ismene's help fail. One might say that this failure has much to do with Ismene's strong—and realistic—sense of delegitimation. The fact that Antigone's rigidity seems to reflect in significant ways that of Creon might be explained not so much by her adherence to similar views about sovereignty, but rather her thorough understanding that her views, feelings, aspirations, and judgments are simply not relevant to Creon, and those of his ilk. If she exhibits a determination that seems to echo Creon's, might this not be attributed to the fact that she is only too well aware of the difficulty of having any kind of voice, or being heard, let alone of her views or actions being considered meaningful, significant, or legitimate? Don't the constraints of her situation compel her forcefulness?

If we push Markell on the question of precisely how Creon's own aspiration to sovereignty might be shored up in a way that insulates him from its impossibility, "leaving others to bear the weight of the contradictions, reversals, and failures that forever frustrate the desire for mastery" (89), we might ask how his attitude to, and response to, Antigone plays out in regard to Creon's aspirations. If Creon "holds false and demeaning views of women" yet at the same time is "driven by his own panicked defense of a position of privilege within a hierarchical social order" (89) this suggests that on the one hand he maintains that Antigone, as a woman, is inferior to him, but on the other hand he is nevertheless threatened by her. In other words, even if it can only be stated negatively, there appears to be some kind of acknowledgment by Creon—largely in his defensive protection of his own privilege—that his position is riven with contradiction. Or, one might say, he is being disingenuous. On the one hand he espouses demeaning views of women, implying their inferiority and incapacity to mount a serious challenge, but on the other hand he acknowledges the precariousness of his own power when confronted with Antigone's challenge to it, insofar as he responds by reasserting his authority. Indeed, Markell says as much. Creon realizes, at some level, that his authority as king depends upon recognition of that authority. To establish an inflexible, iron rule of discipline, and to fail to listen to the views of the public, as Haemon bids him do, is to hold to a general theory of leadership that doesn't bend to the contingencies of the situation.

If Creon's "gender panic" (113) is symptomatic of the threat that Antigone represents, he would not seem to be a figure who insulates himself from his own vulnerability—at least not very effectively. On the other hand, as Markell acknowledges, he does try to enclose Antigone in a space that mimics "the conventional enclosure of women within the *oikos*" (83). What this suggests is that it is not so much a question of Sophocles or Hegel "tracking the threat to . . . sovereignty to a specific social location, and thereby rendering it manageable" (114), but rather a question of those who more or less successfully maintain the illusion of sovereignty doing so by displacing their own vulnerability onto others. It is a question of identifying and containing those others (slaves and women) in highly circumscribed places, and requiring them to work in the mines, to reproduce, to attend to the material aspects of life, but not to participate in political life. In this sense, slaves and women make possible the lives of free men, but they do so in such a way as to allow their persistent subordination. This could be parsed out very much along the lines of Markell's analysis of how Marx's analysis of the commodity form accommodated contradictions in a way that gave them "room to move" (110).

43. Daughters, as Vernant says, were handed over by the "*kurios*, the relative who has authority to arrange her marriage. . . . The act of handing over, or *ekdosis*, consists in the transfer of the woman from one *kurios* to another, from the qualified relative to the husband," *Myth and Society in Ancient Greece*, trans. Janet Lloyd (New York: Zone Books, 1990), 56. Also see Rabinowitz, *Anxiety Veiled: Euripides and the Traffic in Women* (Ithaca: Cornell University Press, 1993), 4–5.

44. See Vernant, *Myth and Society in Ancient Greece*, trans. Janet Lloyd (New York: Zone Books, 1990), 58. Vernant goes on, however, to point out the difficulty of distinguishing between wives and concubines in this respect.

45. As Rabinowitz says, "although women had no political rights, they were essential for passing citizenship on to their sons," *Anxiety Veiled: Euripides and the Traffic in Women* (Ithaca: Cornell University Press, 1993), 3.

46. See Vernant *Myth and Society in Ancient Greece*, trans. Janet Lloyd (New York: Zone Books, 1990), 56 and 62. On the question of blockage, also see Page duBois, "Antigone and the Feminist Critic," *Genre* 19 (1986): 371–383.

47. *Antigone* 523. Storr has "My nature is for mutual love, not hate," *Sophocles in two volumes*, vol. 1, *The Loeb Classical Library* (Cambridge, Massachusetts: Harvard University Press, 1981).

48. Aristotle, "Recognition [anagnórisis] . . . is a change [metabolé] from ignorance or knowledge, leading to friendship [philían] or enmity [échthran]," Aristotle, *Poetics*, ed. and trans. Stephen Halliwell. Longinus on the Sublime, trans. W. H. Fyfe, revised by Donald Russell. Demetrius on Style, trans. Doreen C. Innes, based on W. Rhys Roberts. *Loeb Classical Library*, Aristotle, vol. 23 (Cambridge, Massachusetts: Harvard University Press, 1995), 1452a.

49. Elizabeth Belfiore, *Murder among friends: Violation of* Philia *in Greek Tragedy* (New York: Oxford University Press, 2000), 6–7.

50. Òsófisan takes up this taunt in his refrain of the toad not being friends with the tiger.

51. Aristotle, *Poetics*, ed. and trans. Stephen Halliwell. Longinus on the Sublime, trans. W. H. Fyfe, revised by Donald Russell. Demetrius on Style, trans. Doreen C. Innes, based on W. Rhys Roberts. *Loeb Classical Library*, Aristotle, vol. 23 (Cambridge, Massachusetts: Harvard University Press, 1995), 1454a20.

52. Aristotle, *Poetics*, ed. and trans. Stephen Halliwell. Longinus on the Sublime, trans. W. H. Fyfe, revised by Donald Russell. Demetrius on Style, trans. Doreen C. Innes, based on W. Rhys Roberts. *Loeb Classical Library*, Aristotle, vol. 23 (Cambridge, Massachusetts: Harvard University Press, 1995), 77. For Aristotle, the finest recognition occurs simultaneously with reversal in *Oedipus* (*Poetics* 1452a). Although Aristotle confines his references to *Antigone* in the *Poetics* to a single instance, he refers to the play elsewhere. See, for example, the *Politics* and the *Rhetoric*.

53. Thus, symbolically, both Oedipus and Polynices in different ways, become representatives (although not unambiguously) of the foreigner.

54. Vernant says, "There are several ways of leading a woman to one's home. The most official way is to obtain her from her parents by offering them, in return, the *hedna* that—in principle at least—consist of a certain number of head of livestock, in particular cattle. This constitutes a noble marriage that, through the daughter, seals the alliance between two families. In such a marriage the daughter, just like the herds for which she is exchanged, is an important item of exchange in the network of gifts and counter-gifts. However, one may also obtain a woman without *hedna*, in return for some exceptional exploit or for some service done for the girl's parents, or by winning her by armed force in some warlike expedition, or carrying her off in a foray or piratical raid," *Myth and Society in Ancient Greece*, trans. Janet Lloyd (New York: Zone Books, 1990), 62. Also see Rabinowitz's discussion of Lévi-Strauss in her introduction, *Anxiety Veiled: Euripides and the Traffic in Women* (Ithaca: Cornell University Press, 1993).

55. Rabinowitz, *Anxiety Veiled: Euripides and the Traffic in Women* (Ithaca: Cornell University Press, 1993), 5.

56. Vernant points out that the introduction of the dowry reverses the earlier practice of the *hedna*, since the latter "were gifts presented by the father of the girl to her husband" while the former is "given to the husband by the girl's father," *Myth and Society in Ancient Greece*, trans. Janet Lloyd (New York: Zone Books, 1990), 67.

57. Griffith, "Brilliant Dynasts: Power and Politics in the *Oresteia*," *Classical Antiquity*, 14 (1995), 69.

58. As Griffith points out, "*xenia*-alliances with foreign families . . . were sanctified, not by legal statute, but by traditional religious observance (oaths, feasting, sacrifice) and thus by Zeus," "Brilliant Dynasts: Power and Politics in the *Oresteia*," *Classical Antiquity*, 14 (1995): 71. This provides an explanatory context for Antigone's allegiance to her Zeus, her insistence on the authority of unwritten laws, and her understanding of justice in a sense that diverges from Creon's. For a slightly different understanding of Antigone's appeal to unwritten laws, see duBois, "Antigone and the Feminist Critic," *Genre* 19 (1986): 371–383. For commentary on the significance of Antigone's appeal to "My Zeus" see Samuel Weber, who discusses Hölderlin's translation in this context,

"Antigone's 'Nomos' " in *Theatricality as Medium* (New York: Fordham University Press, 2004), 135.

59. Fisher says, "It seems probable . . . that . . . causal links may be found between a steady growth of chattel slavery, a sharper distinction between slaves and free men, and initial moves towards wider popular participation in government and law. . . . One important result of Solon's laws seems to have been a clearer distinction between citizens, slaves, and foreigners; and in more than one way his laws helped the creation of the Athenian model of a slave-society," *Slavery in Classical Greece* (London: Bristol Classical Press, 1993), 15.

60. In addressing the question of who deserved to be a slave and who did not, Aristotle embarks on arguments whose deficiencies have been exposed by, among others, Rabinowitz, "Slaves with Slaves: Women and Class in Euripidean Tragedy," in *Women and Slaves in Greco-Roman Culture: Differential Equations*, ed. Sandra R. Joshel and Sheila Murnaghan (New York: Routledge, 1998), 57–8. See also Bull "Slavery and the Multiple Self," *New Left Review*, no. 231 (1998): 94–131.

61. Butler, *Antigone's Claim: Kinship Between Life & Death* (New York: Columbia University Press, 2000), 62.

62. duBois, *Slaves and Other Objects* (Chicago: University of Chicago Press, 2003), 110.

63. duBois, *Slaves and Other Objects* (Chicago: University of Chicago Press, 2003), 16, 112, and 118.

64. duBois, *Slaves and Other Objects* (Chicago: University of Chicago Press, 2003), 10, 118, and 220.

65. duBois, *Slaves and Other Objects* (Chicago: University of Chicago Press, 2003), 128.

66. duBois, *Slaves and Other Objects* (Chicago: University of Chicago Press, 2003), 141.

67. Bernard Knox, *The Heroic Temper: Studies in Sophoclean Tragedy* (Berkeley: University of California Press, 1992), 40.

68. Bernard Knox, *The Heroic Temper: Studies in Sophoclean Tragedy* (Berkeley: University of California Press, 1992), 41–2.

69. Bernard Knox, *The Heroic Temper: Studies in Sophoclean Tragedy* (Berkeley: University of California Press, 1992), 40–1.

70. Vlastos suggests that it was not until Plato that the connotation of subjection in a kindly way became well established, which argues in favor of Sophocles' use of *doulos* and related terms in a more literal way, "Slavery in Plato's Thought," in *Platonic Studies* (Princeton: Princeton University Press, 1981), 150.

71. Of course, it needs to be acknowledged that the problem of slavery, although it is typically dubbed "human trafficking" has far from disappeared—in fact its prevalence is alarming. However, I think it is safe to say that it is highly unlikely that Knox has this problem in mind. I thank Mary Beth Mader for reminding of this point, and in general, for her invaluable, incisive questions, which pushed me to clarify crucial points throughout the manuscript.

72. duBois, *Slaves and Other Objects* (Chicago: University of Chicago Press, 2003), 220. Insofar as slavery continues, duBois' statement is problematic.

73. Vernant and Vidal-Naquet, *Myth and Tragedy in Ancient Greece*, trans. Janet Lloyd (New York: Zone Books, 1990), 26–7. See also John Hamilton who quotes Vernant and goes on to point out that, "Antigone's name reveals her function. *Anti-* can mean 'opposed to' or 'in compensation for.' The *gen-/gon-* root is cognate with *genos*, 'lineage,' and *gonē* can even mean 'womb.' Antigone's action validates kinship based on the womb in compensation for its being dishonored; she restores an equilibrium of honor to 'those from the same womb.' . . . In another sense, however, she opposes the *genē* 'lineages,' bloodlines. She is indifferent to Haimon, chooses virginity in death, and opposes in her simple ritual for a dead kinsman the massive burial associated with the funerals of the royal *genē*," "Antigone: Kinship, Justice and the Polis," in *Myth and the Polis*, ed. Dora C. Pozzi and John M. Wickersham (Ithaca: Cornell University Press, 1991), 87–95.

74. Charles Segal, "Antigone: Death and Love, Hades and Dionysus," in *Tragedy and Civilization: An Interpretation of Sophocles* (Norman: University of Oklahoma Press, 1999). See also Zeitlin "Thebes: Theater of Self and Society in Athenian Drama" in *Nothing to do with Dionysos? Athenian Drama in its Social Context*, ed. John J. Winkler and Froma I. Zeitlin (Princeton, New Jersey: Princeton University Press, 1990). Simon Goldhill and Nicole Loraux are amongst those who have developed and built on Vernant and Vidal-Naquet's approach in a variety of ways.

75. Vernant and Vidal-Naquet, *Myth and Tragedy in Ancient Greece*, trans. Janet Lloyd (New York: Zone Books, 1990). See also, for example, David Wiles, who, in an otherwise interesting argument that he casts in opposition to the "positivist" approach of Oliver Taplin, appeals to an apparently unproblematic assumption about outsiders—one that I would want to say is precisely at stake in the very tragedies he is discussing—when he pits "Plato the Athenian" against "Aristotle the cultural outsider," *Tragedy in Athens: Performance Space and Theatrical Meaning* (Cambridge University Press, 1997), 9. See Taplin, *Greek Tragedy in Action* (London: Routledge, 2003). To be sure, Wiles' argument plays out in terms of Plato's experience of tragic performance, versus Aristotle's lack thereof: "Plato, unlike Aristotle, grew up in Athens and experienced fifth-century drama. He conceives tragedy as an event rather than a text" (87). My point, however, is that Wiles neglects the ways in which the notion of outsider is implicated in ideas concerning the barbarian other, foreignness, and slavery. The same can be said with regard to slavery of Zeitlin's otherwise excellent and exhaustive essay. Although it proposes that "Thebes is the place . . . that makes problematic every inclusion and exclusion, every conjunction and disjunction, every relation between near and far, high and low, inside and outside, stranger and kin," slavery is not considered to be implicated in these themes. See "Thebes: Theater of Self and Society in Athenian Drama" in *Nothing to do with Dionysos? Athenian Drama in its Social Context*, ed. John J. Winkler and Froma I. Zeitlin (Princeton, New Jersey: Princeton University Press, 1990), 134. Similarly, the discussion of marriage by Vernant and Vidal-Naquet does a wonderful job of tracing the transition from exogamy to endogamy, but neglects its implications for slavery.

76. Jean Anouilh, *Antigone: A Tragedy by Jean Anouilh*, trans. Lewis Galantière (London: Methuen, 1951). Bertolt Brecht, *Sophocles' Antigone*, trans. Judith Malina (New York: Applause Theatre, 1990). Seamus Heaney, *The Burial at Thebes: A Version of Sophocles'* Antigone (New York: Farrar, Straus and Giroux, 2004). Aidan Mathews, Aidan. Undated. *Antigone: Gone Anti*. Unpublished manuscript, courtesy of the author.

Marianne McDonald, *Antigone by Sophocles* (London: Nick Hern Books, 2005). Tom Paulin, *The Riot Act: A Version of Sophocles'* Antigone (London and Boston: Faber and Faber, 1985), and Brendan Kennelly, *Sophocles' Antigone* (Tarset, Northumberland: Bloodaxe Books, 1996). Janusz Glowacki, *Antigone in New York*, trans. Janusz Glowacki and Joan Torres (New York: Samuel French, 1997). Athol Fugard, Kani, and Ntshona Ntshona, *The Island*. In *Statements: two workshop productions. Sizwe Bansi is Dead*, and *The Island*; and a new play, *Statements after an arrest under the Immorality Act* (London: Oxford University Press, 1974). Fémi Òsófisan, *Tègònni, an African Antigone* (Ibadan, Nigeria: Kenbim Press, 1999).

77. Bemba, Sylvain. "Black Wedding Candles for Blessed Antigone" in *Theatre and Politics: An International Anthology* (New York: Ubu Repertory Theatre, 1990). Griselda Gambaro, "Antigona Furiosa" in *Information for Foreigners: Three Plays by Griselda Gambaro*, trans. and ed. Marguerite Feitlowitz (Evanston, Illinois: Northwestern University Press, 1992). For a wonderful discussion of the wide array of international performative appropriations of *Antigone* see Moira Fradinger's discussion in her prologue to *Feminist Readings of* Antigone, ed. Fanny Söderbäck (Albany: State University of New York Press, 2010), 15–23.

78. Derrida, *Glas*, trans. John P. Leavey and Richard Rand (Lincoln: University of Nebraska Press, 1986), 142 and 8.

79. Derrida, *Glas*, trans. John P. Leavey and Richard Rand (Lincoln: University of Nebraska Press, 1986), 108 and 144.

80. Derrida, *Glas*, trans. John P. Leavey and Richard Rand (Lincoln: University of Nebraska Press, 1986), 167.

81. Derrida, *Glas*, trans. John P. Leavey and Richard Rand (Lincoln: University of Nebraska Press, 1986), 8, 166, 151 and 162.

82. Derrida, *Glas*, trans. John P. Leavey and Richard Rand (Lincoln: University of Nebraska Press, 1986), 162.

83. Derrida, *Glas*, trans. John P. Leavey and Richard Rand (Lincoln: University of Nebraska Press, 1986), 144–5.

84. Derrida, *Glas*, trans. John P. Leavey and Richard Rand (Lincoln: University of Nebraska Press, 1986), 144, 39, 146.

85. Derrida, *Glas*, trans. John P. Leavey and Richard Rand (Lincoln: University of Nebraska Press, 1986), 142.

86. See Weber, *Theatricality as Medium* (New York: Fordham University Press, 2004), 138–9.

87. See Weber, *Theatricality as Medium* (New York: Fordham University Press, 2004), 121.

88. See Weber, *Theatricality as Medium* (New York: Fordham University Press, 2004), 123.

89. See Weber, *Theatricality as Medium* (New York: Fordham University Press, 2004), 125 and 132.

90. See Weber, *Theatricality as Medium* (New York: Fordham University Press, 2004), 125. My difference with Weber here is for reasons similar to the critique I shall make of Agamben's suggestion that the state of exception becomes the rule, and which I have already outlined in the footnote to Markell earlier in this chapter.

91. See Weber, *Theatricality as Medium* (New York: Fordham University Press, 2004), 132.

92. See Weber, *Theatricality as Medium* (New York: Fordham University Press, 2004), 126–7.

93. See Zeitlin, "Thebes: Theater of Self and Society in Athenian Drama" in *Nothing to do with Dionysos? Athenian Drama in its Social Context*, ed. John J. Winkler and Froma I. Zeitlin (Princeton, New Jersey: Princeton University Press, 1990).

Chapter 2

1. See J. Timothy Reiss, *Tragedy and Truth. Studies in the Development of a Renaissance and Neoclassical Discourse* (Yale University Press: New Haven and London, 1980), 11.

2. Miguel de Beistegui and Simon Sparks, *Philosophy and Tragedy* (New York: Routledge, 2000), 3.

3. Beistegui and Sparks, *Philosophy and Tragedy* (New York: Routledge, 2000), 4.

4. Derrida comments on Antigone's resistance to Hegelian dialectics in *Glas*. I want to suggest another way in which *Antigone* remains outside of Hegel's attempt to integrate ethics into dialectical thought.

5. "It was a brother, not a slave [*doulos*] who died" Antigone says to Creon in Sophocles' *Antigone* (line 517). Elizabeth Wyckoff, "Antigone," in *Sophocles I*, ed. David Grene. *The Complete Greek Tragedies*, ed. David Grene and Richmond Lattimore (Chicago: The University of Chicago Press), 1954. F. Storr translates the line "The slain man was no villain but a brother," *Sophocles in two volumes*, vol. 1, *The Loeb Classical Library*, (Cambridge, Massachusetts: Harvard University Press, 1981), 353, while Reginald Gibbons has "It was no slave—it was my brother who died," A*ntigone*, tr. Reginald Gibbons and Charles Segal, *The Greek Tragedy in New Translations*, eds. Peter Burian and Alan Shapiro (Oxford: Oxford University Press, 2003), 76.

6. Jacques Lacan, *The Ethics of Psychoanalysis 1959-1960: The Seminar of Jacques Lacan*, ed. Jacques-Alain Miller, Book VII, trans. Dennis Porter (New York: Tavistock/ Routledge, 1992). Irigaray, Luce. *Speculum of the Other Woman*, trans. Gillian C. Gill (Ithaca: Cornell University Press, 1985). *Speculum de l'autre femme*. (Minuit: Paris, 1974). Judith Butler, *Antigone's Claim: Kinship Between Life & Death* (New York: Columbia University Press, 2000).

7. See, for example, Robert Bernasconi, "Hegel at the Court of the Ashanti," in *Hegel after Derrida*, ed. Stuart Barnett (Routledge: London and New York, 1998), 41–63. See also Robert Bernasconi, "With What Must the Philosophy of History Begin? On the Racial Bases of Hegel's Eurocentrism," *Nineteenth Century Contexts* 22 (2000): 171–201.

8. See G. W. F. Hegel, *Hegel's Aesthetics: Lectures on Fine Art*, trans. T.M. Knox. 2 volumes (Oxford: Clarendon Press), 1988, vol. I: 464. *Vorlesungen über die Ästhetik*. Suhrkamp Taschenbuch Wissenschaft. B. 13–15 (Suhrkamp: Frankfurt am Main) 1970, B. II: 60. Hereafter volume and page numbers will be indicated in the text. The fact that Hegel designates *Antigone* as sublime, yet also describes the play in terms of beauty, can be attributed perhaps to Antigone's unruly, formlessness on the one hand, and the supposed order, balance, and harmony that Creon provides, as a precursor of the modern statesman, on the other hand.

9. Thus, for example, Hegel says "Diana of the Ephesians. . . . has, as her chief content, nature in general, procreation and nutrition. . . . [w]hereas in the case of the

Greek Artemis, the huntress, who kills beasts, this natural aspect recedes altogether into the background in her humanly beautiful maidenly form and independence" (I: 474; II: 72). Every example Hegel provides is intended to demonstrate that "in the new gods the universal elements of nature are disparaged but yet retained" (I: 474; II: 73).

10. Hegel obfuscates the fact that the wholes to which the Greek tragic heroes are said to belong are conceived differently at various points of his own discourse. How to delineate between the "community," "generation" [*Geschlecht*], "family," or "clan" is exactly what is under interrogation in *Antigone.*

11. Hegel does not think slavery should be a thematic topic, but allows that dramatic poetry can let "an ugly thing appear just for a moment [*augenblicklich*] and then vanish again" (I: 205; I: 268). While Hegel acknowledges that "the evil and the bad" are "not excluded from the Ideal" and that they were often "the substance and ground of the heroic and mythic age" from which ancient tragedy drew its themes, he specifies that these times were "wilder" and "removed from a thoroughly developed legal and ethical order" (I: 191; I: 251). He compares this less "ideal state of the world" to that of the Christian ideal," which is "more indifferent to external circumstances" (ibid.). He goes on to add that Greek tragedy with royalty because there we find "perfect freedom of will," in contrast to the "lower classes," in which we see "subjection everywhere" (I: 192; I: 251).

12. If as ethical actors tragic heroes are necessarily particular in their one-sidedness, as artistic figures, tragic heroes are imbued with universality due to their historical character. Memory confers on them a "greater universality" (I: 190; I: 249) than characters drawn from the present would have, since "memory's picture" liberates them "from the accidents of the external world" (I: 189; I: 249). At the same time, in the Heroic age, the individual is not yet confronted by law, and in this sense the poet is more immediately concerned with the "Ideal" (I: 190; I: 249).

13. It might not be stretching the point too far to suggest that Hegel's condemnation of Euripides for slipping into "pity and emotion" (II: 1215; III: 546) could itself be a veiled reference to the proliferation of slaves we find in Euripides, in contrast to the relative paucity of slaves in Sophocles.

14. Charles Segal, "Catharsis, Audience, and Closure in Greek Tragedy," in *Tragedy and the Tragic: Greek Theatre and Beyond*, ed. M.S. Silk (Oxford: Clarendon Press, 1996), 156.

15. The negative effects of the tragic mimesis of grief and lamentation, which he regards as disruptive, are among Plato's concerns about tragedy. See *Republic* 604e1–605a6; for further consideration of these issues see Sheila Murnahagen, "Sucking the Juice without Biting the Rind: Aristotle and Tragic Mimesis," *New Literary History* 26.4 (1995): 750. Plato fears that imitating women and slaves might prove morally harmful (Rep 3.394b3–e5), as might "representing 'womanish' emotions in tragedy" See Plato, *Republic* 10.605c1–e6. For further discussion see Hall "The Sociology of Athenian Tragedy," in *The Cambridge Companion to Greek Tragedy*, ed. P. E. Easterling (Cambridge: Cambridge University Press, 1997), 119.

16. Hall, "Is there a *Polis* in Aristotle's *Poetics*?" in *Tragedy and the Tragic: Greek Theatre and Beyond*, ed. M. S. Silk (Oxford: Clarendon Press, 1996), 302. Hall refers to Plato, *Republic* 601d–e, 607d 6–9.

17. This is complicated further by the fact that ultimately art and philosophy perform the same service, that is, the purification of spirit. See Hegel, *The Philosophy of Mind*, trans. A. V. Miller (Oxford: Clarendon Press, 1971), 297.

18. Hall, "Is there a *Polis* in Aristotle's *Poetics*?" in *Tragedy and the Tragic: Greek Theatre and Beyond*, ed. M. S. Silk (Oxford: Clarendon Press, 1996).

19. J. Peter Euben and Jean-Pierre Vernant are two of the most important critics to have elaborated the idea that tragedy provided Athens with a space for critically reflecting upon the politics in which the tragedians also participated. See, for example, J. Peter Euben, *Corrupting Youth: Political Education, Democratic Culture, and Political Theory* (Princeton: Princeton University Press, 1997). See also Jean-Pierre Vernant, *Myth and Society in Ancient Greece*, trans. Janet Lloyd (New York: Zone Books, 1990).

20. Augusto Boal, *Theatre of the Oppressed* (New York: Theatre Communications Group, 1985), 25.

21. Hall, "Is there a *Polis* in Aristotle's *Poetics*?" in *Tragedy and the Tragic: Greek Theatre and Beyond*, ed. M. S. Silk (Oxford: Clarendon Press, 1996), 303.

22. Hall, "Is there a *Polis* in Aristotle's *Poetics*?" in *Tragedy and the Tragic: Greek Theatre and Beyond*, ed. M. S. Silk (Oxford: Clarendon Press, 1996), 304–5.

23. Hall, "Is there a *Polis* in Aristotle's *Poetics*?" in *Tragedy and the Tragic: Greek Theatre and Beyond*, ed. M. S. Silk (Oxford: Clarendon Press, 1996), 305.

24. Hall, "Is there a *Polis* in Aristotle's *Poetics*?" in *Tragedy and the Tragic: Greek Theatre and Beyond*, ed. M. S. Silk (Oxford: Clarendon Press, 1996), 305.

25. See for example, Hegel, I: 1197; III: 524.

26. See Judith Butler, *Antigone's Claim: Kinship Between Life & Death* (New York: Columbia University Press, 2000). See also Warren J. Lane and Ann M. Lane. "The Politics of Antigone," in *Greek Tragedy and Political Theory*, ed. J. Peter Euben (Berkeley and London, University of California Press, 1986).

27. Hegel ignores the fact that Antigone appeals not only to Dike—a god Hegel associates with the old order, and thus with those gods that are closer to nature—but also to Zeus.

28. Hegel does not engage as fully as he might in accounting for the parameters within which the family emerges as a family understood in modern terms—as distinct from the complex network of kinship relations implicated in archaic exogamous marriages (see I: 188–9; I: 247–8). The question of generation (*Geschlecht*) is implicated not only in terms of which particular kinship configurations are endorsed, and which are excluded by the rhetoric of the Oedipal cycle, but also in how the lineage of a noble family is to maintain itself as distinct from slaves.

29. See for example Hegel, I: 188; I: 247.

30. See Aristotle, *Politics* (1260a13–14).

31. See Roger Just, *Women in Athenian Law and Life* (New York: Routledge, 1991), 191–2. See also Hall, "Is there a *Polis* in Aristotle's *Poetics*?" in *Tragedy and the Tragic: Greek Theatre and Beyond*, ed. M. S. Silk (Oxford: Clarendon Press, 1996), 109.

32. See Aristotle. *Politics*, trans. H. Rackham. *Loeb Classical Library*, Aristotle, vol. 21 (Cambridge: Harvard University Press, 2005), 1260a.

33. Roger Just argues that the grounds on which Aristotle distinguishes between women and slaves are shaky, and that "consequently as a 'set of human beings' women are 'slaves by nature,' " *Women in Athenian Law and Life* (New York: Routledge, 1991), 190. See Aristotle. *Politics*, trans. H. Rackham. *Loeb Classical Library*, Aristotle, vol. 21 (Cambridge: Harvard University Press, 2005), 1254b.

34. See Athol Fugard, John Kani, and Winston Ntshona, "The Island," in *Statements: two workshop productions,* Sizwe Bansi is Dead, *and* The Island; *and a new*

play, Statements after an arrest under the Immorality Act (London: Oxford University Press, 1974).

35. As T. M. Knox's footnote clarifies, Phryne is "The famous courtesan who was the model for Apelles' picture of Aphrodite rising from the sea" (I: 720).

36. Hegel's association of Antigone with the old order of the gods is part of a broader argument regarding the various configurations of the relationship between nature and spirit. Having established that whatever form the "freedom of spirit" takes, it involves the "cancellation [Aufheben] of the purely natural qua spirit's opposite" (I: 443; II: 33), Hegel refers to Hesiod, who notes the successive origination of the gods (see I: 464; II: 60–1). Within the earlier, Titanic gods, Hegel distinguishes three groups, each one less identified with nature. The third group is the one that Hegel takes Antigone to call upon. This group "already borders on what is inherently ideal, universal, and spiritual" but lacks. . . "spiritual individuality," . . . and "retain[s] a closer bearing to what is necessary and essential in nature" (I: 462; II: 57 my emphasis). In describing the new gods, with whom he associates Creon, Hegel maintains that "the Greeks did not in any way regard the natural as the divine. On the contrary, they had the distinct idea that the natural is not the divine . . . As the substance of these gods, therefore, it is not the natural as such which is to be adduced, but the spiritual, the universal, λόγος, intellect, conformity to law" (I: 472; II: 70). Referring to Plutarch, he tells us that the Egyptian gods "had elements of nature as their content to a greater extent than the corresponding Greek gods had" (I: 472; II: 70).

37. Clearly Hegel has in mind the lack of self-consciousness that he judges to be characteristic of the kind of rationality embodied in the tragic outlook (II: 1216; III: 547).

38. Carol Jacobs claims that "Both Hegel and Irigaray glide unproblematically from the figure of Antigone to the role of women in general," *Dusting Antigone. MLN* 111 (1996): 895. With regard to Hegel, in more than one sense Jacobs is entirely right, since Hegel does make assumptions about Antigone on the basis of the fact that she represents the naturalized functions he attributes to women. Yet in another sense, Hegel is invested in marking Antigone's blood kinship to Polynices as a sister, and as such as a member of a natural family, rather than as a woman who enters into a contractual relationship with a husband. Of course, the irony is that there is nothing ordinary about Antigone's blood kin, since Oedipus's status as both her half-brother and her father has precisely confused the familial patterns (contractual versus natural) that Hegel seeks to separate out.

39. For Hegel, marriage is a relationship that involves "obligations" (I: 464; II: 59) even in the absence of love.

40. Hegel specifies the notion of character in terms of pathos: Greek tragic characters "are not what we call 'characters' in the modern sense of the word, but neither are they mere abstractions. They occupy a vital central position between both, because they are both firm figures who simply what they are, without any inner conflict, without any hesitating recognition of someone else's 'pathos,' and therefore (the opposite of our contemporary 'irony'), lofty, absolutely determinate individuals, although this determinacy of theirs is based on and is representative of a particular ethical power" (I: 1209–10; III: 540).

41. Hegel disparages the purely subjective, personal emotions he sees displayed in modern tragedy to the extent that they are not reflective of abiding, communal, ethical concerns, yet he is also suspicious of the formulaic character that the legal framework of modern morality imposes on communal ethics.

42. See also Hegel, I: 212; I: 276. Perhaps there is a subterranean polemic in Hegel with Aristotle about the relative merits of Euripides versus Sophocles, and the significance of pity and fear.

43. Fémi Òsófisan, *Tègònni, an African Antigone* (Ibadan, Nigeria: Kenbim Press, 1999).

44. Lacan Jacques. *The Ethics of Psychoanalysis 1959–1960: The Seminar of Jacques Lacan*, Book VII., trans. Dennis Porter, ed. Jacques-Alain Miller (New York: Tavistock/Routledge, 1992), 263. Carole Pateman's *The Sexual Contract* (Stanford: Stanford University Press, 1988), and Charles Mills, *The Racial Contract* (Ithaca: Cornell University Press, 1999) have drawn out the implications of the contradictions inhabiting social contract theory. For a recent discussion of the impact of Pateman's work, which includes an afterword by Pateman and an essay by Charles Mills, see *The Illusion of Consent: Engaging with Carole Pateman*, ed. Daniel O'Neill, Mary Lyndon Shanley, and Iris MarionYoung (University Park: Pennsylvania State University, 2008).

45. On the one hand women in ancient Greece were seen as a threat due to their allegedly passionate natures, which demanded their containment and control, and on the other hand their emotions were construed as dangerous and contaminating, especially those displayed in the one sphere of public activity granted them, namely religion. In particular, women and hired mourners were subject to controls designed to hem in funereal lamentation, on which a good deal of important and interesting recent work has been done.

46. My argument here is that derogatory, racializing assumptions inform Hegel's judgment of Eastern religions, as distinct from the Christianity with which he identifies. The argument does not depend on any coherent concept of race structuring Hegel's assumptions. It concerns Hegel's attempt to differentiate between the gods of ancient Greece and those of the East, an effort that is inflected by Hegel's identification of ancient Greece as a precursor, and model for, nineteenth century Western Europe.

47. John Sallis has commented on the significance of this term in Hölderlin's translation of Oedipus. See Sallis, *Crossings: Nietzsche and the Space of Tragedy* (Chicago: University of Chicago Press, 1991).

48. For an interesting reading of Hegel on Natural law see Elaine Miller, "Tragedy, Natural Law and Sexual Difference in Hegel," *Bound by the City: Greek Tragedy, Sexual Difference, and the Formation of the Polis*, ed. Denise Eileen McCoskey and Emily Zakin (Albany: State University of New York, 2009), 149–176.

49. One might even read Hegel's championing of Antigone as a repudiation of the exemplary role Aristotle attributed to *Oedipus Rex*, and as implicated in the way Hegel tried to finesse the function of pity for Aristotle.

50. A version of this chapter appeared in *Hegel's Philosophy and Feminist Thought. Beyond Antigone?* ed. Kimberly Hutchings and Tuija Pulkkinen (Basingstoke: Palgrave Press, 2010), 61–85. I thank Kimberly Hutchings for pushing me to clarify the relationship between the master-slave dialectic in Hegel and my argument about tragedy and slavery in Hegel's *Aesthetics*.

51. Bull cites as exemplary of this reading C. Arthur, "Hegel's Master-Slave Dialectic and a Myth of Marxology," *NLR* 143, November–December 1983: 67–75, and P. Osborne, *The Politics of Time* (Verso: London, 1995), 72.

52. I would like to thank Ted George for his careful reading of this chapter, and for our exchanges on it.

Chapter 3

1. Kevin Wetmore suggests that Antigone "might even be considered the 'most transcultured/most transcultural' tragedy," *The Athenian Sun in an African Sky* (Jefferson, North Carolina: McFarland & Company, Inc., 2002), 169.

2. Ismene regards Antigone as excessive. See Mary Whitlock Blundell, *Helping Friends and Harming Enemies: A Study in Sophocles and Greek Ethics* (Cambridge: Cambridge University Press, 1989), 111, and *Antigone* 67f.

3. Reiss, *Tragedy and Truth. Studies in the Development of a Renaissance and Neoclassical Discourse* (Yale University Press: New Haven and London, 1980).

4. See Lacan, *Ethics of Psychoanalysis 1959–1960: The Seminar of Jacques Lacan*, Book VII, trans. Dennis Porter, ed. Jacques-Alain Miller, New York: Tavistock/Routledge, 1992. See also Slavoj Žižek, "From Antigone to Joan of Arc," *Helios* 31 (2004) 51–62. Žižek reads Antigone as a totalitarian figure. For a more sympathetic, and more faithful, reading of Lacan's essay on Antigone, which reads Lacan as making an intervention in Hegel's insistence upon construing Creon's and Antigone's claims as equal to one another, by making Antigone the unambiguous heroine of his reading, see Joan Copjec, *Imagine There's No Woman* (Boston: MIT, 2004).

5. Euben, Introduction, *Greek Tragedy and Political Theory* (Berkeley: University of California, 1986). David Halperin, "Why is Diotima a Woman? Platonic Eros and the Figuration of Gender," *Before Sexuality: The Construction of Erotic Experience in the Ancient Greek World*, ed. David M. Halperin, John J. Winkler, and Froma I. Zeitlin (Princeton, New Jersey: Princeton University Press, 1990).

6. Ormand, "Oedipus the Queen: Cross-gendering without drag," *Theatre Journal* 55 (2003): 1–28.

7. Ironically enough, as Knox says, Sophocles manuscripts would have been copied, says Knox, by "booksellers' employees (probably slaves)," Notes to Robert Fagles, *The Theban Plays* (Harmondsworth, Middlesex: Penguin, 1984), 389. I thank Mary Beth Mader for this reference.

8. Sue-Ellen Case says, "The classical plays and theatrical conventions can . . . be regarded as allies in the project of suppressing actual women and replacing them with the masks of patriarchal production," "Classic drag: the Greek Creation of Female Parts," *Theatre Journal* (1985): 318. Yet Mclure is no doubt right to suggest that "Attic drama should not be understood simply as a univocal, hegemonic discourse in service of civic ideology; it is a complex, polyvocal, and polysemous genre that alternately subverts and reinforces the dominant agenda," *Spoken like a woman: Speech and Gender in Athenian Drama* (Princeton: Princeton University Press, 1999), 5.

9. See Boal, *Theatre of the Oppressed* (New York: Theatre Communications Group), 1985. Greek tragedy is said to specialize in depicting the awful, chaotic, destructive consequences that ensue when women challenge the boundaries of convention, endangering the order of the polis by the very fact that they think and act for themselves, or "move on their own," Borregaard, "The Tragic Heroics of Ancient Greek Extreme Women," *New Antigone*, vol 1. Spring (2005): 68. Tragedy is thus understood as merely confirming the danger that women represent when they violate the expectation that requires them not to be the authors of their own movement, not to act but to obey. Rather than construe tragedy as reaffirming the stability of the border separating politics from

nature, so that if women are positioned "outside of society and its boundaries" they are necessarily "close to nature" (68), tragedy might itself become a way of contesting how those boundaries are drawn. To question how a society draws its boundaries is at the same time a way of demonstrating the politicized nature of those boundaries, of who is recognized as capable of acting politically, and who is legitimated as moving of their own principle and accord, and who is not.

10. Euben, Introduction. *Greek Tragedy and Political Theory* (Berkeley: University of California, 1986), 37.

11. Case "Classic drag: the Greek Creation of Female Parts," *Theatre Journal* (1985): 319.

12. David Halperin, "Why is Diotima a Woman? Platonic Eros and the Figuration of Gender," *Before Sexuality: The Construction of Erotic Experience in the Ancient Greek World*, ed. David M. Halperin, John J. Winkler, and Froma I. Zeitlin (Princeton, New Jersey: Princeton University Press, 1990), 290.

13. See Pomeroy, *Goddesses, Whores, Wives, and Slaves*: *Women in Ancient Antiquity* (New York: Schocken Books 1995), 78.

14. Anne Carson "Putting her in her Place: Woman, Dirt, and Desire," *Before Sexuality: The Construction of Erotic Experience in the Ancient Greek World*, ed. David M. Halperin, John J. Winkler, and Froma I. Zeitlin (Princeton, New Jersey: Princeton University Press, 1990), 156. On Solon's legislative constraints on women see also Pomeroy, *Goddesses, Whores, Wives, and Slaves*: *Women in Ancient Antiquity* (New York: Schocken Books, 1995), 57 and 63, 80. Mclure points out that "male anxieties about women's reproductive power" may well derive from the fact that men could not "know the true paternity of their children" and so were "plagued by uncertainty" about the truth that was only known to women, *Spoken like a woman: Speech and Gender in Athenian Drama* (Princeton: Princeton University Press, 1999), 27.

15. Carson, "Putting her in her Place: Woman, Dirt, and Desire," *Before Sexuality: The Construction of Erotic Experience in the Ancient Greek World*, ed. David M. Halperin, John J. Winkler, Froma I. Zeitlin (Princeton, New Jersey: Princeton University Press, 1990), 156. Pomeroy, *Goddesses, Whores, Wives, and Slaves*: *Women in Ancient Antiquity* (New York: Schocken Books, 1995), 59.

16. Pomeroy, *Goddesses, Whores, Wives, and Slaves*: *Women in Ancient Antiquity* (New York: Schocken Books, 1995), 72–-3.

17. Quoted in Halperin, "Why is Diotima a Woman? Platonic Eros and the Figuration of Gender," *Before Sexuality: The Construction of Erotic Experience in the Ancient Greek World*, ed. David M. Halperin, John J. Winkler, Froma I. Zeitlin (Princeton, New Jersey: Princeton University Press, 1990), 290.

18. Pomeroy, *Goddesses, Whores, Wives, and Slaves*: *Women in Ancient Antiquity* (New York: Schocken Books, 1995), 75.

19. Pomeroy, *Goddesses, Whores, Wives, and Slaves*: *Women in Ancient Antiquity* (New York: Schocken Books, 1995), 74. The fact that Antigone is referred to throughout *Antigone* as a "child" [insert] is reflective both of her inferiority as a woman, and, perhaps of the youth of unmarried females. Pomeroy says "A girl was ideally married at fourteen to a man of about thirty," 64.

20. Pomeroy, *Goddesses, Whores, Wives, and Slaves*: *Women in Ancient Antiquity* (New York: Schocken Books, 1995), 71.

21. Pomeroy, *Goddesses, Whores, Wives, and Slaves*: *Women in Ancient Antiquity* (New York: Schocken Books, 1995), 60.

22. Loraux, Nicole, *Born of the Earth: Myth and Politics in Athens*, trans. Selina Stewart (Ithaca: Cornell University Press, 2000), 23.

23. Carson, "Putting her in her Place: Woman, Dirt, and Desire," *Before Sexuality: The Construction of Erotic Experience in the Ancient Greek World*, ed. David M. Halperin, John J. Winkler, and Froma I. Zeitlin (Princeton, New Jersey: Princeton University Press, 1990), 158–9. See also Borregaard, who observes the ancient Greek fascination with "the woman who is taken beyond the boundaries of order to become an agent of ruination. These female prototypes cross the border into chaos in different ways but this action usually results in self-destruction," "The Tragic Heroics of Ancient Greek Extreme Women." *New Antigone*, vol 1. Spring (2005), 68.

24. Case, "Classic drag: the Greek Creation of Female Parts," *Theatre Journal* (1985): 319.

25. For Mclure, "Although women were largely excluded from the discursive realms in which male civic identity was consolidated in classical Athens, their silence and seclusion have to be understood partly as the fictional constructs of men: women did speak, to their husbands, their sons, to one another; they found a public voice through ritual whereas noncitizen and lower-class women frequently moved through the public world of men," *Spoken like a woman: Speech and Gender in Athenian Drama* (Princeton: Princeton University Press, 1999), 24.

26. Euben, *Corrupting Youth: Political Education, Democratic Culture, and Political Theory* (Princeton: Princeton University Press, 1997), 143. See also Euben's introduction to *Greek Tragedy and Political Theory* (Berkeley: University of California, 1986), esp. 24, 28–9, and 37.

27. Mclure, *Spoken like a woman: Speech and Gender in Athenian Drama* (Princeton: Princeton University Press, 1999), 24.

28. Although there has been some controversy over whether or not women attended performances, Goldhill, "The Audience of Athenian Tragedy," *The Cambridge Companion to Greek Tragedy*, ed. P. E. Easterling (Cambridge: Cambridge University Press, 1997) reaffirms the traditional view that women were not in attendance. See also Wohl, *Intimate Commerce: Exchange, Gender and Subjectivity in Greek Tragedy* (Austin: University of Texas, 1998), xx. The uncertainty still hovering over the question of whether or not women attended tragic plays itself attests to women's marginal status in ancient Greece.

29. See Pomeroy, *Goddesses, Whores, Wives, and Slaves*: *Women in Ancient Antiquity* (New York: Schocken Books, 1995), 80. See also Winkler, Representing the Body Politic: The Theatre of Manhood in Classical Athens, *Perspecta*, 26 (1990): 226.

30. Griffith, "Corporality in the Ancient Greek Theatre," *Phonenix*, 52 (1998), 247.

31. Case "Classic drag: the Greek Creation of Female Parts," *Theatre Journal* (1985): 321. Ormand "Oedipus the Queen: Cross-gendering without drag," *Theatre Journal* 55 (2003): 1. Aristotle discusses how actors in tragedy relied on modulation of the voice. For further discussion see Mclure, *Spoken like a woman: Speech and Gender in Athenian Drama* (Princeton: Princeton University Press, 1999), 18.

32. Ormand "Oedipus the Queen: Cross-gendering without drag," *Theatre Journal* 55 (2003): 23.

33. Until Case took seriously the significance of what she called "Classic drag: the Greek Creation of Female Parts," *Theatre Journal* (1985), the topic had been signaled

only by a dearth in the critical literature on Greek tragedy. Perhaps it is unsurprising that critics have only begun to take seriously the theatrical conventions of ancient Greek theatre since the institution of women's and gender studies as a serious academic pursuit.

34. Ormand "Oedipus the Queen: Cross-gendering without drag," *Theatre Journal* 55 (2003): 28.

35. Foley, *Female Acts in Greek Tragedy* (Princeton: Princeton University Press, 2001, 4). Zeitlin suggests the paradox that "the theater uses the feminine for the purpose of imagining a fuller model for the masculine self and 'playing the other' opens the self to those often banned emotions of fear and pity . . . Woman may be thought to speak double, and sometimes she does. But she also sees double; the culture has taught her that too," *Playing the Other: Gender and Society in Ancient Greek Literature* (Chicago: University of Chicago Press, 1996), 363.

36. Foley, *Female Acts in Greek Tragedy* (Princeton: Princeton University Press, 2001) 4 n.3. See Zeitlin, *Playing the Other: Gender and Society in Ancient Greek Literature* (Chicago: University of Chicago Press, 1996), 363.

37. As Euben puts it, "What is political is itself a political issue. . . . the very contestability of what constitutes politics may be distinctive to it . . . conflicts are not just conflicts about particular beliefs or even principles, but about principles of adjudication themselves. What is at issue is the meaning and scope of accepted political values," *Corrupting Youth: Political Education, Democratic Culture, and Political Theory* (Princeton: Princeton University Press, 1997), 139–144. Contra Creon, who assumes that "the more order he can establish the more secure politics will be," Euben argues that "Politics requires insecurity and rests on contingency in a way that makes political order both a necessity and an oxymoron. The messiness and transformative dimension to politics, cannot be contained either by the singularity of Creon's world or the opposition to it, which remains implicated in that world because of its opposition," 156.

38. I do not mean to signal an uncritical embrace of Hegelian logic; one of the strengths of psychoanalytic thinking is its recognition (even if this recognition is not applied with all the rigor that it might to the assumptions of psychoanalytic thought itself) of variant types of negativity, not all of which can be subsumed under the logic of negation, let alone determinate negation. By taking seriously the indeterminacy of the imaginary, and the various ways in which inconsistency is maintained and illusions are sustained, rather than being debunked—rather than cashing out the logical implications of incompatible premises—psychoanalytic theory is capable of shedding light on how political thought often proceeds. This is not to suggest that Hegel does not acknowledge the variety of subterfuges in which consciousness engages in order to keep itself from confronting and resolving contradictory theses by moving on to a more adequate epistemological position, only that the sheer importance Hegel attaches to dialectical thinking as that which drives thought leads to a privileging of the cashing out of logical contradictions that is not in keeping with the weight that actually attaches to the political fantasies that in fact compel us. Hegel certainly saw that there were a wide variety of ways in which consciousness operates in order to keep itself from confronting the illogicality of contradiction, but whether his privileging of speculative thought allows him to accord the necessary weight to these various modes of negativity is in question.

39. When Lacan applies the logic of the fetish uncritically to Antigone, he simply reformulates the appeal to natural womanly instinct, or women's true reproductive vocation an appeal that will inform otherwise erudite, sophisticated analyses. Knox acknowledges

Antigone's act is political, *The Heroic Temper: Studies in Sophoclean Tragedy* (Berkeley: University of California Press, 1992), 76, while Segal suggests that Antigone's "relation to civilized values" is one of ambiguity, and not simply a repudiation of the social order. Segal says, for example, "By challenging one principle of civilization in the name of another, she generates a tragic division that calls the nature of social order itself into question," "Antigone: Death and Love, Hades and Dionysus," in *Tragedy and Civilization: An Interpretation of Sophocles* (Norman: University of Oklahoma Press, 1999), 182. He also claims that in burying Polynices, Antigone "performs [a] basic civilizing act" (160) yet he falls back on gender stereotypes in his final explanation of Antigone. Ultimately, for Segal, Antigone's comparison of herself with Niobe is reminiscent of "the unfulfillment of her womanhood" (156).

40. The phalloi that were paraded in satyr plays could then be read as a hyperbolic way of drawing attention to the maleness of a character.

41. See my *The Picture of Abjection: Film, Fetish and the Nature of Difference* (Bloomington: Indiana University Press, 2007).

42. As Mclure puts it, it is almost certain that slaves were not allowed to attend, and few women, if any, would have been present; in any case, fifth-century Athenian drama clearly addressed itself to a conceptual audience of male citizens," *Spoken like a woman: Speech and Gender in Athenian Drama* (Princeton: Princeton University Press, 1999), 17.

43. On Borregaard's reading—which, however, ultimately refuses to recognize that Antigone calls for a new political order in such a way as to draw attention to the logic of the excluded other, Antigone's ability to act is acknowledged, but only at the cost of reading her action as a transgression of the properly feminine role, such that she must be punished for her manly action. Death becomes the penalty for daring to challenge the accepted boundaries that require women to conform to "ideals of stillness," "The Tragic Heroics of Ancient Greek Extreme Women." *New Antigone*, vol 1. Spring (2005), 68.

44. A mere detail, rendering the Oedipal deviation from the law null and void, bringing him back to the law.

45. Oedipus proved to be distinctly unreliable as an overseer of reproductive clarity and control, unknowingly marrying his mother in a gesture that unleashes a series of consequences he is unable to contain.

46. Neither the line separating these two different responses that I am characterizing in an overly schematic way would have been clear, nor would their political impact have been unambiguous. Even if it contests the idea that the nature of the boundary separating the *oikos* from the *polis* is pre-political, a performance of Antigone would have reduplicated the conditions that maintained women in their seclusion from active and vocal participation in the political.

47. In contrast to Antigone, who refrains from ordering Ismene to help her bury the corpse of Polynices, and in line with "his characteristic view of his subjects as animals, controlled and subjugated" as Segal puts it Creon's "speech consists in giving orders," "Antigone: Death and Love, Hades and Dionysus," in *Tragedy and Civilization: An Interpretation of Sophocles* (Norman: University of Oklahoma Press, 1999), 159–162.

48. My formulations here are informed by Butler *Antigone's Claim: Kinship Between Life & Death* (New York: Columbia University Press, 2000).

49. Heather Rakes, in an unpublished seminar paper, "Antigone and Idiolect of Abject Anger" (DePaul, 2006), asks "Is it the anger of colonized, occupied, and/or incarcerated subjects [which] is intolerable and unintelligible, or is it the threat of an end to apartheid, segregation, exploitation, the prison industrial complex, by means of exposing their injustices? Is it, perhaps, both?"

50. Hodoshe, a Xhosa word meaning carrion-fly, was the nickname of the prison guard—a name that has peculiar resonance for Sophocles' *Antigone*, in which the corpse of Polynices was exposed to the birds. The guard, then, hovered over his prisoners, who endured a living death, and whose incarceration refigured Antigone's premature entombment by Creon in an underground cave. The guard in question was renowned for his attempt to break the spirits of the prisoners on Robben Island.

51. Errol Durbach, "Sophocles In South Africa: Athol Fugard's *The Island*," *Drama and the Classical Heritage: Comparative and Critical Essays*, ed. Clifford Davidson, Rand Johnson, and John H. Stroupe (AMS Press, Inc.: New York, 1993), 248. In the play *Sizwe Banzi is Dead* Fugard, Kani, and Ntshona explore the central and determining role that the possession of a pass book, or the lack of one, had on constraining the lives of those living under apartheid in South Africa.

52. When Winston's and John's legs are bound together, they are "on four legs," when John sprains his ankle they go "on three," and when they are separated, they go "on two legs." Winston's eye is injured when he is beaten by Hodoshe, and, again, according to the stage directions, he "crawls around the cell, blind with rage and pain" (I 47). Thus the riddle of the Sphinx is invoked, and at the same time, the injuries Oedipus sustains, to his feet as an infant, and to his eyes, at his own hands, as an adult and a criminal, are evoked.

53. Olga Taxidou suggests that Oedipus internalizes the Sphinx, and is thereby feminized, *Tragedy, Modernity and Mourning* Olga (Edinburgh: Edinburgh University Press, 2004), 47, 54, and 69.

54. The Robben Island play that served as the inspiration for *The Island*—which includes a performance of Antigone onstage, complete with mop—failed to raise, in Fugard's words, "even a titter," "*Antigone* in Africa," in *Amid Our Troubles: Irish Versions of Greek Tragedy*, ed. Marianne McDonald and J. Michael Walton (London: Methuen, 2002), 134.

55. Fugard, "*Antigone* in Africa," in *Amid Our Troubles: Irish Versions of Greek Tragedy*, ed. Marianne McDonald and J. Michael Walton (London: Methuen, 2002), 132.

56. Fugard, "*Antigone* in Africa," in *Amid Our Troubles: Irish Versions of Greek Tragedy*, ed. Marianne McDonald and J. Michael Walton (London: Methuen, 2002), 130.

57. Fugard, "*Antigone* in Africa," in *Amid Our Troubles: Irish Versions of Greek Tragedy*, ed. Marianne McDonald and J. Michael Walton (London: Methuen, 2002), 132.

58. Fugard, "*Antigone* in Africa," in *Amid Our Troubles: Irish Versions of Greek Tragedy*, ed. Marianne McDonald and J. Michael Walton (London: Methuen, 2002), 133.

59. Fugard, "*Antigone* in Africa," in *Amid Our Troubles: Irish Versions of Greek Tragedy*, ed. Marianne McDonald and J. Michael Walton (London: Methuen, 2002), 134.

60. Fugard, "*Antigone* in Africa," in *Amid Our Troubles: Irish Versions of Greek Tragedy*, ed. Marianne McDonald and J. Michael Walton (London: Methuen, 2002), 134.

61. Fugard, "*Antigone* in Africa," in *Amid Our Troubles: Irish Versions of Greek Tragedy*, ed. Marianne McDonald and J. Michael Walton (London: Methuen, 2002), 144.

62. Fugard, "*Antigone* in Africa," in *Amid Our Troubles: Irish Versions of Greek Tragedy*, ed. Marianne McDonald and J. Michael Walton (London: Methuen, 2002), 134.

63. See Fugard, "*Antigone* in Africa," in *Amid Our Troubles: Irish Versions of Greek Tragedy*, ed. Marianne McDonald and J. Michael Walton (London: Methuen, 2002), 145.

64. Wetmore also quotes this line, but attributes to it a slightly different connotation, *The Athenian Sun in an African Sky* (Jefferson, North Carolina: McFarland & Company, Inc., 2002), 198.

65. Fugard, "*Antigone* in Africa," in *Amid Our Troubles: Irish Versions of Greek Tragedy*, ed. Marianne McDonald and J. Michael Walton (London: Methuen, 2002), 143.

66. See Òsófisan, *Tègònni, an African Antigone* (Ibadan, Nigeria: Kenbim Press, 1999).

Chapter 4

1. I say paradoxically because Friedrich Nietzsche associates "democratic taste" and the "triumph of *optimism*" with "a decline of strength," without clarifying *whose* strength is at stake, *The Birth of Tragedy*, trans. Walter Kauffman (New York: Vintage Books, 1967), 21.

2. Reiss, *Tragedy and Truth. Studies in the Development of a Renaissance and Neoclassical Discourse* (Yale University Press: New Haven and London, 1980), 2.

3. Òsófisan, "Interview with Fémi.Òsófisan," Interview by Victor Aire and Kanchana Ugbabe, in *Portraits for an Eagle: Essays in Honour of Femi Osofisan*, ed. Sola Adeyemi, Bayreuth: Bayreuth University, 2006, 68.

4. Elizabeth Wyckoff, "Antigone," in *Sophocles I*, ed. David Grene. *The Complete Greek Tragedies*, ed. David Grene and Richmond Lattimore (Chicago: The University of Chicago Press) 1954. F. Storr translates the line "The slain man was no villain but a brother," *Sophocles in two volumes*, vol. 1, *The Loeb Classical Library*, (Cambridge, Massachusetts: Harvard University Press, 1981), 353, while Reginald Gibbons has "It was no slave—it was my brother who died," A*ntigone*, trans. Reginald Gibbons and Charles Segal, The Greek Tragedy in New Translations, ed. Peter Burian and Alan Shapiro (Oxford: Oxford University Press, 2003), 76. As O'Brien notes, "Creon treats Polynices' body as if her were a slave-thing (517)," *Guide to Sophocles'* Antigone (Carbondale and Edwardsville: Southern Illinois University Press, 1978), 40.

5. See, for example, Weber, "Antigone's Nomos," *Theatricality as Medium* (New York: Fordham University Press, 2004), 138 and 383–4 n. 17. See also Lacan, *The Ethics of Psychoanalysis 1959–1960: The Seminar of Jacques Lacan*, Book VII, trans. Dennis Porter. Ed. Jacques-Alain Miller (New York: Tavistock/Routledge, 1992), 254–6. See also Mary Beth Mader, *Antigone's Line. Bulletin de la société Américaine de philosophie de langue Francaise*, 14 (2005): 2, 18–40.

6. See, for example, *Antigone*, line 467.

7. See Wyckoff, *Antigone*, line 199. Joan V. O'Brien comments that Creon speaks of " 'the land of his fathers and the gods of his race' [*Gēn patroi n kai theous tous engeneis*], i.e., the gods and ancestors not just of this father's house of Labdakos but those revered by the whole Cadmean people," *Guide to Sophocles'* Antigone (Carbondale and Edwardsville: Southern Illinois University Press, 1978), 40. O'Brien goes on to

note, however, that while one could see the differences between Antigone's and Creon's outlooks as "relics of the matrilineal and patrilineal outlook of an earlier age," Antigone also "invokes the gods 'of our fathers' (848) and hopes for reunion with both her mother and her father (898ff)," suggesting that Antigone does not align herself exclusively with a matrilineal tradition (40).

8. See Gibbons' translation in, *Antigone*, trans. Reginald Gibbons and Charles Segal, *The Greek Tragedy in New Translations*, ed. Peter Burian and Alan Shapiro (Oxford: Oxford University Press, 2003), 62. See also Storr, *Sophocles in two volumes*, vol. 1, *The Loeb Classical Library*, (Cambridge, Massachusetts: Harvard University Press, 1981), 373. See also Wyckoff, "Antigone," in *Sophocles I*, ed. David Grene. *The Complete Greek Tragedies*, ed. David Grene and Richmond Lattimore (Chicago: The University of Chicago Press, 1954), 185. See also. O'Brien, whose commentary in this regard is valuable. She makes the point that "the abstract noun *douleuma*, 'a slave-thing,' is a more insulting word than the world *doulos*, the concrete noun 'slave,' " *Guide to Sophocles'* Antigone (Carbondale and Edwardsville: Southern Illinois University Press, 1978), 41 and 92.

9. See O'Brien, *Guide to Sophocles'* Antigone (Carbondale and Edwardsville: Southern Illinois University Press, 1978), 41.

10. See Robert F. Goheen, *The Imagery of Sophocles' Antigone* (Princeton: Princeton University Press, 1951), 28–35.

11. O'Brien, *Guide to Sophocles'* Antigone (Carbondale and Edwardsville: Southern Illinois University Press, 1978), 41.

12. See Storr, *Sophocles in two volumes*, vol. 1, *The Loeb Classical Library*, (Cambridge, Massachusetts: Harvard University Press, 1981), 355.

13. See Jacques Derrida, *L'animal que donc je suis*, ed. Marie-Louise Mallet (Paris: Galilée, 2006).

14. For readings of Antigone that emphasize her monstrous, uncanny dimension, see Martin Heidegger, *An Introduction to Metaphysics*, trans. Ralph Manheim (New Haven and London: Yale University Press, 1959). See also, Lacan, *The Ethics of Psychoanalysis 1959–1960: The Seminar of Jacques Lacan*, Book VII, trans. Dennis Porter, ed. Jacques-Alain Miller (New York: Tavistock/Routledge, 1992), 263. Lacan appears to distance himself from understanding Antigone as monstrous, only to read her as beyond Atē, beyond all limits.

15. Butler, *Antigone's Claim: Kinship Between Life & Death* (New York: Columbia University Press 2000), 6.

16. Butler says, "Two questions that the play poses are whether there can be kinship—and by kinship I do not mean the 'family' in any specific form—without the support and mediation of the state, and whether there can be the state without the family as its support and mediation. And further, when kinship comes to pose a threat to state authority and the state sets itself in a violent struggle against kinship, can these very terms sustain their independence from one another?" *Antigone's Claim: Kinship Between Life & Death* (New York: Columbia University Press, 2000), 5.

17. Butler, *Antigone's Claim: Kinship Between Life & Death* (New York: Columbia University Press, 2000), 22–3.

18. See Butler, *Antigone's Claim: Kinship Between Life & Death* (New York: Columbia University Press, 2000), 14. Butler suggests that the Lacanian symbolic is symptomatic of a psychoanalytic fantasy that refuses to question its own authority as

ultimate. For all the lip service paid to contingency, Butler thinks that any significant change of social relations is disavowed by this fantasy. Lacan's "description of the symbolic as intractable law takes place within a fantasy of law as insurpassable authority" and that Lacan "at once analyzes and symptomizes this fantasy" (30). For Butler the symbolic "can acknowledge the contingency of its own structure only by disavowing the possibility of any substantial alteration in its field of operation" (30). Revising her earlier formulations, Butler suggests not that "the symbolic is universal in the sense of being universally valid for all time, but only that, every time it appears, it appears as a universalizing function; it refers to the chain of signs through which it derives its own signifying power. . . . In no way, however, is the universalizing effect of its own operation called into question by the assertion of contingency here" (44). Finally, then, whatever sense of universality the symbolic claims for itself, if its universality is used to shore up its own authority as unassailable and intractable, it would appear to remain immune from any changes in actual, social relations. "If the Oedipus complex is not universal in one way, but remains in another, does it finally matter which way it is universal if the effect is the same?" (45).

19. Butler says, "Consider that in the situation of blended families, a child says 'mother' and might expect more than one individual to respond to the call. Or that, in the case of adoption, a child might say 'father' and might mean both the absent phantasm she never knew as well as the one who assumes that place in living memory. . . . Does it make sense on these occasions to insist that there are symbolic positions of Mother and Father that every psyche must accept regardless of the social form that kinship takes? *Or is that a way of reinstating a heterosexual organization of parenting at the psychic level* [my emphasis] that can accommodate all manner of gender variation at the social level? Here it seems that the *very division between psychic or symbolic, on* the one hand, *and the social,* on the other, *occasions* this preemptory *normalization* [my emphasis] of the social field. . . . The structure is *purely formal,* its defenders say, but note how its very formalism secures the structure *against critical challenge.* What are we to make of an *inhabitant of the form that brings the form to crisis* [my emphasis]?"*Antigone's Claim: Kinship Between Life & Death* (New York: Columbia University Press, 2000), 69–71.

20. Butler, *Antigone's Claim: Kinship Between Life & Death* (New York: Columbia University Press, 2000), 19.

21. Although Butler takes her "distance from both" Hegel and Lacan, she also "endeavor[s] to rework aspects of both positions in the account that [she provides] to these questions: Does Antigone's death signal a necessary lesson about the limits of cultural intelligibility, the limits of intelligible kinship, one that restores us to our proper sense of limit and constraint? Does Antigone's death signal the supersession of kinship by the state, the necessary subordination of the former to the latter? Or is her death precisely a limit that requires to be read as that operation of political power that forecloses what forms of kinship will be intelligible, what kinds of lives can be countenanced as living?" *Antigone's Claim: Kinship Between Life & Death* (New York: Columbia University Press, 2000), 29.

22. Butler, *Antigone's Claim: Kinship Between Life & Death* (New York: Columbia University Press, 2000), 73–4. In fact, while she does not follow out this motif in relation to *Antigone,* Butler does point to an orientalizing trope in *Oedipus at Colonus, Antigone's Claim: Kinship Between Life & Death* (New York: Columbia University Press, 2000), 62.

23. While Mader recognizes this, she does not take account of it in relation to Lacan's distinction between the symbolic and social, which operates in a law-like fashion, but which is itself a normative distinction, one that Butler puts into question. See Mader, "Antigone's Line," *Bulletin de la société Américaine de philosophie de langue Française*, 14: 2 (2005): 18–40.

24. Butler, *Antigone's Claim: Kinship Between Life & Death* (New York: Columbia University Press, 2000), 6). See Mader, "Antigone's Line," *Bulletin de la société Américaine de philosophie de langue Francaise*, 14: 2 (2005): 18.

25. Mader, "Antigone's Line," *Bulletin de la société Américaine de philosophie de langue Francaise*, 14: 2 (2005): 28.

26. Mader, "Antigone's Line," *Bulletin de la société Américaine de philosophie de langue Francaise*, 14: 2 (2005): 35.

27. Cf. Weber suggests that Creon is a tyrant precisely because "he acquires power" rather than inheriting it, pointing out that he is not a blood relative, but is "next of kin," *Theatricality as Medium* (New York: Fordham University Press, 2004), 29, Yet, the distinction Weber seeks to draw is unclear; his familial status is precisely put in question by the confusion of inheritance Oedipus has created. Whether Creon seizes power is thus unclear.

28. See Mader, "Antigone's Line," *Bulletin de la société Américaine de philosophie de langue Francaise*, 14: 2 (2005): 18–40.

29. Mader casts her argument against the background of those of Lacan's and Butler's, Mader, "Antigone's Line," *Bulletin de la société Américaine de philosophie de langue Francaise*, 14: 2 (2005), 18–40. While in both cases, she disputes the status that law or legality play in their arguments, she does not expand her insights in order to draw out their political implications. I want to take seriously both the contemporary theoretical and political reflections with which theorists such as Irigaray and Butler asks us to engage, and the history of political dramatizations of Antigone that recapitulate the principle for which she stands in a wide variety of contexts, and which continue to draw energy from the figure of Antigone even as they refigure her.

30. See Just, *Women in Athenian Law and Life* (London: Routledge, 1989), 87.

31. Cf. Ormand who says "Creon's right to the throne comes to him through his sister, Jocasta. He has no patrilineal relation to the two dead brothers," *Exchange and the Maiden: Marriage in Sophoclean Tragedy* (Austin: University of Texas Press, 1999), 85.

32. Antigone insists on naming Polynices under the description of *autadelphos* (my own brother), and stressing that she shared the same womb (*homosplanchnos*) as him. See Segal, "Antigone: Death and Love, Hades and Dionysus," in *Tragedy and Civilization: An Interpretation of Sophocles* (Norman: University of Oklahoma Press, 1999), 158, 170, and 184. See also Knox, *The Heroic Temper: Studies in Sophoclean Tragedy* (Berkeley: University of California Press, 1992), 79.

33. It is crucial to understand that in emphasizing maternal genealogy, Antigone is not asserting the authority of a natural relationship, but making a symbolic claim. Derrida is right to insist that "a genealogical tie" will always be phantasmatic, *The Politics of Friendship,* trans. George Collins (New York: Verso, 1997), "it always implies a symbolic effect of discourse—a 'legal fiction' " and that "This is also true . . . of maternity." As he points out, any appeal to *phusis* is intended to renaturalize what is always in fact a fiction/phantasm (93).

34. Recall Pericles' law on citizenship. See Loraux, *The Children of Athena: Athenian Ideas about Citizenship and the Division between the Sexes*, trans. Caroline Levine (Princeton: Princeton University Press, 1993), 119.

35. This would not prevent, however, the possibility of Creon adopting a son, a practice that was fairly prevalent in fifth century BCE Athens. See Mader, 18–40.

36. The fact that Creon refers to her throughout as child could be taken to refer to the dual symbolic status Antigone occupies as both daughter and granddaughter of Jocasta—in other words as her own child. However, as Pomeroy observes (see above), wives were viewed as having the status of children, Pomeroy, *Goddesses, Whores, Wives, and Slaves*: *Women in Ancient Antiquity* (New York: Schocken Books, 1995).

37. Cf. Segal, "Antigone: Death and Love, Hades and Dionysus," in *Tragedy and Civilization*: *An Interpretation of Sophocles*. Norman: University of Oklahoma Press, 1999).

38. See Tyrrell and Bennett, who elaborate on the connection between the premature cutting off of Antigone's fertility, and Niobe's petrification, which brings to an end her fertility, *Recapturing Sophocles' Antigone* (Lanham: Rowman and Littlefield, 1998), 143.

39. However, as Rachel Kitzinger points out, Niobe is both parallel and opposite to Antigone: Niobe is a mother, Antigone a virgin; Niobe dies for a boast about giving birth, Antigone for a boast about burying the dead; Niobe defies a goddess to assert her superior power of generation, Antigone defies a king to assert her superior power of her enactment of eternal, divine law." "Sophoklean Dialogues," in *Contextualizing Classics: Ideology, Performance, Dialogue*, ed. Thomas M. Falkner, Nancy Felson, and David Konstan. (Lanham: Rowman and Littlefield, 1999), 216.

40. See Loraux, *Mothers in Mourning*, trans. Corinne Pache (Ithaca: Cornell University Press, 1998), 51.

41. See Mader, "Antigone's Line," *Bulletin de la société Américaine de philosophie de langue Francaise*, 14: 2 (2005): 18–40.

42. That recognition is something that must occur between two humans, rather than something that can proceed from inanimate objects, is one of the lessons that issues in the master-slave dialectic. Markell's discussion of the master slave relationship in this regard is illuminating, *Bound by Recognition* (Princeton and Oxford: Princeton University Press, 2003). The importance of this dialectic for Lacan is well established. Of course, the questions raised by Derrida, in *L'animal que donc je suis*, ed. Marie-Louise Mallet (Paris: Galilée, 2006) throw into crisis the assumption that one should ever appeal to a definitive boundary separating animality from humanity, yet this has not prevented racialized, orientalizing, homophobic, and classist discourses benefiting from precisely such metaphysically problematic appeals.

43. Butler makes the point that from the restriction of certain familial relations it does not follow that other familial relations should follow a specific normative pattern: "From the presumption that one cannot—or ought not to—choose one's closest family members as one's lovers and marital partners, it does not follow that the bonds of kinship that are possible assume any particular form," *Antigone's Claim: Kinship Between Life & Death* (New York: Columbia University Press, 2000), 66.

44. Sheila Murnaghan, "*Antigone* 904–920 and the Institution of Marriage," *The American Journal of Philology* 107 (1986): 192–207.

45. Others also emphasize that Creon implies the replaceability of women as marriage partners. Ormand says that "the woman is a replaceable party in a marriage," *Exchange and the Maiden: Marriage in Sophoclean Tragedy* (Austin: University of Texas

Press, 1999), 84. He cites Neuberg who says "the entire scene between Creon and Haemon implicitly involves the replaceability of the spouse" (1990), 73.

46. Loraux, *Born of the Earth: Myth and Politics in Athens*, trans. Selina Stewart (Ithaca: Cornell University Press, 2000), 3.

47. See Murnaghan, "Sucking the Juice without Biting the Rind: Aristotle and Tragic Mimesis." *New Literary History* 26.4 (1995): 755–773. Quoted by Tyrrell and Bennett (RS 114).

48. Ormand, *Exchange and the Maiden: Marriage in Sophoclean Tragedy* (Austin: University of Texas Press, 1999), 17.

49. Thomas Wiedemann observes that "Only when the citizen community felt itself desperately threatened would slaves be called upon to fight side by side with their masters . . . and even then the fiction that only free men should be involved in the organized violence of warfare was normally maintained by manumitting the slaves in question first," *Greek and Roman Slavery* (New York: Routledge, 2005), 4.

50. Ormand, *Exchange and the Maiden: Marriage in Sophoclean Tragedy* (Austin: University of Texas Press, 1999), 84.

51. Murnaghan also connects *Antigone* to Pericles' law. See "*Antigone* 904–920 and the Institution of Marriage," *The American Journal of Philology* 107 (1986): 192–207.

52. Thus the idea of Antigone as a sacrificial victim, who helps to cement social bonds, needs to be complicated. For a discussion of this idea see Rabinowitz *Anxiety Veiled: Euripides and the Traffic in Women* (Ithaca: Cornell University Press, 1993), 31.

53. In addition to all of this, Antigone's assertion of her right to bury Polynices intervenes at the level of establishing the religious ritual of burial as a decisive part of the political ceremonies of the city, and as a claim of the symbolic importance of mourning.

54. Butler, *Antigone's Claim: Kinship Between Life & Death* (New York: Columbia University Press, 2000), 24.

55. One thinks here not only of Jean Anouilh, *A Tragedy by Jean Anouilh*, trans. Lewis Galantière (London: Methuen, 1951).

56. Felix Budelmann says, "Antigone knows, and instructs others, about the plot and the characters of what is, at one level, her own story. She comes, she says, 'from the Greek and other mythologies' (26). She is a figure of hope who shows the value of fighting oppression, since she has done it so famously elsewhere," "Greek Tragedies in West African Adaptations," in *Classics and Colonialism*, ed. Barbara Goff (London: Duckworth, 2005), 132.

57. Anouilh, *A Tragedy by Jean Anouilh*, trans. Lewis Galantière (London: Methuen, 1951), 20.

58. Jean Anouilh, *A Tragedy by Jean Anouilh*, trans. Lewis Galantière (London: Methuen, 1951). Hannah Arendt, *Eichmann in Jerusalem: A Report on the Banality of Evil* (Harmondsworth, Middlesex: Penguin, 1964).

59. As Barbara Goff says in relation to Antigone, "The story is saved instead of the woman," Antigone's Boat: The Colonial and the Postcolonial in Tegnni," in *Portraits for an Eagle: Essays in Honour of Femi Osofisan*, ed. Sola Adeyemi (Bayreuth: Bayreuth University, 2006), 111–121.

60. There are many aspects of this rich play that I have not been able to address here. Among them is the role of orality and the importance of song. See, for example, Gibbs, James. "*Antigone* and After *Antigone*," in *Portraits for an Eagle: Essays in Honour of Femi Osofisan*, ed. Sola Adeyemi (Bayreuth: Bayreuth University, 2006), 85. See also

Budelmann, "Greek Tragedies in West African Adaptations," in *Classics and Colonialism*, ed. Barbara Goff (London: Duckworth, 2005). Also see Rachel Kitzinger's discussion of song and choral response in Antigone, a reading which could be developed in relation to the call and response structure that informs the tradition of Nigerian drama upon which Òsófisan is drawing. See Kitzinger, "Sophoklean Dialogues," in *Contextualizing Classics: Ideology, Performance, Dialogue*, ed. Thomas M. Falkner, Nancy Felson, and David Konstan (Lanham: Rowman and Littlefield, 1999).

61. Reiss, *Tragedy and Truth. Studies in the Development of a Renaissance and Neoclassical Discourse* (Yale University Press: New Haven and London, 1980), 7.

62. Reiss, *Tragedy and Truth. Studies in the Development of a Renaissance and Neoclassical Discourse* (Yale University Press: New Haven and London, 1980), 8

63. Reiss, *Tragedy and Truth. Studies in the Development of a Renaissance and Neoclassical Discourse* (Yale University Press: New Haven and London, 1980), 10.

64. Reiss, *Tragedy and Truth. Studies in the Development of a Renaissance and Neoclassical Discourse* (Yale University Press: New Haven and London, 1980), 17.

65. Reiss, *Tragedy and Truth. Studies in the Development of a Renaissance and Neoclassical Discourse* (Yale University Press: New Haven and London, 1980), 12.

66. Reiss, *Tragedy and Truth. Studies in the Development of a Renaissance and Neoclassical Discourse* (Yale University Press: New Haven and London, 1980) 11–12.

67. See Terry Eagleton, *Sweet Violence: The Idea of the Tragic* (Oxford: Blackwell, 2003).

Chapter 5

1. Irigaray, Luce. *This Sex Which Is Not One*, trans. Catherine Porter (Ithaca: Cornell University Press, 1985), 167–8.

2. See Foucault, *The History of Sexuality*, vol. I: An Introduction, trans. Robert Hurley, (Harmondsworth, Middlesex: Penguin, 1978).

3. Agamben, *Homo Sacer: Sovereign Power and Bare Life*, trans. Daniel Heller-Roazen (Stanford: Stanford University Press, 1998), 6. Hereafter cited in the text as HS, followed by page numbers.

4. Although Agamben stipulates that the head of an estate and the head of the family are both "concerned with the reproduction and subsistence of life" (HS 2), he addresses neither the gender dynamics nor the dynamics that sustain slavery that are thereby overseen. Thus while he persuasively traces out how the structure of the biopolitical is already implicit in the polis of ancient Greece, he does not attend to the dynamics that were transposed into the biopolitical, dynamics that infused and shaped the oikos.

5. It should be clear that the political formation that excludes those who perform the primary work of the oikos, slaves and women, from participation in politics is part of the polis, even if those excluded do not participate in it, just as it should also be clear that the oikos is ruled over by the male head of household, even if those who perform the work of the oikos, and are thereby excluded from the polis as such, are nonetheless included in the sense that the polis benefits from the fruits of their labor, even as it declines to recognize them as political actors.

6. Heaney, *The Burial at Thebes: A Version of Sophocles'* Antigone (New York: Farrar, Straus and Giroux, 2004). While I am not suggesting that the tyrannical aspects

of George Bush's presidency were totalitarian, historically there is certainly a close relationship between totalitarian regimes and tyranny.

7. Arendt, *Eichmann in Jerusalem: A Report on the Banality of Evil* (Harmondsworth, Middlesex: Penguin, 1964), 26–7.

8. See Butler *Precarious Lives: The Powers of Mourning and Violence* (London: Verso, 2004). See also Andrew Benjamin, Particularity and Exceptions: On Jews and Animals," *South Atlantic Quarterly* 107: (2008): 72–87. See also Agamben, *State of Exception*, trans. Kevin Attell (Chicago: University of Chicago Press), 2005.

9. Clifton Spargo, "The Apolitics of Antigone's Lament (From Sophocles to Ariel Dorfman)," 2007, private manuscript.

10. Spargo comments on this aspect when he says "What the play brilliantly exposes is the extent to which his absolutist advocation of the political organization of life occurs under the contingent circumstances of a recent threat against the throne, in response to a secondary act (Antigone's) that symbolically repeats the original threat (Polynices's) by commemorating its primary agent."

11. Weber observes that "The lack of a firm legitimation of his sovereignty constrains him to begin his rule by attempting to lay out the general principles upon which it will be based," in *Theatricality as Medium* (New York: Fordham University Press, 2004), 130.

12. Spargo, 2007.

13. See Ziarek Ziarek, Ewa Płonowska. "Bare Life on Strike: Notes on the Biopolitics of Race and Gender," *South Atlantic Quarterly* 107 (2008): 89–105. See also Andrew Benjamin, Particularity and Exceptions: On Jews and Animals," *South Atlantic Quarterly* 107: (2008): 72–87.

14. Paul Patton demonstrates that not only does Foucault anticipate much of Agamben's analysis, but that there are also some important respects in which, in comparison to Agamben, Foucault's analysis is much less cavalier than Agamben's. However, although he does not frame it in this way, Patton raises a question about Foucault that echoes Agamben's suggestion that the relationship between sovereign power and biopolitics stands in need of clarification in Foucault. Patton asks, "Where do we find evidence of the emergence of a new conception sovereign political right that corresponds to the emergence of biopower?" "Agamben and Foucault on Biopower and Biopolitics" in *Giorgio Agamben: Sovereignty and Life*, ed. Matthew Calarco, and Steve DeCaroli (Stanford: Stanford University Press, 2007), 216.

15. Deutscher, "The Inversion of Exceptionality: Foucault, Agamben and 'Reproductive Rights,' " *South Atlantic Quarterly* 107 (2008): 55–70.

16. Irigaray is not the only one to draw attention to the dynamic of constitutive exclusion in terms of which she reads *Antigone*. Derrida has also exposed this logic, and others, such as Kristeva, have developed this logic in a different logic under the heading of abjection. See Jacques Derrida, *Glas*, trans. John P. Leavey and Richard Rand (Lincoln: University of Nebraska Press, 1986). See also Julia Kristeva, *Powers of Horror: An Essay on Abjection*, trans. Leon S. Roudiez (New York: Columbia University Press, 1982). It bears considering that Agamben's notion of the state of exception closely resembles the logic of constitutive exclusion.

17. Patton, "Agamben and Foucault on Biopower and Biopolitics" in *Giorgio Agamben: Sovereignty and Life*, ed. Matthew Calarco, and Steve DeCaroli (Stanford: Stanford University Press, 2007), 218. Ernesto Laclau, "Bare Life or Social Indeterminacy?"

in *Giorgio Agamben: Sovereignty and Life*, ed. Matthew Calarco, and Steve DeCaroli (Stanford: Stanford University Press, 2007), 11.

18. Laclau, "Bare Life or Social Indeterminacy?" in *Giorgio Agamben: Sovereignty and Life*, ed. Matthew Calarco, and Steve DeCaroli (Stanford: Stanford University Press, 2007), 11.

19. Agamben explains the terms in this way: "*zoē*, which expressed the simple fact of living common to all living beings (animals, men, or gods), and *bios*, which indicated the form or way of living proper to an individual or a group." He goes on to specify that Foucault "summarizes the process by which, at the threshold of the modern era, natural life begins to be included in the mechanisms and calculations of State Power, and politics turns into biopolitics. 'For millennia,' he writes, 'man remained what he was for Aristotle: a living animal with the additional capacity for political existence; modern man is an animal whose politics calls his existence as a living being into question' (*La volonté*, p. 188)," *State of Exception*, trans. Kevin Attell (Chicago: University of Chicago Press, 1995), 1–3.

20. As we have seen, referring to Aristotle's *Politics*, Agamben says "In the classical world . . . simple natural life is excluded from the *polis* in the strict sense, and remains confined—as merely reproductive life—to the sphere of the *oikos*, 'home' (*Politics*, 1252a, 26-35)," *Homo Sacer* HS 2. Yet, as I suggest, he makes no mention of the gendered politics that inform this confinement. Although he develops the notion of the camp as a paradigm, and thereby takes on the question of racial typographies in relation to Jews, he does not extend that analysis to the slaves of classical Greece, whose labor is incorporated into the polis, but who do not figure in the polis as political subjects.

21. Agamben, *State of Exception*, trans. Kevin Attell (Chicago: University of Chicago Press, 1995), 7.

22. Irigiaray, *An Ethics of Sexual Difference*, trans. Carolyn Burke and Gillian C. Gill (Ithaca: Cornell University Press, 1993), 101.

23. As Deutscher notes, in Foucault's analysis there is a sense in which "women's reproductivity in matters of population control and of reproduction incitement become the political focus," "The Inversion of Exceptionality: Foucault, Agamben and 'Reproductive Rights,' " *South Atlantic Quarterly* 107 (2008): 55–70.

24. See Griffith, "Corporality in the Ancient Greek Theatre," *Phonenix*, 52 (3–4) (1998): 230–256.

25. See Carson, "Putting her in her Place: Woman, Dirt, and Desire," *Before Sexuality: The Construction of Erotic Experience in the Ancient Greek World*, ed. David M. Halperin, John J. Winkler, and Froma I. Zeitlin (Princeton, New Jersey: Princeton University Press, 1990), 135–169.

26. See Mader "Antigone's Line," *Bulletin de la société Américaine de philosophie de langue Francaise*, 14: 2 (2005): 18–40.

27. The irony is that the confusion surrounding the identity of Oedipus came from quite another source—which does not prevent it functioning allegorically for the chaos caused by allowing women freedom of movement and access to public speech.

28. Irigaray, *Speculum of the Other Woman*, trans. Gillian C. Gill (Ithaca: Cornell University Press, 1985), 217.

29. As Irigaray puts it, the veil of "glossing over" is "used to cover a lesser 'value,' and to overvalue the fetish," and "it will equally serve to conceal the interest afforded

by what it claims to protect from devaluation: the interest, for example, one might take in the place of copulation; also, in an other way, of conception. Or again it will fail to inquire how much copulation might cost, for this is obviously difficult to calculate and threatens the validity of the economy in place. If for no other reason than that it cannot and could not, in any circumstances, be seen or known. Thus challenging the systems of representation(s), of coining(s) of profits and losses. Setting fire, it may be, to fetishes," *Speculum of the Other Woman*, trans. Gillian C. Gill (Ithaca: Cornell University Press, 1985), 116.

30. Irigaray, *Speculum of the Other Woman*, trans. Gillian C. Gill (Ithaca: Cornell University Press, 1985), 118.

31. Irigaray, *Speculum of the Other Woman*, trans. Gillian C. Gill (Ithaca: Cornell University Press, 1985), 116, 225.

32. Irigaray, *Speculum of the Other Woman*, trans. Gillian C. Gill (Ithaca: Cornell University Press, 1985), 221, 224.

33. Irigaray, *Speculum of the Other Woman*, trans. Gillian C. Gill (Ithaca: Cornell University Press, 1985) 115–6. See Sigmund Freud, "Infantile genital organization: An interpolation into the theory of sexuality" in *The Standard Edition of the Complete Psychological Works*, trans. James Strachey, vol. 19 (London: Hogarth Press and the Institute of Psycho-analysis, 1953), 143–4.

34. Derrida, *Rogues: Two Essays on Reason*, trans. Pascale-Anne Brault and Michael Naas (Stanford: Stanford University Press, 2005).

35. See G. W. F. Hegel, *Phenomenology of Spirit*, trans. A. V. Miller (Oxford: Clarendon Press, 1979), 271. See also Derrida, *Glas* trans. John P. Leavey and Richard Rand (Lincoln: University of Nebraska Press, 1986), 145. See also Weber, *Theatricality as Medium* (New York: Fordham University Press, 2004), 126. See also Irigaray, *Speculum of the Other Woman*, trans. Gillian C. Gill. (Ithaca: Cornell University Press, 1985), 215.

36. This touches on the problem that Deutscher elaborates in relationship to Derrida and the problematic of autoimmunity, " 'Women and so on': *Rogues* and the Autoimmunity of Feminism," *Symposium: Canadian Journal of Continental Philosophy*, 11, 1 (2007): 101–119.

Chapter 6

1. As W. Robert Connor says, "In many cases citizenship and even place of residence must have been unclear. For example, shepherds must often have moved across the boundary line between Attika and Boiotia, or between Attika and Magara, as they searched for good pasture, or moved from summer to winter meadows," "The Problem of Athenian Civic Identity," in *Athenian Identity and Civic Ideology*, ed. Alan L. Boegehold and Adele C. Scafuro (Baltimore: Johns Hopkins University Press, 1994), 36.

2. When Oedipus marks his body, he crosses another taboo by marking himself as slavish. Slavery is a pervasive metaphor for all that the adult Greek male citizen did not want to be.

3. The Athenians would have been aware of Zorastrian rituals given that Herodotus mentions it. See Huff Archaeological Evidence of Zoroastrian Funerary Practices," *Zorastrian Rituals in Context*, ed. Micahel Stausberg (Boston: Brill, 2004), 593.

4. Peter Hunt, *Slaves, Warfare, and Ideology in the Greek Historians* (Cambridge: Cambridge University Press, 1998), 132. See Aristotle, *Politics*, trans. H. Rackham. *Loeb Classical Library*, Aristotle, vol. 21 (Cambridge: Harvard University Press, 2005) 1255a24–32. See also, Roger Just, *Women in Athenian Law and Life* (London: Routledge, 1989), esp. 188–193.

5. If the answer to this question is affirmative, it might have something to do with the enormous influence Aristotle's *Poetics* has exerted on the reading of tragedy. As Dimitris Vardoulakis observed to me in an email communication, "Since Aristotle, it has been a common place that tragedy is about 'important and complete (*spoudaia kai teleia*)' events, which has been taken to mean events performed by significant people, kings and queens etc." If slavery is in fact a structuring theme not just of Athenian life, but also of Sophocles' Oedipal cycle, then Aristotle's theory of poetics deserves re-evaluation. At the very least the idea that the concerns of tragedy are those represented by characters of noble birth—or indeed what such nobility consists in—deserves reconsideration. I thank Dimitris Vardoulakis for our exchange on this point.

6. While the significance attaching to the ritual of burial as a theme in *Antigone* has long been acknowledged, there has been a shift in scholarship of late away from its interrogation exclusively in the context of the religious significance of the universal, unwritten laws to which Antigone appeals. See, for example, Ehrenberg, *Sophocles and Pericles* (Oxford: Basil Blackwell, 1954) and toward investigations that prioritize the social and political significance of burial ritual.

7. See, for example, Gail Holst-Warhaft, *Dangerous Voices: Women's Laments and Greek Literature* (New York: Routledge, 1992). See also Olga Taxidou, *Tragedy, Modernity and Mourning* (Edinburgh: Edinburgh University, 2004).

8. Taxidou, *Tragedy, Modernity and Mourning* (Edinburgh: Edinburgh University, 2004), 175.

9. Taxidou, *Tragedy, Modernity and Mourning* (Edinburgh: Edinburgh University, 2004), 176. It would seem that funerary lamentation was curtailed not only in order to reduce the ostentation of aristocratic shows of wealth and to harness any glorification to the polis, but also as a way of delegitimating the parading of emotions that female-dominated public grieving flaunted. The control of wealth and of feminizing emotions were thus bound up with one another in that they were concerned with consolidating boundaries separating barbarians from ostensibly civilized peoples, both in terms of amassing wealth and in terms of controlling and harnessing emotions. The difference between Plato and Aristotle on emotions can be approached in terms of Aristotle's attempt to envisage the beneficial aspects of rationality containing emotions, a containment that mirrors both the processes by which women's movements were contained through their legal deprivation of rights and the customs that accompanied this political exclusion, and the procedures according to which Aristotle's *Poetics*, rather than merely outlawing poetry and subordinating emotions, rendered both tragedy and emotions ethically productive. If, in religion, which is so important to Hegel's understanding of art for the Greeks, women might be seen as more or less the equals—or even as superior to men—this might account for the need to introduce measures which closely monitored and oversaw the release of emotions in funeral practices. Limiting the one sphere of activity in which women might appear equal or superior to men was a way of ensuring that such power did not contaminate or bleed over into other spheres of life—politi-

cal rights for example. In this sense the formalization of religion into moral and legal principles was also a consolidation of male control over females.

10. Cartledge, " 'Deep Plays': Theatre as Process in Greek Civil Life" in *The Cambridge Companion to Greek Tragedy*, ed. P. E. Easterling (Cambridge: Cambridge University Press, 1997), 27. However, as Griffith notes, Antigone appeals to "Dike" or Justice, "conventionally imagined as Zeus's daughter," "The Subject of Desire in Sophocles' Antigone" in *The Soul of Tragedy: Essays on Athenian Drama*, ed. Victoria Pedrick and Steven M. Oberhelman (Chicago: The University of Chicago Press, 2005), 111.

11. See Taxidou *Tragedy, Modernity and Mourning* (Edinburgh: Edinburgh University, 2004), 178.

12. See Ormand, *Exchange and the Maiden: Marriage in Sophoclean Tragedy* (Austin: University of Texas Press, 1999); Rabinowitz, *Anxiety Veiled: Euripides and the Traffic in Women* (Ithaca: Cornell University Press, 1993); and Wohl, *Intimate Commerce: Exchange, Gender and Subjectivity in Greek Tragedy* (Austin: University of Texas, 1998).

13. On the imperial means of amassing wealth see Cartledge, " 'Deep Plays': Theatre as Process in Greek Civil Life" in *The Cambridge Companion to Greek Tragedy*, ed. P. E. Easterling (Cambridge: Cambridge University Press, 1997), 29.

14. Hall, "The Sociology of Athenian Tragedy" in *The Cambridge Companion to Greek Tragedy*, ed. P. E. Easterling (Cambridge: Cambridge University Press, 1997), 104–5. Hall also establishes a link between the "denial of burial" and the destruction of the kinship line through the notion of Kataskaphe—razing of the house to the ground, usually a punishment for political crime. This is particularly interesting in terms of the symbolic destruction of Creon's house, and the actual extinction of his familial line.

15. Just, *Women in Athenian Law and Life* (London: Routledge, 1991), 192–3.

16. Hall points out that "[o]nly one extant tragedy, Sophocles' *Philoctetes*, contains no women, and female tragic choruses in the surviving plays outnumber male by twenty-one to ten," "The Sociology of Athenian Tragedy" in *The Cambridge Companion to Greek Tragedy*, ed. P. E. Easterling (Cambridge: Cambridge University Press, 1997), 105.

17. Hall, "The Sociology of Athenian Tragedy" in *The Cambridge Companion to Greek Tragedy*, ed. P. E. Easterling (Cambridge: Cambridge University Press, 1997), 106.

18. Hall, "The Sociology of Athenian Tragedy" in *The Cambridge Companion to Greek Tragedy*, ed. P. E. Easterling (Cambridge: Cambridge University Press, 1997), 126.

19. Hall, "The Sociology of Athenian Tragedy" in *The Cambridge Companion to Greek Tragedy*, ed. P. E. Easterling (Cambridge: Cambridge University Press, 1997), 100.

20. While Edith Hall links Pericles' law to Euripides' *Telephus* in *Inventing the Barbarian: Greek Self-Definition through Tragedy* (Oxford: Clarendon Press, 1989), and while Tyrrell and Bennett forge a connection between the Periclean law and Sophocles' *Antigone* in *Recapturing Sophocles' Antigone* (Lanham: Rowman and Littlefield, 1998), 114, I am not aware of anyone having developed this connection into a reading that situates the implications this law has for the distinction Antigone draws between Polynices and a slave, and the nexus of questions in which this distinction is implicated, in the way that I have suggested.

21. Scafuro, "Witnessing and False Witnessing: Proving Citizenship and Kin Identity in Fourth-Century Athens," *Athenian Identity and Civic Ideology*, ed. Alan L. Boegehold and Adele C. Scafuro (Baltimore: Johns Hopkins University Press, 1994) 156.

22. Scafuro, "Witnessing and False Witnessing: Proving Citizenship and Kin Identity in Fourth-Century Athens," *Athenian Identity and Civic Ideology*, ed. Alan L. Boegehold and Adele C. Scafuro (Baltimore: Johns Hopkins University Press, 1994) 156.

23. Connor, "The Problem of Athenian Civic Identity," *Athenian Identity and Civic Ideology*, ed. Alan L. Boegehold and Adele C. Scafuro (Baltimore: Johns Hopkins University Press, 1994), 37.

24. Philip Manville Brook, "Toward a New Paradigm of Athenian Citizenship," in *Athenian Identity and Civic Ideology*, ed. Alan L. Boegehold and Adele C. Scafuro (Baltimore: Johns Hopkins University Press, 1994), 25–6.

25. Peter Hunt, *Slaves, Warfare, and Ideology in the Greek Historians* (Cambridge: Cambridge University Press, 1998), 131. Connor, "The Problem of Athenian Civic Identity," *Athenian Identity and Civic Ideology*, ed. Alan L. Boegehold and Adele C. Scafuro (Baltimore: Johns Hopkins University Press, 1994), 37.

26. Peter Hunt, *Slaves, Warfare, and Ideology in the Greek Historians* (Cambridge: Cambridge University Press, 1998), 132–3.

27. Peter Hunt, *Slaves, Warfare, and Ideology in the Greek Historians* (Cambridge: Cambridge University Press, 1998), 133.

28. Peter Hunt, *Slaves, Warfare, and Ideology in the Greek Historians* (Cambridge: Cambridge University Press, 1998), 133.

29. I include my own earlier interventions on the topic of Antigone as symptomatic of the tendency to oversimplify by reading Antigone as figuring the excluded other.

30. Josiah Ober, *Mass and Elite in Democratic Athens: Rhetoric, Ideology, and the Power of the People* (Princeton: Princeton University Press, 1989), 5.

31. This last clause is one I borrow from Mary Beth Mader.

32. Ober, *Mass and Elite in Democratic Athens: Rhetoric, Ideology, and the Power of the People* (Princeton: Princeton University Press, 1989), 262, 6.

33. Patterson, "The Case against Neaira and the Public Ideology of the Athenian Family," in *Athenian Identity and Civic Ideology*, ed. Alan L. Boegehold and Adele C. Scafuro (Baltimore: Johns Hopkins University Press, 1994), 201.

34. Philip Manville Brook, "Toward a New Paradigm of Athenian Citizenship," in *Athenian Identity and Civic Ideology*, ed. Alan L. Boegehold and Adele C. Scafuro (Baltimore: Johns Hopkins University Press, 1994), 24–5.

35. Patterson, "The Case against Neaira and the Public Ideology of the Athenian Family," in *Athenian Identity and Civic Ideology*, ed. Alan L. Boegehold and Adele C. Scafuro (Baltimore: Johns Hopkins University Press, 1994), 201.

36. Refer to urbana champagne article on naming of play.

37. Martin Bernal, *Black Athena*: *The Afro-Asiatic Roots of Classical Civilization, The Fabrication of Ancient Greece*, 1785–1985, vol. 1 (Rutgers University Press, 2003). The significance of Bernal's intervention is that it raises crucial questions that the tradition has tended to eclipse, even if it does so, as suggested earlier with reference to Hall, in a way that treats myth in a rather heavy-handed manner.

38. Patterson, "The Case against Neaira and the Public Ideology of the Athenian Family," in *Athenian Identity and Civic Ideology*, ed. Alan L. Boegehold and Adele C. Scafuro (Baltimore: Johns Hopkins University Press, 1994), 202.

39. Caroline, Rooney, *African Literature, Animism and Politics* (London: Routledge, 2000), 29.

40. At the same time it needs to be acknowledged that, as I argued in the preface, contemporary theories about race that interpret race as a social concept function in very similar ways to racial othering in ancient Greece

41. Said, *Orientalism* (New York: Vintage Books, 1979).

42. As Barbara Goff says in relation to Tègònni, "The story is saved instead of the woman," "Antigone's Boat: The Colonial and the Postcolonial in Tegnni," in *Portraits for an Eagle: Essays in Honour of Femi Osofisan*, ed. Sola Adeyemi (Bayreuth: Bayreuth University, 2006), 118.

Bibliography

Agamben, Giorgio. *Homo Sacer: Sovereign Power and Bare Life*. Trans. Daniel Heller-Roazen. Stanford: Stanford University Press, 1998.

Agamben, Giorgio. *State of Exception*, trans. Kevin Attell. Chicago: University of Chicago Press, 2005.

Ahl, Frederick. *Two Faces of Oedipus: Sophocles'* Oedipus Tyrannus *and Seneca's* Oedipus, trans. with an introduction. Ithaca, NY: Cornell University Press, 2008.

Ahl, Frederick. *Sophocles' Oedipus: Evidence and Self-Conviction*. Ithaca, NY: Cornell University Press, 1991.

Anouilh, Jean. *Antigone: A Tragedy by Jean Anouilh*. Trans. Lewis Galantière. London: Methuen, 1951.

Arendt, Hannah. *Eichmann in Jerusalem: A Report on the Banality of Evil*. Harmondsworth, Middlesex: Penguin, 1964.

Aristotle. *Politics*. Trans. H. Rackham. *Loeb Classical Library*, Aristotle, vol. 21. Cambridge, MA: Harvard University Press, 2005.

Aristotle. *Poetics*. Edited and trans. Stephen Halliwell. Longinus on the Sublime, trans. W. H. Fyfe, revised by Donald Russell; Demetrius on Style, trans. Doreen C. Innes, based on W. Rhys Roberts. *Loeb Classical Library*, Aristotle, vol. 23. Cambridge, MA: Harvard University Press, 1995.

Aristotle. *Nicomachean Ethics*. Trans. H. Rackham. Loeb Classical Library, Aristotle, vol. 19. Cambridge, MA: Harvard University Press, 1975.

Bassi, Karen. *Acting Like Men: Gender, Drama and Nostalgia in Ancient Greece*. Ann Arbor: University of Michigan Press, 1998.

Beistegui, Miguel de, and Simon Sparks. *Philosophy and Tragedy*. New York: Routledge, 2000.

Belfiore, Elizabeth. *Murder among friends: Violation of* Philia *in Greek Tragedy*. New York: Oxford University Press, 2000.

Bemba, Sylvain. "Black Wedding Candles for Blessed Antigone" in *Theatre and Politics: An International Anthology*. New York: Ubu Repertory Theatre, 1990.

Benjamin, Andrew. "Particularity and Exceptions: On Jews and Animals." *South Atlantic Quarterly* 107 (2008): 72–87.

Benveniste, Emile. *Indo-European Language and Society*. Trans. Elizabeth Palmer. Miami: University of Miami Press, 1973.

Bernal, Martin. *Black Athena: The Afroasiatic Roots of Classical Civilization*, vol. 1, The Fabrication of Ancient Greece 1785–1985. New Brunswick, NJ: Rutgers University Press, 1987.

Bernasconi, Robert. "Hegel at the Court of the Ashanti" in *Hegel after Derrida*. Edited by Stuart Barnett. 41–63. Routledge: London and New York, 1998.

Bernasconi, Robert. "With What Must the Philosophy of History Begin? On the Racial Bases of Hegel's Eurocentrism." *Nineteenth Century Contexts* 22 (2000): 171–201.

Blundell, Mary Whitlock. *Helping Friends and Harming Enemies: A Study in Sophocles and Greek Ethics*. Cambridge: Cambridge University Press, 1989.

Boal, Augusto. *Theatre of the Oppressed*. New York: Theatre Communications Group, 1985.

Borregaard, Tofa. "The Tragic Heroics of Ancient Greek Extreme Women." *New Antigone* 1, Spring (2005): 68–70.

Brecht, Bertolt. *Sophocles' Antigone*, trans. Judith Malina. New York: Applause Theatre, 1990.

Buck-Morss, Susan. "Hegel and Haiti." *Critical Inquiry* 26, 4 (2000): 821–865.

Budelmann, Felix. "Greek Tragedies in West African Adaptations" in *Classics and Colonialism*. Edited by Barbara Goff. 118–146. London: Duckworth, 2005.

Bull, Malcolm. "Slavery and the Multiple Self." *New Left Review* 231 (1998): 94–131.

Butler, Judith. *Antigone's Claim: Kinship Between Life & Death*. New York: Columbia University Press, 2000.

Butler, Judith. *Precarious Lives: The Powers of Mourning and Violence*. London: Verso, 2004.

Carson, Anne. "Putting her in her Place: Woman, Dirt, and Desire," *Before Sexuality: The Construction of Erotic Experience in the Ancient Greek World*. Edited by David M. Halperin, John J. Winkler, and Froma I. Zeitlin. 135–169. Princeton, NJ: Princeton University Press, 1990.

Cartledge, Paul. *The Greeks: A Portrait of Self and Others*. Oxford: Oxford University Press, 2002.

Cartledge, Paul. " 'Deep Plays': Theatre as Process in Greek Civil Life" in *The Cambridge Companion to Greek Tragedy*. Edited by P. E. Easterling. 3–35. Cambridge: Cambridge University Press, 1997.

Case, Sue-Ellen. "Classic drag: the Greek Creation of Female Parts." *Theatre Journal* (1985): 317–327.

Connor, W. Robert. "The Problem of Athenian Civic Identity," *Athenian Identity and Civic Ideology*. Edited by Alan L. Boegehold and Adele C. Scafuro, 34–44. Baltimore, MD: Johns Hopkins University Press, 1994.

Copjec, Joan. *Imagine There's No Woman: Ethics and Sublimation*. Boston: MIT, 2004.

Derrida, Jacques. *Glas*. Trans. John P. Leavey and Richard Rand. Lincoln: University of Nebraska Press, 1986.

Derrida, Jacques. *The Politics of Friendship*. Trans. George Collins. New York: Verso, 1997.

Derrida, Jacques. *Rogues: Two Essays on Reason*. Trans. Pascale-Anne Brault and Michael Naas. Stanford: Stanford University Press. 2005.

Derrida, Jacques. *L'animal que donc je suis*. Edited by Marie-Louise Mallet. Paris: Galilée, 2006.

Deutscher, Penelope. " 'Women and so on': *Rogues* and the Autoimmunity of Feminism." *Symposium: Canadian Journal of Continental Philosophy* 11, 1 (2007) 101–119.

Deutscher, Penelope. "The Inversion of Exceptionality: Foucault, Agamben and 'Reproductive Rights.' " *South Atlantic Quarterly* 107 (2008): 55–70.

Dodds, E. R. *The Greeks and the Irrational*. Berkeley: University of California Press, 1951.

duBois, Page. "Antigone and the Feminist Critic." *Genre* 19 (1986): 371–383.

duBois, Page. *Slaves and Other Objects*. Chicago: University of Chicago Press, 2003.

Durbach, Errol. "Sophocles In South Africa: Athol Fugard's *The Island*," *Drama and the Classical Heritage: Comparative and Critical Essays*. Edited Clifford Davidson, Rand Johnson, and John H. Stroupe. 241–53. AMS Press, Inc.: New York, 1993.

Eagleton, Terry. *Sweet Violence: The Idea of the Tragic*. Oxford: Blackwell, 2003.

Ehrenberg, Victor. *Sophocles and Pericles*. Oxford: Basil Blackwell, 1954.

Euben, J. Peter. Introduction. *Greek Tragedy and Political Theory*. Berkeley: University of California, 1986.

Euben, J. Peter. *Corrupting Youth: Political Education, Democratic Culture, and Political Theory*. Princeton, NJ: Princeton University Press, 1997.

Finley, M. I. *Ancient Slavery and Modern Ideology*. London: Chatto & Windus, 1980.

Fisher, N. R. E. *Slavery in Classical Greece*. London: Bristol Classical Press, 1993.

Foley, Helen P. *Female Acts in Greek Tragedy*. Princeton, NJ: Princeton University Press, 2001.

Foucault, Michel. *The History of Sexuality*, vol. I: An Introduction. Trans. Robert Hurley, Harmondsworth, Middlesex: Penguin, 1978.

Fradinger, Moira. "Violent Boundaries: Antigone's Political Imagination." *theory@buffalo* 10 (2005): 103–128.

Fradinger, Moira. "Prologue" in *Feminist Readings of* Antigone. Edited by Fanny Söderbäck. 15–23. Albany: State University of New York Press, 2010.

Freud, Sigmund. "Infantile genital organization: An interpolation into the theory of sexuality" in *The Standard edition of the complete psychological works*. Trans. James Strachey, vol 19. London: Hogarth Press and the Institute of Psycho-analysis, 1953.

Fugard, Athol, John Kani, and Winston Ntshona. *The Island*. In *Statements: two workshop productions. Sizwe Bansi is Dead*, and *The Island*; and a new play, *Statements after an arrest under the Immorality Act*. London: Oxford University Press, 1974.

Fugard, Athol. "*Antigone* in Africa" in *Amid Our Troubles: Irish Versions of Greek Tragedy*. Edited by Marianne McDonald and J. Michael Walton. 128–147. London: Methuen, 2002.

Gambaro, Griselda. "Antigona Furiosa" in *Information for Foreigners: Three Plays by Griselda Gambaro*. Trans and ed. by Marguerite Feitlowitz, Evanston, IL: Northwestern University Press, 1992.

Garlan, Yvon. *Slavery in Ancient Greece*. Revised and Expanded Edition. Trans. Janet Lloyd. Ithaca: Cornell University Press, 1988.

Garnsey, Peter. *Ideas of Slavery from Aristotle to Augustine*. Cambridge: Cambridge University Press, 1999.

Gibbs, James. "*Antigone* and After *Antigone*" in *Portraits for an Eagle: Essays in Honour of Femi Osofisan*. Edited by Sola Adeyemi. 79–88. Bayreuth: Bayreuth University, 2006.

Gibbons, Reginald, trans. A*ntigone*. Edited by Gibbons and Charles Segal. *The Greek Tragedy in New Translations*. Edited by Peter Burian and Alan Shapiro. Oxford: Oxford University Press, 2003.

Glowacki, Janusz. *Antigone in New York*. Trans. Janusz Glowacki and Joan Torres. New York: Samuel French, 1997.

Goff, Barbara, and Michael Simpson. *Crossroads at the Black Aegean: Oedipus, Antigone and Dramas of the African Diaspora*. Oxford: Oxford University Press, 2007.

Goff, Barbara. "Antigone's Boat: The Colonial and the Postcolonial in Tegonni" in *Portraits for an Eagle: Essays in Honour of Femi Osofisan*. Edited by Sola Adeyemi. 111–121. Bayreuth: Bayreuth University, 2006.

Goldhill, Simon. "The Audience of Athenian Tragedy" in *The Cambridge Companion to Greek Tragedy*. Edited by P. E. Easterling. 54–68. Cambridge, MA: Cambridge University Press, 1997.

Griffith, Mark. "Brilliant Dynasts: Power and Politics in the *Oresteia*," *Classical Antiquity* 14 (1995): 62–129.

Griffith, Mark. "The Subject of Desire in Sophocles' Antigone" in *The Soul of Tragedy: Essays on Athenian Drama*. Edited by Victoria Pedrick and Steven M. Oberhelman. 91–135. Chicago: The University of Chicago Press, 2005.

Griffith, R. Drew. "Corporality in the Ancient Greek Theatre." *Phoenix* 52 (1998): 230–256.

Habenstein, Robert W., and William M. Lamers. *Funeral Customs the World Over*. Milwaukee, WI: Bulfin Printers, 1960.

Hall, Edith. "When is a Myth Not a Myth? Bernal's 'Ancient Model' " in *Greeks and the Barbarians*. Edited by Thomas Harrison. 133–152. New York: Routledge, 2002. Originally published in *Arethusa* 25 (1992): 181–201; this version from Mary Lefkowitz and G. M. Rogers, *Black Athena Revisited*. Chapel Hill: University of North Carolina Press, 1996.

Hall, Edith. "The Sociology of Athenian Tragedy" in *The Cambridge Companion to Greek Tragedy*. Edited by P. E. Easterling. 93–126. Cambridge, MA: Cambridge University Press, 1997.

Hall, Edith. "Is there a *Polis* in Aristotle's *Poetics*?" in *Tragedy and the Tragic: Greek Theatre and Beyond*, Edited by M. S. Silk. 295–309. Oxford: Clarendon Press, 1996.

Hall, Edith. *Inventing the Barbarian: Greek Self-Definition through Tragedy*. Oxford: Clarendon Press, 1989.

Halperin, David M. "Why is Diotima a Woman? Platonic Eros and the Figuration of Gender." *Before Sexuality: The Construction of Erotic Experience in the Ancient Greek World*. Edited by David M. Halperin, John J. Winkler, and Froma I. Zeitlin. 257–308. Princeton, NJ: Princeton University Press, 1990.

Hamilton, John B. "Antigone: Kinship, Justice and the Polis" in *Myth and the Polis*. Edited by Dora C. Pozzi and John M. Wickersham. 86–98. Ithaca, NY: Cornell University Press, 1991.

Harris, H. S. *Hegel's Ladder*, vol. 2: *The Odyssey of Spirit*. Indianapolis, IN: Hackett Publishing Company, 1997.

Heaney, Seamus. *The Burial at Thebes: A Version of Sophocles'* Antigone. New York: Farrar, Straus and Giroux, 2004.

Hegel, G. W. F. *Hegel's Aesthetics: Lectures on Fine Art*. Trans. T. M. Knox, 2 vols. Oxford: Clarendon Press, 1988. *Vorlesungen über die Ästhetik*. Suhrkamp Taschenbuch Wissenschaft, b. 13–15. Suhrkamp: Frankfurt am Main, 1970.

Hegel, G. W. F. *The Philosophy of Mind*. Trans. A. V. Miller. Oxford: Clarendon Press, 1971.

Hegel, G. W. F. *Phenomenology of Spirit*. Trans. A. V. Miller, Oxford: Clarendon Press, 1979.

Heidegger, Martin. *An Introduction to Metaphysics.* Trans. Ralph Manheim. New Haven and London: Yale University Press, 1959.

Holst-Warhaft, Gail. *Dangerous Voices: Women's Laments and Greek Literature*, New York: Routledge, 1992.

Honig, Bonnie. "Antigone's Laments, Creon's Grief: Mourning, Membership, and the Politics of Exception," *Political Theory*, February 2009 37: 5–43.

Huff, Dietrich. "Archaeological Evidence of Zoroastrian Funerary Practices" in *Zorastrian Rituals in Context.* Edited by Micahel Stausberg. 593–630. Boston: Brill, 2004.

Hunt, Peter. *Slaves, Warfare, and Ideology in the Greek Historians.* Cambridge, MA: Cambridge University Press, 1998.

Irigaray, Luce. *Speculum of the Other Woman.* Trans. Gillian C. Gill. Ithaca, NY: Cornell University Press. 1985. *Speculum de l'autre femme.* Minuit: Paris, 1974.

Irigaray, Luce. *This Sex Which Is Not One.* Trans. Catherine Porter. Ithaca, NY: Cornell University Press, 1985.

Irigaray, Luce. *An Ethics of Sexual Difference.* Trans. Carolyn Burke and Gillian C. Gill. Ithaca, NY: Cornell University Press, 1993.

Isaac, Benjamin. *The Invention of Racism in Classical Antiquity.* Princeton, NJ: Princeton University Press, 2004.

The Island [videorecording]. Brooklyn Academy of Music. Alan H. Fishman, chairman of the board; William I. Campbell, vice chairman of the board; Karen Brooks Hopkins, president; Joseph V. Melillo, executive producer, presents The Royal National Theatre and The Market Theatre of Johannesburg production; [written] by Athol Fugard, John Kani, and Winston Ntshona; originally directed by Athol Fugard; [video prod. company] Character Generators, Inc. (2003).

Jacobs, Carol. "Dusting Antigone." *MLN* 111 (1996): 889–917.

Just, Roger. *Women in Athenian Law and Life.* London: Routledge, 1989.

Kennelly, Brendan. *Sophocles' Antigone.* Tarset, Northumberland: Bloodaxe Books, 1996.

Kitzinger, Rachel. "Sophoklean Dialogues," in *Contextualizing Classics: Ideology, Performance, Dialogue.* Edited by Thomas M. Falkner, Nancy Felson, and David Konstan. 205–220. Lanham: Rowman and Littlefield, 1999.

Knox, Bernard M. W. *The Heroic Temper: Studies in Sophoclean Tragedy.* Berkeley: University of California Press, 1992.

Konstan, David. "The Classics and Class Conflict." *Arethusa* 27 (1994): 47–70.

Kristeva, Julia. *Powers of Horror: An Essay on Abjection.* Trans. Leon S. Roudiez. New York: Columbia University Press, 1982.

Lacan, Jacques. *The Ethics of Psychoanalysis 1959–1960: The Seminar of Jacques Lacan*, Book VII. Trans. Dennis Porter. Edited by Jacques-Alain Miller. New York: Tavistock/Routledge, 1992.

Laclau, Ernesto. "Bare Life or Social Indeterminacy?" in *Giorgio Agamben: Sovereignty and Life.* Edited by Matthew Calarco and Steve DeCaroli. 11–22. Stanford, CA: Stanford University Press, 2007.

Lane, Warren J., and Ann M. Lane. "The Politics of Antigone" in *Greek Tragedy and Political Theory.* Edited by. J. Peter Euben. Berkeley and London: University of California Press, 1986.

Liverani, Mario. "The Bathwater and the Baby" in *Black Athena Revisited.* Edited by Mary R. Lefkowitz and Guy Mclean Rogers. 421–427. Chapel Hill: University of North Carolina, 1996.

Loraux, Nicole. *Born of the Earth: Myth and Politics in Athens.* Trans. Selina Stewart. Ithaca, NY: Cornell University Press, 2000.

Loraux, Nicole. *Mothers in Mourning.* Trans. Corinne Pache. Ithaca, NY: Cornell University Press, 1998.

Loraux, Nicole. *The Experiences of Tiresias: The Feminine and the Greek Man.* Trans. Paula Wissig. Princeton, NJ: Princeton University, 1995.

Loraux, Nicole. *The Children of Athena: Athenian Ideas about Citizenship and the Division between the Sexes.* Trans. Caroline Levine. Princeton, NJ: Princeton University Press, 1993.

Mader, Mary Beth. "Antigone's Line" in *Bulletin de la société Américaine de philosophie de langue Française* 14: 2 (2005): 18–40.

Manville, Philip Brook. "Toward a New Paradigm of Athenian Citizenship" in *Athenian Identity and Civic Ideology.* Edited by Alan L. Boegehold and Adele C. Scafuro, 21–33. Baltimore, MD: Johns Hopkins University Press, 1994.

Markell, Patchen. *Bound by Recognition.* Princeton and Oxford: Princeton University Press, 2003.

Mathews, Aidan. Undated. *Antigone: Gone Anti.* Unpublished manuscript, courtesy of the author.

McClintock, Anne. *Imperial Leather: Race Gender and Sexuality in the Colonial Contest.* New York: Routledge, 1995.

McDonald, Marianne. *Antigone by Sophocles.* London: Nick Hern Books, 2005.

Mclure, Laura. *Spoken like a woman: Speech and Gender in Athenian Drama.* Princeton, NJ: Princeton University Press, 1999.

Miller, Elaine. "Tragedy, Natural Law and Sexual Difference in Hegel" in *Bound by the City: Greek Tragedy, Sexual Difference, and the Formation of the Polis.* Edited by Denise Eileen McCoskey and Emily Zakin. 149–176. Albany: State University of New York, 2009.

Mills, Charles. *The Racial Contract.* Ithaca, NY: Cornell University Press, 1999.

Murnaghan, Sheila. "Sucking the Juice without Biting the Rind: Aristotle and Tragic Mimesis." *New Literary History* 26.4 (1995): 755–773.

Murnaghan, Shiela. "*Antigone* 904–920 and the Institution of Marriage," *The American Journal of Philology* 104 (1986): 192–207.

Nietzsche, Friedrich. *The Birth of Tragedy and The Case of Wagner.* Trans. with commentary by Walter Kaufmann. New York. Vintage Books, 1967.

Nippel, Wilfred. "The Construction of the 'Other' " in *Greeks and the Barbarians.* Trans. Antonia Neville. Edited by Thomas Harrison. 278–310. New York: Routledge, 2002.

Ober, Josiah. *Mass and Elite in Democratic Athens: Rhetoric, Ideology, and the Power of the People.* Princeton, NJ: Princeton University Press, 1989.

Oliver, Kelly. "Antigone's Ghost: Undoing Hegel's *Phenomenology of Spirit,*" *Hypatia*, vol. 11, no. 1 (Winter) (1996): 67–90.

Omi, Michael, and Howard Winant. *Racial Formation in the United States: From the 1960s to the 1990s.* New York: Routledge, 1994.

O'Neill, Daniel I., Mary Lyndon Shanley, and Iris Marion Young, ed. *Illusion of Consent: Engaging with Carole Pateman.* University Park: Pennsylvania State University, 2008.

Ormand, Kirk. "Oedipus the Queen: Cross-gendering without drag." *Theatre Journal* 55 (2003): 1–28.

Ormand, Kirk. *Exchange and the Maiden: Marriage in Sophoclean Tragedy*. Austin: University of Texas Press, 1999.

Òsófisan, Fémi. "Theatre and the Rites of 'Post-negritude' Remembering." *Research in African Literatures* 30 (1999): 1–11.

Òsófisan, Fémi. *Tègònni, an African Antigone*. Ibadan, Nigeria: Kenbim Press, 1999.

Pateman, Carole. *The Sexual Contract*. Stanford, CA: Stanford University Press, 1988.

Patterson, Cynthia. "The Case against Neaira and the Public Ideology of the Athenian Family" in *Athenian Identity and Civic Ideology*. Edited by Alan L. Boegehold and Adele C. Scafuro, 199–216. Baltimore, MD: Johns Hopkins University Press, 1994.

Patterson, Cynthia. *Pericles' Citizenship Law of 451–50 BC. Monographs in Classical Studies*. Salem, NH: Ayer Company, 1988.

Patterson, Cynthia. " 'Not Worth the Rearing:' The Causes of Infant Exposure in Ancient Greece." *Transactions of the American Philological Association* 115 (1985): 103–23.

Patterson, Orlando. *Slavery and Social Death: A Comparative Study*. Cambridge, MA: Harvard University Press, 1982.

Patton, Paul. "Agamben and Foucault on Biopower and Biopolitics" in *Giorgio Agamben: Sovereignty and Life*. Edited by Matthew Calarco, and Steve DeCaroli, 203–218. Stanford, CA: Stanford University Press, 2007.

Paulin, Tom. *The Riot Act: A Version of Sophocles'* Antigone. London and Boston: Faber and Faber, 1985.

Plato. *Republic I and II*. Trans. Paul Shorey. *Loeb Classical Library*. Harvard University Press: William Heinemann, 1978.

Plutarch. *The Rise and Fall of Athena: Nine Greek Lives*. London: Penguin, 1960.

Pomeroy, Sarah B. *Goddesses, Whores, Wives, and Slaves: Women in Ancient Antiquity*. New York: Schocken Books, 1995.

Rabinowitz, Nancy Sorkin. *Anxiety Veiled: Euripides and the Traffic in Women*. Ithaca, NY: Cornell University Press, 1993.

Rabinowitz, Nancy Sorkin. "Slaves with Slaves: Women and Class in Euripidean Tragedy" in *Women and Slaves in Greco-Roman Culture: Differential Equations*. Edited by Sandra R. Joshel and Sheila Murnaghan, 56–68. New York: Routledge, 1998.

Razmjou, Shahrokh. "Religion and Burial Customs" in *Forgotten Empire: The World of Ancient Persia*. Edited by John Curtis and Nigel Tallis, 150–156. Berkeley: University of California, 2005.

Reiss, Timothy J. *Tragedy and Truth. Studies in the Development of a Renaissance and Neoclassical Discourse*. New Haven and London: Yale University Press, 1980.

Rooney, Caroline. *African Literature, Animism and Politics*. London: Routledge, 2000.

Rubin, Gayle. "The Traffic in Women: Notes on the 'Political Economy' of Sex" in *Toward an Anthropology of Women*. Edited by Rayna R. Reiter. New York: Monthly Review Press, 1975.

Said, Edward. *Orientalism*. New York: Vintage Books 1979.

Sallis, John. *Crossings: Nietzsche and the Space of Tragedy*. Chicago: University of Chicago Press, 1991.

Scafuro, Adele C. "Witnessing and False Witnessing: Proving Citizenship and Kin Identity in Fourth-Century Athens" in *Athenian Identity and Civic Ideology*. Edited by Alan L. Boegehold and Adele C. Scafuro. 156–198. Baltimore, MD: Johns Hopkins University Press, 1994.

Segal, Charles. "Catharsis, Audience, and Closure in Greek Tragedy" in *Tragedy and the Tragic: Greek Theatre and Beyond.* Edited by M. S. Silk, 149–172. Oxford: Clarendon Press, 1996.

Segal, Charles. "Antigone: Death and Love, Hades and Dionysus" in *Tragedy and Civilization: An Interpretation of Sophocles.* Norman: University of Oklahoma Press, 1999.

Spargo, Clifton. "The Apolitics of Antigone's Lament (From Sophocles to Ariel Dorfman)," personal manuscript. 2007.

Spivak, Gayatri Chakravorty. *Critique of Postcolonial Reason: Toward a History of the Vanishing Present.* Cambridge, MA: Harvard University Press, 1999.

Storr, F. trans. *Sophocles in two volumes*, vol. 1, *The Loeb Classical Library*, Cambridge, MA: Harvard University Press, 1981.

Taplin, Oliver. *Greek Tragedy in Action.* London: Routledge, 2003.

Taxidou, Olga. *Tragedy, Modernity and Mourning.* Edinburgh: Edinburgh University Press, 2004.

Tyrrell, Wm. Blake, and Larry J. Bennett. *Recapturing Sophocles' Antigone.* Lanham: Rowman and Littlefield, 1998.

Vernant, Jean-Pierre. *Myth and Society in Ancient Greece.* Trans. Janet Lloyd. New York: Zone Books, 1990.

Vernant, Jean-Pierre, and Pierre Vidal-Naquet. *Myth and Tragedy in Ancient Greece.* Trans. Janet Lloyd. New York: Zone Books, 1990.

Vlastos, Gregory. "Slavery in Plato's Thought" in *Platonic Studies*, 147–63. Princeton, NJ: Princeton University Press, 1981.

Weber, Samuel. "Antigone's 'Nomos' " in *Theatricality as Medium*, 121–140. New York: Fordham University Press, 2004.

Wetmore, Jr., Kevin J. *The Athenian Sun in an African Sky.* Jefferson, NC: McFarland & Company, Inc., 2002.

Wiedemann, Thomas. *Greek and Roman Slavery.* New York: Routledge. 2005.

Wiles, David. *Tragedy in Athens: Performance Space and Theatrical Meaning.* Cambridge, MA: Cambridge University Press, 1997.

Willett, Cynthia. The *Soul of Justice: Social Bonds and Racial Hubris.* Ithaca, NY: Cornell University Press, 2001.

Williams, Bernard. *Shame and Necessity.* Berkeley: University of California Press, 1993.

Winkler, John. "Representing the Body Politic: The Theatre of Manhood in Classical Athens." *Perspecta* 26 (1990): 215–229.

Wohl, Victoria. *Intimate Commerce: Exchange, Gender and Subjectivity in Greek Tragedy*, Austin: University of Texas, 1998.

Wyckoff, Elizabeth, trans. "Antigone," in *Sophocles I.* Edited by David Grene. *The Complete Greek Tragedies*, ed. David Grene and Richmond Lattimore. Chicago: The University of Chicago Press, 1954.

Zeitlin, Froma I. "Thebes: Theater of Self and Society in Athenian Drama" in *Nothing to do with Dionysos? Athenian Drama in its Social Context.* Edited by John J. Winkler and Froma I. Zeitlin, 130–167. Princeton, NJ: Princeton University Press, 1990.

Zeitlin, Froma I. *Playing the Other: Gender and Society in Ancient Greek Literature.* Chicago: University of Chicago Press, 1996.

Ziarek, Ewa Płonowska. "Bare Life on Strike: Notes on the Biopolitics of Race and Gender." *South Atlantic Quarterly* 107 (2008): 89–105.

Žižek, Slavoj. "From Antigone to Joan of Arc." *Helios* 31 (2004) 51–62.

Index